PORTRAYING PERSONS WITH DISABILITIES

AN ANNOTATED BIBLIOGRAPHY OF

NONFICTION

FOR CHILDREN AND TEENAGERS

SERVING SPECIAL NEEDS SERIES

AN ALL NEW VOLUME IN THE TRADITION OF
ACCEPT ME AS I AM.

PORTRAYING PERSONS WITH DISABILITIES

AN ANNOTATED BIBLIOGRAPHY OF

NONFICTION

FOR CHILDREN AND TEENAGERS

SECOND EDITION

JOAN BREST FRIEDBERG
JUNE B. MULLINS
ADELAIDE WEIR SUKIENNIK

R. R. BOWKER
A REED REFERENCE PUBLISHING COMPANY
New Providence, New Jersey

MAI 290 2015 √

Published by R. R. Bowker, a Reed Reference Publishing Company
Copyright © 1992 by Reed Publishing (USA) Inc.
All rights reserved
Printed and bound in the United States of America

Library of Congress Cataloging in Publication Data

Friedberg, Joan Brest, 1927–
    Portraying persons with disabilities : an annotated bibliography
of nonfiction for children and teenagers/Joan Brest Friedberg,
June B. Mullins, Adelaide Weir Sukiennik.—2nd ed.
      p.   cm.—(Serving special needs series)
    Includes indexes.
    ISBN 0-8352-3022-8
    1. Children's literature—Bibliography. 2. Bibliography—Best
books—Children's literature. 3. Young adult literature—
Bibliography. 4. Bibliography—Best books—Young adult literature.
5. Physically handicapped—Juvenile literature—Bibliography.
6. Mentally handicapped—Juvenile literature—Bibliography.
7. Mentally ill—Juvenile literature—Bibliography. I. Mullins,
June B., 1927– . II. Sukiennik, Adelaide Weir, 1938–
III. Title. IV. Series.
Z1037.9.F735 1992
[PN1009.A1]
011.62′083—dc20   92-15047
                                             CIP

ISBN 0 - 8352 - 3022 - 8

9 780835 230223

To all those who have so courageously
lived the lives described herein

CONTENTS

PREFACE

The aim of this volume—as in our first, *Accept Me as I Am* (Bowker, 1985)—is to present a selection of books that foster constructive attitudes toward human differences on the part of readers, disabled or not, through the use of interesting, informative, and well-written nonfiction. These books have been designated with reading levels preschool through young adult by the three authors, who are experienced education and library professionals. The following reading-level designations are used: Preschool (ages 2 to 5), grades K–3 (ages 5 to 8), grades 4–6 (ages 9 to 11), grades 7–9 (ages 12 to 14), and grades 10–12 (ages 15 to 17, with many titles in this category of interest to adult readers). These divisions are necessarily arbitrary and many young readers can enjoy books from more than one grade category. The entries portray real people and real situations. The disabling conditions represented are inclined to be those affecting younger rather than middle-aged or elderly people and are those with which they must cope throughout their lives.

In the main, the books included have been selected from titles published since 1984; however, on occasion, we have discovered earlier books of merit going back as far as 1964. Those books that are out of print are readily accessible in library collections.

Chapters 1 to 4 are narratives. Chapter 1 details the criteria by which the books were selected. Chapter 2 puts the subject of disability into social and historical perspective. Chapter 3 offers a list of reference sources about disabilities or about persons with disabilities. Chapter 4 examines the patterns and trends that have emerged in these books.

Chapters 5 to 8 comprise annotations of the books that we have selected, organized according to broad categories of disabling conditions for easy access. In each category books are listed alphabetically by author and then by title. Each entry begins with a complete bibliographic citation and an indication of the reading level. The specific disability is then given, followed by a summary of the book and a critical analysis that often suggests specific uses for the book, as well as its strengths and weaknesses. The volume concludes with author, title, and subject indexes. The Subject Index includes names of notable people who have been described in the works. In addition, these indexes include all of the titles that were included in *Accept Me as I Am.* In each index, entries from the earlier book appear with an "A" preceding the page number. The user can easily locate that entry in *Accept Me as I Am* for detailed information.

This guide will be of use to librarians, teachers, counselors, health professionals, and parents. In school libraries it will be a resource for students and teachers, particularly those in classes that mainstream children with disabilities. School personnel will find it useful for parents who want to locate books for their children that foster understanding of disabled classmates, family, or friends. Parents, both disabled and able-bodied, who are working to help their children with disabilities to achieve the maximum possible independence and satisfaction will find support in this literature.

Newly published titles included were identified by consulting current issues of library reviewing tools such as *Booklist* and *School Library Journal.* In addition, Amy Kellman and the other librarians at the Children's Room of The Carnegie Library of Pittsburgh called our attention to new titles in children's literature that they had identified. Hillman Library of the University of Pittsburgh is the repository of many of the selections included as appropriate for teenagers and young adults. In cases where we were unable to obtain copies of books locally, Patricia Colbert and the staff of the Interlibrary Loan Department of Hillman Library borrowed titles for us from a wide variety of collections throughout the United States. We acknowledge the help of these people and of the many other students and staff members at the University of Pittsburgh who in various ways have assisted us in this project. We also wish to thank Marion Sader, publisher, and Judith Balsamo, managing editor, and the rest of the staff at R. R. Bowker, who have communicated with us frequently and helpfully and prepared the manuscript for publication.

ABBREVIATIONS

REVIEW SOURCES

American Historical Review	AHR	Byte	Byte
Antioch Review	AntR	Children's Book News	CBN
Appraisal: Science Books for Young People	ASBYP	Children's Book Review Service	CBRS
Atlantic	Atlan	Children's Literature Association Quarterly	CLAQ
Best Sellers	BS		
Book Guide	BG	Children's Literature in Education	CLE
Book Report	BR		
Booklist	BL	Choice	CH
Books	Books	Computer Book Review	CBR
Books for Young People	BYP		
Books in Canada	BIC	Contemporary Psychology	CP
Bookwatch	BW	Curriculum Review	CR
British Book News	BBN		
Bulletin of the Center for Children's Books	BCCB	English Journal	EJ
		Horn Book Magazine	HB

Instructor	Inst	Punch	Pun
Interracial Books for Children Bulletin	IBCB	Queen's Quarterly	Queens Q
		Quill & Quire	Quill&Q
		Reading Teacher	RT
Journal of Learning Disabilities	JLD	Reference Services Review	RSR
Journal of Visual Impairment & Blindness	JVIB	Reference & Research Book News	R&RBKN
Kirkus Reviews	KR	School Librarian	SL
Kliatt Young Adult Paperback	KLIATT	School Library Journal	SLJ
		Science Books and Films	SBF
Lambda Book Report	LAM BK Rpt	SE Childhood Education	SE
Los Angeles Times Book Review	LATBR	Small Press Book Review	SPBR
Library Hi Tech News	LHTN	Stand Magazine	Stand
		Time	Time
Library Journal	LJ	Times Educational Supplement	TES
Library Quarterly	LQ		
London Review of Books	LRB	Times Literary Supplement	TLS
Nation	Nat	Tribune Books	TB
New Directions for Women	NDW	Village Voice Literary Supplement	VLS
New York Review of Books	NYRB	Voice of Youth Advocates	VYA
New York Times	NYT	Volta Review	VR
New York Times Book Review	NYTBR	Wall Street Journal	WSJ
New Yorker	NY	West Coast Review of Books	WCRB
Newsweek	NW		
Parents Magazine	Par	Wilson Library Bulletin	WLB
Personnel & Guidance Journal	PGJ	Women's Review of Books	WRB
Phi Delta Kappa	PDK	Yale Review	YR
Psychology Today	PsyT		
Publishers Weekly	PW		

DATES

Ja	January	O	October
F	February	N	November
Mr	March	D	December
Ap	April	Sp	Spring
My	May	Su	Summer
Je	June	MS	Midsummer
Jl	July	Fl	Fall
Ag	August	W	Winter
S	September	MW	Midwinter

1

CRITERIA FOR SELECTION OF BOOKS

These are not just books, lumps of lifeless paper, but minds alive on the shelves . . . by taking down one of these volumes and opening it, we can call into range voices far distant in time and space, and hear them speak to us, mind to mind, heart to heart.
—Gilbert Highet

This is a continuation of the comprehensive nonfiction collection about disabilities, addressed to readers in their formative years, compiled by Friedberg et al. (*Accept Me as I Am,* 1985). The usefulness of such books has been attested to by classroom teachers from preschool through college, by curriculum developers who want to foster healthy social attitudes, by mental health therapists who have long used bibliotherapy, and by young readers themselves who frequently seek out this literature.

Selection of these books has been guided by the eight criteria that follow.

1. WORKS THAT FOSTER ACCEPTANCE AND UNDERSTANDING

In our reading, we have heard a repeated message. "Look at us, listen to us," the voices say. "We are people first, individuals first. Our disabilities are part of us, but only part. We are more than our impairments. Count us in the world." As a society, we have made progress since the days when people with mental disorders were manacled to the walls and those with physical abnormalities were displayed in circus freak shows. These are injustices on a gross scale, and we recoil from the memory. Nonetheless, we need to be alert to prejudices and misconceptions that any of us might still labor under; we need to help our children acquire the knowledge and sensitivity to enable them, whatever their particular individual condition, to reach out to others with understanding and acceptance.

A 9-year-old boy, named Jordan, questioned by a writer who was talking to him about his blindness, said, "I feel left out of the world sometimes" (*Seeing in Special Ways,* by Thomas Bergman, p. 45). *Portraying Persons with Disabilities* has been prepared as a guide for young readers and listeners who range in age from preschoolers to high school and college students; its aim is to help these children and adolescents increase their knowledge and understanding of disabling conditions so that isolation can be bridged and blind children like Jordan can feel included in the human circle, not left out of the world.

2. YOUNG AUDIENCE

The scope of this collection is specifically focused on nonfiction books that would be of particular interest to those still in their developmental period—preschool age through the teen years. The annotated titles address the problems of self-realization and social integration, which are common tasks for all young people, but which are highlighted and intensified by the challenge of disability. For the reader beset by an uncommon problem, such books can comfort, teach, and reassure. For the "ordinary" reader, such books foster the appreciation of diversity and the positive response to adversity that are necessary tasks for the development of a mature personality.

This collection overlaps to some extent with others, including the various lists of books for and about parents of disabled children. (These lists have yet to be gathered into a book.) Because teenagers are approaching or have reached reproductive age, they may identify with very young parents who are faced with a baby born with problems; some of the titles annotated here describe such situations.

A few books are written from the perspective of a child whose parent is disabled—for example, Lou Ann Walker's *A Loss for Words,* which is about a hearing child with deaf parents. Adulthood demands an evolution in the parent-child relationship to a point where parents acknowledge their offspring's maturity and the child accepts the parents' vulnerability and shortcomings. Again, the fact of disability intensifies these processes and makes them more clear.

Most of the books deal with the childhood of their main protagonist. Exceptions to this include accounts in which the writer felt his or her life transformed at the onset of the disease or disability, so that the story proceeds from that time. Many of the books about AIDS are in the latter category.

3. PORTRAYAL OF ACTUAL PEOPLE

Nonfiction books about disability may be more or less didactic. There are some books on the preschool and elementary school level that are written clearly for the purpose of describing a problem and/or explaining how the person with the problem can be treated and thought about. If books describe real people and real situations, not simply the disabling condition, they have been included; for example, *Overcoming Disability* by Brian Ward, describes 17 disorders by focusing on individuals with the conditions. Science books including life skills guides or texts on any level are generally omitted. However, some of the books in the collection presented here can make fine supplemental reading for science, health, social science, or literature classes.

4. PORTRAYAL OF CHRONIC DISABILITIES WITH WHICH PROTAGONISTS LIVE

In the main, disabilities are included that are nonfatal and that affect younger rather than middle-aged or elderly people. Therefore, fatal diseases of early childhood, such as Tay-Sachs, are not often represented, nor are problems of older age, such as Alzheimer's. On the other hand, problems such as breast cancer, that confront young adults and those in early maturity, are the focus of some stories.

Books are included only when disability is a major influence in the story. The disabilities described are always significant ones; consideration of minor imperfections, either physical or psychological, would not merit inclusion in this collection.

Some of the books follow the course of a life, such as in the biographies of notable women and men with disabilities. Other books describe a setting, such as a camp, school, or hospital, where the characters are described in a case study format.

5. ACCESSIBLE READING LEVEL

Because this collection consists of trade books of general interest, selection has been limited to a top reading level of grade 12. Designation of reading level is at best subjective, and it even varies by country. For example, the style of British juvenile books places a greater burden on the reader than comparably classified American books. Furthermore, a third-grader might enjoy reading or listening to a book described as being at the preschool level, and a competent middle school student might handle with ease a title listed as appropriate for those in senior high school. Nonetheless, the three authors have attempted reading level classifications with the caveat that even very simply worded stories may express profound thoughts and that the prose of other narratives might present too much of a challenge to any but very capable readers. Such judgments appear in the annotations, but those who use this guide will want to apply their own evaluations for the young readers they know.

6. LITERARY STANDARDS

In making our selections, we have looked for writing that is distinguished by style and also by the sense of immediacy conveyed by the author. We have omitted books marked by banal language, overwriting, sentimentality, and unclear explanation and description. Occasionally, an account may be so informative and compelling that these qualities overcome weaknesses of form and word choice. Generally, however, we have included books that by their subject matter and presentation not only will attract young readers but will also be worth their reading. All, we hope, give an honest picture of and represent accurately the condition being described. We have looked for scientific plausibility and, at the same time, for work that acknowledges pain, bitterness, frustration, and failure, in addition to celebrating extraordinary triumphs of the will and spirit, and for writing that, however difficult and tragic the condition described, speaks with a positive voice.

7. REPRESENTATIVE CATEGORIES OF DISABILITY

As in our first guide (*Accept Me as I Am*, 1985), we have used the word "impairment" to describe a physical deviation from what is considered normal in structure, function, physical organization, or development. Such a condition is clearly objective and measurable, such as spina bifida or missing limbs. "Disability" refers to the functional limitation caused by the impairment; although it may be to some extent measurable and objective, its severity may be related to subjective factors such as age, intelligence, and temperament. For example, a person with a missing leg (the impairment) will be unable to walk without crutches or a prosthesis (the disability). "Handicap" is the disadvantage caused by the impairment or disability and is a subjective experience that will vary depending on many factors such as the period and culture in which people live as well as their own personalities. For example, when children with Down's syndrome were more routinely placed in institutions than is now the case, both their experience and that of their family were profoundly influenced by medical and societal practices and expectations.

Annotations of each title included appear in Chapters 5–8, and each chapter focuses on a different set of problems: physical problems, sensory problems, cognitive and behavior problems, multiple/severe disabilities and those we categorize as various disabilities. Books dealing with physical problems are found in Chapter 5 and cover health problems, AIDS, and orthopedic/neurological disabilities. Perhaps the most dramatic change between the literature surveyed for *Accept Me as I Am* (1985) and that covered in this guide has been the outpouring of books on AIDS, and thus this new category has been added. Books in Chapter 6 dealing with sensory problems cover those about the deaf-blind category, hearing impairments, and visual impairments. Books in Chapter 7 dealing with cognitive and behavior problems include emotional disturbances, learning disabilities, and mental retardation. Finally, Chapter 8 covers books dealing with multiple/severe disabilities, and with various disabilities that are represented in a single book.

Each annotation includes a factual description of the book and a short critical analysis. Citations of reviews that have appeared in various periodicals are also given, and this marks a change from the 1985 guide.

8. ACCESSIBILITY OF THE COLLECTION

The Carnegie Library of Pittsburgh, Pennsylvania, has undertaken a project to collect the books cited in the reference books pertaining to disability published by R. R. Bowker: Baskin and Harris, *Notes from a Different Drummer,* 1977, *More Notes from a Different Drummer,* 1984; Friedberg et al., *Accept Me as I Am,* 1985; and the two new volumes *Portraying Persons with Disabilities* covering fiction and nonfiction works. To enhance the usefulness of the collection both as a research source and also to reach the general public, the collection will include at least two copies of each of these titles. One copy will remain in a reference collection available for research on the premises. At least one copy of each title will become part of the regular circulating collection.

The Carnegie Library of Pittsburgh participates in the ACCESS Pennsylvania program linking public, school, and academic library collections throughout the state in one database. Through ACCESS and OCLC, an international database to which the Carnegie Library belongs, the collection will be available for interlibrary loan statewide and to a national and international audience.

2

DISABILITY AND HISTORICAL TRENDS

M. Scott Peck, writing in The Different Drum: Community Making and Peace *(1987), quotes a statement made by John Winthrop, Massachusetts Bay Colony governor, which calls to us poignantly across the years: "We must delight in each other, make each other's conditions our own, rejoice together, mourn together, always having before our eyes our community as members of the same body."*

HISTORICAL TRENDS

From the dawn of history, human beings have demonstrated ambivalence about those who have had extreme physical, sensory, or behavioral deviations from what is considered usual or ordinary or normal. On the one hand, societies have frequently killed, isolated, or rejected such persons. Infanticide has been practiced by many cultures, including not only defective infants, but on occasion girl babies, twins, and those with other distinctive characteristics. Older persons as well who can no longer contribute to their group have been expected to die. Thus in some societies today individuals are still sacrificed for the survival of the group.

On the other hand, societies have felt fascination with the gamut of human differences and have portrayed odd and disabled people in the arts and literature from the time of the ancient Egyptians to the present day. Tenets from various religions, in addition to popular superstitions, have influenced social attitudes about exceptionalities, sometimes to the benefit but more often to the detriment of persons possessing them.

As societies have developed the technical, medical, and educational resources to better the lot of more of their members, more attention has been given to the well-being of individuals, including weaker or more vulnerable members, such as children, women, the aging, eccentrics, and handicapped persons. Thus, in technically highly developed societies, which are ruled by laws and guided by reason and morality, there is the expectation that disabled individuals will be offered just and humane treatment.

DEVELOPMENTS IN THE UNITED STATES

In the centuries preceding the present one, disabled people had to rely on charity or the whims of the powerful for their care and survival, and institutions were generally custodial rather than remedial. In the eighteenth and nineteenth centuries in France, England and America, educators became increasingly interested in the possibility of educating deaf, blind, autistic, and mentally retarded children.

Indeed, American educators became overoptimistic about their ability to ameliorate the effects of handicapping conditions. By the end of the nineteenth century, more and more handicapped people were entering specialized institutions. However, too few were graduated from them, so that often geographically isolated state "schools" and "hospitals" grew in size and impersonality, until they became vast warehouses for those whom society deemed rejects. By the end of the century, misinterpretation of Darwinism (social Darwinism) gave a rationale for the practices of institutionalization and segregation of disabled people (as well as the subjugation of poor and minority people).

By the turn of the century, the concept of universal education was a reality in the United States, but it was not until 1918 that all states in the Union had legally effective compulsory education. This practice did not extend universally to handicapped children by any means.

At the beginning of the present century, public education classes for children with illnesses and impairments were gradually established in the larger cities. After World War I, there was increased interest in vocational education and rehabilitation for disabled adults as wounded soldiers returned from the battlefields. In the 1920s, a number of organizations were formed to benefit various groups of disabled people, including the Council for Exceptional Children (CEC) in 1922. CEC's emphasis was on the education of special children and on the establishment of professional standards for special education teachers. Today, CEC is an organization of almost 50,000 members, including teachers, administrators, parents, professionals, and advocates of handicapped and gifted children and adults.

Whereas slow progress was made toward better medical and educational sources for children in the beginning of this century, ambivalence toward the disabled can be illustrated by the pattern of exclusion of handicapped children from access to public schools, which was typical of this period. In 1919, in a challenge to such exclusion, a suit was brought to a Wisconsin court by parents of a child with cerebral palsy. Their son's exclusion was upheld because he produced "a depressing and nauseating effect upon teachers and school children" (State ex rel. *Beattie vs. Board of Education,* 1919).

As recently as 1962, only 16 states included even only mildly mentally retarded children in their compulsory school attendance laws (Roos, 1970; Trends and issues in special education for the mentally retarded. *Education and Training of the Mentally Retarded,* 5[2]: 51–61).

In 1954, in the landmark ruling in *Brown vs. Topeka Board of Education,* the Supreme Court outlawed the widespread practice of maintaining racially segregated schools. The court maintained that the separate schools denied black students their right, as guaranteed by the Fourteenth Amendment, to equal educational opportunity. A decade later, the Civil Rights Act clarified the definition of "equal educational opportunity." Although progress toward racial equality was accelerated by these events, the goal of equal access and opportunity is still elusive in many school systems.

Following the momentum engendered by the civil rights activists, advocates of disabled children and adults began to exert their influence in the courts and legislatures on behalf of their constituencies. Efforts to ensure free and appropriate education for disabled children culminated in 1975 in Public Law 94-142, the Education of All Handicapped Children Act, passed by Congress and signed by President Ford. Incorporating as it did the due process procedures available to parents and the financial incentives available to the states, it was a landmark event in the struggle to obtain the same rights for handicapped students as exist for other children.

In the same year, however, professional practices by those responsible for the well-being of exceptional children, particularly with regard to classification and labeling, were analyzed and questioned in a source book (N. Hobbs, *Issues in the Classification of Children: A Source Book on Categories, Labels, and Their Consequences,* Jossey-Bass, 1975). This report was commissioned by Secretary of Health, Education and Welfare Elliot Richardson in 1972 and involved ten federal agencies and 93 leading experts. They reported an overrepresentation of poor, minority, and male students labeled as mentally retarded. It was noted that this pejorative label has a negative effect on a child, regardless of subsequent remediation. Their 40 recommendations in addition to other recommendations were timely for the formulation of P.L. 94-142. In 94-142, the former situation is addressed to some extent in the provisions that the evaluation mechanisms must be racially and culturally fair. To some extent the latter objection is addressed by the stipulation that the Individualized Educational Program of students identified as handicapped must be reviewed annually to ascertain its appropriateness.

PUBLIC LAW 94-142 IN JEOPARDY

In the *Washington Post* of April 18, 1985, the following news was reported: Education Secretary William J. Bennett appointed as his special assistant for the Office of Educational Philosophy and Practice, Eileen Marie Gardner, an analyst who had written in the previous year that "the handicapped constituency displays a strange lack of concern for the effects of their regulations upon the welfare of the general population." Senator Lowell P. Weicker (R., Conn.), waving a May 1984 article for the American Heritage Foundation by assistant Eileen Marie Gardner, quoted her as writing that regulations specifically aimed at the disabled have "probably weakened the quality of teaching and falsely labeled normal children."

In the study for the American Heritage Foundation, drafted in 1983, and in her testimony before the Senate Appropriations Committee, Health and Human Services Subcommittee, philosopher Gardner was quoted as saying she will be involved in "setting the tone for the department." She stated: "They [handicapped children] and their parents are 'selfish.' " "They are draining badly needed resources from the normal school population" [to the extent of $1.2-billion]. "Nothing comes to an individual that he has not (at some point in his development) summoned. . . . Each of us is responsible for his life situation." She also stated that hers are "private religious views, a fundamentalist doctrine of Christian existentialism." "There is no injustice in the universe . . . a person's external circumstances do fit his level of spiritual development. . . . Children and all who suffer affliction were made that way to help them grow toward spiritual perfection," she answered in response to questions from Lowell Weicker. She supported the elimination of all federal assistance to the handicapped. We are violating the "order of the universe" by trying to help these people, she maintained.

The conservative right wing wished to abolish the Office of Education as a cabinet post, and some actually wanted to dismantle the public school system. Thus, Secretary Bennett's office was to some extent a philosophical battleground for those of varying educational philosophies. Bennett first disassociated himself from Gardner's remarks, then asked for and received her resignation. In the *New York Times* of April 18, 1985 (A 25), it was reported that Lawrence A. Uzzell, another newly appointed aide, also advocated ending most federal education programs, including those for the handicapped. Bennett said these comments on federal laws "do not in any way reflect the views of the Administration or the Secretary of Education."

At the Council for Exceptional Children's 63rd Annual Convention (April

1985), a resolution of opposition was accepted with regard to the appointment of Gardner. Specifically they found her position, notably that programs for the handicapped have been purchased at the expense of academically talented students, unacceptable. "We find it appalling for an official of an Administration that has abolished the federal program for gifted and talented students and the Office for the Gifted and Talented to have blamed the lack of services for such children on handicapped children" ("Resolution of Opposition," *Exceptional Children* vol. 52 #1, 1985, p. 86).

On April 19, 1985, the two officials Gardner and Uzzell were reported to have left the Department of Education. The Secretary of Education expressed surprise that so many citizens had attended hearings and voiced their opposition to any attempts to weaken P.L. 94-142. Written testimony was submitted by many groups on behalf of handicapped people. For example, in February 1986, a ten-page testimony and appendix was submitted by the director and the supervisor of Perkins School for the Blind on behalf of deaf-blind services, which reach a small, discrete low-incidence population.

In October 1986, further amendments to 94-142 were passed by both the House and Senate, enlarging educational responsibility. Perhaps the most noteworthy change is the mandate for educational services for handicapped children from birth through 5 years of age. President Reagan signed this piece of legislation.

CHRONOLOGY: EVENTS INFLUENCING DISABLED PEOPLE

This chronology details events that have significantly influenced disabled children and adults in the United States. These events comprise educational practices, instructional policy, court actions, legislation, political happenings, citizens' advocacy, and scientific advances. The events have altered the nature of problems to which people are prone and changed the quality of life and opportunities for fulfillment of disabled and health-impaired people.

1790   Ben Franklin invents bifocal lenses.

1800   Benjamin Waterhouse performs the first vaccination in the United States against smallpox.

1817   First educational program for any exceptional children and youth is formally established in the United States: the American Asylum for the Education and Instruction of the Deaf (now the American School for the Deaf), in Hartford, Connecticut.

Thomas Gallaudet establishes an asylum for instruction of people who are deaf mutes and employs a deaf teacher, Laurent de Clerc.

1829   First residential school for blind pupils, New England Asylum for the Blind, is established in Watertown, Massachusetts (now Perkins School for the Blind).

1834   Louis Braille publishes Braille code, using six raised dots in combination.

1839   Laura Bridgeman, the first deaf-blind person to be educated in the United States, is admitted to Perkins School for the Blind.

1840   Rhode Island passes the first state compulsory education law.

1851   A school for "the idiot and the feeble minded" is founded in Massachusetts after Eduard Sequin, a student of Jean-Marc Gaspard Itard, in France, described his educational procedures.

1852   Compulsory school attendance is introduced in Massachusetts.

1859   Nation's first residential school for people with mental retardation is started in South Boston under the name Massachusetts School for Idiotic and Feeble-Minded Youth. Samuel Gridley Howe, then head of Perkins School for the Blind, is most influential in enlisting legislative and public support for this new facility.

1861–   Civil War: 61 percent of the total number of deaths among Union forces are
1865   due to disease, showing the enormous influence of infectious diseases in this century.

1862   Cerebral palsy (Little's disease) is defined by Winthrop Phelps.

1864   Gallaudet College for deaf students is founded in Washington, D.C.

1869   First daytime classes for any exceptional children are begun for deaf pupils in Boston, Massachusetts.

1879   Funds are appropriated by Congress, establishing the American Printing House for the Blind (in Kentucky).

1882   Robert Koch discovers the tubercle bacillus as the cause of tuberculosis (consumption).

1890   Helen Keller begins oral speech and symbolic communication with Anne Sullivan.

1892   Braille typewriter is developed by Frank Hall.

1895   Diphtheria antitoxin is produced on a worldwide scale, greatly reducing the death rate from this disease and spurring research on other antitoxins.

1896   First public school day classes for mentally retarded are begun in Providence, Rhode Island.

1899   First public school classes for children with physical handicaps are started in Chicago, Illinois.

1900   First electrical amplifying device for hard-of-hearing people is designed.
        First public school for blind children is begun in Chicago, Illinois.

1906   First public school class for epileptic children opens in Cleveland, Ohio.

First public school classes for children with heart disease are held in New York.

1909   First classes for persons with epilepsy begin in Baltimore, Maryland.

1913   Roxbury, Massachusetts, starts first classes for partially sighted pupils.

1914–   World War I: Disabled veterans focus national attention on rehabilitation.
1918

1917   Braille code is accepted for blind people as the universal American standard for the written word.

1918   All states achieve legally effective compulsory education.

1919   Federal Board for Vocational Education is directed to program vocational education for disabled veterans.

1920   Classes for hard-of-hearing students begin in Lynn, Massachusetts.

Training programs for teachers of handicapped children begin in colleges and universities, and states give partial reimbursements to local schools serving handicapped students; many state special education departments are established.

1921   Smith-Fess Act is passed—a joint federal-state program of vocational education for physically handicapped persons.

National Society for Crippled Children is founded.

American Foundation for the Blind is founded.

1922   The Council for Exceptional Children is organized. Emphasis is on education of special children (rather than on identifying them) and on establishing professional standards for special education teachers.

Frederick Banting and Charles Herbert Best report the discovery of insulin, making diabetes a controllable disease.

1928   Seeing Eye dogs for blind people are introduced in the United States.

1931   Modern library service for blind people begins, culminating in the Library for the Blind in the Library of Congress (Pratt-Smoot Act).

1935   Social Security Act is passed to aid crippled children and blind people. It defines "blind" for legal purposes.

1937   National Foundation for Infantile Paralysis is organized with President Roosevelt's support. Efforts finally culminate in a successful vaccine.

First blood bank opens in Cook County Hospital, Chicago, Illinois, and leads to new treatment to aid people with hemophilia, sickle-cell anemia, and thalassemia.

1939–   World War II spurs interest in physical medicine, rehabilitation procedures,
1945   and vocational rehabilitation.

1941   Retrolental fibroplasia is increasing greatly, causing over 10,000 blind babies.

1943   A new effect remedy for epilepsy (diphenylhydantoin) is developed.

Poliomyelitis epidemic occurs.

1945   World War II ends.

1946   Penicillin is manufactured synthetically, a lifesaving aid in infectious diseases, including rheumatic heart disease, and in protection from kidney disease for those with spina bifida.

1947   President's Committee on Employment of the Handicapped is organized.

1948   The United States joins the World Health Organization to work with other countries toward achieving the highest possible level of health for all people.

1948   United Cerebral Palsy Association is organized to help bring about reform in educational policy and practices.

      National Epilepsy League is established in Chicago.

      Linus Pauling and coworkers come to understand the mechanism of sickle-cell anemia and its heredity factors.

1950   National Association for Retarded Citizens is formed; other parent groups with focus on specific exceptional conditions also begin to press for special education and other necessary services.

      "The pill" is popularized by Margaret Sanger. Birth control technology allows persons with hereditary and other disabilities a reproductive choice. Thus sex and marriage become more viable options for exceptional persons.

1953   National Institute of Neurological Diseases and Blindness begins study culminating in the discovery that retrolental fibroplasia is related to overadministration of oxygen to infants, thus greatly reducing this cause of blindness.

      DNA molecule is described by James Watson and Francis Crick, heralding genetic and chromosomal research such as gene splicing and in utero detection of inherited disease.

1954   Jonas Salk introduces a poliomyelitis vaccine.

      First successful kidney transplant from an identical twin heralds a new age of organ transplants.

      Brown vs. Topeka: Supreme Court rules that segregated schools violate the Fourteenth Amendment.

1959   Oldest documented case of AIDS, in a 25-year-old man in Manchester, England, with tissue analysis made 3 decades later.

1961   American National Standards Institute designates minimum design regulations consisting of 16 different aspects of a building for acceptability and usability by physically handicapped people.

      U.S. Public Health Service licenses the Sabin vaccine against poliomyelitis. It is taken by mouth, at low cost, and confers longer-lasting immunity.

1962   Thalidomide disaster in Europe leading to birth of deformed babies, is a stimulus to strengthening of drug amendments adopted by Congress, limiting human experiments, and mandating informed consent.

1963   Congress legislates funds both to support training of educators for all recognized groups of handicapped children and youth and to subsidize research regarding their education.

1964   Widespread epidemic of rubella occurs, producing congenital defects in 20,000 infants.

P.L. 88-352, Civil Rights Act of 1964, is passed, prohibiting discrimination on the basis of race, color, religion, sex, or national origin.

1967   Bureau of Education for the Handicapped is established by congressional action.

1968   Architectural Barriers Act (P.L. 90-480) is passed: assurance of barrier-free access for the handicapped to all public school facilities, federally occupied buildings, and buildings funded by federal assistance.

Rubella vaccine distribution is begun by the U.S. Public Health Service, eliminating a disease that exerts a damaging effect on the fetus of an infected mother.

Chromosome abnormalities associated with Down's syndrome are discovered by Court Brown.

1969   Passage of the Handicapped Children Early Education Program. Federal funds are allocated for programs to train the handicapped from birth to the age of 9.

Pennsylvania Association for Retarded Children vs. Commonwealth of Pennsylvania and *Mills vs. Board of Education of the District of Columbia* establishes that exclusion of handicapped children from public education may be a violation of due process and equal protection.

1973   Sections 503 and 504 of the Rehabilitation Act of P.L. 93-112 become the "Bill of Rights" for the handicapped, including the following: new barrier-free facilities, accessible programs or activities, right to employment, a free public education for every handicapped child.

1974   National Endowment for the Arts Amendments (P.L. 93–380) designate art education for the handicapped.

P.L. 93-247 Child Abuse Prevention Act becomes law.

1975   Project on the Classification of Exceptional Children results in the publication of *Issues in the Classification of Children: A Source Book on Categories, Labels, and Their Consequences* (Nicholas Hobbs, ed.).

P.L. 94-142, Education of All Handicapped Children Act, is passed to ensure the right of all exceptional children to an education. Those aged 3 to 21 will be served unless contrary to state law.

1976   All states have regulations subsidizing public school programs for exceptional children and youth.

1978   P.L. 94-142, Education of All Handicapped Children Act, becomes effective, ensuring all handicapped children a full public education and a variety of accompanying rights.

Gifted and Talented Children's Education Act is passed.

1981   International Year of the Disabled Person (United Nations).

1983   Essential features of 94-142 are upheld in the amendments passed by Congress.

Environmental Protection Agency concludes that lead levels (raised primarily by use of leaded gasoline) have put large numbers of American children (especially low-income urban dwellers) at risk.

1985   Organ transplants performed on infants and young children become common.

1986   P.L. 99-457, Education of the Handicapped Act, amendments require all states to offer educational services to children between the ages of 3 and 5 who have handicaps.

1989   Centers for Disease Control have 1,859 recorded cases of children under 13 years old nationwide having full-fledged AIDS.

1990   Americans with Disabilities Act covers 43 million handicapped people, including recovering drug and alcohol abusers and people with AIDS.
   • Law bans discrimination in employment in all businesses with more than 15 employees.
   • Every retail establishment must be made accessible.
   • Public and private transportation must provide lifts and other facilities in all new vehicles.
   • Telephone companies must provide special equipment for hearing and speech impaired.
   • P.L. 101-476 amended P.L. 94-142, Education for All Handicapped Children Act, to eliminate all references to "handicapped children," replacing this phrase with "children with disabilities."

Some of the events in this chronology were culled from a previous publication: June B. Mullins, "Events Influencing Physically Handicapped and Health Impaired People in the United States." *DPH Journal* Vol. 9, No. 1, Fall 1986.

3

REFERENCE BOOKS ON DISABILITIES AND ON PERSONS WITH DISABILITIES

> *Liberty demands not only equality of opportunity but a variety of them. It also means a tolerance for those who fail to conform to standards that may be culturally desirable but are not essential for society to continue. Present day society often fails to offer this tolerance.*
> —Bruno Bettelheim in *The Informed Heart, Autonomy in a Mass Age* (1960)

The early 1970s marked the beginning of the disability rights movement; the passage of legislation designed to ensure the right to education, access, and jobs for people who are disabled; and a correspondingly greater public awareness of the problems of people with disabilities. Naturally, the need for information on disabilities and on those who are disabled grew in direct proportion to these other factors. One result has been the publication of additional reference books dealing with disabilities and with persons who are disabled. The following bibliography, briefly annotated, contains 71 reference titles on all aspects of disabilities and the people who have them. Most tend to be oriented toward the United States, although there are a few from Great Britain and a few that deal with other countries as well. The majority of them have been published since 1980, although a few earlier titles have been included selectively.

One group of reference titles that has not been included is guides to the use of language dealing with disabilities—language as it is used in everyday writing and speaking and thus in bibliographic indexing and searching. For a detailed discussion of this topic, see *Accept Me as I Am: Best Books of Juvenile Nonfiction on Impairments and Disabilities,* fully cited in the bibliog-

17

raphy below. Discussions of this topic appear in Chapter 2, "Evolution of Attitudes, Practice, and Terminology," pages 7–16, and Chapter 3, "Treatment of Disabilities in Printed Sources," pages 17–30.

The only really up-to-date source for terminology that uses language in a way that is dignified, nonjudgmental, and lacking in stereotypical qualities is the *Thesaurus of ERIC Descriptors* (Phoenix, Ariz.: Oryx Press, any edition beginning with the 10th, 1984). The crux of language use when referring to disabilities or discussing persons who are disabled is that the emphasis should always be on the person, not on the disability. "We are people first," is an often quoted maxim among many minority groups. This statement is also the key to appropriate language use. For example, a group of children playing in the schoolyard of a school for deaf children are "children who are deaf" and not "deaf children." People who are blind or deaf or who use a wheelchair should be referred to this way, not as "the blind," "the deaf," or "the disabled."

Instead of the word "handicapped," which has come to have negative connotations, one might use the word "disabled," which is more neutral in tone and content. Or one might, as has been the recent trend, also decide that "disabled" is also somewhat negative, because it states a lack of some sort of ability, and might choose to use terminology such as "physically challenged" or "differently abled." The term "impairment" is sometimes used also. We prefer to use "impairment" when speaking of the actual physical condition and "disability" when speaking of the results of that condition. For example, a detached retina is a physical impairment that can result in the disability called low vision or blindness.

We see "handicap" as a description of a perceived social role. One can, for example, have an impairment that results in the disability of blindness, deafness, or paraplegia. Whether these disabilities are handicaps is a social perception, both on the part of those who have them and on the part of others who interact with individuals who are disabled. See the pages cited above in *Accept Me as I Am: Best Books of Juvenile Nonfiction on Impairments and Disabilities* for a more lengthy discussion of these ideas.

An excellent source of information on how one might approach positively the use of language dealing with disabilities and with people who have them is a small pamphlet published by the National Center on Educational Media and Materials in Reston, Virginia, *Guidelines for the Representation of Exceptional Persons in Educational Materials.* Most of the best articles on this topic were written in the 1970s. However, society, people, and language change slowly, and progress has not been all that rapid, even though people generally recognize that language is a main source for the perpetuation of stereotypes. A recent news article in the *DPH Newsletter* (Vol. XIII, No. 1, Spring 1991), published by the Division for Physically Handicapped of the Council for

Exceptional Children (note the name of the division as an example of how slowly language use changes), states that "Person First Language" is mandated in P.L. 101-476, which was passed in 1990 as an amendment to P.L. 94-142, the Education for All Handicapped Children Act. This amendment removes all references to "handicapped children," replacing this terminology with the phrase "children with disabilities" and thus placing the emphasis on people, not on disabilities.

Obviously, use of language is a personal choice and as such cannot be prescribed, but one should be aware that many people with disabilities are offended by most of the language used to discuss them and their physical impairments. The reference books here make use of a wide variety of language. The list is not intended to be comprehensive; rather, the items have been selected as examples of the types of reference works that are available. One could identify others by a bibliographic search. In addition, there are many excellent journal articles dealing with information on programs and services for people with disabilities, and we have made no attempt to cover them.

BIBLIOGRAPHY

Abrams, A. Jay, and Margaret A. Abrams. *The First Whole Rehab Catalog: A Comprehensive Guide to Products and Services for the Physically Disadvantaged.* White Hall, Va.: Betterway Publications, 1990.
A recent catalog of equipment, supplies, and services available in the United States for persons who are disabled.

Access to Mass Transit for Blind and Visually Impaired Travelers. Ed. by Mark M. Uslan et al. New York: American Foundation for the Blind, 1990.
A recent guide to travel and local mass transit in the United States for persons who are blind.

American Occupational Therapy Association. *Guidelines for Occupational Therapy Services in School Systems.* Rockville, Md.: American Occupational Therapy Association, 1987.
A handbook giving guidelines for occupational therapy in schools, especially in mainstreamed situations.

Angels and Outcasts: An Anthology of Deaf Characters in Literature. 3rd ed. Ed. by Trent Batson and Eugene Bergman. Washington, D.C.: Gallaudet College Press, 1985.
A revised edition of *The Deaf Experience* (2nd ed., 1976). Contains excerpts from fiction by and about persons who are deaf.

Baskin, Barbara H., and Karen H. Harris. *More Notes from a Different Drummer: A Guide to Juvenile Fiction Portraying the Disabled.* New York: Bowker, 1984.

Detailed reviews of fiction books for children and young adults about persons who are disabled. A follow-up to *Notes from a Different Drummer,* below.

Baskin, Barbara H., and Karen H. Harris. *Notes from a Different Drummer: A Guide to Juvenile Fiction Portraying the Handicapped.* New York: Bowker, 1977.
Detailed reviews of fiction books for children and young adults about persons who are disabled.

Case Studies: Serving Handicapped Children from Birth to Age Five. Ed. by Roberta Weiner, Executive Editor. Alexandria, Va.: Capital Publications, 1987.
Case studies on the care and education of young children in the United States who are handicapped, together with a directory of services available.

Children with Special Needs: ACT's Guide to TV Programming for Children. Ed. by Maureen Harmonay; foreword by Julius B. Richmond. Cambridge, Mass.: Ballinger, 1977.
Somewhat old but still a valuable tool to use when considering television programming for children with disabilities.

Civil Service Recruitment Program for Persons with Disabilities. Washington, D.C.: U.S. Department of State, Bureau of Personnel, 1988.
A brief guide to the possibilities for civil service jobs for persons who are disabled.

College and Career Programs for Deaf Students. Washington, D.C.: Gallaudet College and Rochester, N.Y.: National Technical Institute for the Deaf, 1986.
A directory of higher education programs in the United States and Canada for students who are deaf.

Davis, William Edmund. *Resource Guide to Special Education: Terms, Laws, Assessment Procedures, Organizations.* 2nd ed. Boston: Allyn and Bacon, 1986.
A general but comprehensive directory of special education in the United States.

Directory/Handicapped Children's Early Education Program. Chapel Hill, N.C.: Technical Assistance Development System, University of North Carolina, 1984– .
Annual.
A U.S. government publication listing preschool education programs in the United States for children who are handicapped. Some issues distributed to depository libraries in microfiche.

Directory of College Facilities and Services for People with Disabilities. 3rd ed. Ed. by Carol H. Thomas and James L. Thomas. Phoenix, Ariz.: Oryx Press, 1991.
A recent directory of colleges and universities in the United States and Canada that offer access and other related services for students who are physically handicapped.

Directory of National Information Sources on Handicapping Conditions and Related Services. U.S. Department of Education, Office of Special Education and Rehabilitative Services, Clearinghouse on the Handicapped. Washington, D.C.: U.S. Government Printing Office, 1982.
A somewhat dated but still useful directory of services in the United States for persons who are handicapped.

Directory of Residential Facilities for the Mentally Retarded. Willimantic, Conn.: American Society on Mental Deficiency. Annual.
A directory of public and private schools, hospitals, and homes in both the United States and Canada for persons who are mentally retarded.

Directory of Services for Blind and Visually Impaired Persons in the United States. 23rd ed. New York: American Foundation for the Blind, 1988– . Biennial.
Formerly titled *American Foundation for the Blind Directory of Agencies Serving the Visually Handicapped in the United States.* A comprehensive guide to services available in the United States.

Directory of Special Education. Prepared by the Special Education Section of UNESCO. Paris: UNESCO, 1986.
One of the few comprehensive international sources available.

Encyclopedia of Special Education: A Reference for the Education of the Handicapped and Other Exceptional Children and Adults. Ed. by Cecil R. Reynolds and Lester Mann. 3 vols. New York: Wiley, 1987.
A recent three-volume encyclopedia and an excellent comprehensive reference source.

The Exceptional Child: A Guidebook for Churches and Community Agencies. Ed. by James L. Paul. Syracuse, N.Y.: Syracuse University Press, 1983.
A guide to services for children with disabilities, focusing on religious education.

The FCLD Learning Disabilities Resource Guide: A State-by-State Directory of Special Programs, Schools, and Services. New York: Foundation for Children with Learning Disabilities Systems, Inc., 1985.
A 408-page state-by-state listing of programs, schools, and services for children who are disabled.

Financial Aid for the Disabled and Their Families. 1988–89 vol. Ed. by G. A. Schlachter and R. D. Weber. Redwood City, Calif.: Reference Services Press, 1988– . Biennial.
A directory of scholarships, fellowships, and other forms of financial aid for people who are disabled and for their families.

Friedberg, Joan Brest, June Mullins, and Adelaide Sukiennik. *Accept Me as I Am: Best Books of Juvenile Nonfiction on Impairments and Disabilities.* New York: Bowker, 1985.
A bibliography with detailed reviews of nonfiction books about persons who are disabled, geared to children and teenage readers.

Gallaudet Encyclopedia of Deaf People and Deafness. 3 vols. Ed. by John V. Van Clefe. New York: McGraw-Hill, 1987.
A landmark three-volume encyclopedia dealing with all aspects of the lives of deaf persons, information on deafness both historical and current, and biographical data.

Golin, Anne K., and Alex J. Ducanis. *The Interdisciplinary Team: A Handbook for the Education of Exceptional Children.* Rockville, Md.: Aspen Systems Corporation, 1981.
A handbook and manual on the teaching of children with disabilities, with an emphasis on the interdisciplinary approach and team teaching.

Gordon, Sol. *Living Fully: A Guide for Young People with a Handicap, Their Parents, Their Teachers, and Professionals.* New York: John Day, 1975.
Somewhat older than most books in this bibliography but still one of the best all-around guides to daily living for teens with disabilities and also for their parents, their teachers, and the professionals who work with them.

A Guide for Managers and Supervisors: Employment of People with Disabilities in the Federal Government. Washington, D.C.: U.S. Equal Employment Opportunity Commission, 1990.

A manual for employers of persons with disabilities, aimed at federal government managers but useful generally as well.

A Guide to Colleges for Hearing Impaired Students. Ed. by Mary Ann Liscio. Orlando, Fla.: Academic Press, 1986.

A directory of colleges and universities in the United States in terms of their accessibility and services for students who are hearing impaired.

A Guide to Recreation, Leisure, and Travel for the Handicapped. Toledo, Ohio: Resource Directories, 1985.

A directory and guide to travel, recreation, and sports for persons with disabilities.

Handicapped Funding Directory. Oceanside, N.Y.: Research Grant Guides. 1978– . Biennial.

A comprehensive funding directory dealing with services, federal aid, general economic assistance, grant seeking, and fund raising for persons with disabilities, as well as for programs for persons with disabilities. Latest edition is 1990.

Hanson, David P. *A Desk Reference of Legal Terms for School Psychologists and Special Educators.* Springfield, Ill.: Thomas, 1980.

A dictionary of legal terms dealing with special education issues, especially useful for school psychologists and special education professionals, as well as for parents and activist groups.

Heron, Timothy E., and Kathleen C. Harris. *The Educational Consultant: Helping Professionals, Parents, and Mainstreamed Students.* Boston: Allyn and Bacon, 1982.

A handbook for educational consultants, focusing especially on mainstreaming issues.

Katz, Alfred Hyman, and Knute Martin. *A Handbook of Services for the Handicapped.* Westport, Conn.: Greenwood, 1982.

Another handbook and manual on services for persons with disabilities, slightly older but still useful.

Klobas, Lauri E. *Disability Drama in Television and Film.* Jefferson, N.C.: McFarland, 1988.

A comprehensive, nearly 500-page review of the portrayal of persons with disabilities in television and motion pictures, with emphasis on stereotyping.

Lipkin, Marjorie B. *The School Search Guide to Private Schools for Students with Learning Disabilities.* Belmont, Mass.: Schoolsearch, 1989.

A more than 300-page guide to private schools in the United States geared to students who have learning disabilities.

Liscio, Mary Ann. *A Guide to Colleges for Mobility Impaired Students.* Orlando, Fla.: Academic Press, 1986.

A guide to colleges and universities in the United States with access and services for mobility-impaired students.

McIntyre, Thomas. *A Resource Book for Remediating Common Behavior and Learning Problems.* Boston: Allyn and Bacon, 1989.

A manual and handbook of behavior modification techniques, useful in working with children who are disabled, with potential for parents as well as for educators.

McKee, Nancy Carol. *The Depiction of the Physically Disabled in Preadolescent Contemporary Realistic Fiction: A Content Analysis.* Ann Arbor, Mich.: University Microfilms International, 1987.

A doctoral dissertation done at Florida State University in 1987 based on a content analysis of contemporary realistic fiction for children.

Mental Health Directory. Bethesda, Md.: U.S. Department of Health, Education and Welfare, Public Health Service and Washington, D.C.: Superintendent of Documents, 1985.

A directory of state and national agencies dealing with mental health and mental retardation.

NARIC Quarterly. Vol. 1, No. 1, Spring 1988. Silver Spring, Md.: National Rehabilitation Information Center, 1988– . Quarterly.

A quarterly journal published by the National Rehabilitation Information Center and a good source of various types of information useful to persons with disabilities.

National Directory, Training and Employment Programs for Americans with Disabilities. Washington, D.C.: U.S. Department of Health and Human Services, 1985.

A comprehensive directory of rehabilitation centers and opportunities for vocational rehabilitation and training in the United States.

National Endowment for the Arts. *The Arts and 504: A 504 Handbook for Accessible Arts Programming.* Washington, D.C.: National Endowment for the Arts; Superintendent of Documents, 1985.

A handbook and manual dealing with accessible art facilities for persons with disabilities.

Nutrition Services for Children with Handicaps: A Manual for State Title V Programs. Los Angeles: Children's Hospital of Los Angeles, 1982.

A handbook on nutrition and health services for children with disabilities, targeted for Title V programs in the states but with generally useful information.

OSERS News in Print. Vol. 1, No. 1, Autumn 1985. Washington, D.C.: U.S. Department of Education, Office of Special Education and Rehabilitative Services. Quarterly.

A quarterly guide to federal programs for persons with disabilities.

Perspectives: A Handbook in Drama and Theatre by, with, and for Handicapped Individuals. Ed. by Ann M. Shaw, Wendy Perks, and C. J. Stevens. Washington, D.C.: Drama and Theatre by, with, and for Handicapped Individuals, 1981.

A handbook on drama and theater by, with, and for persons with disabilities, developed by the American Theatre Association with the support of the National Committee on Arts for the Handicapped.

Peterson's Guide to Colleges with Programs for Learning-Disabled Students. 2nd ed. Ed. by Charles T. Mangrum II and Stephen S. Strichart. Princeton, N.J.: Peterson's Guides, 1988.

A nearly 400-page guide to colleges and universities in the United States with programs adapted to students who are learning disabled.

Pilkington, Thomas A. *Guide to Films on Mental Handicap: A List of Films on All Aspects of Mental Handicap Classified by Subject and Suggested Audiences.* London: National Society for Mentally Handicapped Children, 1973.
Included for its historical interest but may have some titles for current use.
Postsecondary Education and Career Development: A Resource Guide for the Blind, Visually Impaired, and Physically Handicapped. Baltimore, Md.: National Federation of the Blind, 1981.
A handbook and manual on higher education and careers for persons who are blind, visually impaired, or physically disabled.
Quicke, John. *Disability in Modern Children's Fiction.* Brookline, Mass.: Brookline Books and London: Croom Helm, 1985.
A book on disability as portrayed in contemporary fiction for children.
Ratzka, Adolf Dieter. *Independent Living and Attendant Care in Sweden: a Consumer Perspective.* New York: International Exchange of Experts and Information in Rehabilitation, World Rehabilitation Fund, 1986.
A description of living arrangements for persons with disabilities in Sweden.
Ready Reference Press. *Directory of Information Resources for the Handicapped: A Guide to Information Resources and Services for the Handicapped.* Santa Monica, Calif.: Ready Reference, 1980.
A guide and directory of resources and services for persons with disabilities, somewhat older than several similar ones listed in this bibliography but still of use.
Respite Care: A Listing of Resources: A report of the Select Committee on Children, Youth, and Families, 101st Congress, 2nd Session, House of Representatives. Washington, D.C.: Superintendent of Documents, Congressional Sales Office, 1990.
A directory of home care services for disabled and ill children in the United States.
Rickert, William E., and Jane Bloomquist. *Resources in Theatre and Disability.* Lanham, Md.: University Press of America, and Dayton, Ohio: Association for Theatre and Disability, 1988.
A recent directory on the theater in the United States for persons with disabilities.
Rogers, Michael A. *Living with Paraplegia.* London and Boston: Faber and Faber, 1986.
A directory on rehabilitation services and other facilities and services for persons with paraplegia in Great Britain.
Rosenberg, Michael S., Lawrence J. O'Shea, and Dorothy J. O'Shea. *Student Teacher to Master Teacher: A Handbook for Preservice and Beginning Teachers of Students with Mild and Moderate Handicaps.* New York: Macmillan and Toronto: Collier Macmillan Canada, 1991.
A recent handbook for training teachers of children with disabilities.
Scheiber, Barbara, and Jeanne Talpers. *Unlocking Potential: College and Other Choices for Learning Disabled People: A Step-by-Step Guide.* Bethesda, Md.: Adler and Adler, 1987.
A directory to colleges and universities, as well as to other postsecondary options in the United States, for people with learning disabilities.
Schuchman, John S. *Hollywood Speaks: Deafness and the Film Entertainment Industry.* Urbana: University of Illinois Press, 1988.

A history and the present situation of deafness and persons who are deaf in the American film industry.

Slovak, Irene. *BOSC Directory: Facilities for Learning Disabled People.* Congers, N.Y.: BOSC, 1985.

A directory of schools and training facilities for children who are learning disabled.

Sourcebook of Aid for the Mentally and Physically Handicapped. Ed. by Judith Norback and Asst. Ed. Patricia Weitz. New York: Van Nostrand Reinhold, 1983.

A directory of services for persons in the United States who are disabled.

The SpecialWare Directory: A Guide to Software Sources for Special Education. Columbus, Ohio: LINC Associates, 1983.

A directory of computer-assisted instruction available in the United States for the education of children with disabilities.

Spinal Network. Ed. and produced by Sam Maddox. Boulder, Colo.: Spinal Network, 1987.

"The total resource for the wheelchair community," according to its cover, a book that provides detailed information on all aspects of living with a spinal cord injury.

Synoground, S. Gail., and M. Colleen Kelsey. *Health Care Problems in the Classroom: A Reference Manual for School Personnel Emphasizing Teacher Classroom Observations and Management Techniques.* Springfield, Ill.: Thomas, 1990.

A recent handbook and reference manual for teachers on how to deal with health problems in the classroom.

Thorin, Suzanne E., and Shirley Piper Emanuel. *International Directory of Braille Music Collections.* Washington, D.C.: National Library Service for the Blind and Physically Handicapped, Library of Congress, 1987.

A reference work listing worldwide collections of music in Braille.

Training in the Community for People with Disabilities, by Einar Helander et al. One vol. in 35 parts. Geneva: World Health Organization, 1989.

A handbook on home care, rehabilitation, family relationships, independent living skills, and community health services for persons who are disabled in the developing countries of the world.

Videocassette and Film Programs for Special Education. Washington, D.C.: U.S. Department of Education, 1987.

A brief list of films and videotapes useful in special education settings.

Vocational Rehabilitation and the Employment of the Disabled: A Glossary. Geneva: International Labour Office, 1981.

A dictionary/glossary, in English, French, and Spanish, of terms used by persons involved in the occupational rehabilitation and employment of persons who are disabled.

Weisenstein, Gregory R. *Administrator's Desk Reference on Special Education.* Rockville, Md.: Aspen, 1986.

A handbook/manual for school administrators dealing with special education, especially with laws surrounding special education and mainstreaming.

Westling, David L. *The Special Educator's Handbook.* Boston: Allyn and Bacon, 1988.

A handbook/manual for new special educators giving guidelines and tools for carrying out one's job.

Westman, Jack C. *Handbook of Learning Disabilities: A Multisystem Approach.* Boston: Allyn and Bacon, 1990.

A comprehensive, 854-page guide to learning disabilities and to the education of children with learning disabilities.

Williams, Philip. *The Special Education Handbook: An Introductory Reference.* Milton Keynes, UK: Open University Press, 1990.

A basic dictionary of terminology used in special education.

Wright, Keith C., and Judith F. Davis. *Library and Information Services for Handicapped Individuals.* Englewood, Colo.: Libraries Unlimited, 1989.

A practical directory on how to provide library services, including school library services, for persons with disabilities.

Ziegler, Carlos Ray. *The Image of the Physically Handicapped in Children's Literature.* New York: Arno, 1980.

Reprint of a 1971 doctoral dissertation written at Temple University on the ways that physically disabled persons are portrayed in children's literature.

4

PATTERNS AND PRESENT TRENDS

Biologically, physiologically, we are not so different from each other; historically, as narratives we are each of us unique.
—Oliver Sacks

The world breaks everyone and afterward some are strong at the broken places.
—Ernest Hemingway

In our first volume, published in 1985 *(Accept Me as I Am)*, 350 nonfiction books portraying disabled people were reviewed. These books were often targeted for a particular reading level or age group. Some adult and other trade books were also deemed appropriate for young people and were included. In the ensuing years, significant additions to this genre of literature have motivated publication of the present, all-new edition, *Portraying Persons with Disabilities*. Some of the recent books have been best sellers, and some have received prestigious awards. A number of their plots have been adapted for movies and television. Their authors have been interviewed on talk shows and in newspapers and magazines. The popularity of this type of literature obviously continues, thereby maintaining the significant literary trend noted five years ago. Other patterns and trends that were evident in the previous collection have remained constant as well. These are reviewed in this chapter and illustrated by updated examples from the present volume. Some new emphases are noted that mirror contemporary developments and changing times.

WHO ARE THE AUTHORS OF THIS LITERATURE?

Disabled authors continue to contribute importantly to the collection. Ved Mehta's new, ongoing biographical recollections, serialized in *New Yorker* magazine, have been published in book form; the author has been blind since early childhood. One of the youngest contributors is Jason Gaes, who has written his book for kids, like himself, fighting cancer. Some writers are just embarking on their adult career, such as lawyer Angela Muir Van Etten, a dwarf, who tells about her childhood in New Zealand and her struggle for higher education, career, and marriage. At the other end of the age continuum, in Agnes deMille's book, are the insights of a very wise, old woman who has only lately confronted serious disability and illness. Among others, Hugh Gallagher has written a biography of Franklin Delano Roosevelt, adding strong emphasis about the effects of polio and paraplegia on the personality and actions of the great statesman. Gallagher brings unique insights to this work, since he himself was disabled by polio in young adulthood.

Relatives of disabled children and adults have provided many entries. Englishwoman Janet Taylor has crafted a moving memorial to her adolescent daughter's life, cut short by cancer. Writer Josh Greenfeld has continued the saga of his autistic son into the boy's approach to manhood. Randy Harper collaborated with his brother to write of Tom's bout with testicular cancer while at naval college at Annapolis. Jill Krementz recorded the voices of children who talked about how it feels when a parent dies.

A number of workers in the helping professions have penned accounts about their students, clients, and patients. Educator Mary MacCracken continues to beguile with her latest chronicle about her students and an aide, whose unique needs and problems were addressed in her special education class. Psychiatrist Judith Rapoport's best seller offers case histories of patients with the newly recognized obsessive-compulsive disorder that she has done much to identify. Perri Klass has reflected movingly in her journal about her interaction with hospitalized people while she was a medical student.

The literature is further enriched by a number of contributors who are professional writers and photographers. Curt Kaufman provided the black-and-white photos of his wife's elementary school class, where physically disabled Rajesh was mainstreamed. Investigative reporter Eric Lax has written a thriller about life and death on a transplant ward. Columnist Erma Bombeck appeals to all ages in her book of interviews of young people with cancer. Essayist Nancy Mairs writes more than incidentally of her seriously incapacitating multiple sclerosis but also offers an integrated, beautifully stated philosophy of life that embraces a far-reaching world view.

Some writers have had to use very ingenious methods to get their message across. Nonverbal and paralyzed Christopher Nolan relied on his mother to interpret his thoughts and type the words of his best-selling autobiography. Sienkiewiecz-Mercer literally raised her eyes to say yes to Steven Kaplan, who taught her to use a communication board in the institution where she had spent her childhood.

WHAT ARE THE SUBJECTS OF THESE BOOKS?

Some of the biographies and autobiographies discussed above recount the life of ordinary people. Or it might be more accurate to say the people were ordinary until they and their family responded to the burden of disability with extraordinary courage and grace. Other protagonists are celebrated for their outstanding achievements in politics, the arts, religion, and science. In some cases, it may not be generally known that the noted person was disabled. For example, in the case of Franklin Delano Roosevelt, it was public policy to hide the extent of his disability. Painter and nonsense writer Edward Lear kept his epilepsy a secret to all but his closest family members and friends for his entire life. There is yet another children's book about Louis Braille, who developed a notation system for blind readers. Several more books on various reading levels have been added to the already extensive coverage of Helen Keller, the famous deaf-blind scholar and activist. A few more children's books recount the life of scientist Thomas Edison, who had a hearing loss.

A number of entries reflect public interest in the vast institutions that, until recently, have tended to warehouse mentally retarded, emotionally disturbed, and other neglected people in society. A special indictment can be found in *Minds Made Feeble,* in which David Smith reexamines the whole history of the descendants of a supposedly tainted girl who was institutionalized for life. This celebrated case had shocking consequences for social policy, although it was apparently based on flawed research and prejudiced thinking. Other books, like *Winnie: My Life in the Institution* (Pastor-Bolnick, 1985) have provided a view from the institutionalized residents' often appalling perspective.

A number of books have had a foreign setting. For example, the well-known author Dominique Lapierre describes the milieu of a leper colony in a Calcutta slum. This intriguing book, *City of Joy,* translated from the French, begins with the activities of a Polish priest, who has come to India to be a holy man. Like that of Ved Mehta, Lapierre's rich prose illuminates a land and a culture fantastically different from our own. In a book on former times, *Everybody Here Spoke Sign Language,* Nora Ellen Groce researches the history of a population on an isolated island off the coast of New England, where a high incidence of hereditary deafness necessitated that everyone learn to sign through many generations.

Earlier in this century, disabled members of cultural minorities were apt to be ignored. This trend has been reversed in the professions and is reflected in trade literature as well. For example, the plight of present-day Native Americans is documented by Michael Dorris, who eloquently details both the heartbreak and the opportunities facing his people. The "Silent Twins" are black Americans who were raised on military bases in England. Their minority status no doubt exacerbated the mismanagement and misunderstanding that contributed to the waste of their gifts and their lives. Among the troubled children of Santa Clara with whom young Elizabeth Marek worked were Spanish Americans and members of other minorities.

Debra Kent, in *Images of the Disabled, Disabling Images* (A. Gartner and T. Joe, eds.; Praeger, 1987), analyzed works of fiction and drama to assess the image of disabled women in literature. With the exception of two recent collections of writings, she found that writers have usually focused on the most negative, inferior aspects in the life of disabled characters. Therefore, few positive role models have emerged on their pages for handicapped youth, and then only models of awe and pity for nonhandicapped readers. This situation is in contrast to the strong and positive images of disabled women that are present in this collection of nonfiction. Of course, famous women such as Jane Addams and Helen Keller are represented, but lesser known subjects also show the many life-styles available to disabled girls and women.

Animals are the subject of several books, most often in their capacity to provide special services for blind or physically disabled people. Perhaps the strangest animal subject noted is the blinded English jackdaw, Blind Jack. The story of his rehabilitation illustrates some of the best principles of special education, even though he was only a bird and his teacher was a full-time housewife and mother.

REPRESENTATION OF DISABILITIES

The most notable addition to the literature since the earlier compilation is a new category of books: those about acquired immune deficiency syndrome, AIDS. This disease first was identified in 1981 and is now recognized as one of the major health problems in the world today. Over 100,000 cases have been confirmed in this country alone, and estimates of new cases continue to rise. High-risk populations include drug abusers, as well as homosexual and bisexual males, but the disease is spreading to the population at large.

More than 1,700 American children under the age of 13 have been diagnosed with AIDS, and many others, including infants, are HIV positive for the disease. Television has dramatized the trials of one family whose two hemophiliac boys contracted the disease from blood transfusions. Because curtailing the spread of AIDS is linked to safe sexual practices and, in the case of drug abusers, to the use of clean needles, further education in these areas is crucial. A plethora of books targeted at junior high and high school age readers have appeared, as have a few for younger children. In addition, many books have been written about the young adults who have contracted AIDS. Rapid advancements in research tend to quickly date medical information in this area, but some of the older books may serve as a useful starting point to introduce the subject, and one, *And the Band Played On,* is regarded as a classic. It should be remembered that books that are solely didactic and informational in content have largely been excluded from this collection, which favors books dealing with real people and actual situations.

Advances in the area of organ transplantation have led to wide use of this treatment to replace an increasing number of organs in patients of all ages. The trend is reflected in books such as English professor Lee Gutkind's foray into a modern transplant center to write an exciting book for better readers. Margery Facklam explains to younger children the subject of spare parts. The organ recipient's perspective is usually very important in such books.

A few disabilities have received almost no attention in the literature before now or were perhaps barely identified until recently. Michael Dorris has written about the absolutely preventable and, therefore, more tragic fetal alcohol syndrome that beset his adopted son. Neurologist Oliver Sacks devotes a chapter of his best seller to an account of a young man with Tourette's syndrome—a disorder that some still fail to acknowledge. Judith Rapoport has publicized obsessive-compulsive disorder, a behavioral syndrome that was considered rare until she clarified the problem and described its fairly successful treatment. Joanna Permut has contributed an autobiographical account of her struggle to learn to live with lupus. A relatively new illness, posttraumatic stress syndrome, is graphically described by stewardess Sandra Purl *(Am I Alive?),* who survived an airplane crash in which there were many fatalities.

MAJOR THEMES

All of the books that have been included are deemed scientifically accurate and therefore provide information about impairments and disabilities. When appropriate, there may be a strong emphasis on prevention, on treatment and rehabilitation, or on education about a category of problems. The many books by the Silversteins for elementary age children focus on the under-standing of disabilities as their main emphasis.

In concert with general professional opinion, most authors stress integra-tion of disabled children in school and of adults in the community. A won-derful picture book for young children, *Our Teacher's in a Wheelchair,* por-trays a young man with paraplegia who teaches in a day care center. Notable exceptions to the trend toward integration appear most often in deaf educa-tion. Marcia Forecki, for example, eventually enrolled her young son in a state residential school for deaf children. Oliver Sacks' and Harlan Lane's books illustrate an increasing interest in deaf people and in sign language. New signing dictionaries, some for very young children, continue to reach the market.

We have noted above some works that offer a strong indictment against large institutions for retarded or emotionally disturbed people. However, these institutions, as well as others such as specialized hospitals, group homes, and medical schools, are frequently the settings in which the protago-nists find themselves.

As in the first compilation, a few books here are humorous and even irreverent. Cartoonist John Callahan has a serious message, but his story, the illustrations of his alcohol-related accident, and his rehabilitation as a quad-riplegic are full of laughs along the way.

FUTURE DIRECTIONS

Until recently the concept "learning disabilities" embraced those disorders of cognition generally associated with communication, memory, problem solv-ing, and logic. Most of the books in the present volume and *Accept Me as I Am* (1985) describe children and adults who have such problems, and often consequent emotional reactions to their inabilities and lack of social accept-ance.

Recently, researchers have turned their attention to the nonanalytical, right side of the brain, which seems to play a crucial role in direct conscious-ness and in recognition of reality. Oliver Sacks' book, *The Man Who Mistook His Wife for a Hat* (1985), addresses the development of people with various kinds of learning disabilities. Sacks offers some new insights on the value of literature, or narrative as he calls it. He says that narrative or symbolic power, which is concrete reality in the imaginative form of symbol and story, is comprehended by children before abstract and schematic thought is achieved, and that this mode persists in giving any individual, even a grossly retarded one, "a sense of the world."

Carol Lawson, writing in the *New York Times* ("Once Upon a Time in the Land of Bibliotherapy," Nov. 8, 1990, p. B1) describes the startling change that has occurred in contemporary children's literature. The new books reflect a stark realism that contrasts with the innocence and fantasy of most children's books a generation ago. Lawson says that publishers and librarians group these books—both fiction and nonfiction—into the category "bibliotherapy." Her first example is a book for six-year-old readers, *Losing Uncle Tim,* by Mary Kate Jordan, a vivid and poignant treatment of AIDS. Lawson also points to the trend for special-issue books to include photographs of "real people and places instead of drawings, long a standard feature of children's books" (p. B6).

Special issues include, but are not exclusively limited to, the subjects of disability, sickness, and death. The executive director of the American Library Association's children's division, Susan Roman, reports that the children's book industry has gone from 3,000 to 4,500 titles a year and that books on special issues are proliferating as part of this general growth.

While there is some controversy about whether children should be exposed to harsh realities, the books reviewed in this volume are almost always positive in the sense that they portray real people successfully coping with problems and enriching themselves and others through the process. Those portrayed do not always survive, but their courage and spirit command our admiration.

5

BOOKS DEALING WITH PHYSICAL
PROBLEMS

And as for sickness: are we not almost tempted to ask
whether we could get along without it? Only great
pain is the ultimate liberator of the spirit.
> —Nietzsche

Deep under ashes . . .
Burning charcoal chilled now by
*   his hissing tears.*
> Bashō Matsuo in *The Mourning Father*

Titles in this chapter are classified under two sections: Health Problems and
Orthopedic/Neurological Disabilities. Within each section, citations are al-
phabetical by author, except for the subsection on AIDS, included under
Health Problems, that is alphabetized separately.

The first section, Health Problems, annotates titles covering disorders
such as allergies, cancer, and kidney failure.

Books listed under Orthopedic/Neurological Disabilities include brain
injury, cerebral palsy, epilepsy, quadriplegia and multiple sclerosis.

There is an inherent overlapping of diagnoses in the two sections. Books
about people with cancer are usually listed in the first section, Health Problems, although the subjects may have various orthopedic or neurological
problems as a result of their disease. A book about a person who is paraplegic
due to poliomyelitis is listed in the second section, although the individual
was originally stricken with a viral disease. A book about someone disabled
by a birth defect or by an accident also appears in the second section. The
section labeled AIDS deals with all phases and manifestations of this epidemic.

HEALTH PROBLEMS

■ Abrams, Bernard S., and Mike Harden. *Fight for Life.* Silverwood, 1987. 125pp. (0-9618145-0-0) Reading Level: Grades 9–12.
Disability: Epilepsy; Lennox-Gastaut syndrome

Dr. Bernard S. Abrams, a Columbus, Ohio, optometrist, and his wife, Shirley, adopted Felice as an infant. She was their fourth child. They knew little of her medical history, but she was a healthy, happy child. At the age of 6, however, she began to suffer severe seizures, which were eventually diagnosed as epilepsy. The usual drug therapy did not help, and the seizures became more frequent and more traumatic.

Felice's parents, her three siblings, who ranged in age from 11 to 22, and her kindergarten teacher rallied around and provided all the support they could. It soon became evident, however, that her prognosis was bleak. A trip to Johns Hopkins resulted in the diagnosis of myoclonic epilepsy, or Lennox-Gastaut syndrome, a form of epilepsy that did not respond to most drugs. Its long-term effects frequently included mental retardation, which would eventually result unless the seizures could be controlled.

Abrams learned of a drug, sodium valproate, that had been used successfully for years in the treatment of severe seizures. Because of questions about side effects, however, the Federal Drug Administration (FDA) had never approved it for use in the United States. Encouraged by Dr. Earl Sherard, a Columbus neurologist, himself a paraplegic, and by Father Robert Hunt, a priest friend, Abrams began a campaign to gain approval for the drug that eventually led NBC-TV to undertake national televised coverage of Felice and the issue of sodium valproate. Abrams took Felice to Birmingham, England, for initial withdrawal from her other drugs and the inception of treatment with sodium valproate. Felice responded well and eventually was able to resume the life of a nondisabled child, belying the second opinion diagnosis of a local neurologist who had recommended that Felice be permanently institutionalized and treated by the usual drugs.

Even after Felice was stabilized, Abrams continued his campaign, which finally resulted in official FDA approval of the drug, but not before Abrams and Fr. Hunt found it necessary to smuggle in 5,000 tablets of sodium valproate from England for use by dozens of people who had appealed to them to help their children. At the same time, other parents were also smuggling the drug from Mexico.

In an epilogue, Abrams reflects both on the "professional arrogance" and callousness that he often encountered from American medical professionals, public health officials, and pharmaceutical company officials, on the double-track American health system for the rich and for the poor, and on the quest that brought together an Orthodox Jewish father, a black paraplegic physician, a Roman Catholic priest, and large numbers of desperate parents.

Analysis: Highly recommended for high school aged readers, this book is outstanding both for its story of the way Abrams and his family dealt with Felice's disability and for its advocacy of citizen action to accomplish necessary changes in government and society. It is surprising that a trade publisher did not pick up the rights for this work. It is literate, intense, and gripping, and its themes represent universal questions.

■ Aladjem, Henrietta, and Peter H. Schur. *In Search of the Sun: A Woman's Courageous Victory over Lupus.* Scribner, 1988. 264pp. (0-684-18759-0) Reading Level: Grades 10–12. (KR 1 Ja88; LJ 15 Mr88; PW 8 Ja88)
Disability: Lupus

This is a revision of Aladjem's book *The Sun Is My Enemy,* published in 1972, in which she first described her struggle with lupus. In the present volume, Dr. Schur's medical chapters are interspersed with Aladjem's story.

In a detailed introduction, Schur defines systemic lupus erythematosus (SLE or lupus), a chronic inflammatory disease characterized by autoimmune phenomena that may affect the skin, joints, kidneys, lungs, nervous system, tissue linings, or other organs of the body. The abnormal immune response may be triggered by infections, ultraviolet light, drugs, pregnancy, stress, or other factors. The clinical course of the illness may involve periods of remission and relapse that can be acute or chronic. Lupus develops nine times more frequently in females, although boys and girls up to the age of adolescence are affected almost equally. Most patients experience their first symptoms as young adults. It is more common among blacks, Chinese, and some Indian tribes than among whites. The prognosis has continued to improve in recent years, so patients now have a 90 percent chance of survival for at least ten years.

Aladjem wrote stories for the *Boston Globe* from Paris during the Vietnam peace talks. She was instrumental in founding the National Lupus Foundation of America and has written four books about the disease. Her battle for her own life began with a strange array of ailments, including fatigue, nausea, and swelling of her skin, which assailed her on a trip to Holland with her husband and her three young children. The symptoms were similar to those she had experienced as an 18-year-old in her native Bulgaria after a ski trip. Back in Boston, it would be three years before physicians would confirm a diagnosis of her mysterious disease. Like one third to one half of lupus patients, she had become photosensitive, and she developed skin rashes from exposure to the sun. Lupus has been described as "a chronic civil war within the body" (p. 29).

At that time, in the 1950s, little was known about lupus, and simply reaching a diagnosis of the problem was a long and agonizing process. After a winter walk in the Canadian mountains, the author developed a red butterfly facial rash, a hallmark of lupus. She continued feeling excruciatingly weak and tired, and her kidneys became seriously affected. She was treated by a host of drugs, some of which exacerbated the discomfort. Finally, she was given injections of a vitamin, nicotinamide, that a Bulgarian doctor had used to cure her nephew of lupus some years before. For whatever reason, she had a complete remission after 20 years of symptoms, and the case was reported in the *Journal of the American Medical Association.*

With her newfound health and a need for independence, she spent a month in Paris as a reporter, later publishing her story and beginning a career of helping lupus sufferers. The Lupus Foundation of America now has a membership of over 30,000, with chapters in every state and international affiliates. Aladjem received the President's Volunteer Action Award for health in 1985, in the presence of her granddaughter.

The book ends with several chapters of questions and answers, a glossary, references, a list of resources, and an index.

Analysis: Aladjem writes crisp, colorful prose. Her interesting story can be read without reference to the interspersed medical chapters. On the other hand, Dr. Schur's more scholarly text deepens the reader's understanding of lupus. His ruminations on medical responsibility and the doctor-patient relationship are thought provoking. It should be noted that Aladjem's experiences with lupus are not necessarily typical, in either severity or eventual outcome, as she herself indicates.

■ Almonte, Paul, and Theresa Desmond. **Diabetes.** Illus. Crestwood, 1991. 47pp. (0-89686-604-1) Reading Level: Grades 2–6.
Disability: Diabetes

Part of The Facts About . . . series, this book is written to present diabetes to young readers. Topics covered include types and causes of diabetes, treatments and daily routines, effects of the disease, and special problems. The writers illustrate their text with miniprofiles of diabetic children and adults. Full-color photographs show youngsters injecting insulin, taking blood for tests, and engaging in activities like swimming and boating. The final pages give sources for more information and a glossary/index.

Analysis: This is an excellent book both for children with diabetes and for the general reader. The text is informative and clearly written, the type is large and readable, and the brief case histories personalize the facts being transmitted.

■ Bearison, David J. *They Never Want to Tell You: Children Talk about Cancer.* Harvard Univ. Pr., 1991. 194pp. (0-674-88370-5) Reading Level: Grades 7–12.
Disability: Cancer; Leukemia

Bearison is a professor in developmental psychology at the City University of New York. In the foreword, he says he initially intended to write a book just for children but found that children's concerns were also those of anyone who has cancer, and the children were often able to speak more candidly about issues than adults, who have absorbed the conventionalized behavior and attitudes of society. The introduction instructs adults in how to talk to children about cancer, a disease associated with so much uncertainty. The author advocates that parents and professionals be open with children in terms of the course of treatment, in welcoming questions, and in encouraging the expression of feelings. He would deemphasize both the specific diagnosis and the probabilities for recovery.

Bearison personally met with 75 children, either in the hospital or in an outpatient pediatric oncology clinic. He selected the stories of the eight children who, in their own voice, are the focus of the book. These narratives consist of the children's own words and dialects to tell about what it is like to have cancer. Many of the children interviewed said they wished that they had had such a book either to read when they found out they had cancer or to give to their family and friends. The children ranged in age from 3 to 19, and they came from many economic classes and ethnic backgrounds.

Several children spoke of their disappointment when their tumors reappeared, necessitating another arduous course of chemotherapy and radiation. Several had considered suicide as a way out of their predicament. Some spoke of friends who were scared of catching the disease, but most found that their friends stood by them. To a person, they described the terrible toll their illness had on their parents. Some parents tried, unsuccessfully, to hide information from them.

The first narrator spoke of the time when nurses tried to keep him from knowing that a good friend on the ward had died. In the end, he did a graffiti project on the handball court in memory of his friend. One girl said her boyfriend left her because she was going to lose her hair through chemotherapy and because she could not dance anymore. An athletic boy who was planning to try out for college tennis was told that because part of the bone in his leg must be replaced, he could never ski or play tennis again. He later learned he must have lung surgery as well, which really bothered him. A preschool boy had a bone marrow transplant donated by his 8-year-old brother.

Following the narratives, the common themes that have run through them are listed: "Why Me?," the role of God and prayer, fears about having cancer, losing hair, advice for others who have cancer, how having cancer tests friendships, how having cancer has changed the subjects' attitudes and social behavior beyond the context of cancer, and talking about talking about cancer. Discussion of each of these follows, illustrated with commentary by children. In an afterword, Bearison writes a dialogue of a typical case conference as a way of demonstrating how very well medical staffs are attuned to the psychological reactions and emotional needs of their young patients.

Analysis: This well-written book attests to Bearison's ability to communicate with youngsters. Even the preschool narrator speaks out with honesty and wisdom. His advice for parents, professionals, and friends is easy to understand but of profound significance. The narratives are easy to read and in the vernacular of the children. We are told nothing about the contributors except what is gleaned from their presentations. Even the gender of some is not clear. Thus, the voices are somewhat disembodied. However, the universal themes discussed have been made very accessible to young readers, which was the stated purpose of the book.

■ Bergman, Thomas. *One Day at a Time: Children Living with Leukemia.* Photographs by Thomas Bergman. Gareth Stevens, 1989. 56pp. (1-55532-913-6) Reading Level: Grades 2–6. (BCCB F90; BL 15 Ja90; KR 1 N89)
Disability: Cancer; Leukemia

In this photo-essay, Bergman follows two children through eight months of treatment for leukemia. Hanna is 2 years old and had been sick for two weeks when Bergman began her story; the opening pictures show the little girl and her parents in the first days of diagnosis and treatment. Frederick was 3 and had been sick for six months. Although both children have the same disease and are being treated at the same hospital and with similar protocols, each story includes some different details. The focus is on the hospital, its staff and procedures, and the two small patients, but both children are also shown at home: Hanna sits at the table hungrily spooning in food from a full plate of her mother's cooking; Frederick goes fishing with his father and his brother.

The final pages include questions and answers about cancer and leukemia, suggestions for young readers who might want to try to help children with cancer, a list of sources of information and books, and a glossary of words about leukemia and its treatment.

Analysis: Bergman approaches this difficult subject with remarkable sensitivity and honesty. Thirty years ago, nearly all children with leukemia died within 18 months; now, thanks to advances in treatment, more than half of leukemia patients recover and grow up. Yet, as Bergman shows, the treatment itself is difficult and painful, and the outcomes uncertain for a long time; the reader cannot escape the thought that, if more than half the patients with childhood leukemia survive, almost half of them do not.

Bergman's text is straightforward, with well-chosen details. The photographs are at once moving, poignant, and informative; Bergman does not flinch from showing children (and parents) living through terrible moments. The resource pages at the end are an important part of the book.

Young readers will gain a clear picture of Hanna's and Frederick's experiences and the causes and treatment of this disease. Older readers, gazing at close-ups of these beautiful children, will be moved by their vulnerability, their courage, and their strength.

■ Blakely, Mary Kay. *Wake Me When It's Over: A Journey to the Edge and Back.* Times Books/Random, 1989. 273pp. (0-8129-1699-9) Reading Level: Grades 10–12. (BL J189; KR 15 Je89; LJ J189; NYTBR 6 Ag89) *Disability:* Multiple health problems (diabetes and pulmonary disease); Coma

Mary Kay Blakely is a professional journalist who has written for national magazines and newspapers; at the time of publication of this book, she was a regular contributor to *Lear's* and taught writing at the New School for Social Research. In 1984 she was at a frenetic point in her life. Her marriage had ended, and she and her former husband had worked out an amicable custody agreement that involved her shuttling between Ann Arbor, where their two young sons lived, and New York, where she had many professional commitments and a relationship with a man named Larry; she and Larry planned to move to Connecticut and to have the boys with them for her share of their time. She had severe health problems—diabetes and a mysterious lung condition—and had recently submitted to a lung biopsy, which required insertion of a tube for drainage. Eventually, five different infections found their way into her lungs, probably as a result of this procedure. Although she was clearly ill when she flew to New York on March 21, 1984, she ignored the seriousness of her symptoms, in part, as she says, because her "early-warning system was shot." Two days later, she was in St. Vincent's Hospital in New York, in a deep coma that was to last nine days.

The focus of Blakely's book is the coma, but she moves from the hospital room to scenes of her life with her parents and siblings, husband and children, friends and colleagues, and lover. She grew up in a devout Catholic family, one of five children; her older brother Frank became manic-depressive and committed suicide in 1981 after years of battling his illness. Brilliant in both sanity and madness, Frank had profoundly influenced the other members of his family. Blakely missed him acutely.

As she lay seemingly unconscious, watched over by Larry, her younger sister Gina, her mother, and the hospital staff, Blakely experienced visions and dreams and yet, although often aware of what was going on around her, she was powerless to respond. In spite of her inaccessibility and the terrible fear that she had suffered irreparable brain damage, her family, Gina especially, spoke to her, read to her, touched her, as if she were still "there." Eventually, she fought her way out of the coma and back to a slow, sometimes painful, but successful recovery. As the book ends in the fall of 1984, Blakely and Larry are living in Connecticut; the boys have spent the summer with them and have returned to Ann Arbor to live with their father for nine months—a painful wrench, but one that she is prepared to accept. And she is resuming her work.

Analysis: An accomplished professional, Blakely writes with great fluency and style; sometimes, perhaps, her bright, witty voice seems in danger of overburdening her text with word play. Nonetheless, this is a compelling story. Although the reader knows the outcome, in the final pages the suspense heightens just as it must have for all those who surrounded Blakely's hospital bed and for the friends and family around the country who waited for news by telephone. Blakely is an acute observer of people and relationships, of herself, and of the manifestations of illness both physical and mental. She is at once honest and loving in her analyses, and the scope of the book is much broader than an account of collapse and recovery.

The length of this book and its complex structure demand an able and sophisticated reader. It can certainly be recommended to senior high school students, who would be interested in both the medical drama and the descriptions of human relationships.

■ Bombeck, Erma. *I Want to Grow Hair, I Want to Grow Up, I Want to Go to Boise: Children Surviving Cancer.* Special American Cancer Society ed. Illus. Harper & Row, 1989. 174pp. (0-06-016171-X) Reading Level: Grades 9–12. (BL Ag89; KR 1 Ag89; PW 11 Ag89)
Disability: Cancer

Erma Bombeck, the nationally known humorist, newspaper columnist, and author, has written a book about how children cope with and often survive cancer. Her research consisted of visiting children in hospitals and summer camps, where she informally interviewed them, their parents and siblings, and the medical staffs that treat and care for them. The result is a book that is at once wonderfully light and humorous and yet grimly serious and realistic.

Using quotes, narratives, and even pictures that the children have drawn, Bombeck portrays very real kids, full of pranks and jokes but also fear and pain. Many of the children she writes about do survive, but not all of them. She describes the effects of chemotherapy, including hair loss, and the other realities of cancer. She also spends a great deal of time describing and discussing the reactions of parents, friends, and especially siblings.

Analysis: The book would be useful for any child whose sibling or friend has cancer, for a child who has cancer, and for families of children with cancer. Bombeck succeeds amazingly in using humor to present a truly realistic picture of the life of young cancer patients. A follow-up on adults dealing with cancer would be in order. Highly recommended for high school readers, but also of potential use as a read-aloud book for younger children and as a possibility for junior high/middle school youngsters whose life is affected in some way by cancer.

■ Bowen-Woodward, Kathy. *Coping with a Negative Body Image.* Rosen, 1989. 197pp. (0-8239-0978-6) Reading Level: Grades 6–12. (BRPT Mr90; SLJ N89)
Disability: Emotional disturbance; Anorexia; Bulimia

This book gives detailed, practical advice to teenage girls who have a negative body image, which is true of a large majority of them, according to research referred to in the text. The author cites case studies, some of which are individual cases and others of which are composites of many cases. She then discusses each case in detail, pointing out to the reader why the situation has developed as it has and what the subject of the case could do to help herself. She usually does not give an actual resolution for the case.

This analysis is then followed by a further explanation of the facts that are known about the problem—usually anorexia or bulimia—and how these facts may apply to the reader. Each chapter ends with a set of "exercises" designed to encourage the reader to apply to her own life the facts she has learned. At the end, an entire chapter is devoted to similar exercises. An appendix gives addresses and telephone numbers for some associations dealing with anorexia and bulimia. There is also a suggested reading section, containing annotated citations of a few selected books on eating disorders and of a number of other books that treat problems of growing up.

Analysis: The author is a clinical psychologist who is highly experienced in the treatment of patients with eating disorders and with a negative body image. She writes clearly and in a simple, interesting, and non-condescending style, presenting the facts about the origins of the pervasive problem that faces so many young women today, that of dissatisfaction with their body size. Most of them, she recounts, think that either all of their body or at least parts of their body are too fat. As a consequence, they begin to diet, and many are led into various obsessive-compulsive behaviors that sometimes result in anorexia nervosa and/or bulimia—serious eating disorders that result either in severe damage to their health or even in death. The goal here is to encourage young women already caught in the endless dieting-gaining cycle to analyze their behavior and take positive steps to change it before it becomes an eating disorder.

The book is highly recommended for all preteen and teenage girls and women for its logical information about body size and dieting as well as for its information on eating disorders. Its matter-of-fact, informational, and nonjudgmental approach ensures that its message will affect a large number of its readers.

■ Buchanan, William. *A Shining Season.* Illus. Coward, 1978. 249pp. (0-698-10888-4) Reading Level: Grades 10–12. (BL 1 My79; LJ 1 D78; SLJ Mr79)
Disability: Cancer

In 1969, John Baker, a 24-year-old elementary school physical education teacher, was preparing for the Olympics to be held in Munich in 1972. Ranked eighth best among the world's indoor track runners and the veteran of a long, amateur running career, he was a potential medalist for the upcoming games. Young, handsome, successful, and healthy, he was living the "perfect American dream" of a life. However, one morning while running, Baker blacked out and awoke suffering severe pain extending from his pelvis to his neck. Subsequent physical examination revealed that a lump on his testicle was malignant.

Surgery to remove the lump, accompanied by extensive tests, showed that the cancer had already spread throughout his entire body. Very little could be done to save him. Baker contemplated suicide but ultimately decided that as a competitor, he should end his life in one "shining season" rather than give in to despair. Medical treatment bought him 18 months of time, during which he devoted himself to working with problem children and disabled children, coaching them through sports training and participation. He also formed a girls' track team that was on its way to compete in a national meet at the time he died.

Analysis: This is a moving and inspirational story, well written and detailed, and which reads more like a novel than like nonfiction. One way the author achieves the effect is by the extensive use of dialogue. In a prefatory note, Buchanan states, "This story is true. It is recounted as closely as possible to eyewitness accounts or to John Baker's revelation of events to his family and closest friends." Nevertheless, this technique does move the book into the realm of fictionalized biography. It is still highly recommended as an absorbing true tale of how a young man chose to cope with a devastating illness.

■ Chamberlain, Shannin. *My ABC Book of Cancer.* Illus. by Shannin Chamberlain. Synergistic Pr., 1990. 40pp. (0-912184-07-8) Reading Level: Grades PS–4.
Disability: Rhabdomyosarcoma

Shannin Chamberlain was 9 years old in February 1989, when a malignant tumor was discovered in her pelvis and diagnosed as rhabdomyosarcoma. She has been treated at the University of Michigan Children's Hospital in Ann Arbor, 233 miles from her home, and has undergone four operations on her pelvis and lungs, radiation treatments, and chemotherapy. She wrote and illustrated her book while at Camp Catch-a-Rainbow, a facility operated by the American Cancer Society.

Using crayons and colored ink and tying every letter into her experience with cancer and treatment, Shannin goes through the alphabet. The capital letters are in red, the text in black, and a few of the letters illustrated; for example, under the text for the letter I, a drawing shows Shannin, with stick-figure arms and legs and a slightly quizzical half smile, lying on a bed receiving medication intravenously. She uses medical definitions for some letters ("B is for Blood. White Blood cells which cannot be transfused. Red Blood cells or hemoglobin and Platelets.") while for other letters she chooses nonmedical words and sometimes abstractions ("J is for Joy for each day I have, for none of us knows when the day will no longer come for any of us.").

At the end of Shannin's book there is a page about Shannin's case and cancer, followed by a glossary of terms, a resource list, and a bibliography of suggested titles for both children and adults.

Analysis: Even without the comments from doctors and her mother that are included at the end, the reader would recognize in Shannin a child of heroic courage and determination. The survival rate for her particular type of cancer is not encouraging. Despite her frequent hospital stays and school absences, she is a successful student; she missed 77 days of school in fifth grade but finished the year with all As and Bs.

This book would be an excellent choice for children undergoing treatment for cancer and for their siblings and friends; it is also appropriate for readers without a personal connection to the subject, for it conveys not only simply phrased information but also a sense of one child's fortitude and realistic optimism. In her definition of H, Shannin poignantly links Hospital and Hope.

■ Chernin, Kim. *The Obsession: Reflections on the Tyranny of Slenderness.* Harper & Row, 1981. 206pp. (0-06-014884-5) Reading Level: Grades 10–12. (BL 15 O81; LJ 1 S81; PW 28 Ag81)
Disability: Eating disorders; Anorexia nervosa

Kim Chernin calls her first chapter "Confessions of an Eater" and in it describes memories of her first bout with compulsive eating, when she was 17 and living for a time in Berlin. Eventually, after 20 years of living with the disorder, pondering it, and talking to other women about it, she came to understand much more clearly its causes and manifestations. She sees her hunger for food as a symbolic cover for other hungers—loneliness, for example, or a desire for escape from constricting and socially imposed roles. When a person denies herself food, as in anorexia nervosa, she is denying the sensual aspects of her nature. With recovery, Chernin accepted herself, came to see the beauty in the female body in its natural, rounded, even fat, contours and became able to give herself permission to eat, "to gratify my appetite. . . . My body, my hunger and the food I give to myself, which have seemed like enemies to me, now have begun to look like friends," she writes.

In subsequent chapters, Chernin looks at the social and cultural causes and implications of eating disorders. She makes reference to the experiences and stories of other women but does not focus on any particular individual until a chapter close to the end, in which she writes about Ellen West, the pseudonym given a patient by the existentialist psychiatrist Ludwig Binswanger, who wrote about her in 1944, "piecing [her story] together from his research into her medical history, her own writings, and his direct experience with her." West was a young woman who lived in an unnamed European country; although over the years she consulted many medical experts, they were unable to help her break away from a destructive cycle of unnatural eating, denial, and purging. Indeed, her own writings indicate that in some ways she understood her illness better than they, though she was unable to reach the insight that Chernin feels could have saved her—"the idea that she was hungering for a state of being, a unified condition of the self, rather than for a piece of food." She committed suicide at the age of 33.

Analysis: Chernin's book is complex, reflecting her observations, reading, thought, and understanding of the nature and causes of eating disorders. It was published in 1981, when both medical experts and the public were becoming increasingly interested in eating disorders. In the decade since then, many other books have appeared, written both by those who have lived with the disorder and by professionals who attempt to guide and heal patients. *The Obsession,* while difficult for younger readers, could be recommended to mature high school students.

■ Chisholm, Anne. *Faces of Hiroshima: A Report.* Jonathan Cape, 1985. 181pp. (o.p.) Reading Level: Grades 7–12. (BL 12 F86; TLS 9 Ag85) *Disability:* Burns

In the book's preface, the author explains that she is British and hopes to treat dispassionately the story of the 25 schoolgirls, a group later known as the Hiroshima Maidens, who were badly burned and disfigured in one of the atomic bomb attacks on Japan. Her narrative is based on interviews with journalists, surgeons, and others with firsthand experience, as well as with six of the women, now middle-aged, themselves. She is motivated by the statement by war correspondent Martha Gillhorn that "Memory and imagination, not nuclear weapons, are the great deterrents."

The book is divided into three parts. Part one begins with firsthand reports by the schoolgirls and others of the early hours and days after the bomb attack. Efforts, or, rather, lack of efforts, to aid the survivors, or "hibakusha," as they were called, on the part of the Japanese and U.S. government demonstrated the inertia of both the medical establishment and society. A complex set of ambivalent attitudes, including guilt, denial, shame, and distrust of leftists, arose from the consequences of occupation of an enemy country and preoccupation with the Cold War.

Through a long and involved struggle, a private effort, whose best-known proponent was Norman Cousins, succeeded in bringing 25 badly scarred and somewhat crippled girls to the United States for surgery and for, what turned out to be even more important, months of loving care in the homes of Quaker families in the New York area. Further, the only plastic surgeon in Hiroshima also came to learn techniques that had not been known in his country.

The surgeons performed 127 operations on these 25 women, who ranged in age from 17 to 30. As a result, one of them could close and open her left eye for the first time in ten years, and another could open her mouth to eat a hot dog. One 26-year-old tragically died of cardiac arrest.

Even more important to the women than the positive physical and medical improvements was the loving treatment they received. The women increased their morale, and they suddenly "blossomed as people" in the words of one of the surgeons. To illustrate, one of them said to the social worker as she was wheeled into the operating room, "Tell Dr. Barsky not to be worried because he cannot give me a new face. I know this is impossible, but it does not matter. Something has already healed here inside" (p. 108). One of the chief surgeons had referred to the group as "a loving, grateful, wonderful bunch of kids" (p. 101).

In the aftermath of the experience, all but two returned to Japan for good. Thirteen of the 24 women married, 9 of those producing 19 children, and some are now grandmothers. A number found work or opened shops. Some still suffered after their return to Hiroshima because of the continuing feelings of guilt, resentment, and helplessness that they felt and that Japanese society felt about them.

Analysis: The beginning of the book is somewhat difficult reading, because the facts about nuclear war are most unpleasant. However, the reader soon becomes caught up in the stories of the young girls, who suffered so much and yet showed great courage and wisdom. Their engrossing adventures with their host families served to bridge the cultures of two nations that had been at war. The struggle by the many sponsors to overcome bureaucratic negativism is exciting and disquieting. (Indeed, the volunteered Air Force plane that transported the women took off only because the general in charge "didn't have his glasses," so he could not read the last-minute State Department directive canceling the venture.)

With regard to the terrible facial disfigurements with which the book is concerned, it becomes clear that the inner character or flaws of character were far more important than the disabilities themselves; hence psychological rehabilitation was more important than the admittedly helpful physical treatments. The author had a unique opportunity to view "the girls" 40 years later. While their bodies and lives were still scarred by the bombings, they were as diverse as most people in their subsequent experiences and accomplishments.

■ Dickens, Monica. *Miracles of Courage: How Families Meet the Challenge of a Child's Critical Illness.* Dodd, 1985. 196pp. (0-396-08554-7) Reading Level: Grades 7–12. (KR 15 Ja85; LJ2 Ap85; PW 15 Mr85) *Disability:* Cancer; Leukemia

Monica Dickens, a former nurse in England and now a professional writer, began the research for this book after one of her twin grandsons, barely a year old, suffered a near-fatal illness. During the baby's hospitalization, Dickens became aware of the special, constricted world of parents whose children are desperately ill. After the child's recovery, she sought out Dr. John Truman, founder and head of the Hematology/Oncology Children's Clinic at Massachusetts General Hospital. Dr. Truman, who contributed a brief but poignant introduction to the book, was known for the skill and wisdom evident in his treatment of young patients with cancer and for the trust that both youngsters and parents placed in him. Beloved by all who worked with him or were treated by him, he seemed to combine the best aspects of good practice and research in medicine with a profound hope, respect, and gentleness for his patients, their families, and his busy staff.

"How do ordinary people become giants?" asks Dickens. She attempts to answer this question by telling the stories of children with blood and bone cancers. She describes their illnesses, inpatient and outpatient routines, staff and patient interaction, the waiting and suffering, and many courageous and humane interactions in this unusual environment, which the ill youngsters and their parents get to know as well as home. Dickens also writes about the founding of a new house, where families from other areas and other countries could stay inexpensively and communally while their children were under treatment. Here, families comforted each other in their precarious new world. The author discusses professional and self-help support groups, including those of the children themselves. The feelings of the siblings of sick children are explored as well.

Some of the children die in the course of her research, and some sustain long periods of remission; one boy, who appears repeatedly in the text, is pronounced cured. One vignette ends in social action, when a mother whose child was only one of many in her area to contract leukemia eventually testified in Congress; as a result, two neighborhood wells polluted with toxic chemicals were closed. Another vignette recounts the well-publicized case of parents who, refusing conventional treatment for their son, took him to Mexico, where he died; they later faced criminal charges.

The book is infused with a philosophy of hope and enormous respect for the children and families in their ordeal. It ends with a quote from John Truman: "I'm lucky. In this job I see people at the worst time of their lives, but I see them at their best" (p. 196).

Analysis: Though Dickens says that her medical skill is now limited to taking pulse rates and blood pressures, she brings to this study familiarity with the world of medicine. She also brings a keen observing eye, an informal and readable style, and an empathy that manages to skirt sentimentality; her book gives a moving and realistic picture of the altered lives of those confronted by critical illness. It is very loosely organized; Dickens does not offer a series of stories, nor logically sequential chapters. She gives, rather, a gripping and optimistic look at the interaction of families in need within a modern medical environment.

The children and parents she describes are courageous beyond what would seem possible. They may rage against their fate, cry with pain and exhaustion, shout that they cannot go on, weep the bitter tears of excruciatingly painful loss. But children and parents do go on, finding the strength to accept and bear what has been dealt them. Dr. Truman speaks of his "noble mothers," and nobility is a characteristic that Dickens, too, conveys while at the same time convincing us that the people whose stories she tells are, indeed, ordinary.

Many young readers are drawn to books about illness and disability, as the popularity of the fiction of Jean Little or the books about Karen Killilea attests. This title will have similar appeal. Middle school and high school students who are thinking about a career in medicine could be inspired by the work of Dr. Truman and his staff. Although Jason Gaes's *My Book for Kids with Cansur* is written for younger children, readers of *Miracles of Courage* might well want to look at the two books together for the insight both offer into the experience of critical illness.

■ Erlanger, Ellen. *Eating Disorders: A Question and Answer Book about Anorexia Nervosa and Bulimia Nervosa.* Illus. Lerner, 1988. 64pp. (0-8225-0038-8) Reading Level: Grades 4–9.
Disability: Anorexia; Bulimia

As the subtitle indicates, Erlanger's book poses questions and provides answers. After a first chapter describing the eating disorder of an eighth-grade girl, the text moves on to consider signs and symptoms, causes and cautions, help and hope. The fifth chapter presents two first-person stories, one by a recovered anorexic young woman, the other by a recovered bulimic. The bibliography comprises not only books, a professional journal, and a newsletter but also a lesson plan for grades 7–12 and a list of audiovisual materials. A list of self-help and support groups and an index follow. The book is illustrated with black-and-white drawings and engravings from nineteenth-century sources.

Analysis: Erlanger directs her text toward readers who know someone with an eating disorder rather than toward patients themselves. However, patients could of course find themselves described in these pages. The direct and simple style of the writing makes it accessible to elementary and middle school readers; the type is very large, and it is to be hoped that youngsters will not therefore consider the book babyish. Details in the section on treatment should be helpful, but the two first-person accounts could perhaps have offered more specifics in describing the hard road to recovery. The arrangement of the material and the presumed audience for the book (that is, readers who do not themselves have a disorder) should make it particularly well suited for classroom use and discussion.

■ Facklam, Margery, and Howard Facklam. *Spare Parts for People.* Illus. by Paul Facklam. Harcourt, 1987. 131pp. (0-15-277410-6) Reading Level: Grades 7–12. (BCCB 087; BL 15 D87; VYA Ap88) *Disability:* Heart disease; Tissue rejection; Burns

The Facklams have published a number of award-winning science trade books for children. They state their hope that this book will inspire young readers to seek a career in "spare parts" medicine. The book was written with input from over a dozen medical and technical specialists from all over the country. The text is illustrated with a few drawings and many black-and-white photographs both of people who have benefited from artificial implants, transplants, and prostheses and of those who developed procedures for their use.

The first several chapters put their subject in historical and biological perspective. The immune system and its importance in tissue and organ rejection is explained. Subsequent chapters cover such subjects as heart transplantation and pacemakers, kidney dialysis and transplant, and artificial or electrically controlled limbs. Cosmetic implants are not discussed.

One chapter explores issues surrounding organ donation; another, hopes for the future. A short glossary defines technical terms, and a short bibliography and index close the book.

Analysis: In relatively nontechnical language, the authors provide enough background information to make the biological engineering explanations meaningful. The focus is on specific professional people and on recipients of parts, rather than on abstractions. Anecdotes about various efforts and discoveries are well chosen to whet interest.

In this field, practices and procedures soon become outdated. For example, a new antirejection drug will probably supplant the "magic bullet"—cyclosporine—that is discussed in the book. Very innovative research on the forefront of bionic medicine is included, so the account seems as up-to-date as possible. However, the authors may be in error when they state that it is ethically impossible to use brain tissue from human fetuses. In fact, this use (of aborted fetuses) is most promising in the treatment of Parkinson's disease.

The Facklams are careful to emphasize the experimental nature of some of the procedures they describe. They are objective and optimistic in their narrative, and there is little mention of the pain suffered by many recipients of spare parts. Nonetheless, these accounts of scientific discoveries and their application for the benefit of sick and disabled people are exciting and inspiring.

■ Fine, Judylaine. *Afraid to Ask: A Book for Families to Share about Cancer.* Lothrop, Lee & Shepard, 1986. 178pp. (LB 0-688-06195-8) Reading Level: Grades 7–12. (BCCB Mr86; BL 1 Mr86; VYA Ag86) *Disability:* Cancer; Leukemia; Lymphoma

Fine, a professional writer, has arranged her material in two sections. Part I, Afraid to Ask, answers the questions "What is cancer?" and "Who gets cancer?" and discusses prevention, treatment, and dying. Narratives about people with cancer and their families are interwoven in the text. Part II, The Common Cancers, goes systematically through the carcinomas, the lymphomas, the leukemias, and the sarcomas. For each category, Fine looks at the part of the body involved, its normal function, and what happens when cancer appears. She poses and answers questions about who is most likely to get the disease in this form, what are the causes, signs, and symptoms, how diagnosis is made, and what treatment is indicated. The book concludes with a bibliography and an index.

Analysis: Fine writes with a combination of straightforward objectivity and sympathetic understanding, particularly when discussing the reactions of family members and family units to diagnosis and treatment of this devastating disease. Without glossing over those forms of the illness that are likely to end in death, she still offers hope—not only in steadily improving methods of diagnosis and treatment but also hope for the capacity of human beings to respond with courage and unquenchable spirit, whatever the prognosis and outcome. In one area, breast cancer, Fine indicates that the usual procedure when biopsy reveals cancer is for the cancerous breast to be removed while the patient is still under general anesthetic; however, it is our understanding that at least in more recent times the patient is given some time to explore options and to participate in the choice of treatment.

An excellent book for, as the subtitle suggests, families facing the drastic changes that a diagnosis of cancer creates in their life.

■ Frist, William H. *Transplant: A Heart Surgeon's Account of the Life-and-Death Dramas of the New Medicine.* Atlantic Monthly, 1989. 267pp. (0-87113-322-9) Reading Level: Grades 10–12. (BL 15 Je90; LATBR 20 Ag90; LJ 15 Je90) *Disability:* Health problems; Heart disease

William Frist, a heart transplant surgeon currently at Vanderbilt University, trained as a resident under Dr. Norman Shumway, the pioneer in heart transplants, at Stanford. In this book, Frist recounts his life from his days as a resident on through his present job. Teenage readers, as well as adults, will enjoy the narrative style—vivid, detailed, and realistic.

His story follows for a period of time the life of several patients under treatment. They are real people, unique and alive, more than just case histories. Other members of the transplant team—the physicians, coordinators, and nurses, for example—are also examined. Frist pays special attention to the coordinators, whose job he sees as the most emotionally demanding. They are the ones, he says, who most often become very close to the patients and their situation and who burn out very fast.

Frist takes the reader on a late-night flight to a small community hospital to pick up a heart, which he harvests, places in a red-and-white ice chest, and rushes back to Tennessee, where one of his patients, a man who needs a second transplant, is speeding toward the hospital. This man, Jim Hayes, becomes a major theme of the book. He does well with his second transplant but later needs a third one. Frist is ultimately under pressure from his peers about what they perceive as his overinvolvement with Hayes, who nearly dies but ultimately recovers.

Frist, who has a wife and three children, also discusses the problematic personal life of physicians, especially the residents who must spend so much time at the hospital, and he gives the reader a glimpse into his own personal life, including his last-minute decision not to marry a woman who also was going to medical school. He then describes and discusses the various sensitive ethical dilemmas surrounding transplants.

Analysis: Overall, the story is very dramatic and realistic but not melodramatic. The author uses several quotes from conversations in which he participated, and this technique adds drama, immediacy, and realism without fictionalizing the writing to any extent. Highly recommended.

■ Gaes, Jason. **My Book for Kids with Cansur.** Illus. by Tim and Adam Gaes. Melius & Peterson, 1988. Unp. (0-937603-04-X) Reading Level: Grades K–3. (NW 4 J188; SPBR N87)
Disability: Cancer; Burkitt's lymphoma

Jason Gaes's cancer was discovered when he was 6 and diagnosed as Burkitt's lymphoma, a rare and extremely fast-growing form of the disease. He was treated with radiation, surgery, and chemotherapy; at one point, miserable from the effects of treatment, he wanted to stop. As his mother said, "Jason was scared of things they'd do to him when he was alive—operations, the pain. He had no paralyzing fear of death—that was my fear." She promised him anything he wanted if he continued, and exactly two years after the cancer was discovered, Jason got his wish: "the biggest party in the world, where all the ladies wear new dresses and all the men drink beer." Jason began this book while he was still under treatment, because he had been given a storybook in which the young patient died and he wanted to tell the story of one who lived. At the time of publication, three years after diagnosis, Jason was described as fully recovered.

The book is reproduced exactly as Jason wrote it, with his printing and spelling. Each spread is illustrated with full-color drawings by his twin brother, Tim, and older brother, Adam.

Analysis: This is an honest, gallant, moving book. Jason gets to his subject immediately ("I am 8 yrs. old and I have cansur"), describing the discovery of the first tumor in his mouth and the subsequent treatment of this lesion and other cancerous sites. Addressing his readers directly, he tells them what the various procedures were like and which were worse. "Sometimes keymotharupy makes you sick and you throw up. Sometimes you looz your hair from it but you can wear hats if it bothers you. Mostly kids don't care when your bald. And if they laff or make fun there not very good friends anyway." He tells children what to bring to the hospital and suggests ways to deal with pain and fear, acknowledging that "spinals and bone mairos are bad no matter how far you count but they go faster if you curl up tight and try to relacks" and giving his phone number so that other children can call him for reassurance. Jason has been brought up to believe in heaven, a comfort not all parents can offer their children, but readers should not find these pages offensive no matter what their beliefs. Jason intends to grow up to be a doctor "who takes care of kids with cansur so I can tell them what it's like."

The drawings by Jason's brothers are vivid and lively, and faces are usually smiling. It is unfortunate that many of them have been printed with the red plate out of alignment.

Though cataloged as a title for preschool and elementary school readers, Jason's book could be suggested to readers of all ages, whether they themselves are ill or they simply are interested in one child's response to disease and treatment.

■ Garfield, Johanna. *The Life of a Real Girl.* St. Martin's, 1986. 373pp. (0-312-48399-6) Reading Level: Grades 7–12. (LJ 1 Je86; PsyT J187) *Disability:* Weight loss/gain; Drug addiction

Writing in the first person, the author chronicles both the vast fluctuations in weight and the eventual dextroamphetamine addiction that she, "Jo Jo," battled from the age of 14. She was raised in an extremely privileged materialistic environment, but the demands of a perfectionist father and the neglect by her narcissistic mother contributed to her growing turmoil as she approached adolescence. Part one covers the high school and college years of this attractive and intelligent girl from Long Island whose behaviors masked an underlying and excruciating insecurity. She perceived her struggle as one between her worthless real self and "The Other Me" whose exuberant personality and thin appearance were only the artificial creation of her diet pills. In college, she began a long relationship with Ross, the man she would finally marry, but at the time she felt she must hide from him the person she really was.

Part two begins with Jo Jo's commitment in a private mental hospital. Her task was to learn "who she was, and where she was going from here." Among the sick but interesting and friendly patients was Lee, a handsome young man who had been a psychiatrist before his illness. As a deep and loving relationship developed between them, Jo Jo achieved a new confidence and a budding sense of self. In time, Lee died alone under ambiguous circumstances.

Eventually Jo Jo was weaned both from reliance on drugs to maintain a normal weight and from the need for the security of the mental institution. She graduated from college, taught school, and married her ever-faithful Ross.

Analysis: The author is a free-lance writer whose prose is free flowing, easy to read, and entertaining. Although many of the situations described in the story are devastating, the entire chronicle seems a bit muted by time because the book refers to events of over 30 years ago. In addition, the reader knows from statements made at the beginning that all will turn out well for the affluent, perceptive, and not too crazy Jo Jo. The author refrains from in-depth psychiatric explanations, but her common sense observations about her predicaments ring true.

■ Gohlke, Mary, and Max Jennings. *I'll Take Tomorrow.* Evans, 1985. 204pp. (0-871-31458-4) Reading Level: Grades 7–12. (BL 15 Ap85; KR 1 Mr85; LJ 1 My85)
Disability: Primary pulmonary hypertension; Heart-lung transplant

Mary Gohlke was a middle-aged woman, advertising director of a daily newspaper in Phoenix, Arizona, married and with two teenage sons, when she felt a change in her normal energetic health. Doctors discovered that she had primary pulmonary hypertension, a disease that causes the blood vessels in the lungs to close up; the heart has to work increasingly hard to pump blood through these vessels, and then it becomes enlarged. There was no treatment and certainly no cure, and she was told that her illness was terminal. The decline in her health was more rapid than the doctors had expected, and her fatigue increased; even her thought processes became affected, as her brain reacted to a diminished supply of oxygen.

Eventually, a newspaper article and the memory of a book read some years earlier prompted her to call Dr. Bruce Reitz, who had been performing heart-lung transplants on monkeys at Stanford University. Gohlke was accepted for a transplant and then had to wait for a donor, becoming increasingly weaker. At last, in March 1981, the surgery was performed, the first heart-lung transplant procedure on a human patient. She successfully weathered the operation, the long recuperative period, and subsequent setbacks both physical and emotional. For a time, she returned to full-time work on the newspaper, but at the time of writing this book, she had retired from her job.

Analysis: The author is clearly a woman of courage, determination, and energy. She describes with honesty not only the details of her illness and treatment but also many aspects of her life, including her growing up and her marriage. She writes vividly about the terrible loneliness of a person facing death, acknowledges the displacement she felt when she returned home from Stanford and realized that things could never be the same again, and touches on the depression that sapped her strength after she had recovered physically. Details about the surgery and convalescence are clearly presented. Max Jennings, her coauthor, is a colleague from her newspaper. Despite the fact that both writers are professionals, the chronological arrangement of events is not always the clearest or most elegant; on the other hand, Gohlke's voice comes through with an authentic ring. Recovery from her depression, which seems to have arisen from her having to retire from her job, is rather sketchily treated.

Middle and high school readers with an interest in stories of human drama as well as in transplant surgery should find this an attractive and accessible book.

■ Gordon, Jacquie. *Give Me One Wish.* Norton, 1988. 350pp. (0-393-02518-7) Reading Level: Grades 10–12. (BL 1 Ap88; NYTBR 19 Je88; PW 12 F88)
Disability: Cystic fibrosis

Christine, the elder of Jacquie Gordon's two daughters, died of cystic fibrosis in 1982 at the age of 21. Her mother, a fashion industry worker in New York, has written this moving biography of their life together.

Christine's illness was first diagnosed as celiac disease, an intolerance of gluten that interferes with digestion, but in 1966 the diagnosis was changed to cystic fibrosis. At that time, the average life span of a child with this disease was little more than seven or eight years. Christine was frequently ill, and she and her mother learned to live with this chronic illness, which was at times severe and at other times mildly manifested.

Although a lively, intelligent, and precocious child, Christine thrived in a smaller school environment, rather than in a large, impersonal New York public school. Jacquie therefore sent Christine to various private schools, which sometimes proved to be a financial burden, because Jacquie had neither a high-paying job herself nor, in the beginning, much help from Christine's father, Jerry, from whom she was divorced when Christine was very young. Jerry was an actor and puppeteer, who for many years struggled to earn a living; eventually, however, he returned to New York from California because Chris and Jacquie both pleaded with him to be nearer for Chris's sake, especially during her bouts of illness. Shortly thereafter, he became part of the Muppets television show, and his career has been in ascendence ever since.

Despite her illness, Chris lived a full, active, and highly social life. She read widely and wrote often, keeping detailed journals on which Jacquie based this book along with the use of interviews with schoolmates and other friends, in addition to Chris's physician's detailed records.

Analysis: The book contains reconstructed conversations and situations that Jacquie herself never witnessed. She explains this in the introduction and describes how she wove her story by using these extensive interviews and written documentation. The story, therefore, reads like a novel, and the use of quoted conversations and secondhand accounts of events in Chris's life in no way interferes with the credibility of the book. Chris, rather, comes alive, and the reader feels deep pain and sorrow as her life inevitably comes to a close. Many high school students will be intrigued by this book, not only for the realistic and moving story of Chris's short life, lived to the full despite her illness, but also for the high-interest teenage story line describing her school and social life set against New York's popular culture scene. Highly recommended.

■ Gravelle, Karen, and Bertram A. John. *Teenagers Face to Face with Cancer.* Messner, 1986. 118pp. (LB 0-671-54549-3) Reading Level: Grades 7–12. (BL 15 Ja87; KR 1 D86; SLJ F87)
Disability: Leukemia, Lymphoma; Sarcoma

Gravelle has a doctorate in biopsychology and John is a psychologist. In this book, they examine the experiences of 16 adolescents who have all had cancer as teenagers or, in one case, had a best friend who died of the disease. The young people represent a diverse group in terms of their homes and economic circumstances and racial identification; their cancers are acute lymphocytic leukemia, acute myelocytic leukemia, non-Hodgkin's lymphoma, and osteogenic sarcoma. Some face very uncertain futures, and four have had recurrences; one young woman has had both acute lymphocytic leukemia and non-Hodgkin's lymphoma. Others appear to have recovered. All have undergone difficult and frequently painful treatment. The authors quote extensively from the teenagers, who are given pseudonyms. The book is divided into six parts: The First Encounter: "I Have Cancer"; The Aftershock; Fighting Back; Relationships with Others; Planning for the Future; and Coming to Terms. A glossary of terms, a short list of suggested readings, and an index complete the book.

The authors emphasize that "the tasks of adolescence, as a developmental stage in life, and the tasks involved in conquering cancer are on a direct collision course." Adolescents are dealing with their changing relationships with parents and family, with their feelings about their bodies, with emerging sexuality, and with friendships and romantic involvements, as well as with thoughts about future educational and occupational directions. Cancer throws all these issues into question. For example, illness keeps these adolescents dependent on adults (parents and medical personnel) at just the time when they are establishing new independence. It makes them feel ugly and physically different when they want so badly to be attractive and comfortable in their own bodies. It forces them to confront mortality at a time when most healthy teenagers believe that life stretches on forever.

Analysis: At first, the authors' method of arranging their material may seem confusing. Each section of the book concentrates on a particular area, and the text is interlaced with quotes from the young people; it is difficult sometimes to remember that, for example, Amy had osteogenic sarcoma and an amputation and that it is Laura who has been sick for five years with acute lymphocytic leukemia and then non-Hodgkin's lymphoma. However, although one may be deeply moved by these stories, the individual histories come to matter less than the several voices speaking directly to the reader on such topics as friendships, independence, and thoughts about having children of their own.

This is a very valuable book for the general readership and especially for those whose life is directly affected by cancer. The authors write clearly and fluently, and the voices of the teenagers sound authentic. Neither the authors nor the young people themselves flinch from an honest accounting. These teenagers have had to face extraordinary trials, and they are extraordinarily courageous; no one pretends that they will be rewarded with a good outcome. Most families, friends, teachers, and medical staff have been supportive and understanding, but not all. Parents draw away from physical and emotional contact, teachers say hurtful things, doctors are rushed, friends disappear. In a short final chapter called "Last Thoughts," the quotations are "intended to emphasize these themes [of the book] in the way the adolescents who discussed them intended." The youngsters tell other cancer patients to live as positively as possible, and they tell other people that illness has not made them different: "We're not different. We're the same people [that we were before we got sick]." Thus they echo the cry of nearly everyone with a disability: they demand to be seen not as a condition but as an individual.

■ Grollman, Sharon. *Shira: A Legacy of Courage.* Illus. Doubleday, 1988. 84pp. (Paper 0-385-24114-3) Reading Level: Grades 4–9. (BL 15 Je88; KR 1 My88; SLJ Ag88)
Disability: Diabetes

Shira Putter was diagnosed with diabetes at 5½. A serious but usually treatable disease, the illness proved in Shira's case to be rare and intractable; she died at the age of 9. Sharon Grollman has written her biography in the form of Shira's diary, using the child's own journal entries and poems in addition to the materials assembled by Shira's mother, Ann Marie Putter, and Mrs. Putter's taped memories of her daughter's life. The 3½ years of illness were filled with hospitalizations in different institutions and cities (over 500 days), operations (more than 15), and treatments, as doctors and the family searched for a way to control the ravages of the disease. Shira also participated as far as she was able in the more ordinary aspects of a child's life—school, holidays, family outings, homework, and parties. The last entry in Shira's voice is a poem dated April 3, 1983. In an epilogue, Ann Marie Putter gives a brief account of Shira's life with diabetes and describes her daughter's final days: worn out by pain and infection, Shira asked to be taken off all support equipment and to be allowed to go home from the hospital; she knew what this meant and wanted to die at home, which she did, on July 26, 1983.

The book begins with a "Note to Parents and Teachers," written by Rabbi Harold Kushner, whose child also died and who has written about loss and sorrow. In the preface, the author describes how she came to know about Shira and explains her decisions about how to handle the material. Shira's own journal had gaps and omitted many details the reader needed in order to follow the story, but Grollman "hoped that a book could be written that would not only recapture Shira's story, but her inner voice, the way she was." To achieve this, the author used Shira's writings, the materials assembled by her mother, and the tape recordings made by Ann Marie Putter as she and Grollman worked together, so that in the end, the author says, "I started to write a journal I thought Shira might have written, using words that I thought Shira might have used." The epilogue is followed by a list of recommended resources (organizations, hospices, and books for both children and adults) and a glossary.

Pencil drawings illustrate the text. The final page notes that the artist has dedicated his work to the memory of his wife, who also died as a result of diabetes.

Analysis: Reading about the painful illness and slow death of a child can be almost unbearable—one wants to push away such pain. Nevertheless, this is not a depressing book, though it is an intensely sad one. Grollman has achieved what she set out to do, presenting Shira as she was, as she actually expressed her ideas, and as Grollman imagined her writing in her own voice. People who knew Shira all indicated that she was unusually gifted not only in her abilities but also in her personality and character. Grollman avoids the pitfalls of presenting her as a saint, however. The reader sees her anger, depression and her fear, as well as her courage. One particularly affecting entry describes Shira's reactions when her mother told her that her current doctor was not going to be treating her any more because " 'sometimes adults have a hard time dealing with children who are sick, especially when adults have a special relationship with those children.' I said, 'Yeah, and when those adults know that those children are dying. Well, I'm not dead yet.' " Then she is frightened, because if one doctor can leave her, so can the next, and "maybe Mom and Grandma and Rachel [a nurse] will someday come up to me and say, 'Sorry, Shira. We can't deal with your illness anymore so you'll have to find someone else.' Who will take care of me then?" As Rabbi Kushner notes in his introduction, this is not an unusual fear for seriously ill children.

Although this is perhaps not a book to suggest to children with treatable diabetes, it could certainly be read by healthy youngsters, who would gain insights into what it means to face life-threatening illness. It might offer comfort to sick children with conditions other than diabetes. For adults, it gives a valuable picture of what a child in Shira's position might be thinking and feeling.

■ Gutkind, Lee. *Many Sleepless Nights: The World of Organ Transplantation.* Univ. of Pittsburgh Pr., 1990. 378pp. (Paper 0-8229-5905-4) Reading Level: Grades 10–12. (BL 15 Je88; LJ 1 S88) *Disability:* Organ failure; Organ rejection

The author did the bulk of research for this book over a four-year period in Pittsburgh hospitals. His introduction recapitulates the 35-year span of transplant research, from risky, experimental beginnings to the present time, when procedures are considered legitimate and lifesaving. However, he delineates the many difficulties that remain, even after an operation deemed successful: the never-ending threat of organ rejection, costly medications with possible side effects, and an often curtailed quality of life for the patient.

Part 1, "The Surgeon," traces in detail the evolution of the transplant field, including the crucial discovery of cyclosporine, which wards off rejection of the transplanted organ. The pioneer work of Thomas Starzl, currently in Pittsburgh, and those he has trained figures prominently. Part 2, "The Donor," opens with the story of a teenager who had sneaked his mother's sports car out for a joyride. His wild showing off for his friends led to a terrible accident that left him alive but brain dead. The agonizing decision process that led to multiple organ donations is explored from the standpoint of family, professionals, and the potential recipients. Part 3, "Pittsburgh," describes in much detail the site of the largest transplant center in the world. Part 4, entitled "The Wait," chronicles the often long and tedious days of waiting of a number of actual candidates for transplants. Some were finally matched with compatible organs, whereas others underwent a relentless descent to death. Part 5, "The Procedure," follows the surgical team's simultaneous harvesting from the brain-dead donor and the removal, often a helicopter trip away, of the diseased organ from the chosen recipient. Part 5, "Life After Transplantation," gives an essentially optimistic account of those survivors who now have "a beautiful, but often flawed, second chance."

A brief epilogue ends with the description of a meeting Gutkind arranged between a pregnant recipient and the family of the teenager who had been a donor. The father drew the young woman close, touching his ear to her body. "Dick Becker listened for the last time to the absolutely astounding miracle of organ transplantation: the heart and lungs of his dead son, Richie, beating faithfully and unceasingly inside this stranger's warm and living chest" (p. 359).

Analysis: Although Gutkind has (in another context) described himself as "obsessed" with the world of organ transplantation, he offers here an evenhanded, factual piece. Both the dedication of professionals and the courage and fortitude of the patients are inspiring in this highly readable, fast-moving account. A strength of the book is the author's ability to write medical explanations succinctly and clearly.

■ Harper, Randy, and Tom Harper. *I Choose to Fight: Tom Harper's Courageous Victory over Cancer.* Prentice Hall, 1984. 201pp. (0-13448-911-X) Reading Level: Grades 6–12.
Disability: Testicular cancer; Lung cancer

Tom Harper and one of his brothers have written this first-person narrative of Tom's first two years as a midshipman at the United States Naval

Academy at Annapolis. At age 19, he and 1,300 other young men were sworn in during the summer of 1973. Tom was a 205-pound high school football player, and he had high hopes of making the Navy varsity team as a tight end while still a freshman.

The intense, often difficult life of a plebe was mitigated by summer football drills. Halfway through "Plebe Summer," Tom began to experience pain and swelling in his testicle. He endured increasing pain as the fall academics and ball practice began, but was loath to complain or to interfere with his school schedule. Just before his team left for an all-important game against the University of Michigan, the team doctor insisted he check into the hospital for tests.

Tom describes the ebbing of his hopes of joining his team as he underwent strenuous and painful medical tests. A biopsy confirmed a diagnosis of cancer, which had metastasized to his lungs.

The major portion of the story describes Tom's fight to overcome his cancer as he undergoes the grueling treatments necessary to improve the prognosis of three months to live, typical of his illness at that time. He lost his hair, muscle tone, and strength. The drug and radiation therapy gave him severe acne, constant diarrhea, and vomiting and caused his fingernails to fall off. Throughout the ordeal, he committed himself both to playing football again and to a return to the Naval Academy. He writes that in literature he could not find a cancer patient to serve as a role model; one "that concentrated on a real awareness of what I was going through, that had life as its constant thread, and the quality of life at that. I prayed earnestly to God and had always been answered before, perhaps in ways I could not understand, so I decided to be my own model, to be my own hero, and someday to relate my experience to others to help them better understand and react to the affliction" (p. 100).

Finally, the cancer began to subside, and Tom began rebuilding his wasted body in the weight room and on the running field. He had been afraid that the academy would not take him back, but the superintendent, Vice Admiral Kinnard McKee, ruled that "Tom Harper can stay here until he either dies or graduates" (frontispiece).

Tom did rejoin the football team, although with his decreased lung capacity, he worked as a coach, not as the fine player he had once been. He graduated from the Naval Academy and was commissioned. He became a spokesman for the American Cancer Society and for his courage received recognition from the White House, on the "Today" show, and from many friends he had inspired. An epilogue, written in 1983, states that he is married and has fathered a child.

Analysis: This book is written in a fast-moving forthright style. Tom Harper's lack of pretentiousness and his warm personality come through on every page. Fortunately, in hindsight, he did not lose the perspective of an exuberant teenager, who found humor even in the midst of his terrible ordeal.

Diagnosis and treatment of testicular cancer, a rather frequent disease of young men, have progressed since 1973. Nevertheless, the feelings and experiences expressed by Tom Harper still have the ring of truth today.

■ Haskell, Molly. *Love and Other Infectious Diseases: A Memoir.* Morrow, 1990. 302pp. (0-688-07006-X) Reading Level: Grades 10–12. (BL 1 F90; KR 1 F90; PW 16 F90)
Disability: Cytomegalovirus; Encephalitis; Paralysis

This true story opens as Molly Haskell and Andrew Sarris, both movie reviewers, are returning to their beloved Manhattan, after an exhausting trip to the Cannes Film Festival. She, of a southern background, and he, a child of urban Greek immigrants, have been married for 15 years.

Andrew was admitted to the emergency room of New York Hospital with a raging fever and disorientation. He then had a seizure and had abnormal enzymes. Many tests failed to identify the underlying cause of his baffling illness. As he worsened, he became paranoid, incoherent, and occasionally violent, signaling encephalitis. Haskell writes, "Someone had kidnapped Andrew's soul and all I could do was minister to the anti-Andrew that remained" (p. 85). Andrew's crisis deepened. He was operated on for perforation of the colon and was given a temporary colostomy. Then his legs became paralyzed. Cytomegalovirus was finally discovered to be the underlying culprit.

As Andrew hovered between life and death, Molly began to reexamine her marital relationship in terms of her background, needs, and gender. Her deceased father, her mother, and her mother-in-law figured prominently in her reflections. The strong, supportive women represented outdated feminine models for her. She mused on the differences in expectations for men and women in the hospital, on the tennis court, and in life in general. She became aware of her complete financial, intellectual, and emotional dependence on her husband.

Four months after his initial hospitalization, Andrew was well enough to be transferred to the Rusk Rehabilitation Institute—another prolonged ordeal for himself and his exhausted wife. As he recovered, they were able to collaborate on two lectures on French cinema, which Molly delivered in Andrew's stead at City College of New York.

While Andrew recuperated at the rehabilitation center, Molly had an operation for recurrence of an intestinal blockage, a problem that would continue to plague her. Finally, Andrew returned to their apartment to be nursed by his wife. She writes, "The male patient is as unaware of his own exorbitant needs and the demands he makes, and as content to be taken care of as a newborn calf" (p. 267).

As a way of achieving independence of spirit, Haskell created this book from her journals. The very week of its completion, Andrew had emergency surgery on a bowel obstruction. "This new crisis, this coda, was like a restaging of the original horror, enabling me to see just what I had been about" (p. 294). In the end, all the crises and the nearness of death led Haskell to become a more self-accepting and independent person with a deep and maturing love for her husband.

Analysis: The dust jacket describes this book as "medical grand opera," with "stages of Andrew's illness becoming way stations in the anatomy of a marriage." Written with humor and grace, it is full of insights about families, the role of friends, and the pitfalls of a close conjugal relationship. Flashbacks offer a sparkling picture of the author's girlhood in gracious, patriarchal Richmond, Virginia. The world of motion picture criticism is well described. The brilliant, quirky Andrew is brought alive on the pages. Haskell emerges as a funny, honest, and compassionate person.

At one point, Haskell says that she and her husband have opted not to have children, because at heart they are still children themselves. The quest described in the book is a youthful one—that of understanding one's childhood and finding identity and meaning in the adult world, even in the face of death. Overall, the book illustrates the plight of the sad and perplexed companion who stands helplessly by a sick loved one, alternately diminished and supported by the medical bureaucracy and by well-meaning friends and relatives.

■ Holdren, Shirley, and Susan Holdren. **Why God Gave Me Pain.** Loyola, 1984. 115pp. (0-8294-0469-4) Reading Level: Grades 7–12. (BL 1 F85; VYA Je85)
Disability: Leukemia

This book is written by the mother of Susan, a teenage girl who contracted leukemia while still in high school. Also included are extensive entries from Susan's diaries.

Susan was a runner on the track team and artistically inclined, when she went through the all-too-familiar misdiagnoses that are associated with acute childhood leukemia. Ultimately, she received intensive and uncomfortable treatments with chemotherapy and radiation, which took her disease into remission and enabled her to start college courses in art. By now her boyfriend was fading out of her life.

Forgetting about her illness, Susan made plans to teach art to children who are deaf, because one of her track team friends was a girl who was deaf. She had good times with a new boyfriend.

A second onset of the cancer put her back into the hospital, where her present boyfriend visited her for the last meeting they would ever have. Although she was sad about losing this relationship, she began to lose her customary shyness as well and to interest herself in other hospital patients.

In her next remission, she arranged her priorities and delved for the meaning of her life. "If I can't do great things, I want to do small things great" (p. 54). She realized that she had learned to help others and felt this was a God-given gift, related to the suffering she was enduring. Her summer college courses would be the last ones she could take, for the remission became more and more problematic.

Surrounded by friends in and out of the hospital and her loving family, she fought her disease as long as possible but died peacefully at 20 years old.

Analysis: This book does not have the strong religious orientation that the title might suggest, although it does describe a family with strong Christian faith. The narrative is straightforward and factual, although Susan's diary entries have an adolescent floridness, which contrasts with her mother's simply written prose. Although the book describes grief, it does not end in bitterness, and it is even uplifting in its description of a life well lived.

■ Hyde, Margaret O., and Lawrence E. Hyde. *Cancer in the Young: A Sense of Hope.* Westminster, 1985. 96pp. (0-664-32722-?) Reading Level: Grades 7–12. (BCCB O85; BL 1 My85; SLJ N85)
Disability: Cancer

The authors examine such topics as the prevalence and types of cancer among children and young people, tests and treatments, and outlooks for remission and recovery as well as for future improved treatments. Brief patient histories are scattered throughout the text. There is a chapter called "Young Cancer Patients Speak Out" and another on camps and special programs for youngsters with the disease. The book concludes with a glossary, a list of suggested books for young readers, information about a variety of resources, a list of camps arranged by state for cancer patients and their siblings, and an index.

Analysis: The tone of this book is sober, nonsensational, realistic, and hopeful. The authors present information clearly and integrate the experiences and statements of young patients into the text. While never minimizing the threat to life presented by cancer, or holding out false promises, they nevertheless do offer readers a sense of hope. There is perhaps too frequent use of the words "victim" and "suffer" in connection with the patients, and the authors have confused the words "hone" and "home." These quibbles should not, however, detract from the book's usefulness, both for children with cancer and their families and for young readers in the general public. A survey such as this one might well be read in conjunction with personal accounts of cancer.

■ Jaffe, Hirshel, James Rudin, and Marcia Rudin. *Why Me? Why Anyone?* St. Martin's, 1986. 193pp. (0-312-87803-6) Reading Level: Grades 10–12. (BL 15 F86; LJ 15 F86; PW 7 F86)
Disability: Leukemia

Hirshel Jaffe, at the time of the writing of this book, was the rabbi of a congregation in Newburgh, New York. He was successful, a community as well as a religious leader. A marathon runner, he ran with a torch through New York City to promote the cause of Soviet Jews, and he ran long miles to keep in condition during the 11 days he spent in Tehran with a group of American leaders working to facilitate the release of the Iranian hostages. An active, always healthy person, he was stunned when an apparently minor illness became worse and proved to be hairy-cell leukemia, one of the most difficult types of leukemia to treat.

Jaffe did have several forms of treatment, which, by the end of the book, had miraculously put him into a solid, stable remission that in time it was hoped would become a cure. The book itself is written by Jaffe, by his rabbi friend James Rudin, and by Marcia Rudin, James's wife. Each one writes in the first person and chapter by chapter presents a different perspective on Jaffe's experiences. They not only tell Jaffe's story, but they also reflect on the philosophical meaning of illness and death and on its relationship to God and to religion. Although no one ever quite answers the "Why me? Why anyone?" question posed in the title and at the end of a chapter, Jaffe concludes at the close of the book, as he is ready to resume his rabbinical duties, that what is important is not the adversities in one's life, but one's attitude toward those adversities and one's ultimate ability to have a purpose at all times and to be guided by that purpose.

Analysis: The narrative is well written, interesting, and not overly convoluted or complex despite its musings on the meaning of life and death. The three writers' styles mesh well. Highly recommended for thoughtful teenage readers.

■ Kinoy, Barbara P., Estelle B. Miller, and John A. Atchley. *When Will We Laugh Again? Living and Dealing with Anorexia Nervosa and Bulimia.* Columbia Univ. Pr., 1984. 139pp. (0-231-05638-9) Reading Level: Grades 7–12. (KLIATT W85; LJ 1 Je84; VYA F85)
Disability: Anorexia; Bulimia

The book opens with a foreword by Arthur H. Crisp, a British researcher in this field, and an introduction by Estelle B. Miller, mother of a recovering anorexic and a psychotherapist who was also founder and director of the American Anorexia/Bulimia Association (AA/BA). There follows a brief section describing a recovered anorexic woman who one day a week answers the phone at the AA/BA. John Atchley and Susan Heeger contribute a chapter defining the illness, and then come three chapters called "Family Text," which look at the illness, the family of the patient, and treatment and recovery. "In Their Own Words" consists of transcripts of taped therapy sessions and letters written by patients, all of whom are young women. The last section is a commentary written by the Book Committee of the American Anorexia/Bulimia Association and presenting the "themes, observations, and conclusions [that] seemed to emerge" as they looked at the material gathered for the book. Appendixes give statistics on hospitalization and weight and alcohol problems reported by parents in addition to addresses of associations and resource people. A suggested reading list and an index follow.

Analysis: Unlike many other books on this topic, *When Will We Laugh Again?* concentrates in its first section not on the individual experience of the illness but on the family, with extensive quotations from parents and siblings. Thus the reader comes to the patient's account from the outside in, as an observer, just as professionals and families do. Both the personal statements and the authors' text corroborate the experiences of patients and the findings of writers and specialists that are seen in other books presenting descriptions of the disorders, probable causes, and varieties of treatment. The text contains much factual material; the view of the authors is both realistic and hopeful, their attitude nonjudgmental and supportive. The final chapter of commentary might be particularly helpful as survey and analysis of these conditions. High school students, whether themselves "sufferers" (to use the word chosen by the authors) or simply interested in the subject, should find the book informative and readable.

■ Kjosness, Mary A., and Laura A. Rudolph, eds. *What Happened to You Happened to Me: A Book for Young People with Cancer.* Illus. Children's Orthopedic Hospital and Medical Center of Seattle, 1980. 37pp. Reading Level: Grades 4–12.
Disability: Cancer

Like Jason Gaes's book, this work has been written especially for children and teens who have cancer. The authors are children and teens, ranging in age from 6 to 19, who themselves are being treated for cancer or who have recently undergone treatment for this disease. They have written brief notes, signed with their first name and age, that are incorporated into sections with a defined theme: How I Felt in the Beginning, Hospital Experiences, Surgery, Radiation, Clinic Visits, Hair Loss, Side Effects, Back to School, My Activities, Feelings and Experiences, How We've Changed, and Thoughts.

Analysis: The book is really a paperbound pamphlet, printed on bright yellow paper and illustrated with black-and-white drawings done by the children. The format is appealing and effective, but some reinforcement or rebinding is recommended.

This is not a book about terminal illness and death. It is about living with and recovering from cancer. The child and teen authors give detailed, accurate facts about the disease and its treatments, and they expose quite bluntly their fears and concerns. Highly recommended as good reading and as an educational tool about cancer whether or not the reader has cancer.

■ Lancaster, Matthew. *Hang Toughf.* Illus. by Matthew Lancaster & Pamela Huffman. Paulist Pr., 1983. 13pp. (0-8091-2696-6) Reading Level: Grades 4–6. (LATBR 22 S85)
Disability: Cancer; Ewing's sarcoma

On the back page of this small book is a photograph of the author with a page of narrative presumably not meant for young readers. It states that Matthew Lancaster lived with Ewing's sarcoma for a year and a half, knowing in his heart that he had little hope. "That understanding made him want to leave behind the way an ordinary 10-year-old took on life when the only thing left to do was 'hang toughf.' " The publication of this book, in his own printing and drawing, was a posthumous fulfillment of his dream.

The boy dedicates his book "to all people with cancer." He tells of the diagnosis of the sarcoma in his leg and how scared and upset he was. He details his "kymotherapy" opposite a humorous drawing of a "mad doctor" as Dracula. He describes how relaxation and imagery helped to get him through many invasive procedures. After a year of several hospitalizations, he had more "tumours," and he could no longer walk. "If your friends laghf at you they are not very good friends" (p. 6), he writes. He discusses pain and medication, hope and religion.

Analysis: The text captures the serious side of a spunky, sensitive youngster who is writing to help others in his same predicament. The drawings are caricatures of medical personnel and medical treatments. The handwriting and spelling are not exemplary; they do serve to remind the reader how young Lancaster was. The inaccuracies might pose a problem for some children, although a bright 10-year-old told the reviewer he could easily decipher the prose.

■ Lapierre, Dominique. *The City of Joy*. Trans. from the French. Double-day, 1985. 464pp. (0-8161-4114-2) Reading Level: Grades 10–12. (LJ 1 N85; NYRB 29 My86; NYTBR 3 N85)
Disability: Leprosy; Starvation; Tuberculosis

The setting of this story is a slum district called the City of Joy in the midst of Calcutta, India. Here, in the vast city known for its culture and wealth, 70,000 penniless refugees, driven by droughts and floods from their rural lands, inhabit hovels or even areas of the street. They struggle to find work, and they endlessly battle starvation, disease, and untimely death. A Polish priest, Stephen Kovalski, came to live among these poorest of the poor in order to share their lives and suffering. Moslems, Hindus, a few Christians, and a colony of lepers lived in the contiguous quarters of the vermin- and pestilence-ridden area. The priest's crowded neighborhood included aborigines, a household of eunuchs, sweatshops for children, and cow pens. Kovalski found that these people had a capacity for joy, loving, and sharing that transcended their often agonizing life situations.

The author tells how the priest befriended the residents of the segre-gated lepers' quarter, where he found conditions unbelievably more horri-fying than any he had encountered before. By a great act of will, he was able to love the mutilated and dying lepers as his brothers and sisters, and he vowed to set up a dispensary to give them medical treatment. Therefore he sought help from Mother Teresa, who ministered to the dying in a section within the busy Temple of Kali. Mother Teresa had founded the Mission of Charity, whose mission of service to the most neglected people had spread from Calcutta throughout India and to all the continents.

Another strand of the story follows the family of Harsari Pal, which had to leave a drought-ridden rice paddy to seek subsistence while camp-ing in Calcutta's streets. Harsari had the good fortune to find work as a human horse, one of thousands who transported people by rickshaw in the frenzied, crowded streets of the city. After months of hard work, the Pals earned enough money to pay the local Mafia for a space in the slum, where they became neighbors of Big Brother Stephen.

Halfway through the book, an American connection emerges: In Miami, a young Jewish medical student, Max, has just graduated. He is the son of a prodigiously wealthy Miami physician. He vows to postpone his internship to work for a year in the City of Joy helping Kovalski to set up his clinic.

During the course of the narrative, the inhabitants of Calcutta experience several natural catastrophes. Among these were an eight-day monsoon rain and an ensuing flood that caused much death and disease. Even so, the flood brought financial benefit to Harsari, because only rickshaw drivers could negotiate the knee-high overflow of sewers and sluices that engulfed the city. Harsari, like so many of his coworkers, was in the final stages of tuberculosis. His fervent wish was to arrange a dowry and suitable marriage for his daughter before he died. He joyfully showed his new riches, further enhanced by the advance sale of his skeleton, to the priest. Kovalski was privy to the lengthy marriage negotiations transacted between the prospective bride's and groom's fathers and the matchmaker. In the course of the elaborate marriage ceremony, Harsari quietly died.

On a Christmas morning, a terrible cyclone decimated much of the land in the state of Bengal. After more death and destruction, the surviving people in the City of Joy were to be seen celebrating India's detonation of the hydrogen bomb.

An epilogue tells of substantial changes in Calcutta since the end of the story. The public and private efforts for reform demonstrated that the lot of the Indian people could be improved. The priest was granted the Indian citizenship he coveted, along with a Bengali name, translated as "Blessed is he who is loved by God."

Analysis: Lapierre has a number of well-known books to his credit. This work is constructed like a tapestry, weaving together the lives of men, women, and children of countless castes and classes—all against the background of a city, opulent and degenerate beyond the imagination of many westerners. The descriptions are dazzling, often humorous, and at times graphically horrifying. Fiction could not be more fascinating than this true tale of the life and death struggles of some of the poorest, sickest, and yet most resilient people on earth. The account of the spiritual quest of those who joined the City of Joy as a mission is inspiring for people of all faiths.

■ Lax, Eric. *Life and Death on 10 West.* Times Books, 1984. 267pp. (0-81-291-0270) Reading Level: Grades 10–12. (LJ 1 Mr84; NYTBR 25 Mr84; Time 4 My84)
Disability: Cancer; Leukemia

The author has written numerous articles and a book for the popular press. He spent seven months on a ward of the UCLA Medical Center, where, under the stewardship of Dr. Robert Gale, patients with leukemia and other life-threatening blood diseases come for extraordinary and experimental medical procedures such as bone marrow transplantation that might save their life. He tells the story of a young woman, Linda, who, at

26 was expecting her first baby in three months. During a routine check, she was to get the diagnosis that would so alter her life and that of her family—leukemia.

Linda bravely achieved her first goal, to carry the baby to term before beginning treatment for her disease. After nine days of labor, little Angela Hope was born.

The next part of Linda's story involved medical treatment to get her into remission and enjoy a brief but happy respite at home with her baby and husband. Finally Linda decided to undergo a bone marrow transplant, since her chances of survival with that procedure were considerably greater than the 10 percent of persons who remained in remission after conservative treatment.

The story weaves around Linda, the other patients, and the dedicated doctors and nurses who are responsible for the medical decisions and procedures in 10 West. The tremendous commitment of all of the people involved is explored in depth. By the end of the book, Linda's release into death has become a part of the fabric, rather than a main theme of the book, that describes hope, pain, and laborious medical progress.

Analysis: This book has been well received by such literary figures as Norman Cousins. It is a fast-moving work and yet explains technical matters clearly and without medical jargon. One of the unusual strengths of the book is its portrayal of the perceptions and feelings of all of the characters involved in the life and death dramas in this cancer unit—those of physicians, nurses, patients, and families. Rather than being optimistic or pessimistic, it might best be categorized as compassionate, and it is a compelling book as well.

■ Leinwand, Gerald. *Transplants: Today's Modern Miracles.* Franklin Watts, 1985. 88pp. (LB 0-531-04930-2) Reading Level: Grades 7–9. (BCCB S85; BL 1 Je85; SLJ S85)
Disability: Organ transplants

The author, an educator and writer, begins his book with the first human heart transplant, performed by Dr. Christiaan Barnard in South Africa. He then defines some of the terms common to this procedure. In subsequent chapters, he gives a history of transplants (including the information that "[t]he earliest record of transplantation surgery, about 2000 B.C., described the grafts of skin from the neck or cheek to repair a mutilated nose, lip, or ear" [p. 8]) and brings the story up to the present time. He presents the ethical, legal, and medical issues raised by transplantation and sketches the future of transplantation surgery. There is a short bibliography for further reading, and the book concludes with an index.

Analysis: Leinwand writes with admirable clarity and directness. He presents complicated physiological and medical concepts so that they can be grasped by the lay reader and is equally strong in his presentation of the difficult questions and dilemmas of transplantation surgery. He has woven brief vignettes about real people into the text, a good technique for involving the reader. The book is well suited for use in classroom discussion and would also be helpful to young people who have experienced transplantation either for themselves or for someone close to them. It might well be paired with *The Gift of Life,* by Paricheh Yomtoob and Ted Schwarz.

■ Lerner, Max. ***Wrestling with the Angel: A Memoir of My Triumph over Illness.*** Norton, 1990. 210pp. (0-393-02846-1) Reading Level: Grades 10–12. (BL 1 Je90; LJ J190; NYTBR 8 J190)
Disability: Cancer

Max Lerner, noted author and teacher for more than 60 years, has written an autobiographical memoir of his wrestlings with the angel of death that began with lymphoma when he was 79. Over the next eight years, Lerner recovered not only from that cancer but also from a bout of prostate cancer and a heart attack. Still active as a writer and teacher at age 88, he reviewed his journal notes and wrote this philosophical, passionate narrative about his years of illness and recovery.

Analysis: This book is not for every high school age reader, because a book about an older adult's disability usually has little to attract or sustain the interest of a teenager. This one, however, has much to offer readers of any age and is "young" enough so that a mature teenager who is a good reader will find it an interesting and rewarding experience. First and foremost, Lerner is a superb writer and an excellent storyteller. His language and his attitudes are remarkably youthful. His reflections about the developmental course of life have much to attract a mature teenager. Highly recommended for a select group of teens.

■ Malcolm, Andrew H. ***This Far and No More: A True Story.*** Time Books, 1987. 247pp. (0-8129-1606-9) Reading Level: Grades 10–12. (BL 1 Ap87; LJ 1 Je87; NYTBR 26 Ap87)
Disability: Amyotrophic lateral sclerosis

Malcolm, Chicago bureau chief of the *Chicago Times,* became interested in the ever-increasing phenomenon of families who must make decisions regarding a relative's death—a process that used to be "in the hands of God" but is now subject to medical technologies that can significantly prolong life and dying. After several months of research, he found a family (called the Bauers in the book) that was willing to share its three-year-long ordeal. The mother, who died, kept a diary until her end. Other family members, professionals, and friends agreed to be interviewed. It is the author's belief that the experiences and insights to be gained from this compelling story will be helpful to other families and professionals who must face life and death issues.

"It started with a stumble" (p. 3). Pregnant Emily Bauer caught her foot on the sidewalk as she jumped from the taxi, coming home from work.

Emily had focused her first 15 years of adulthood on graduate education and a subsequent career in the teaching and practice of psychology. At age 34, she met Bob, a free-lance film producer. They began a modern marriage: Emily, the chief bread winner, operating weekdays from a small city apartment, joining Bob in their country home for weekends.

She had a daughter when she was 38 and was pregnant again on her 40th birthday. After the birth of her second daughter, the dropsied foot that had caused her stumble became worse. After a series of tests, she was diagnosed with amyotrophic lateral sclerosis, or Lou Gehrig's disease, which results in a progressive wasting of the body's muscle and early death.

The narrative and Emily's diary tell of the family's descent into illness. Emily faced ever greater losses—becoming unable to mother or keep her job or help her husband. She lost the ability to move, to breathe, and eventually to speak. While still at home, her respirator failed, and she agreed to be resuscitated and hospitalized.

Two years after the onset of the illness, her attentive husband, Bob, was exhausted physically, psychologically, and financially. Emily had been a flamboyant, even strident, organizer, and she tried to keep control of her family and friends even as she lost control of her faculties. Eventually she was transferred to a nursing home, attended by round-the-clock nurses. Yet, she derived much pleasure from seeing her family and friends and from simple objects such as a vase of flowers. She was able to continue her diary by using a printing machine operated by head movement.

Finally Emily made peace with her fate and was ready to die. Her husband contacted a lawyer and then a doctor from the organization Concern for Dying in order to help her arrange for her end. She returned to their apartment to receive last good-byes from family and friends. When all had left, the doctor administered a sleeping potion and un-plugged her respirator. The book ends on a note of hope, as the survivors rejoice in the brave spirit of Emily, and they go on to appreciate their lives more fully because of her life and death.

Analysis: This book does not have chapters. The narrative moves as relentlessly as the illness that felled Emily in the prime of her life. Ethical issues, such as the right to die, are illustrated more by the story line than by abstract discussion. The author is adamant about facing the reality of intractable illness, but not what to do about it. The ambivalence and guilt of loved ones, the suffering of all those whose lives touched the victim, and her own, are sensitively addressed.

■ Miller, Caroline Adams. *My Name Is Caroline.* Illus. Doubleday, 1988. 278pp. (0-385-24208-5) Reading Level: Grades 10–12. (BL 15 F88; LJ 15 F88)
Disability: Bulimia

The black-and-white photographs of the author show an exceptionally pretty, blonde girl who was raised in affluence in the Washington, D.C., area. She had gone to the "best" schools from preschool through college. She was encouraged in academics, sports, and music by her rather perfectionist parents. She dated a preoccupation with her weight from the age of 8, when, in a restaurant, her father referred to her as "heavy." She faced enormous competition in the achievement-oriented Cathedral School. Although she was outwardly a success in all areas, she felt insecure, lonely, and inadequate inside. She began her compulsive eating and purging in preparatory school and continued in college and then into her marriage, for a total of seven years. By this point, her physical health and her sanity were in jeopardy.

The author begins her story with the description of a secret binge of eating and vomiting that she indulged in while a student at Harvard. She devoured succulent ice creams, milk shakes, and cookies. She ended the evening making a disgusting mess in the history department women's room. She not only deceived her friends about her activities, but she also resorted to shoplifting food and laxatives to sustain her habit.

Much of the book chronicles the rocky road to recovery from her compulsion. After her marriage, in desperation, she answered an advertisement for a self-help group for bulimics. Here she was linked to a sponsor who would support her. Eventually she undertook that role herself with newer members. Her therapy involved letting go of the obsession about being thin and learning to appreciate herself for what she was. She had to learn to eat normally, preparing proper foods in moderation, so that she would not have the need to purge. She began to honestly accept her problem and her responsibility for getting better. She learned to put her trust in a higher power. She could finally stand up in her group and say, "Hi, my name is Caroline, and I'm a bulimic and compulsive overeater" (p. 128).

A test of her newfound strength arose when her husband had a grand mal seizure from what turned out to be a lesion in his brain. She was able to face the crisis without breaking down or turning to food. Her "chain reaction of improvement" led to her getting a new wardrobe, a new hairstyle, and a new job. After a final binge-and-purge incident after an attempt to leave the support group, she became active in groups for recovering alcoholics and drug addicts as well, because she had also, at times, abused these substances.

Her final task was to make amends to the people she had offended, lied to, or stolen from, as a result of her compulsion. The most daunting experience was apologizing to her parents. They ultimately participated with her in a group session, after which the family became closer and more loving than ever. The writer is convinced from her experiences and contacts that bulimia is widespread in schools, among athletes and models, and among men as well as women. She does not suggest that her type of therapy is the only one that can work, but she is convinced that bulimia is a disease for which help should be sought.

Following the story there are a bulimia self-test and one for family and friends of a suspected bulimic. Various helpful organizations and references are listed. In an afterword, Miller states her intention to start a nonprofit foundation to educate people about bulimia.

Analysis: This well-written account shows the dark side of an honest, humorous, and talented young woman. Her rich, graphic descriptions convincingly portray the seductiveness of the binging compulsion. The stages of therapy are clearly presented, and the insights she gained are well expressed. This book should be, as the author intended, helpful to others in understanding the bulimia malady and the possibilities for overcoming it.

■ Miller, Robyn. *Robyn's Book: A True Diary.* Scholastic, 1986. 179pp. (0-590-33787-4) Reading Level: Grades 7–12. (BL J186; BR N86; PW 30 My86; SLJ S86; VYA D8)
Disability: Cystic fibrosis

In her opening chapter, "Who I Am," Robyn Miller gives some details of her background, including her piece "An Autobiography of Sorts," first published in Scholastic's *Voice* magazine. At the time of writing of this book, she was 21 years old; born in 1964, she was diagnosed as having cystic fibrosis when she was a year old. She was relatively healthy until the age of 16, when she began to experience progressively frequent and severe episodes of lung infection necessitating hospitalization. Despite her illness, she finished high school with an excellent record and became a student at Barnard College.

Each chapter has an introductory section, printed in italics. In the material that follows, she includes short stories, poems, profiles of friends, a discussion of cystic fibrosis as "the hidden handicap," and some of the correspondence that resulted from the issue of Scholastic's *Voice* magazine (November 2, 1984) that was devoted to her work, with emphasis on her experience as a person with a progressive disability. She received about 3,000 letters from students all over the world, and the April 26, 1985, issue of the magazine was devoted to some of these letters and Miller's answers.

The afterword, written by an editor of *Voice,* tells the reader that Robyn Miller died in August 1985, just as her book was ready to go to press.

Analysis: This is a moving, almost unbearably poignant book. Robyn Miller was clearly a gifted young woman. She was bright, curious, an accomplished writer; as the afterword puts it, "Robyn had a rare gift, to make public language speak to the private person." She was also perceptive, honest, and courageous—with the kind of courage that does not deny fear and rage. Most of the friends she describes were children and young people she met in the hospital; they had cystic fibrosis, too, or cancer, and they were dying, and, like Robyn, they faced their lives with brave spirits. All were determined, consciously or unconsciously, to wring joy and beauty from pain, outfacing death by the way they lived.

Cystic fibrosis is a cruel disease. The life expectancy of children with cystic fibrosis has improved with better treatment techniques, but thus far the end has not been changed, only postponed. Robyn Miller was sure that one day a cure will be found but equally sure that she would not live to see it. She took satisfaction in the knowledge that through her writing she had helped to make readers aware not only of this disease but also of the effects of living with any disability.

■ Miller, Thomas, and Jayne Miller. *Baby James: A Legacy of Love and Family Courage.* Illus. Harper & Row, 1988. 192pp. (0-06-250584-X) Reading Level: Grades 7–12. (BL 15 088; KR 1 My88) *Disability:* Cardiomyopathy

Named Baby James for purposes of press releases, Nicholas Lawrence Miller was the adopted son of Jayne and Thomas Miller. He was apparently a perfect, healthy infant when he was born in February 1985, in the hospital in northern California where Jayne worked as a respiratory therapist; his birth parents released him for adoption immediately, without seeing him. The Millers had been trying for some time to adopt an infant, and this beautiful baby seemed truly the answer to their prayers, for they were actively devout and committed Catholics. Within hours of his birth, however, Nicholas experienced a life-threatening medical crisis caused by infection; he survived pulmonary hemorrhage, cardiac fibrillation, and peritonitis from a bacterial infection that entered his system through the incision made for dialysis. The infections were conquered, but the baby's heart was damaged. When the Millers took their son home from the hospital nine weeks after his birth, they embarked on a routine of carefully monitored medications, care, and continuous evaluation.

In his first months, Nicholas made good progress in many areas and developed into a bright, energetic, very attractive baby. However, his medical problems continued; after a bout with pneumonia and congestive heart failure, doctors performed an extensive echocardiogram that confirmed the pediatric cardiologist's view that the baby's heart was so badly damaged that he was a candidate for a heart transplant. The Millers' medical insurance for Nicholas, provided by the state for adopted children, covered transplant surgery only at Stanford University Hospital; however, Jayne Miller did some research and concluded that Loma Linda University Hospital in southern California, which had already done heart transplants on infants, was preferable; Loma Linda accepted Nicholas without charge. The surgery was performed there in April 1986 by Dr. Leonard L. Bailey, pediatric cardiology surgeon.

When Nicholas was released from the hospital 18 days later, Jayne and the baby stayed nearby. After an episode of organ rejection, Tom got a leave of absence from his job and joined them. They spent the summer in a rented apartment in a mountain town not far from Loma Linda. Nicholas's weekly checkups in August, four months after the surgery, were very encouraging, and he was to move to two-week examinations. However, after two unexplained episodes of vomiting only three days later, the Millers took Nicholas back to the hospital, where tests showed that he seemed headed for another rejection episode. This time, his condition rapidly deteriorated; the medical staff tried desperately to save him, even registering him for another transplant, but Nicholas died in his mother's arms. He was 18½ months old.

In the last section, called "Conclusion," the Millers describe their immediate devastating grief, the carefully planned funeral service, and their lives since their son's death. They describe the mourning process, different for each of them, and the way each learned to respect the other's grief. They found not only that they missed Nicholas, with acute, terrible pain, but also that they missed being parents; they write that they are "committed to creating our family anew through adoption." In an afterword, subtitled "A Physician's Perspective," Dr. Bailey gives his account of his meeting the Millers, Nicholas's medical condition, and the surgery and its aftermath. At the end, he writes, "[h]arsh reality chilled us to the bone. Nicholas was dying, and nothing we tried was making a difference. A part of each of us was dying with him."

Analysis: Thomas Miller is a professional writer and editor of technical material. In the first section of the book, the reader is told that the Millers have chosen to tell the story of their son together; sometimes they refer to Jayne's thoughts and experiences, sometimes to Tom's, and sometimes they use "we." Deeply committed to their religious faith and to their marriage, they nevertheless have not hesitated to include their doubts and anger and the strains that Nicholas's illness caused to their relationship. Their son seems, from their descriptions and the photographs, to have been a child of unusual compelling grace and attractiveness, a little boy whose body and spirit fought courageously and who, if he had not been assaulted by illness, would have grown into a fine adult. Though at times they raged against the terrible unfairness of fate, the Millers were able ultimately to believe that God had a purpose in bringing them together with Nicholas and that their beautiful child had entered heaven and eternal peace. In the conclusion they write, "Whatever else we might seek or learn in our attempts to make sense of it all . . . we truly believe that Nicholas was a gift to us, and that we were chosen by God to share his brief but happy life." The work contains black-and-white photographs.

■ Morrell, David. *Fireflies.* Dutton, 1988. 216pp. (0-525-24680-0) Reading Level: Grades 10–12. (BL 1 S88; LJ 1 O88; PW 30 S88)
Disability: Cancer; Ewing's sarcoma

David Morrell is the award-winning author of *First Blood,* the novel on which the Rambo film series is based, and a former professor of American literature. This book is the true story of the illness, death, and burial of his son, Matthew, who, at 15, developed a rare form of bone cancer, Ewing's sarcoma. Two mystical themes also run through the narrative. The first deals with three events that happened to David Morrell after Matthew's death, one of which was attested to by the dozen people who witnessed the placing of his urn in a mausoleum. The second lies within the fictional framework that Morrell builds near the beginning and near the end of the book in the process of telling the true story. In a closing section, he sorts out the truth from the fiction and discusses the significance of using this device. In the fictional framework, Morrell sees himself as an old man, dying some 40 years later, then going back in time and saving Matthew from dying.

Analysis: The Library of Congress has classified this book as fiction. However, it has been decided to include it in this bibliography of nonfiction works, because in the judgment of the authors, the nonfictional aspects are clearly delineated and are paramount to the fictional aspects. In addition, it is wonderfully written and a superlative tribute by a father to his son, and it is quite clear that Morrell has written it as Matthew's biography, with emphasis on his teenage years, his death, and their relationship.

The entire book is beautifully written. Morrell was very close to Matthew, and his writing often becomes lyrical and poetic. It is also sensitive and intensely painful. Highly recommended for teens, who will feel an immediate affinity with Matthew.

■ Mullan, Fitzhugh. *Vital Signs: A Young Doctor's Struggle with Cancer.* Farrar, 1982. 220pp. (0-374-16864-4) Reading Level: Grades 10–12. (BL 15 N82; KR 15 N82; LJ 15 Ja83; NYTBR 27 F83; PW 17 D82) *Disability:* Cancer; Seminoma

In March 1975 Dr. Fitzhugh Mullan was a 32-year-old pediatrician practicing in a community clinic operated by the Public Health Service in Santa Fe, New Mexico, when he ordered chest X rays for a sick baby. Though he felt healthy and had no reason to suspect anything serious, he had had occasional chest pain at night for three months and a cough after a recent bout with flu, so he decided to have an X ray also. To his stunned and horrified astonishment, the film revealed a lump the size of a grapefruit in his chest. The next day he was on his way east to the National Naval Medical Center in Bethesda; his wife and 3-year-old daughter followed.

Mullan was a writer as well as a physician, and at the time of the onset of his illness he was preparing his first book, *White Coat, Clenched Fist: The Political Education of an American Physician,* for publication. His parents gave him a tape recorder when he entered the hospital; eventually, he says in the introduction, "I came to want to tell the story, partly to leave something behind if I died and partly because it helped relieve my anger at my condition." His book covers the years from the discovery of the mass through diagnosis and treatment to his reaching the magic five-year mark.

The first step was diagnostic mediastinoscopy, so that a tissue diagnosis could be made. Unfortunately, things went seriously awry during this procedure, and Mullan nearly died. The biopsy bled, and the surgeons had to perform an emergency thoracotomy to stop the bleeding; the tumor was revealed to have invaded his chest, nerves, blood vessels, and right lung, and it was decided to remove as much as possible right then. The tumor was a seminoma, "a cancer of testicular tissue that usually starts as a swelling in the scrotum of young men."

The subsequent years were difficult and painful, marked by life-threatening crises and debilitating treatments. Mullan swelled up from blockage of the superior vena cava, and radiation therapy had to be started a week early; radiation burn of the esophagus made swallowing and eating nearly impossible for months; chemotherapy attacked malignant and healthy cells alike, and left him nauseated and weak. Later, a small opening in the incision, which refused to heal, called for more surgery; the persistent infection failed to respond to therapy, and ultimately the sternum was removed. Mullan then had plastic surgery that required tedious procedures, including attaching his arm to his chest to nourish the transplanted flap of skin. Though he was encouraged and supported by a fine medical staff, by friends, and by his close and loving family, especially his wife and parents, he suffered from loneliness and depression so profound that he once contemplated suicide. He knew no one else his age who was facing the same kind of mortal assault, and he had to deal with anger at the abrupt change in his expectations and with a sense of betrayal and terrible loss as his once responsive healthy body became emaciated, scarred, and feeble.

Eventually, Mullan left the hospital for the last time. His recovery was helped by the support group that he and his wife attended, by his gradual return to work with the Public Health Service in Washington, and by events signaling affirmation and joy. A few weeks after diagnosis, his wife discovered that she was pregnant. They debated whether to continue the pregnancy, given their uncertain family future; the conception had taken place before Mullan had therapy, so that possible damage to his sperm from treatment was not an issue, but his life expectations were tenuous. They decided to have the baby, and determination to live to see her gave him a goal; the birth of this second daughter led Mullan to reflect that whatever the eventual effect of his illness, "I had been fulfilled on at least one count—I *had* lived to see my child born. I had shared life with Caitlin. In my own cosmos, that was monumentally important." His first book was published, another milestone for rejoicing. And two years later, the Mullans adopted a 3-year-old boy.

In the final chapter, "Taking Stock," Mullan concludes, "In many ways life had more flavor and more verve after my illness than before it. In no way do I mean to recommend or endorse serious sickness, but living through it has, I think, left me with a fuller sense of life."

Analysis: Mullan is a fine writer, able to describe scenes, events, feelings, and thoughts with vivid clarity. Though the reader knows that his survival is not in doubt, the medical crises marking his illness and slow recovery propel the narrative forward. The thoughtful passages concerning introspection and analysis are marked by an honest, sometimes wry, and humorous self-awareness. Acknowledging his own weaknesses and flaws, describing the terror of critical illness and the tortuous process of recovery, he avoids both self-pity and self-congratulation. In his introduction, Mullan explains that as he thought about his own experience and that of other people he had heard of, "I came to believe that the problems of young people with cancer were more complex and far less explored than I had ever realized. This made me the more eager to share my experiences in the hope that they would be helpful to other young adults facing cancer or similar life-altering crises." In acknowledging his pain, rage, and isolation and describing the process by which he regained much of his health as well as a measure of acceptance of the blows dealt him, Mullan has written a book that indeed speaks to healthy and ill readers alike.

■ Murray, Gloria, ed., and Gerald G. Jampolsky. *Another Look at the Rainbow: Straight from the Siblings.* Celestial Arts, 1982. 92pp. (0-89087-341-0) Reading Level: Grades 4–12.
Disability: Health problems

A group of 34 children who attended support groups at a Center for Attitudinal Healing wrote and illustrated this intriguing and highly realistic piece of work about how siblings cope with the severe illness and ultimate death of a brother or sister. The essays and illustrations are organized into chapters with themes such as "Our First Reactions," "Fear, Loneliness, Jealousy, and Guilt," "Facing Death," "Making Life an Upper—You Have a Choice," and "Thoughts for Others on Going Through Life."

The brief essays and drawings are written simply and straight from the heart. Besides expressing anger and fear, the two most overwhelming reactions seem to be the age-old questions of "Why?" and "Why not me?" In addition, there is jealousy: "Why does she get all the attention and presents?" accompanied by guilt, as the sibling admits that she or he understands all too well the "why" of all this extra attention.

Analysis: This book would be extremely useful for a child dealing with the severe illness of a brother, sister, or friend. It would also be useful for teachers, medical and mental health professionals, and social workers in their interactions with families. Sections could easily be read to and discussed with children younger than those in grade 4, especially because of the drawings that accompany them. Highly recommended.

■ Nolen, William A. *Surgeon Under the Knife.* Dell, 1977. 221pp. (Paper 0-440-18-388-X) Reading Level: Grades 7–12. (LJ 15 My76; NYTBR 9 Ja77; PW 29 Mr76)
Disability: Coronary artery disease

William Nolen is a general surgeon who has combined his medical career with writing books and articles for the lay public, as well as one book for children *(Spare Parts for the Human Body).* At the age of 47, he had a successful practice, a writing career, and a large, happy family. He was athletic and followed a reasonably healthy life-style. Only his father's early death from heart disease and his own high blood pressure presaged his angina (heart pain) and subsequent diagnosis of coronary artery disease.

The book begins with an explanation, in layman's terms, of the main functions of the heart, a pump which supplies oxygen and nutrient-rich blood to all parts of the body, including the heart itself. The clogging of the small corneal arteries supplying blood to the heart can lead to pain and eventual muscle damage or death; it is these that must be bypassed with one, two, or three or more segments of veins from the body when one has single, double, or triple or more bypass surgery.

The author details his own successful double bypass surgery from the time of diagnosis, when he unabashedly wept, through his recuperation, when he resumed his surgical duties. Treatment procedures and regimens are detailed. The book ends with brief vignettes about others who have successfully and gratefully gone through the same ordeal.

Analysis: The author writes in a personal style and seems straightforward and honest about his feelings and experiences. He has a knack for describing medical issues in simple terms understandable to young readers. He stresses the contributions of all the dedicated people in the hospital setting: the nurses, technicians, young interns, and residents, as well as the more seasoned physicians whom he sought out for his surgery.

In 1976, when he began his book, the prospect of bypass surgery was a relatively new and often lifesaving alternative to traditional medical treatment for arterial heart disease. Undoubtedly, some of the procedures and findings detailed in the book have been amended in the intervening years, but the basic message still rings true today.

■ Ostrow, William, and Vivian Ostrow. *All about Asthma.* Illus. by Blanche Sims. Whitman, 1989. 40pp. (LB 0-8075-0276-6) Reading Level: Grades 2–7. (BCCB D89; BL 15 D89)
Disability: Asthma

William Ostrow had his first attack of asthma when he was about 8 years old, after a bout of pneumonia. He and his mother have written their book to explain the disease to other children and to reassure those who also have this chronic disability. Short chapters describe William's life with asthma, his treatment and medications, and ways he has found to help himself. The authors explain what happens in an asthma attack and discuss possible causes. In William's case, triggering agents include dander (he had to give up his cat), cold air, dust, certain foods, and smoke; he comes from a family in which his mother and uncle both have mild asthma.

In a postscript, William writes that for him, "the key to successfully managing my asthma was learning as much about it as I could. I hope this book helps you to learn so you can understand and cope with your asthma better." When he first became ill, he felt very much alone and wished he had another youngster in the same situation to talk to: now he invites his young readers to write to him and promises to answer, ending with his address.

Every spread includes large cartoon-style drawings done in black, gray, white, and blue-green. Asthma is pictured as a big-eyed, hairy little creature who sometimes sits on William's shoulder and is always his opponent.

Analysis: The authors write in an informal, lively first-person voice. Information is conveyed clearly as they explain what asthma is and is not. William acknowledges the feelings of isolation, embarrassment, and anxiety brought on by his attacks when they first began and describes persuasively the treatments, attitudes, and activities that he uses to help him live with this chronic condition. The text gives explicit directions about dealing with attacks, explaining, for example, that one should respond with treatment immediately. Throughout, the emphasis is on taking an active role in meeting the disease, controlling it with proper medication and exercise, and developing the most effective techniques to temper its severity. The authors explain that attacks are controllable and their effects reversible. The tone is light without being trivial and is matched by amusing and informative illustrations, which show William in a variety of situations; the other children represent a multiethnic group. The book is attractively designed and well laid out typographically.

Asthma can be frightening, frustrating, and difficult to control. This book should go far toward explaining it to asthmatic and nonasthmatic readers alike. As William says, the more he knows about his asthma and what he can do to help himself, the more relaxed he can be during an attack. Knowledge is power.

■ Permut, Joanna Baumer. *Embracing the Wolf: A Lupus Victim and Her Family Learn to Live with Chronic Disease.* Cherokee, 1989. 175pp. (0-87797-166-8) Reading Level: Grades 10–12. (BL 15 S89; LJ Ag89; NYTBR 19 N89)
Disability: Lupus

In her 20s, Permut was the mother of a young daughter, Lisa, and an employee of Yale University, where her husband had an academic appointment. After several busy and happy years, she began to experience pain and fatigue that would eventually be diagnosed as symptoms of lupus. Her disease is a type of arthritis that bears the Latin name for "wolf," hence giving her book its title. By the time Permut was 30, she had become so generally debilitated that she had to forsake her job—a very hard blow to her sense of worth and identity. She could no longer horseback ride with 10-year-old Lisa, and she needed help with housework and gardening. In addition, she and her grieving father were facing the imminent death of her mother. She had "joined the ranks of malcontents. Self hatred bred self pity" (p. 49).

Permut looked healthy, but she experienced unpredictable flare-ups with psychomotor seizures, dry eyes, weakness, and pain that interfered with the family's social life and everyday activities. Her husband, Steven, could not comprehend her helplessness and moodiness. After scenes and recriminations, the couple would reunite apologetically in recurring cycles. Permut was ashamed of this illness that she personified as a stalking wolf.

A turning point came when she decided that she could no longer afford to be held hostage to her disease. She consulted a psychiatrist, in large measure to save this, her second marriage. She learned to express her feelings in her psychotherapy and at home, and she began to understand her husband's perplexity with the "wolf" that had entered her family. She revived an old practice—writing poetry to relieve her emotional tensions. She slowly expanded her circle of friends and became a volunteer managing editor on a local poetry magazine.

The lingering problems Permut had with her husband seemed to be dispelled when he learned to express his anger over lupus and to realize that the disease was a mutual problem rather than exclusively his wife's. "Regardless of which partner the disease hits, the other's hell has only just begun" (pp. 164–65). Eleven years after her diagnosis, at the time of her writing, Permut felt a fulfillment in her life that she believed was possible only through the broadening experience of dealing with a serious chronic disease.

An appendix and a glossary, contributed by several physicians, deal with medical terms. A short bibliography ends the book.

Analysis: Few books for the layman address the experience of having lupus. This account gives a graphic description of the effects of the disease, including the consequent anger, frustration, and despair that so often beset a young adult suddenly struck down with chronic illness. Laudable as well is the author's attention to the problems of her husband and daughter, which were exacerbated by lupus.

Permut is an articulate, honest writer with a somewhat moralistic and pedantic style that is nevertheless readable. Her unique personification of her disease as a wolf to be tamed and even admired might enhance the narrative for some.

■ Reisman, Barry. *Jared's Story: A Boy in a Bubble and How His Family Saved His Life.* Crown, 1984. 185pp. (0-517-55423-2) Reading Level: Grades 10–12. (KR 1 S84; LJ 1 N84; VYA Ap85)
Disability: Allergies

Jared Reisman was 12 years old when his father wrote this book, beginning with these words: "This is the story of a little boy who lost his right to live. He can no longer see a doctor, attend school with other children, or receive a religious education. His only right is to an institution and a death without dignity. His crime: he survived an illness so debilitating that it was diagnosed, incorrectly, as severe retardation. The agony and the limitation placed on him continue to this day" (p. 3).

Jared developed severe allergies to airborne substances when he was 18 months old. As of 1984, when his father wrote this book, Jared was a vibrant, healthy, intelligent child, but he could remain this way only by living in his dust-free, air-filtered home or by leaving this environment wearing a bubble device attached to a portable air filter.

As if this way of life is not complex and difficult enough, the Reisman family's existence has been further complicated by a diagnosis of mental retardation and autism, made when Jared was a toddler and so ill from allergic rhinitis that he was nearly deaf and lacking in the mental and physical alertness needed to take an IQ test.

Under California law, this diagnosis was officially recorded by a social services unit and, unless changed by a physician, would remain in effect until Jared was 18, thus making him eligible only for special schooling for severely retarded children and ineligible for the services needed to provide him with a special physical environment in his regular school's classroom. The Reismans' attempts to change this diagnosis have met with a closing of the medical ranks to protect the original diagnosis and the physician who made it, despite the fact that he really needed no protection from the Reismans. This resistance has been carried to incredibly complex lengths, to the point where some of the events described in the book are even the stuff from which espionage stories are woven.

At the writing of this book, Jared remained at home, being tutored by his mother with the reluctant cooperation of a local school. His health was good, and his parents still hoped that he would eventually outgrow this immune system problem and be able to function in a broader environment.

Analysis: The theme of conflict with the various medical, educational, and social services professionals whose very reason for being is to provide assistance to children and their families is a common thread that runs through many stories about the lives of children with disabilities or chronic illnesses (as well as through the stories of many differently abled adults). *Jared's Story* presents one of the clearest, most direct, and most powerful accounts of the breadth and depth that these conflicts can assume.

A stark example of what the term "arrogance of power" means, the story is an indictment of mindless educational bureaucracy and of the medical profession's frequent unwillingness to admit an error and its dedication to protecting its own, no matter what the truth may be or how unnecessary that protection is. Finally, it is an example of the importance of patient and family participation in health care and in the planning of social and educational services. Without his parents, Jared would have died at a young age. The irony here is that instead of applauding the family's triumph over Jared's illness, professionals have assiduously denied it, and in the process, they have made the boy's life, as well as the life of his family, problematic and stressful.

This is a work with great significance for anyone who has or ever will have to deal with a complex illness or injury. Recommended for high-school-level readers.

■ Sacker, Ira M., and Marc A. Zimmer. ***Dying to Be Thin: Understanding and Defeating Anorexia Nervosa and Bulimia.*** Warner, 1987. 259pp. (Paper 0-446-38417-8) Reading Level: Grades 6–12. (KLIATT S87; VYA D87)
Disability: Anorexia; Bulimia

Dr. Sacker is medical director of the Eating Disorders Program and chief of Adolescent Medicine at Brookdale Hospital in Brooklyn, New York. Dr. Zimmer is director of the Biofeedback and Psychotherapy Center in Valley Stream, New York. Both have worked extensively in the field of eating disorders. Their book is divided into six sections dealing with understanding the conditions, overcoming them through a variety of treatment plans, and helping one's children, friends, and students with eating disorders; the section on resources lists organizations as well as programs, organized by state. The authors include a short bibliography and an index.

The book incorporates extensive material from patients who have agreed to the publication of their statements, journals, and letters. Although adolescent girls and young women are generally held to be the more usual patients, Sacker and Zimmer include histories of somewhat older women and of young men. They present the symptoms and typical course of the disorders, discuss causes, and describe treatment programs, stressing repeatedly that each case is unique and that each therapy plan must be designed for the individual patient. All of the histories are about people who have recognized and acknowledged their illness and are taking steps toward recovery; some patients came close to death before being able to accept their condition.

Analysis: While never underestimating the seriousness of these disorders or their fatal potential, the authors use a nonjudgmental tone, recognizing that attempting to place blame and guilt accomplishes nothing. At the same time, they make clear the necessity for the anorexic or bulimic person to take the necessary and difficult steps toward acknowledging illness and seeking treatment. They are both realistic about the difficulty and pain involved in the slow process of recovery and optimistic about the possibility of a return to health; they are supportive both of the patient and of her or his family.

The book contains much helpful, valuable information. It is also somewhat repetitive, as it seeks to emphasize points. In at least one case history, there were errors in some nonmedical details, but such lapses do not appear to extend to the medical/psychological material. The authors treated the patients whose voices are heard here; they do not hesitate to record praise of themselves. This may sometimes startle the reader but does not detract from the value of the book for people who suffer from eating disorders or for their families, friends, teachers, and those who attend them professionally.

■ Severno, Richard. *Lisa H.: The True Story of an Extraordinary and Courageous Woman.* Harper & Row, 1985. 180pp. (0-06-015405-5) Reading Level: Grades 9–12. (BL 1 F85; KR 1 D84; NYTBR 6 F85) *Disability:* Neurofibromatosis

Lisa H. is the pseudonym of a young woman, born in 1960 in southeastern Pennsylvania. The fifth child of loving, family-oriented, working-class parents, she was born with glaucoma, which eventually left her with very poor vision. A physician eventually discovered that the cause of the glaucoma was pressure exerted by fibrous tumors growing in the cranial and facial areas and that these tumors were manifestations of neurofibromatosis, commonly called elephant man's disease.

Lisa's mother, Mary, was determined that her daughter would receive all possible medical help and also that she would grow up in the same way as the other children in the neighborhood. Mary sent Lisa to school with these children, took her to church, social events, and shopping malls, and generally reared her as she had reared her four other children. As a result, Lisa became an outgoing, determined, spirited child, who was accepted on an equal footing by her schoolmates. However, especially as she grew older, she became the object of stares as well as jeering, cruel remarks. Although some of this harassment came from children, more came from adults, and nearly always these people were strangers to the family: the school bus driver who told Lisa she was the ugliest thing that he had ever seen, the woman who approached Mary in a dress shop and told her she had no right to bring such a deformed creature out in public, and the person who told Lisa she did not need a Halloween mask, to name only a few of the indignities to which she was subjected. Most of the time, Mary and Lisa's two sisters suffered as much from these events as did Lisa herself.

As Lisa went through adolescence into early adulthood, however, her differences became more critical to her. She desperately wanted to look "normal" so that she would eventually be able to achieve her most prized goal—a husband and a family. As a result, Lisa underwent massive surgery in December 1981 that nearly took her life, followed by four more operations in the next 21 months, for a lifetime total of 16 operations on her face and her head, or an average of one surgery for each 17 months of her life. The major surgery in December 1981 included the removal of one eye that had become virtually useless. At the conclusion of the book, Lisa is learning to accept her new self, even though her face, while improved, still does not present the standard of beauty she would like to achieve.

Analysis: This is an excellent book for those dealing with all kinds of obvious physical differences. It is also useful in dealing with the larger issue of body image. It emphasizes Lisa's warm personality, her sensitivity, and her intelligence, as well as her physical problems and the resulting emotional stresses, in an honest, factual, unsentimental manner. Very little is available about people with neurofibromatosis, and this book fills a real need.

■ Sharkey, Frances. *A Parting Gift.* St. Martin's, 1982. 162pp. Reading Level: Grades 7–12. (BL 15 Ap82; KR 15 Ja82; LJ 1 Ap82; PW 5 F82; SLJ S82)
Disability: Cancer; Leukemia

In the preface to her book, Frances Sharkey describes how for 20 years after she became a doctor, she believed that she had chosen pediatrics as a specialty because she enjoyed children and because a pediatrician could, with the help of antibiotics, help children recover from illness and grow to adulthood. Then, following the death of an 8-year-old patient to whom she had become very attached and who with her help had died at home, she realized that her decision had been influenced by her fear of death. Children usually die in hospitals, she says, because the impersonality there comforts the doctors, shielding them "from the emotional impact of seeing a dying child in his very own bedroom where his life and individuality are so much in evidence." Doctors believe too that they spare parents by this choice and that no one considers the child's preference. "The death of a child is always, I think, the most somber event anyone ever encounters," she writes. "But it is a tragedy that can be compounded by a second tragedy: the denial of death. I hope that my book will help persuade people not that there is ever a good way for a child to die, but that there are some ways that are better than others."

As a medical student, Sharkey encountered death in the old, in the cadaver she dissected, and in an adolescent girl who in six months had gone from being a talented ballet student to a desperately sick and frightened child dying of bone cancer that had spread to her lungs. Over the next years, Sharkey was able to save patients who, before current medical advances, would have been lost, and she derived great satisfaction from her work. She also read *On Death and Dying,* by Elisabeth Kubler-Ross and began to understand her own denial of death. When a 15-month-old patient died of monocytic leukemia, she wept with the family at the child's bedside—the first time, she says, that she had ever "let a family know how much I really did care. Why had it taken me so long to realize that it was all right?"

In 1971, a beautiful 2-year-old boy was referred to her. The diagnosis was leukemia. He responded very well to treatment and appeared to have recovered. Over the years, Sharkey monitored his progress carefully. David was a child of unusually compelling character who impressed people immediately by his intelligence, his calm, and his courageous acceptance of everything that had to be done for and to him. When he was 8, as Sharkey did her periodic examination of his testes, she thought she might have detected a slight increase in size, but they seemed to be normal as compared to her previous measurements and to other boys his age. The doctors could have used radiation therapy on the testes, as they had earlier done on his brain to prevent spread there, but such procedure was not recommended without clear symptoms. Sharkey went to India for the summer to work as a volunteer doctor; when she returned, she found that David had relapsed. He had a hard spot on one of his testes and malignant cells in his bone marrow. Therapy was ineffective, and it became clear that he was dying. Together, Sharkey and David's parents planned for his death, at home. Before he left the hospital, the doctor told him that he was dying. Once home, David's physical condition continued to worsen, but his spirits improved even as his body weakened. Some days later, while his mother was out doing a necessary errand and his father was in the kitchen getting him some juice, David died.

Analysis: This is a book that compels tears. Frances Sharkey is clearly a doctor with great sensitivity to both her patients and their parents, who has the courage to examine her own thinking and motives and the intelligence to reach new insights. She is an acute observer and writes with unaffected eloquence and compassion. Her description of events in her practice as well as the long section on David could appeal to many young readers and their parents, whether or not they face serious medical conditions. In addition, it might inspire those considering a medical career.

■ Siegel, Bernie. *Love, Medicine and Miracles: Lessons Learned about Self-Healing from a Surgeon's Experience with Exceptional Patients.* Illus. Harper & Row, 1986. 242pp. (0-06-091406-8) Reading Level: Grades 10–12. (BL 1 My86; LJ 15 My86; PW 28 Mr86) *Disability:* Cancer

This book has been a best seller and has been reviewed favorably by well-known people in health, the ministry, and psychology. It qualifies as a self-help book for anyone who is beset with life and death concerns.

Siegel, a surgeon, writes about his partnership with his patients, most of whom have cancer. He suggests a complete change from the traditional medical perspective to a humanistic one. One of the book's main tenets is that a healthy attitude and self-love can favorably influence the course of almost all disease. Much anecdotal material and some research studies buttress this contention. While he focuses more on the quality of life than on the avoidance of death, he discusses the psychosomatic aspects of illness in order to teach patients to take charge of their own life. Siegel conducts therapy groups in which he encourages honesty and free expression of negative feelings.

The healing powers of laughter, good nutrition, and stress reduction are discussed. Perhaps most important to the author is the power of love, both love of oneself and love of others, to bring healing and peace of mind. In the last chapter, Siegel discusses precognition and other psychic mysteries, all of which he or his associates have witnessed.

An appendix describes a method of meditation step-by-step. The book also lists various tapes and lectures that the reader can purchase.

Analysis: While Siegel insists that he does not promise or expect cure of disease to follow from his approach, he constantly cites examples of people given up for dead whose tumors "melt away" after they have changed their thought patterns and improved their relationships. Unwary readers might find false hope in the book, or worse, believe themselves to blame if they could not turn their disease around. This book is not annotated, and it would certainly not pass scrutiny as a scientific work. With these caveats, it can be said both that the basic tenets are worthwhile and that the quotations and vignettes are always interesting. The style is compelling, revealing the author's strong and likable personality.

■ Solkoff, Joel. *Learning to Live Again: My Triumph over Cancer.* Holt, 1983. 242pp. (0-030-57647-4) Reading Level: Grades 7–12. (KR 1 Ap83; LJ 1 Je83; PW 29 Ap83)
Disability: Lymphatic cancer; Hodgkin's disease

In 1976, Joel Solkoff was a 28-year-old writer living in Washington, D.C. He had discovered a lump under his arm, which was diagnosed as lymphatic cancer, or Hodgkin's disease. After surgery to remove his spleen, he was given a course of radiation treatment. Five years later, he was declared cured and sat down to write this book. He describes in detail his reaction to the diagnosis, his treatment, and the effect of his illness on his work, his thinking, and his relationships, particularly with his mother and with the woman he was in love with and planned to marry. Their love affair, he writes, "became a casualty of the cancer cure," and he subsequently met and married another woman.

Analysis: Solkoff appears to be an honest young man, able to analyze himself and to describe his less attractive traits—his self-absorption, neediness, impatience, and anger, all of which were exacerbated by his illness and its treatment. In addition to his personal story, he includes objective, factual material on this disease. Advances in medical knowledge have made it possible for many people to survive what was once almost inevitably fatal.

This is a book for the mature young reader. It might be disturbing, since Hodgkin's is an illness that most often attacks young adults, but it is also hopeful because of the rate of successful treatments.

■ Taylor, Janet. *Brigie, A Life, 1965–1981.* St. Martin's, 1984. 224pp. (0-312-09628-3) Reading Level: Grades 10–12. (BL 15 D84; KR 1 N84; SLJ My85)
Disability: Cancer; Rhabdomyosarcoma

In a short introduction, the author expresses her compelling need to share all she could about the life of her daughter. She has also written the story of a family.

Brigid Anne Moorhouse was one of four children, with an older sister and brother and a younger brother. The family lived first in a London suburb; then, some time after the parents had divorced and had each remarried, Taylor and her second husband and the children moved to the Dales in Yorkshire. Brigie loved horses and eventually had one of her own. In most ways a typical adolescent, she went to school and had part-time jobs; she listened to popular music, giggled with her friends, thought about boys, and squabbled with her siblings. Her mother describes her as independent, even contrary, original, witty, and fun loving.

In the summer of 1981 Brigie noticed a lump between her thumb and finger, which was diagnosed as a ganglion. Later, a persistent cough and breathlessness alarmed her family; tuberculosis was suspected, but she did not respond to medication. Eventually, in October, the correct diagnosis was made; Brigie had rhabdomyosarcoma. Taylor had promised to tell her daughter what the doctors said, so Brigie knew from this time the nature of her illness. The family decided to follow the advice of the specialist who told them that aggressive therapy—"blunderbuss chemotherapy"—would not only not be helpful but would not be kind. "It's a sarcoma," the doctor told her parents, "starting from that lump on her hand, very rapid, very aggressive, and by now widely dispersed through her whole body. It's the only thing that kills girls her age. Boys kill themselves on motor bikes and girls die of this" (p. 102). Brigie was given medication to relieve distress, and an operation was performed to reduce the fluid in her lungs.

The last half of the book describes the leave taking. Brigie used the short period left to her to mature and to deeply appreciate her family, her friends, and the life she had lived. Surrounded by family and friends, Brigie spent her last months on the settee in the sitting room at home, and she died there on December 1, 1981, about six months after the first unrecognized symptom (the "ganglion") had appeared.

Taylor describes not only the course of the illness but also the way in which the family drew together to support Brigie with love and even laughter. A religious person herself, Taylor worried about how to prepare her daughter for death. Although Brigie had not had a particular interest in religion and made no formal acceptance of religious practice, she did achieve calm and peace before she died. In the words of the jacket copy, "The energy of her youth metamorphosed into a reservoir of calm inner peace." Her funeral was, as Taylor wished, a "thanksgiving—for her life, however short, and for her spirit, and for the closeness and love that we had all experienced."

There are two appendixes: "The Tillich Meditation" and the address made at Brigie's funeral by Bishop John Robinson.

Analysis: As Taylor makes clear in her introduction, she has written a very personal account: "I did not see everything, nor can I judge what it was really like for others involved. What was undoubtedly true was that a lively sixteen-year-old girl, taken in the full flush of her teenage obsessions and with no previously obvious spiritual resources, came to accept death peacefully."

This is a mother's story. We see Brigie through her eyes and through the letters and diary excerpts of others that are quoted. Soon after Brigie's death, Taylor says in the introduction, she wanted to write down everything she could remember about what had happened. She includes moments of impatience, irritability, exhaustion, despair, and joy. The family appears to be an extraordinary one in its ability to give support to each other; Brigie's father and stepmother as well as her mother and stepfather were all involved in her care. Her older sister and brother came home to be with her, and the house was open to all of the family's many friends.

Taylor writes extremely well, albeit the language and vocabulary are distinctly British. She gives a verbal picture of people, conversations, diary entries, thoughts, and all the foods eaten and who made them, as thoughts stream almost obsessively from her consciousness.

The mother is comforted by a simple faith, by gratitude for the help and love of those around her, and, probably not the least, by the knowledge that she gave everything she could of herself for her dying daughter. She does not push her private religious beliefs, though her own spiritual quality is evident. The final effect of the book is like the impact of Brigie's life, leaving the reader with both painful grief that a glowing, hopeful life can be so brutally cut off and a sense of triumph because love and devotion sustain both the dying Brigie and those she leaves behind.

■ Yomtoob, Paricheh, and Ted Schwarz. *The Gift of Life: One Family's Story.* St. Martin's, 1986. 229pp. (0-312-32714-5) Reading Level: Grades 7–12. (BL 15 S86; KR 1 O86; NYTBR 2 N86)
Disability: Wilson's disease

In the spring of 1981, 12-year-old David Yomtoob became seriously ill with what was eventually diagnosed as Wilson's disease, a rare hereditary condition that interferes with the body's ability to eliminate copper. He deteriorated rapidly from being a healthy, active youngster to one on the brink of death. The only hope was a liver transplant. The Yomtoobs took David from their home in Michigan to Children's Hospital in Pittsburgh, where Dr. Thomas Starzl, only recently arrived from Denver, was continuing his pioneering work in the transplantation of organs. After a wait that grew more agonizing with each day, an appropriate liver was at last located for David, and when he was literally only hours from dying, he went into surgery. The operation was successful and was followed by difficult weeks of recovery in the hospital and at the Rehabilitation Institute of Pittsburgh. David's bar mitzvah, to celebrate his becoming a man according to Jewish tradition, had been planned for October 1981. It eventually took place in March 1982, a year after his illness first became noticeable and six months after the transplant.

An appendix lists "some of the nonprofit, voluntary health agencies that seek to improve understanding, prevention, and treatment of liver diseases." There is also a list of transplant centers in the United States and Canada, with the names, office phone numbers, and, in most cases, the home phone numbers of the doctors to contact.

Analysis: Both Dr. Starzl and people who have undergone organ transplantation have received a good deal of media attention recently. This book offers a fascinating picture of this relatively new treatment for potentially fatal organ degeneration and malfunction. Though readers know from the beginning that David recovers, they can share the Yomtoobs' suspense and the pain of their position: they recognize that the liver they pray for for David must come from a child who has died.

The book is written in two voices: passages in italics are by Yomtoob, David's mother, and those in roman type are by Schwarz. This is not explained at the beginning, and because the book's acknowledgments are written by Yomtoob and are printed in regular type, some initial confusion is possible. Yomtoob writes with direct honesty and immediacy. Both she and her coauthor describe not only David's illness and treatment but also the complications of personality, protocol, and politics observed in different hospitals and on different medical services. Unfortunately, though Schwarz is described on the dust jacket as the author of more than 40 books, his writing is frequently sloppy. Nevertheless, the book is still worth reading and should be of interest to young readers who want to know more about the remarkable challenges and opportunities presented by transplant surgery.

■ Zumwalt, Elmo, Jr., and Elmo Zumwalt III, and John Pekkanen. *My Father, My Son.* Macmillan, 1986. 224pp. (0-8161-4307-2) Reading Level: Grades 7–12. (LJ 15 S86; WCRB v.12 86)
Disability: Cancer; Lymphoma; Hodgkin's disease

This story is told in the first person by Adm. Elmo Zumwalt, Jr., his son Elmo III, and others who played important roles at various times. The reader is introduced to four generations of Zumwalts, but the life of Elmo III receives the most attention.

Elmo was born just after his father had graduated from Annapolis and was beginning a long career in the Navy. This career would include appointments as commander of naval forces in the Vietnam war and subsequently as chief of naval operations, the highest rank in the Navy. Adm. Zumwalt was the youngest man in history to achieve this appointment.

Elmo was raised with a brother and sisters in a close-knit, loving family. He had a congenital heart defect that curtailed his physical activities until undergoing a corrective operation at age 12. He also had a light case of poliomyelitis as a young child. His health problems and various childhood experiences in school, on the playground and in summer jobs (some positive and some negative experiences), helped to develop his characteristic determination, courage, and sense of humor.

Young Elmo always had to work hard to succeed in school. When he graduated from college, he enlisted in the Navy at the time of the Vietnam war. As a lieutenant, he volunteered to command one of the swift boats that patrolled the dangerous rivers of the Mekong Delta. He and his crew were involved in many narrow escapes and heroic undertakings as they endeavored to stop the flow of ammunition that was being smuggled in small boats by the enemy from North Vietnam to the Vietcong in the south.

Although the elder Zumwalt had serious reservations about the rationale for and conduct of the Vietnam war, he accepted the appointment as commander as his patriotic duty. He worked to turn the Navy into an efficient, contributing force whose functions could be transferred to South Vietnamese forces in the foreseeable future. In order to secure the Navy's area of operation, the Mekong Delta, Zumwalt ordered copious use of the defoliating chemical agent orange to be applied to the surrounding jungle. He never wavered in his belief that this procedure saved the lives of his men from snipers who would take refuge in thick vegetation. Ironically, his son, Elmo, had maximum exposure to the spray, which is now known to be harmful to humans.

Adm. Zumwalt was appointed chief of naval operations, leaving for Washington before the conclusion of the war. His task was to modernize an outdated Navy, and he instituted a number of reforms, including the abolition of institutionalized racism.

About the same time as his father was assuming his new duties, a much decorated Elmo was also leaving for the States. He was discharged from the Navy and made plans to go to law school. He married his longtime girlfriend and established a home and family. His second child was diagnosed with significant learning problems. At 6, the youngest Elmo was placed in special education. His father associated the child's problems with agent orange.

While Elmo III was still in his 30s, he developed two cancers simultaneously: lymphoma and Hodgkin's disease; he felt that these were also a consequence of his exposure to agent orange. Chemotherapy was not successful in his case, and some doctors predicted an early death. His only hope was a painful, problematic bone marrow transplant procedure. Five months after the completion of the story, Elmo seemed to have beaten the odds and regained his health. As always, he expressed his great love for his family.

Analysis: Because this story is told in the voices of the protagonists, it is very fast and easy reading. The firsthand account of the Vietnam war is absorbing and evenhanded. The Zumwalt family comes through as genuine and forthright. Their high-minded patriotism offers a fine example to all Americans, especially young people. This book should be a most welcome addition to school libraries.

HEALTH PROBLEMS – AIDS

■ Alyson, Sasha, ed. *You Can Do Something about AIDS.* Illus. Stop AIDS Project, Inc., 1988. 188pp. (0-945972-02-4) Reading Level: Grades 10–12. (BL 1 Je88; KLIATT S88; LJ 1 Jl88)
Disability: AIDS

Like *AIDS: The Deadly Epidemic* and *AIDS: Trading Fears for Facts,* this work deals with both the disease and the people who have it. A public service project of the publishing industry, it had the sponsorship of many publishers, vendors, and trade associations and the help of dozens of individuals. The book consists of six sections of short, topical essays and three appendixes, including a directory of AIDS-related organizations, a bibliography of the best books about AIDS, and a list of phone numbers of local and state organizations.

James Michener has written the preface, Elizabeth Taylor has written the introduction, and many of the essays have been written by well-known people such as Greg Louganis. Louganis talks about his friendship with Ryan White, the young boy whose discriminatory treatment by his school and community when he contracted AIDS drew national attention. Louganis goes on to urge readers to join "buddy" projects in which a volunteer organization pairs them up with a person with AIDS who needs human contact and sometimes some help with transportation, shopping, and the like.

Other essays written by AIDS activists, by public officials, and by ordinary citizens also urge involvement in various ways. Many of these people recount their own experiences with individuals who have AIDS; one woman is a foster mother of children with AIDS.

Analysis: This book is excellent for its encouraging and practical approach, which not only views the tragedy of AIDS but also focuses on what people can do to help. Highly recommended for high school readers. It is also accessible and appropriate for good readers at junior high school grade levels.

■ Armstrong, Ewan. *The Impact of AIDS.* Illus. Gloucester, 1990. 62pp. (0-531-17225-2) Reading Level: Grades 7–12. (BL 15 My90; SLJ JI90) *Disability:* AIDS

Ewan Armstrong, who is described as having "both medical and health education qualifications," is a lecturer in health education at a technical school in London. In his first chapter, called "What Is HIV Infection?" he explains viruses and HIV, the ways in which infection is spread, AIDS symptoms, and tests for AIDS. Subsequent chapters discuss people with AIDS and HIV and look at global issues and community response. Brief profiles personalize cases, illustrating fears, treatment, and coping strategies. A list of helpful agencies, a brief glossary, and an index complete the book. There are many full-color photographs.

Analysis: This brief, clearly written, and nonjudgmental book is a good source of information for young readers. Sexual practices such as anal and vaginal intercourse are briefly but explicitly defined; the worldwide scope of the illness is described. Brief profiles of individuals make the factual material more accessible and provide variety in the exposition. This is a good addition to the growing number of books about the fatal illness that in the past ten years has come to seem our present-day plague.

■ Bevan, Nicholas. *AIDS and Drugs.* Illus. by Aziz Khan. Franklin Watts, 1988. 62pp. (0-531-10625-X) Reading Level: Grades 7–12. (TES 9 S88) *Disability:* HIV infection; Kaposi's sarcoma; Pneumonia

This book is one of a series of eight entitled Understanding Drugs. In the introduction, a few common misapprehensions about acquired immune deficiency syndrome (AIDS) are dispelled. The magnitude of the problem and the terrible relentlessness of AIDS are described. Chapters that follow cover aspects of the disease that would be of particular interest to those considering sexual activity or intravenous drug use or who have been even only tempted to experiment. High-risk groups, such as homosexuals and intravenous drug users, are discussed and shown in photographs.

The various ways that AIDS is spread are illustrated by concrete examples. The term "safe sex" (or "safer sex") is explained, with a gradient of behaviors from "no risk" to "extremely risky" clearly explained (p. 36). Infection of newborns and those with hemophilia is also discussed.

The treatment of AIDS with the drug AZT and other drugs is explained and illuminated in drawings. Possible direction toward an eventual cure receives mention. The last chapter, "If You're Worried," stresses practical strategies to prevent contracting or passing on human immunodeficiency virus (HIV). Counseling for related problems is strongly advocated. The book closes with more facts, sources of help, a glossary of terms, and an index.

Analysis: Although this book may make for easy reading at the junior high school level, it imparts its message with a clarity and completeness that is sometimes lacking in more sophisticated material. The author is without censure of the people who engage in the life-styles and sexual practices associated with AIDS. In fact, he expresses sympathy for those who were driven to illegal drug use by previous problems, who now have the additional drug use problem, and who must reckon with AIDS as well. He shows admiration of people with AIDS who have spoken out to help others. The controversy over supplying free drugs or clean needles to addicts is mentioned as it relates to the spread of AIDS but, again, without judgment on the issue.

The color photographs range from those clearly showing young people shooting drugs, to pregnant African women awaiting an HIV test, to a bowl of condoms. Perhaps the most wrenching picture shows two winsome, alert infants—one black, the other white—with the caption, "These babies have the AIDS virus. For them, life will be short" (p. 34).

■ Colman, Warren. *Understanding and Preventing AIDS: A Guide for Young People.* Illus. Childrens Pr., 1987. 125pp. (LB 0-516-00592-8) Reading Level: Grades 7–12. (BCCB Jl88; BL Jl88; KR 15 Mr88) *Disability:* AIDS

The author addresses his book to teenagers. He begins with the case of Ryan White, a youngster infected with AIDS from a blood transfusion; Ryan was barred from attending school until his lawyer fought successfully to have him readmitted. In the following chapters, Colman describes the first appearance of the disease, discusses the way the illness operates, looks at how it is transmitted, and writes about other plagues. He includes information about prevention, treatment, and possible controls and cures. The text is illustrated with photographs, diagrams, and drawings, in color and black and white. The book ends with a short bibliography, a list of organizations and both federal and state government agencies, and an index.

Analysis: This is an excellent book. Colman's presentation is clear, the tone serious but not hysterical. He includes personal stories as well as scientific material. Illustrations augment the text, which includes parenthetical pronunciation guides for scientific words. Colman emphasizes how people can protect themselves against AIDS by avoiding both unprotected sexual activity and intravenous drug use, and he does not shrink from describing anal sex or giving explicit instructions about the proper use of the condom. Although the book is intended for teenagers, its short chapters and clarity should make it accessible to somewhat younger readers as well.

■ Eagles, Douglas A. *The Menace of AIDS: A Shadow on Our Land.* Illus. Franklin Watts, 1988. 71pp. (0-531-10567-9) Reading Level: Grades 7–12. (BL 15 D88; SLJ Ja89)
Disability: AIDS

This is one of a series of First Books written on health subjects. The author states that his purpose is to provide facts about AIDS for young people. He stresses that simple precautions should be taken to guarantee protection from this always fatal disease.

The book starts with a description of the medical problems sustained by some of the first AIDS patients. The opening chapter discusses the cause of the disease and its stages, from HIV (human immunodeficiency virus) infection, to ARC (AIDS-related complex), to full-blown AIDS. A following chapter explains the workings of the immune system. The transmission of the AIDS virus through exchange of body fluids is described and contrasted with other, nonlethal, sexually transmitted diseases. It is made clear that AIDS is not acquired through casual contact. A photograph shows several children with AIDS interacting with their healthy playmate. A chapter is devoted to the nature of a virus compared with the nature of a living cell. The process of AIDS virus reverse transcription of the genetic material RNA to the white blood cells of the host is explained and illustrated in drawings.

A chapter called "Projections" informs young adolescents of the seriousness and relevance of the AIDS epidemic. The possibility of a cure is explored, but the need for protection until that eventuality is deemed crucial. A last chapter touches on social issues, such as the morality of homosexuality and compulsory testing to identify HIV-positive people.

A page of suggested readings includes several other books reviewed in this annotated bibliography. An index follows.

Analysis: The text is often less ambiguous than the photographs. For example, whereas transmission of contaminated blood by needle injection is carefully explained, the picture indicating drug use is a close-up of a boy's face with a vial by his nose—a frightening rather than enlightening pose. Another photograph, introduced a few pages before a discussion of the use of condoms, shows the contents of a sex kit given to students at Dartmouth College. However, the print in the photo of the kit's pamphlet is too small to read, and what is presumably a condom is still in a package. A number of words have synonyms in parentheses for clarity, e.g., "fetus (unborn baby)" (p. 36).

The text is clear and explicit about the transmission of the AIDS virus by semen to heterosexual and homosexual partners. The discussion of homosexuality is obviously meant to be evenhanded but errs on the side of overobjectivity. To say, without further comment, that "homosexual AIDS victims often receive little sympathy for their condition, and become hated and feared outcasts of society" (p. 87) seems somewhat crass after the accounts of terrible suffering that were described earlier. Nevertheless, this book has merit for its well-articulated message for literate young teens.

■ Glaser, Elizabeth, and Laura Palmer. *In the Absence of Angels: A Hollywood Family's Courageous Story.* Illus. Putnam, 1991. 318pp. (0-399-13577-4) Reading Level: Grades 10–12. (PW 21 O90) *Disability:* AIDS

In 1981, after a difficult pregnancy, Elizabeth and Paul Glaser's daughter, Ariel, was born, delivered by cesarean section. Immediately after the baby's birth, Elizabeth began to hemorrhage, and she received seven units of transfused blood. Their second child, Jake, was born in 1984.

Elizabeth Glaser had been a preschool teacher until her marriage; Paul Glaser was a television star and movie director. Until Ariel came down with a mysterious illness in 1985, they lived a comfortable, privileged life. Then, in 1986, Ariel's illness was diagnosed as AIDS. When the rest of the family members were tested, it turned out that only Paul had escaped; Elizabeth and Jake were both HIV positive. Elizabeth had been infected by tainted blood in her transfusion; she had passed the infection to Ariel in her breast milk and to Jake in the uterus.

Numb and stricken, the Glasers had to contend not only with their terrible anxiety but also with the fears and misinformation of others. Aware of the ostracism experienced by the Rays—the family with three infected boys—and by Ryan White—another infected youngster—they decided to tell their secret to as few people as possible. Many of their friends withdrew, afraid to let their children play with Ariel and Jake. Moreover, Paul was so well-known in the film and television world that news of this kind would have made headlines, breaching their privacy. Rather than reveal the diagnosis, they took Ariel out of nursery school; later, she was able to attend public kindergarten and eventually, after the school had arrived at an AIDS policy, to start first grade in the private school the Glasers had chosen the year before.

Normal T-cell counts range between 500 and 1,500. When they were diagnosed, Elizabeth's count was 210; Ariel's was 4. Ariel was given regular shots of gamma globulin to bolster her immune system, and for some time all went well. In the summer of 1987, however, she began to weaken and to experience severe stomach pain. When Elizabeth asked that Ariel be given AZT, she was told that it had not yet been approved for pediatric use. Ariel started first grade but after two weeks had so much pain that she could not attend; a teacher came to tutor her at home. She spent a month in the hospital, where it was found that she had acute pancreatitis, which caused the pain and interfered with her ability to digest food. She had to be fed intravenously by a complicated system called total parenteral nutrition. Elizabeth Glaser learned how to administer this therapy, though it took her two hours every evening at first, and then was allowed to take Ariel home. At the same time, AZT finally became available for her. However, her decline continued until she could no longer walk, speak, read, or write. Some months later, Ariel was back in the hospital with pneumonia. A magnetic resonance imaging test showed that her central nervous system had deteriorated and her brain was atrophying. The doctors expected her to die then, but she pulled out of the crisis.

Elizabeth Glaser became determined to act to save her family and decided that she must start at the top, with President Reagan. Ariel's pediatrician supported her and advised her to talk about pediatric AIDS. Elizabeth met with Surgeon General Koop when he came to Los Angeles, and then she went to Washington. She writes, "I wanted to find out why there was such a delay in getting AZT out for children. I wanted to find out why the federal budget for clinical trials in pediatric AIDS was only $3.3 million, why there were so few clinical trial units and so little research." She talked to many people, including Dr. Phil Pizzo of the National Institutes of Health, who told her that they had had good results with AZT administered intravenously to children in a clinical study. When she confronted her doctor at home, he told her that he knew of this work but had been unable to obtain the medication for other patients; the drug company, Burroughs Wellcome, had refused, claiming insufficient testing. However, because of the government officials Elizabeth Glaser had talked to, her doctor was able to put pressure on the drug company and get the medication. For some weeks, Ariel experienced an amazing comeback. Elizabeth made another trip to Washington, this time meeting with the Reagans for an hour. Everywhere that she told her story, she asked listeners to respect her plea for confidentiality, so that the wall she and her husband had built around their family's privacy would not be breached.

In the summer of 1988 Ariel had to be readmitted to the hospital. Her white blood count had fallen low and she had to be taken off intravenous AZT for a time; she had an intractable fever. Nevertheless, the Glasers were determined to bring her home. As they were preparing to do so, Ariel died, a week after her seventh birthday.

Jake had remained healthy and was developing normally. After Ari's death, Elizabeth Glaser threw herself into the effort to find support for research that would save her son's life. With two friends, working first at their kitchen tables, she formed the Pediatric AIDS Foundation. They had discovered that almost no attention was being given to pediatric AIDS research. They made trips to Washington, they contacted important people in government and medicine, they raised money from individual contributions·(their first one, in the amount of half a million dollars, came from a wealthy relative) and from benefits. After a year, they learned that "ten million dollars had been directed to pediatric AIDS research."

Eventually, the Glasers got word that the *National Enquirer* planned to run a sensational story on them. After much anguish and discussion, they decided to forestall this by offering to let the *Los Angeles Times* do an article. Public awareness and knowledge about AIDS had sufficiently changed so that the article brought them sympathy and support from almost everyone who learned of their tragedy. A CBS "60 Minutes" segment on the Glasers was seen by about 50 million people. In March 1990, Paul and Elizabeth Glaser testified before the House Budget Subcommittee on health issues.

At the end of the book, Jake is still well and has started kindergarten. Elizabeth, who had been on AZT, began to have adverse effects from it and had to change to DDI (dideoxyinosine). She is vigorous and active, determined to be involved in helping to find solutions for some of the world's problems.

Analysis: This is a painful book, particularly in the first half while following the terrible tragic consequences of a blood transfusion that poisoned a family. Unlike the stories of people who have contracted AIDS as a result of their life-styles, the narratives of those who, like the Glasers, were infected by a presumably life-giving procedure carry particular horror because they could have happened to anybody.

Glaser and Palmer have written a compelling, readable book. Elizabeth Glaser talks honestly about her rage, her feeling of powerlessness, and her grief, as well as her anger about some of the characteristics of U.S. politics and government. She describes her relationship with her husband and the way their marriage nearly collapsed in the wake of their loss. She recognizes that she is privileged and that she has been able to make things happen because of her background, abilities, money, and especially contacts, but when she fights for Ariel and Jake, she is fighting for all children with AIDS. She feels that she has learned a vital lesson about love.

In the epilogue, she describes a therapist who helped her in such a way that she felt she heard Ari telling her that she always would be with her and urging her to enjoy life. "In the beginning I felt there were no angels to help us. . . . But over the years, angels have come into our life. . . . Now that I know Ari is always with me, I need not hold on to the sadness and grief. They can float away, and in their place I find great joy. Every day now is a miracle and knowing that makes me smile."

■ Hancock, Graham, and Enver Carim. *AIDS: The Deadly Epidemic.* Gollancz, 1986. 191pp. (Paper 0-575-03837-3) Reading Level: Grades 10–12. (TES 9 My86; TLS 18 Jl86)
Disability: AIDS; Health problems

This is one of several books about AIDS that will be reviewed in this volume even though they are only partly about people who have the disease. Like Alyson's *You Can Do Something about AIDS* and Hein's *AIDS: Trading Fears for Facts, AIDS: The Deadly Epidemic* deals primarily with the disease itself and secondarily with the people who have it. Also, like the other two, it does intersperse the expository information about AIDS with plenty of narrative. In this book, the narrative is both factual and objective but also personal.

In restrained, scholarly, yet simple prose, the authors elaborate on the historical and social contexts of AIDS throughout the world. They also offer vignettes from the lives of a number of individuals who have been touched by the disease in a variety of ways, including persons who have contracted it and subsequently died. In addition, they explain what AIDS is, how it is transmitted, how individuals may protect themselves from it, why it is not only a sexually transmitted disease, and why and how nearly anyone can get this disease.

Analysis: Recommended for mature teenagers for its factual yet dramatic and scientific yet readable approach to the physical etiology of AIDS and to its complex social context.

■ Hausherr, Rosmarie. *Children and the AIDS Virus: A Book for Children, Parents, & Teachers.* Illus. Houghton (Clarion), 1989. 48pp. (0-89919-834-1) Reading Level: Grades 2–6. (CBRS Jl89; HB S89; SLJ Jl89)
Disability: AIDS

Hausherr has organized her presentation of this complex subject by moving from the general to the particular, from the impersonal to the personal. Addressing her reader directly, she explains cells, microorganisms, and viruses. She explains what happens when a person has a cold and how one catches the illness, defines immunity, and then reaches her subject: HIV— the AIDS virus—and ARC—AIDS-related complex. She explains how the infection is not spread before focusing on the means of transmission. Then she presents two children with AIDS: Jonathan, age 5, who contracted the disease from a transfusion of infected blood given to him soon after his premature birth, and Celeste, who at age 10 "is the oldest known survivor born with AIDS." Both Celeste and her brother were infected with HIV by their parents, intravenous drug users; her parents and brother have died, and she is being raised by her grandmother.

The text is illustrated with many black-and-white photographs taken by Hausherr. Most pages have text in large type for young readers and, below that, more complex information in smaller type intended for older children and adults. The final pages tell the reader more about Jonathan and his mother and Celeste and her grandmother. Then follow a list of health care precautions, suggestions about what the reader can do in the face of this disease, a list of resources, a bibliography, and an index.

Analysis: Ten years ago, it would probably have seemed incredible to see books on AIDS written for such young readers. It is a terrible commentary on our situation that we need such books but a hopeful sign when we have one as good as this one. Hausherr's text is clear, her tone compassionate without sentimentality. Although she does not minimize the horror of possible outcomes (Celeste's brother died at 5), she does not close out optimism (Celeste and Jonathan are both helped by injections of gamma globulin, and, though Jonathan's mother "knows [he] could die soon . . . she hopes he will live a long life"). Moreover, the author emphasizes that both children live normally as far as possible, attending school and playing like other youngsters.

The information on sexual transmission of AIDS is very brief, and this may be seen as a weakness; homosexuality is not mentioned, even in the text intended for older readers, but the condom is defined. In the large print on the next page, the writer says, "As you get older, you may have questions about sex. Ask a parent, teacher, or another adult you trust for answers. Or you may want to read some of the wonderful and informative children's books on the subject of sex that are available at most school and public libraries."

Hausherr's black-and-white photographs are striking and effective and show a variety of ethnic strains. The little girl with a cold being given cough medicine by her father is Asian (and in the next picture the father has the cold and she is spooning medicine into his mouth), a scientist is African American, black and white hands clasp each other, and Celeste is Hispanic. This is certainly a book to be recommended for public and school libraries. One hopes that every child who borrows it will have an older person to share it with and to turn to for further information and discussion.

■ Hawkes, Nigel. *AIDS.* Illus. Gloucester, 1987. 32pp. (LB 0-531-17054-3) Reading Level: Grades 4–9. (KR 1 O87; SLJ Ap88; TES 11 S87) *Disability:* AIDS

This book is written by a British newspaper correspondent whose consultant is a clinical immunologist at a London medical school. Hawkes presents a history of AIDS and its usual course. He describes the AIDS virus, explains how it is transmitted, looks at the symptoms, and discusses prevention of the disease. He concludes with pages on living with AIDS and on the outlook for the future. The book is illustrated with many photographs, and the pages are designed with sidebars. There is an index.

Analysis: Though we are seeing increasing numbers of AIDS patients who have contracted the virus passively (e.g., infants born to infected mothers and people given transfusions of infected blood), most people become ill as the result of behavior. Thus it becomes imperative that we educate ourselves and our children about the disease and ways to prevent it. Such education is best started early, and this book can be used with elementary school students. It has large type and many illustrations, the sidebars provide visual variety and attract attention, and the information is clearly presented. The author does not specifically describe either heterosexual or homosexual activity, and young readers may be uncertain about what is going on (the writer does, however, define a condom), but a book of this kind is best read with an adult who is available to answer puzzling questions.

■ Hein, Karen, and Theresa Foy DiGeronimo, eds. *AIDS: Trading Fears for Facts*. Illus. Consumers Union, 1989. 196pp. (0-89043-269-4) Reading Level: Grades 7–12. (LATBR 23 Jl89; SBF Ja90; VYA F90) *Disability:* AIDS

Like *AIDS: The Deadly Epidemic* by Hancock and *You Can Do Something about AIDS* by Alyson, this is a book not strictly about people with the disease. It is about the disease itself. In this case, the emphasis is upbeat, factual, and matter-of-fact without ever losing sight of the fact that AIDS ultimately means death. The writing style is unabashedly didactic but at the same time colloquial and energetic. The intended audience is teenagers, and the text is addressed directly to them, using the second person as though a dialogue is taking place.

The authors, one of whom is a physician who works with adolescent AIDS patients, uses plenty of real-life individuals to illustrate the various points that the text makes as it explains the facts about AIDS, ways of preventing it, and methods of diagnosis and treatment. There is also a heavy emphasis on the individual's and the community's responsibilities for people with AIDS.

Analysis: The writing style is pithy and informal. Black-and-white photographs and drawings, including one showing how to use a condom, liberally illustrate the book. Headings, subheadings, and boxed information in a variety of typefaces present an attractive, readable format with maximum eye appeal.

A chapter that lists state-by-state resources for people with AIDS and an index conclude the volume, which is highly recommended for high school students as well as mature junior high readers.

■ Hyde, Margaret O., and Elizabeth H. Forsyth. *AIDS: What Does It Mean to You?* Illus. Walker, 1987. 116pp. (Paper 0-8027-6747-8) Reading Level: Grades 9–12. (BCCB O85; BL 1 My85; SLJ N85)
Disability: AIDS

Margaret Hyde is a professional author who has written many nonfiction books for young readers, some of them in collaboration with Dr. Elizabeth Forsyth, a psychiatrist. Here, they tackle a critical public health challenge, an illness that has received enormous media coverage since the first cases were diagnosed in 1981 but that also produces irrational responses based on ignorance of causes and transmission. After a chapter that repeats the title question, the authors examine such subjects as living with AIDS, avoiding the disease, and AIDS as an international infection; they discuss plagues in other eras, the fear provoked by this particular illness, and medical progress made toward treatment and prevention. One chapter is a transcription of two speeches made by Michael Callen, a young musician with AIDS who addressed the New York Congressional Delegation in 1983 and the annual meeting of the American Public Health Association in 1986. Another section reproduces the report of Dr. C. Everett Koop, surgeon general of the United States. At the end of the book, the authors list groups that offer AIDS information and support. There are also a glossary and an index.

Analysis: Hyde and Forsyth have written an informative, readable book in which occasional case histories or references to individuals, as well as Michael Callen's moving statements, are woven into the scientific and factual material. The authors place considerable emphasis on refuting myths about AIDS and dispelling panicky and baseless fears while at the same time never glossing over their presentation of this illness as a horrible destroyer of lives and families. They are very clear about what steps people must take to protect themselves, a message repeated in the surgeon general's forceful report. A useful resource for readers of all ages from middle school grades and up, this book could well be recommended to students preparing reports and to teachers for use in classroom discussion.

■ Hyde, Margaret O., and Elizabeth H. Forsyth. *Know about AIDS.* Illus. by Debora Weber. Walker, 1987. 68pp. (Paper 0-8027-6738-9) Reading Level: Grades 4–6. (BCCB Mr88; SLJ N87; WLB Mr88)
Disability: AIDS

Hyde has written many nonfiction books for young readers, several in collaboration with Dr. Forsyth. Here, they discuss AIDS as a new disease, answer the question "Who gets AIDS?" and offer information about viruses and AIDS. Using vignettes, the authors present fictional cases, for example, a child with AIDS and a bisexual father dying of the disease. They write about the outlook for finding a cure and discuss the question of testing. They then offer suggestions for further reading and include an index.

Analysis: The authors are skillful at presenting information to readers in this age group, and here they do so in a calm, straightforward manner that should help to dispel myths and temper hysteria. Perhaps because they are writing for such young children, they do not give explicit definitions of homosexual intercourse (or heterosexual intercourse, for that matter). For example, in one spot they say, "Bob goes out with girls, but he is not ready to become sexually involved with them. He does, however, like to experiment sexually with other boys. He is risking infection with AIDS" (p. 57). Will a young boy reading this understand well enough what is meant so that he can protect himself? Probably not, unless he has additional sources of information. Nevertheless, this is a good introduction to information about a tragic disease.

The short bibliography includes fictional treatments of homosexuality and books about death, hemophilia, the immune system, drugs, and the heart and blood. Curiously, it also lists the very book that the list appears in.

■ Kubler-Ross, Ellsabeth. *AIDS: The Ultimate Challenge.* Macmillan, 1987. 330pp. (0-02-567170-7) Reading Level: Grades 9–12. (LJ 1 Mr88; SBF S/O88)
Disability: AIDS

Kubler-Ross, a Swiss physician, pioneered in the study of death and dying, work which was described in her 1969 book of the same name. She elucidated the "stages of dying" and advocated a more honest and helpful approach toward those in the midst of that inevitable process. Later she studied and wrote about the special responses and needs of dying children. She has promulgated the establishment of hospices in Europe and the United States, including those to serve terminally ill youngsters. In addition, she has conducted innumerable workshops to foster understanding and acceptance of those undergoing the dying process.

It was a natural next step that she concern herself with the sufferers of the new AIDS epidemic, the subject of the present book. The author encountered initial denial of the problem on the part of professionals, similar to that which had hampered her earlier work. During that earlier time, she had been told, "We have no terminally ill patients." Now, she was hearing, "We have no populations of persons with AIDS," in prisons, for example.

The book is replete with stories that illustrate the consequences of public fears, prejudices, anger, and even cruelty toward AIDS patients of all ages and toward their friends and families. An early chapter discusses the increasing number of children with AIDS, many of whom are abandoned in hospitals at birth by mothers unwilling or unable to care for them. Kubler-Ross attempted to establish a caring environment for these dying children on her newly acquired Virginia farm. Several chapters contain dialogues from the public hearings and the letters (some published in newspapers) that resulted from a futile effort to gain community acceptance for the project. The dialogues represent the entire spectrum of popular opinion regarding AIDS.

Another chapter presents dialogues with young men dying of AIDS. A chapter about the AIDS support system in San Francisco recounts a lengthy report by a health worker of her most memorable experiences in serving AIDS patients at their end. She expresses deep religious faith and a conviction that AIDS offers an opportunity for spiritual healing and growth both for patients and for those who care for them. A final chapter deals with the problem of the disease in prisons. Prisons have been among the least responsive and sensitive to those vulnerable to AIDS and those who have AIDS. Reinforced and reiterated overall is the message that human beings have control over the quality of life rather than quantity of life and that all can strive for a loving and peaceful heart. An epilogue and appendix summarize the issues raised in the book.

Analysis: The author's strong belief in the healing powers of love and acceptance makes the tone of this book one of the most positive and hopeful of the growing literature on AIDS. Kubler-Ross does have a rather eclectic Christian perspective, and she is adamant without preaching about the reality of the afterlife. She is convincing in her attitude of total acceptance of all the human beings whom she encounters.

Her consideration of both heterosexual victims who are not drug users and children with AIDS will increase this book's relevance as the disease continues to spread among these two groups. Again, the prison population will also warrant increased attention.

The writing is simple, clear, and forceful. There are few statistics; rather, the ideas are expressed in human terms. The anecdotes, descriptions of group encounters, and the interviews are moving. A fault may be a certain lack of organization and coherence of style; nevertheless, the book is gripping and timely.

■ Kuklin, Susan. *Fighting Back: What Some People Are Doing about AIDS.* Illus. Putnam, 1989. 110pp. (0-399-21621-9) Reading Level: Grades 7–12. (SLJ F89; VYA Ap89; WLB S89)
Disability: AIDS

Kuklin's book is based on the nine months she spent with a group of volunteers organized by the Gay Men's Health Crisis to provide support for people with AIDS. The volunteers, called buddies, are trained to do whatever the ill person needs, from routine tasks like shopping and house-cleaning to the difficult challenge of trying to prepare for death. Kuklin presents the patients (usually without giving their real names), the volunteers, and the doctors. She describes buddy meetings, interactions between volunteers and their clients, the different aspects of the disease, and courses of treatment. The book is illustrated with black-and-white photographs and concludes with a glossary.

Analysis: By focusing so immediately on the people involved, Kuklin brings this difficult subject to her readers in a most humane way. In her introduction, she speaks of what she has learned from her work: "This is a tale of living, living with the right priorities." Ironically, in a book dealing with a horrible and inevitably fatal disease, a dominant theme is indeed the struggle not only to live but to live well and then to die as well as one can. The people described include a middle-aged nun who gives lectures on safe sexual practices and uses a banana to demonstrate condoms, a drug and alcohol addict who contracted AIDS from sharing dirty needles, and many young men. The scientific material is woven into the text, but conveying this information is not the primary purpose of the book. Kuklin never describes homosexuality or explains what homosexuals do that puts them at particular risk, but it seems that this must have been a deliberate choice on her part. She assumes that knowledge in her readers and concentrates on what happens to human beings when they fall ill with AIDS as well as on the responses and actions of those who volunteer to help them and the physicians who treat them. She has written a compelling book and made the people she describes come vividly alive.

■ Kurland, Morton L. *Coping with AIDS: Facts and Fears.* Illus. Rosen, 1988. 210pp. (0-8239-0779-1) Reading Level: Grades 8–12. (CLE 3 D87; SLJ My88; VYA Ag88)
Disability: AIDS

This is one of a series of about 25 coping books published for adolescents. The purpose of the book is stated in the introduction: "We shall describe what the disease is and how it can be prevented, controlled, and ultimately cured" (p. ix).

The author, a physician, acknowledges that there are differing moral positions with respect to the acquisition and transmission of AIDS, but he takes a scientific, rather than a moral position. He emphatically asserts that this disease is a threat to everyone, not only to certain minority groups. He does suggest that sexual abstinence is the best means of preventing AIDS, but he devotes many pages of advice to sexually active heterosexual, bisexual, and homosexual men and women regarding how to increase the likelihood of safe sexual procedures. For example, he suggests specific opening dialogues to be engaged in with a potential sex partner to ascertain whether he or she has had a blood test to detect the presence of the human immunodeficiency virus (HIV). He suggests abstaining from sex 90 days after an initial test so it can be repeated. He insists on the use of condoms, particularly to protect women during intercourse. He stresses that such precautions should be carried out in the spirit of mutual caring and respect on which an intimate relationship is based.

Short vignettes about young people illustrate these points: Kurland describes a homosexual young man who was infected before the disease was understood. He tells the story of a young heroin addict who supported her habit through prostitution, until she was infected with a dirty needle and died tragically. A young health worker was doomed when she cut her hand while attending an infected accident victim.

Descriptions of the AIDS virus and its effect on the human immune system are enhanced by diagrams. The disease is compared with previously deadly venereal diseases and plagues. Kurland is optimistic that a cure for AIDS will be found, and he discusses helpful treatments, such as AZT, which are available at present; he warns against procedures without a valid scientific basis. He stresses the need to respond to the feelings of patients and their families. Chapter 13 ends the narrative section with a series of specific questions and answers about AIDS that should help to dispel irrational fears and encourage safe sexual practices and procedures.

The last hundred pages of the book are devoted to a glossary, a bibliography, and an extensive list of AIDS crisis centers within each state.

Analysis: This straightforward account is couched in a simple, yet authoritative style. The author neither minimizes the scourge of AIDS nor evokes panic and guilt. He takes as positive a view as possible. The vignettes and the similes used to illustrate medical facts are appropriate for young people.

Kurland presupposes a certain amount of sexual sophistication in his readers: He does not elucidate what oral or anal sex is or what a condom is, for example. The book is a helpful addition to the growing literature on this ominous problem. It targets a vulnerable group to whom education and rational persuasion can make a vital difference.

■ Landau, Elaine. **We Have AIDS.** Franklin Watts, 1990. 126pp. (0-531-15152-2) Reading Level: Grades 7–12. (BL 1 Mr90; KR 15 F90; SLJ Ap90; VYA Ag90)
Disability: AIDS

Landau has focused on nine teenagers with AIDS. Each chapter begins with a thumbnail sketch of the young person whose extended interview then makes up the rest of the section. Between each chapter, brief sections called "Facts about AIDS" deal with such subjects as transmission, high-risk groups, AIDS-related complex, silent carriers, sexual behavior, and safe practices. The teenagers have contracted AIDS through sexual relations, intravenous drug use, and blood transfusions; one young woman has had a baby, and another is pregnant. All have been diagnosed, but some do not yet have symptoms. All understand the seriousness of their situation and know that the almost certain outcome for them is early death; a brief author's note at the end of the first chapter tells the reader that Karen, the speaker, died about three months after the interview.

At the end of the book, Landau has included a list of organizations and informational groups, a suggested bibliography, and an index.

Analysis: Using a straightforward, dispassionate style for factual material and letting her subjects tell their own story, Landau has put together a poignant, moving book. Although sometimes the fluent, polished style of the interviews seems to indicate that they have been somewhat edited, the voices of these tragically doomed young people come through with poignant intensity. Whether they contracted the disease through their own actions or were unknowingly infected by tainted blood, they are touched by innocence—even when their history has included promiscuous sexuality and intravenous drug use. They have not only suffered the symptoms of AIDS and the terror of facing early death but have also had to endure the frightened prejudice and paranoia of communities, friends, and families—even parents—so that their isolation is heightened. Even when the family is loving and supportive, death must be met alone.

In the last chapter, Paul describes the final illness of his brother Danny, two years older; both boys were hemophiliacs and had been transfused with infected blood. Danny's brain was affected by the virus. Paul says, "You could see that Danny was in terrible pain right before he died. We stroked his shoulders and arms. Everyone tried to comfort him. But I don't think it helped. In the end, he didn't recognize us. Our whole family stood around his bed, but Danny couldn't have died more alone."

Without preaching, Landau has given young readers a powerful picture of the devastation wrought by AIDS and practical information about how to protect themselves against this scourge.

■ Lapierre, Dominique. *Beyond Love.* Trans. from the French by Kathryn Spink. Warner, 1991. 400pp. (0-446-51438-1) Reading Level: Grades 10–12. (BL 1 Ja91)
Disability: AIDS; Leprosy

Two of the strands in this story follow the fates of people dealing with one of the oldest plagues known to man, leprosy, and of those involved in the world's newest plague, AIDS. The first disease is still endemic in India.

The book opens in the holy city of Benares, where lepers were attracted, sure of alms from the pilgrims who had come to improve their karma at the sacred banks of the Ganges River. Here the teenager Ananda, an untouchable, sieved the foul water for gold teeth and other valuables from the rich corpses whose ashes were consigned to the river. On the eve of what was to be her betrothal day, a lesion on her face was diagnosed as leprosy. She was banished from her family and driven into the streets. Destitute and desperate, she finally came to Mother Teresa's Sisters of Charity, which operated a haven for the poorest of the poor and the dying. The sisters undertook the arduous care of "the little Ganges vulture" and helped her overcome her feeling of debasement due to her low caste.

The AIDS part of the story begins in California in 1980, where San Francisco was known as the gay capital of the world, in a country with an estimated 17 million gays and lesbians. Here, a 25-year-old hairdresser was to present the puzzling pneumocystis pneumonia, a bell ringer for the yet undetected AIDS virus. This signaled the start of the medical adventure still in the making to this day.

Painstaking research led to the identification of the AIDS retrovirus at the Pasteur Institute in Paris and in Dr. Robert Gallo's laboratory in Bethesda, Maryland. The intense rivalry between the two research teams is documented. After the identification of the AIDS virus and in the face of an ever-expanding and agonizing epidemic, the Burroughs Wellcome pharmaceutical company commenced the search for a cure, working in their facilities in Research Triangle Park, North Carolina. The company's enormous research efforts led to the discovery that the substance AZT, a powdered form of herring sperm, was effective in slowing the course of the disease. Twenty-one men and women constituted the human subjects who tested what is still the best treatment, but not cure, for AIDS.

A third thread of the story involves a young Arab monk who was friendly with a homosexual American archaeologist, Joseph Stein, in Israel. While they were descending a cave under excavation in Geser, a tragic misstep plunged Brother Malouf into the abyss, rendering him quadriplegic. Eventually, the monk would offer up his suffering in a worldwide network supporting the work of the Sisters of Charity. Mother Teresa proclaimed his spiritual marriage to the dark and beautiful Ananda, who had joined the order.

In 1985, the first New York center to take in destitute people with AIDS was created with the help of Cardinal O'Connor and Mayor Koch. However, initially, no local people would serve the 20 residents. As a result, Mother Teresa agreed to take charge of this new home. Ananda was summoned from Calcutta to the new hospice. Joseph Stein became one of the first patients in the home, and he eventually died there, holding the Indian girl's hand.

An epilogue and index conclude the book.

Analysis: As with all of Lapierre's well-known books, this one is beautifully written and well translated. Although the book is long, its chapters are short, alternating the separate strands, and the plots of each are suspenseful. Before the reader can become disappointed that one adventure has been left hanging, the new story becomes engrossing. The strands come together at the end of the book in a satisfying conclusion.

This latest book on AIDS is a welcome update to the rapidly changing face of this epidemic. Since its publication, new data have emerged concerning the French-American controversies over the discovery of the AIDS virus. In *Science* magazine of June 7, 1991, Joseph Palca summarizes the unfinished saga in a short article, "Gallo Concedes Contamination (Again)" (p. 1379). On the same page, Palca describes the U.S. government's effort to break the Burroughs Wellcome monopoly on the production of AZT.

Lapierre brings a needed international perspective to this subject. It affords a glimpse into other interesting cultures and religions. The reader is left with an appreciation of both the diversity of people and the singleness of purpose among the worldwide scientific community and among others dedicated to the relief of human suffering.

■ Lerner, Ethan A. *Understanding AIDS.* Illus. Lerner, 1987. 64pp. (LB 0-8225-0024-8) Reading Level: Grades 4–6. (BCCB N87; Inst S87; SBF My88)
Disability: AIDS

The author is a researcher in immunology and tropical diseases and has treated AIDS patients. In this book addressed to young (elementary school) readers, Dr. Lerner begins each chapter with a short fictional sketch of a person with an illness, which he uses as a springboard to discussion of an aspect of AIDS. For example, in the first chapter a boy wakes up with a fever and swollen glands and is diagnosed as having strep throat; this leads to a discussion of infections. Subsequent chapters deal with sexuality, transfusions, hemophilia, drug abuse, and AIDS itself. Each chapter concludes with a question-and-answer section. At the end of the book, the reader will find a short list of resources, a glossary, and an index. Black-and-white illustrations depict the people described.

Analysis: Lerner's combination of fictional profiles written in easy, naturalistic style and followed by clearly presented facts works well to transmit information to young readers. The design, with effective use of boldface print and question-and-answer format, is also effective. The chapter on homosexuality and the one on a college student who contracts AIDS through a homosexual relationship do not specifically describe homosexual practices, and the term "anal sex" does not appear in the glossary or index. "Condom," however, is defined.

This could be a valuable book for young readers, especially if there are adults close at hand with whom readers feel comfortable about extending the discussion. Although it is clear as far as it goes, the text could give rise to questions that should be answered if children are to have the kind of full information they need to protect themselves.

■ Lester, Bonnie. *Women and AIDS: A Practical Guide for Those Who Help Others.* Continuum, 1989. 143pp. (0-8264-0501-0) Reading Level: Grades 10–12. (ABR My90; BW Ag89)
Disability: AIDS

Lester is a psychologist whose interest in AIDS and its effect on women was occasioned by the tragic death of a close friend, a 39-year-old homosexual man who died of an AIDS-related infection. One of the chapters is devoted to his story. Other chapters deal with the relation and attitude of women to such subjects as heterosexual transmission of the disease, the media, AIDS testing, talking to children about AIDS, and educational programs in the schools. Lester interviewed a number of women, including some infected by the disease, some who had been exposed to it, and others who had no reason to think that they would become ill. Their responses are woven through the text. There is an appendix that lists national and international organizations to contact for further information, as well as the telephone numbers of state departments of health.

Analysis: This is a specialized book but one that could be helpful and informative for high school students, both male and female, as well as for their teachers, counselors, and parents. Lester's style is easy and readable, and the stories she writes are compelling. One of the most affecting is told by a school counselor who became very attached to an 8-year-old boy whose mother was dying of AIDS.

■ LeVert, Suzanne. *AIDS: In Search of a Killer.* Illus. Messner, 1987. 145pp. (LB 0-671-62840-2) Reading Level: Grades 7–12. (BL Ag87; SLJ S87; WLB S87)
Disability: AIDS

Beginning with a chapter called "Ten Important Questions and Answers about AIDS," the author goes on to present information about the immune system and to describe the first appearance of AIDS in this country. Then follow chapters on opportunistic infections and how they work, the kinds of people who are most at risk to get the disease, AIDS and civil rights, treatment, and hopes for cures. LeVert includes vignettes of people with AIDS, for example, a young homosexual man and a woman who used drugs. She discusses the ways in which the disease is transmitted, with explicit reference to homosexual practices. A glossary, a list of resources, and an index complete the book.

Analysis: LeVert has written a clear, detailed, and careful book, one that demands attention from the reader. Her descriptions are detailed, and her presentations of sexual information are frank, unlike some texts that do not explain such phrases as "anal sex" or habits of homosexual behavior. At the end, she speaks out strongly for prevention and for responsible behavior.

This is a book to be recommended to the mature reader. It could be very useful as the basis of group discussion in the middle and upper grades.

■ McCarroll, Tolbert. *Morning Glory Babies: Children with AIDS and the Celebration of Life.* Illus. St. Martin's, 1988. 161pp. (0-312-02255-7) Reading Level: Grades 7–12. (BL O88; KR 1 S88; PW 19 Ag88)
Disability: AIDS

Tolbert McCarroll has lived for a number of years in a small monastic community, Starcross, that he and two women established on a farm in northern California. All three are what McCarroll describes as "progressive Catholics" whose "relationship with the official structure is friendly but autonomous." At various times the community has included other adults, and for a number of years they provided a foster home for neglected, abused, and troubled children. In 1986, when they saw a television program on babies with AIDS living in hospitals, they decided to open their home to such children. They already had one baby, McCarroll's adopted son.

Their first infant was Melissa, who came to them after living her first five months in the hospital. She had been born prematurely to a mother who had had no prenatal care, and she was addicted to heroin and cocaine at birth. Already beautiful and charming even after this harsh beginning, she thrived and developed in the warmly nurturing and stimulating environment of the Starcross community. Later, she was joined by two other AIDS-infected babies. One, Aaron, died shortly after his first birthday, but at the time of the writing of this book, Melissa and Rachel were alive and reasonably healthy.

McCarroll describes the development of the babies and of the Starcross community members, interlacing the narrative with accounts of interaction with social service, government, and medical agencies as well as with neighbors. These relationships have often been prickly and difficult, as people react out of fear, ignorance, and rigid adherence to regulations. However, the Starcross community has also received support, advice, and practical help from many professionals and friends, as well as attention from the national media. McCarroll writes too of the daily life—the farm chores, meditation and worship, celebrations, the turn of the seasons, and delight in the growth of the babies.

Black-and-white photographs show the babies with members of the Starcross community.

Analysis: As McCarroll says in his prologue, the birth of babies with AIDS "is one of the most poignant aspects of the AIDS plague." Not only are these infants born with the prospect that their life will be cruelly brief, but because of the very nature of the virus, they also are usually deprived of parental love and care; their mothers, often very young and themselves fatally ill, cannot nurture them. Yet, tragic though his subject is, this is not a depressing book. McCarroll believes in concentrating on living rather than on dying, and on seeing the babies as separate individuals defined by that individuality, not by their disease. He makes no claim to superior understanding, dedication, or skills, but he and the other members of his community have made a commitment to try to meet needs they see. In writing about the funeral service for Aaron he says that they had to face the "troublesome question" of how God could allow this death, and he answers himself by saying, "In a sharing of feelings we took responsibility for the situation. Aaron was dead because of society's folly, not because of God's will."

■ Martelli, Leonard J., Fran D. Peltz, and William Messina. *When Someone You Know Has AIDS.* Crown, 1987. 238pp. (0-317-52879-3) Reading Level: Grades 10–12. (BL 15 Je87; KR 15 Je87; LJ J187) *Disability:* AIDS

Leonard Martelli is a writer and AIDS carepartner, and his coauthors are therapists who counsel people with AIDS or AIDS-related complex and their friends and family; the introduction is by Dr. Joyce Wallace, a physician specializing in the treatment of AIDS. The authors define a carepartner as "a person who is providing continuing emotional support and physical care to a person with AIDS or AIDS-Related Complex (ARC)" and a caring friend as someone who "is involved . . . in the same ways as a carepartner, but to a lesser degree."

In their book the authors deal with such topics as attitudes toward AIDS; its medical symptoms and manifestations; treatments (including experimental drugs); the practical matters of care, housekeeping, insurance, and wills; the effect of AIDS on relationships; and dealing with death and its consequent grief and loss. They convey much of the information by the use of vignettes, describing the experiences of people and returning to the same individuals repeatedly. The AIDS patients include homosexual men, a heterosexual man who contracted the disease through treatment for his hemophilia, and a woman intravenous drug user. Their carepartner may be a lover, friend, wife, or sibling.

The text takes the reader through the course of AIDS, from first symptoms to diagnosis through different patterns of infection and treatment to final days and hours. Appendixes look at different possible causes of this syndrome and the pros and cons of the human immunovirus (HIV) antibody test; another appendix offers guidelines for safer sex. The authors include a national directory of AIDS-related organizations, a glossary, a bibliography, and an index.

Analysis: This is an AIDS book with a slightly different slant, because Leonard Martelli is a homosexual who has been a carepartner and has himself had many of the experiences covered in the text. The information is explicit and detailed, conveyed in a fluent style and enlivened by the individual histories. Much has already changed in the intervening years since the book was published; for example, the most recent information about the efficacy of AZT as early treatment puts a different slant on the question of testing for HIV. The literature on AIDS has, of course, grown, so that the bibliography given here would now be only a starting point. Nevertheless, these are not major drawbacks.

Perhaps one of the most valuable aspects of the book lies in its compassionate, nonjudgmental outlook. The authors do not minimize the horror of this illness, and they describe realistically what may be demanded of those who support and care for victims of the disease; they understand that, for a variety of reasons, friends and family may turn away from the sick person, often because they cannot move beyond the prejudices of society and fear of condemnation. Yet the writers also make clear that those who can offer the commitment of love will find their relationships enriched and deepened and their understanding of life irrevocably changed. Beyond its applicability to a particular illness, the book might also be read as commentary on human interaction, on response to challenge, and on individual decision and control over the course of one's life.

Because of the length of the book and the explicit nature of the material, it should be recommended to able, mature readers. Classroom teachers might wish to use some sections as a basis for group discussion.

■ Moffatt, BettyClare. *When Someone You Love Has AIDS: A Book of Hope for Family and Friends.* Borgo, 1986. 154pp. (LB 0-8095-6551-X) Reading Level: Grades 10–12. (BL 1 S86)
Disability: AIDS

The author is described as "a writer, teacher, counselor and public speaker in holistic healing." She is also the mother of a young man who has been diagnosed as having AIDS. The emphasis in her book is on the power of love to effect understanding and forgiveness and ultimately to heal, a process involving both the people with the symptoms and all the other people in their life. Moffatt describes her own reactions when her son Michael, who had long been estranged from many family members, called to tell her about his illness. Other voices speak too: those who, like Michael, have AIDS, Michael's grandmother, a psychiatrist, and practioners of techniques such as rebirthing.

Two chapters are devoted to alternative therapies. Moffatt and her family and associates believe that it lies within the individual's power to decide how he or she wishes to live; they reject the notion of the person with AIDS as victim, preferring the term "AIDS person." All the AIDS persons who figure in the book have made decisions about their life patterns, from choosing a healthy diet to opening the way for new understanding with family (especially parents) and friends. Emphasis is on living rather than dying, whatever the number of days or years that may be left. The last chapter, "Beyond Life and Death," is subtitled "Acceptance and Inner Peace."

A bibliography and a list of resources come at the end, followed by two questionnaires: one for people who have or have had AIDS, and the other for "parents, co-workers, friends, support personnel, etc., of people who have AIDS."

Analysis: Whereas Moffatt is careful to say that she does not attempt to promote any particular belief systems or religions, she has found help and support in movements and groups that will seem to many to stand outside the mainstream—for example, the Love Your Self–Heal Your Body Center, the technique called rebirthing, and a group named Expect a Miracle. She never rejects conventional medicine; rather, she believes that physicians, therapists, the AIDS person, and everyone in that person's world can work together toward healing.

Moffatt writes with clarity and sincerity. Certainly some of her ideas are controversial, and readers may approach them with skepticism. Used with a group of high school students, her book might provoke animated discussion of individual responsibility, the relationship between mind and body, and treatment of life-threatening illness.

■ Monette, Paul. *Borrowed Time: An AIDS Memoir.* Harcourt, 1988. 342pp. (0-15-113598-3) Reading Level: Grades 10–12. (BL Je88; LATBR 5 Je88; NYTBR 11 S88)
Disability: AIDS

Poet, novelist, and script writer Paul Monette has written a bittersweet, heart-wrenching memorial to his lover, Roger Horwitz, who died of the complications of AIDS in 1986, 19 months after his diagnosis. Reviewers have applied various descriptive terms to this book, such as shattering, eloquent, the universal arena of human loss, a gallant, courageous love story at once unbearable and fascinating. It is a difficult book to describe. On the surface it is a lucid, intensely personal, detailed account of the last few years of an intimate relationship between two men who were so close that one became the other. It is often painful reading. One follows the reluctance, the dread, the denial, the horror, and finally, acceptance in the form of coping by attempting to go on with life as usual, even though the usual is gone forever.

Analysis: Monette and Horwitz are cultured, intelligent, urbane, witty intellectuals who travel in a circle of literate, sensitive peers. This sophistication may appear to work against the average teenager who reads this book. Nevertheless, the author is so sincere, direct, and unpretentious that many teens will be drawn to and compelled to finish the gripping story that Monette tells about love, AIDS, and loss. Highly recommended for thoughtful teens with mature interests.

■ Nourse, Alan E. *AIDS.* Illus. Franklin Watts, 1986. 128pp. (LB 0-531-10235-1) Reading Level: Grades 7–12. (BL 1 J987; SLJ Mr87; WLB S87)
Disability: AIDS

Nourse, a physician, has written extensively for both adults and children; his name is probably familiar to many readers through his "Family Doctor" column in *Good Housekeeping* magazine. In this work he looks at the history of the recent AIDS plague, its possible origins, the forms it takes, and the symptoms it exhibits. He devotes one chapter to "Truths and Falsehoods about HTLV-III Infections" and another to ways in which people can protect themselves from infection. A glossary and index complete the book, which is illustrated with black-and-white photographs, drawings, and charts.

Analysis: Nourse has a readable and inviting style, probably developed in his years as the author of a popular magazine column, and he is able to present complex concepts with clarity. He is particularly to be commended for the honesty with which he presents sexual activity and for his refusal to apply moral standards to homosexuality and promiscuity. He remarks that promiscuity "has had a bad press because it is so often associated with sexual activities that many people regard as improper, abnormal, wicked, or bad" and then goes on to give the dictionary meaning of "promiscuous" and to discuss it in terms of risk of infection. Young people who read this book should be left with no doubt about what behaviors will put them in danger and what will protect them. Nourse has made a valuable contribution to the growing body of texts on AIDS written for the general public and for the preadolescent and adolescent reader.

■ Peabody, Barbara. *The Screaming Room: A Mother's Journal of Her Son's Struggle with AIDS.* Illus. Oak Tree, 1986. 254pp. (0-380-70345-9) Reading Level: Grades 8–12. (NDW S86; RSR W87; SBF Ja87) *Disability:* AIDS

This day-by-day journal began at the end of 1983, when 28-year-old Peter was already hospitalized and terribly sick with pneumonia. Peabody had been summoned to New York by her estranged husband to tend to their eldest son. Peter had already given up his job as a waiter, which had been sustaining him while he established a singing career. He had also broken off with his lover, although the young man did visit Peter in the hospital in New York. Peabody advised her son to have an AIDS test, which was positive. Surrounded by caring relatives and buoyed by persistent medical treatment, he grew well enough to return to his mother's home in San Diego.

Back in California, Peter and his mother joined several support groups, including an AIDS project and a group called The Worried Well. They continued to battle the incessant assault of opportunistic infections that tend to plague AIDS sufferers. Most alarming was an increasing mental involvement, beginning with memory lapses, and proceeding to violent and debilitating seizures. Peter's ever-prescient mother was tireless in monitoring his symptoms, ministering to his physical needs, and divining his hopes and fears for his recovery. In her journal, she could express the internal "screaming" that her outward appearance of strength and calm belied.

Care of Peter became a demanding 24-hour-a-day vigil for his mother and a conundrum for his host of physicians and nurses as they treated the relentless invasion of painful and humiliating afflictions. Even as he became blind, and often demented, Peter displayed a quirky sense of humor and a determination to survive. In the end, his mother refused further intervention for a recurrent pneumonia, and Peter died, as he had wished, in the midst of his loving family, almost a year after his first illness.

In the aftermath, Peter's relatives, and his mother in particular, have dedicated part of their life to AIDS patients and to the eradication of this disease.

Analysis: Nearly the whole of this book details the day-by-day, even minute-by-minute, physical sufferings of one AIDS patient. These manifestations were a result both of the disease itself and of the sophisticated and increasingly aggressive medical treatments recommended for Peter's comfort and survival. Peabody's selfless dedication to her son's well-being seemed almost superhuman, and the endurance of her son was equally heroic.

The author is straightforward in her objective acceptance of homosexuality. Peter's uncle was homosexual; she was not surprised when her son revealed his sexual preference in his early 20s. Peter also confided to his parents that he had been a drug abuser even in high school; his parents had suspected nothing. While Peter's mother became intimate with every aspect of his physical being over the course of his illness, she does not seem to acknowledge the young man that Peter must have become in his nine-year stint in New York. Indeed, after seeing a movie with scenes of the New York skyline, he told her, sobbing, how much he missed that city. She dismissed the literal interpretation and wrote that he missed "living," not New York. The reader might wonder what happened to Peter's lover and about what memories he did have of this young man and his own former life.

By the time we are introduced to Peter, he is very sick. Even at the book's beginning, he seems to have reverted to the role of child, albeit brave and forbearing, in the care of a devoted and grieving mother. The physical consequences of AIDS are starkly and compellingly presented in this disturbing account.

■ Petrow, Steven. *Dancing Against the Darkness: A Journey Through America in the Age of AIDS.* Heath, 1990. 218pp. (0-669-24309-4)
Reading Level: Grades 7–12. (R&R BKN D90)
Disability: AIDS

In 1986, Steven Petrow, then 29 years old, discovered a mark on his calf; a homosexual, he had worked at the San Francisco AIDS Foundation and was no stranger to anxieties about the disease. The doctors he consulted told him not to worry about the blemish, but some months later he went back to his doctor, who then ordered a biopsy. The diagnosis was AIDS. But when Petrow had an AIDS antibody test some days later, it was negative. Petrow had been reprieved from death (for the second time, since he had had testicular cancer two years earlier). In the time between the misdiagnosis and the negative results, Petrow—a writer and interviewer who was working on a dissertation—made a bargain with God, promising that if he was allowed to live for 18 months, he would "use that time to help other people understand what it means to live with this disease and to die with it." This book is the result of his bargain.

Petrow conducted an extensive investigation to learn about the virus and to find people who would represent different aspects and experiences. Each chapter focuses on a person or people with AIDS: the hemophiliac Ray brothers, who contracted the virus from blood transfusions; a woman who became ill as the result of intravenous drug use and another who was infected by her male lover; the newspaper writer Bill Cox who in his paper, the *Honolulu Star-Bulletin,* went public about his homosexuality and his illness; a couple who with their two little boys lived a seemingly perfect life until the husband came down with AIDS and died within seven months without ever telling his wife how he had gotten the disease; a gay man from Kansas who lived a wildly promiscuous sexual life gave widely differing descriptions of his relations with his family, and claimed that having AIDS changed his life for the better; and a bright, handsome young man who entered into active homosexual behavior as a young teenager and died at 19. The people Petrow focuses on have had varying experiences as their disease became known. Some, like the Rays, experienced brutal aggression, some were rejected by their families even when they were dying, others were supported by loving friends and family members. Some died angry and bitter, others reached acceptance and reconciliation. In an afterword, Petrow brings the reader up-to-date on the situations of the survivors, both the families and those of his subjects who are still living.

A glossary and a list of AIDS organizations conclude the book.

Analysis: Petrow has written an absorbing, highly readable book. The people he interviewed seemed to have talked to him at length and with considerable frankness, and he presents their stories and conversations sympathetically, without unduly judgmental evaluations. Probably his own misdiagnosis, the anguish of the days that followed, and the subsequent feelings of relief and escape contributed to the empathy and compassion of his approach. His descriptions are vivid, sharply observed, and when he is writing about manifestations of the disease, graphic and sometimes horrible.

Although written for adults, this is a book that can be recommended to able readers as young as junior high school students; it will increase both their knowledge and their understanding.

■ Rieder, Ines, and Patricia Ruppelt, eds. *AIDS: The Women.* Cleis, 1988. 251pp. (0-939416-20-4) Reading Level: Grades 10–12. (BL 15 Ja89; LJ 1 F89; WRB Ap89)
Disability: AIDS

The editors have gathered an anthology of pieces about AIDS as it has affected women in the 1980s, grouping the essays and occasional poems in such categories as "Family, Lovers and Friends," "The Professional Caregivers," and "Prostitution in the Age of AIDS." The contributing writers come from the United States, Europe, Brazil, and Haiti. All have had personal experience with the disease through personal and professional contact; some are ill themselves. All emphasize the fact, now widely recognized, that AIDS is not limited to homosexual men and intravenous drug users. The appendix has a glossary, a list of resources, and a selected bibliography that includes films and videos.

Analysis: This is not a book for the fainthearted or the unsophisticated. The voices one hears are sometimes angry, sometimes despairing, sometimes hopeful and even triumphant; they speak in direct, explicit language, whether it is with the objective tone of the scientist or the grieving voice of loss. The overall note is one of respect and compassion, even for people who seem to be most willfully and hopelessly exposing themselves to repeated risk. Those who have contracted the disease have done so from a variety of sources of infection, including both homosexual and heterosexual activities, intravenous drug use, blood transfusions, and artificial insemination. The emphasis, of course, is on the experience of women, although there is little material that directly describes the birth and subsequent life of infected infants.

This adult book is certainly within the range of mature, able readers.

■ Sanders, Pete, and Clare Farquhar. *The Problem of AIDS.* Illus. Gloucester, 1989. 32pp. (0-531-17191-4) Reading Level: Grades 3–7. *Disability:* AIDS

The authors are an English primary school head teacher (Sanders) and an educational psychologist and researcher who has studied children's knowledge of human immunodeficiency virus (HIV) and AIDS (Farquhar); their consultant (Angela Grunsell) is "an advisory teacher specialising in development education and resources for the primary school age range." They have structured the book with two-page segments, each responding to a question that appears in large type at the top of one page with a facing color photograph. Questions include "What is the difference between HIV and AIDS?" "Could I get the virus?" and "How can these body fluids go from one person to another?" Each set of pages also has an informative sentence highlighted with a heavy border and a contrasting color, for example, "If used correctly condoms can help stop body fluids getting inside another person." A short, one-page glossary and a brief index complete the book.

Analysis: Since the authors are professionally in close touch with elementary school children, they are probably drawing here on questions that youngsters usually ask. The information presented in response is clear, and the emphasis is on what readers can do to protect themselves as well as on what they can do without fear of infection, such as swimming in pools and kissing on the mouth. Attention is also paid to the help and support available to people with AIDS.

However, one might question whether this book goes far enough, even given the young age of its target audience. For instance, the page on drugs does not mention the reasons a person might use such substances or their effect, and there is no indication that the readers may themselves have to make decisions about drug use; most children nowadays have perforce become very sophisticated about substance abuse and need persuasive information to help them resist the attraction. The page on sexuality does include the words "penis," "vaginal," and "condom," stating that "One way that may help to stop fluids from being passed on is to use a condom on the penis when having sex." However, neither heterosexual nor homosexual acts are described, and the authors use those vague phrases "making love" and "having sex."

This book could probably be best used when a knowledgeable adult who is prepared to be frank is at hand. It might be part of a school or public library collection that would also include other informational books on this subject.

■ Shilts, Randy. *And the Band Played On: Politics, People, and the AIDS Epidemic.* St. Martin's, 1987. 630pp. (0-312-00994-1) Reading Level: Grades 7–12. (NYTBR 8 N87; SLJ Ap88; TLS 11–17 Mr88)
Disability: AIDS

The author is a journalist whose full-time assignment from 1982 was to cover the AIDS story for the *San Francisco Chronicle*. This reporting constitutes the core of the long tome.

The 55 persons, politicians, health care personnel, researchers, and AIDS patients whose names and stories constitute the text are listed in a beginning dramatis personae. The federal bureaucratic organizations involved in research and services with respect to AIDS are reviewed in a foreword.

In a prologue, the author reveals his mission in writing the work: "It is a tale that bears telling, so that it will never happen again, to any people, anywhere." (p. xxiii).

The story, told in nine parts, begins July 4, 1976, when the vast celebration in New York for the Bicentennial brought guests from all over the world. This event provided one of the first opportunities for transmission of the AIDS virus to the United States. The story proceeds chronologically, weaving together strands from many sources here and abroad up to early 1987, when the epidemic had become of great political, scientific, and personal import to the nation and to the rest of the world.

Much of the story is about the gay communities in New York and San Francisco where AIDS first appeared. The Gay Freedom Day Parade at the 1980 Democratic National Convention, where the San Francisco Gay Freedom Day Marching Band played to a joyful homophile mecca, symbolized a new era of freedom and self-pride for gay people. This group, homosexual men, was to suffer most from the new disease and thereby to develop strategies to counter it. Eventually, focus shifted to concerted scientific efforts toward identifying the causative agent (a retrovirus transmitted by exchange of body fluids), controlling transmission, and treating patients. As the book went to press, over 36,000 Americans had been diagnosed with the disease, and over 20,000 had died.

Analysis: This is a very long, explicit book with a number of strands woven through it—historical, geographic, scientific, political, and personal. The reader may become forgetful or confused over the myriad of detail. However, the forthright descriptions of personalities and events are troubling and compelling. The facts themselves are sensational and horrendous. The author may not have needed to moralize as much as he did about political obtuseness, professional vanity, pervasive irresponsibility, prejudice, and stupidity. The band still plays on, and this book is still widely respected as a definitive one in the growing literature about AIDS.

■ Taylor, Barbara. *Everything You Need to Know about AIDS*. Illus. Rosen, 1988. 64pp. (0-8230-0809-7) Reading Level: Grades 4–9. (BL 15 S88; SLJ O88)
Disability: HIV infection; Kaposi's sarcoma; Pneumocystis carinii

This is one of a series of Need to Know books edited by Evan Stark. The author is a writer/editor at *Weekly Reader* in Middletown, Connecticut. The prose consists of uncomplicated, short sentences. Technical or difficult words are defined on the spot and also included in a glossary. Illustrations range from simple diagrams to color photographs. Seven chapters cover an explanation of the mechanisms involved in propagation of and infection by the AIDS virus, the history of the disease from the perspective of past plagues, and explicit, practical ways to avoid contracting human immunodeficiency virus. A final chapter asks and answers 17 specific questions about sexual activity, transmission of the virus, and where to seek help. A short reading list and an index close the book.

Analysis: This title offers clear, precise, and complete coverage of the AIDS situation for young readers. The book comes out strongly against drug abuse in general and dirty needles in particular. There are no moral judgments concerning homosexual and heterosexual practices, but readers are urged to protect themselves if engaging in sexual intercourse. A drawing shows an erect penis fitted with a condom, so that there is no mistaking the meaning of one of the author's admonitions concerning safe sex. The book states in easy language some truths about AIDS that are often not grasped even by adults—the fact that the virus cannot be transmitted by casual contact, for example. The questions at the end, written in the first person, are direct and to the point. The text is never condescending. In sum, this appears to be one of the very best of the many children's books about AIDS.

■ Tilleraas, Perry. *Circle of Hope: Our Stories of AIDS, Addiction & Recovery.* Hazelden, 1990. 364pp. (0-89486-610-9) Reading Level: Grades 10–12. (LAM BK Rpt Ag90)
Disability: AIDS; Addiction

Perry Tilleraas describes himself as a person recovering from addiction to drugs and alcohol and from AIDS; about the latter, he says, "More and more, AIDS is becoming a chronic, survivable illness." He points out that many people with AIDS must also battle addictions, including compulsive sexual behavior. He believes that cofactors contributing to AIDS must be part of the study and treatment of the disease and that support groups can help people triumph over their addictions and their illness.

The first six chapters of the book deal with such subjects as living with AIDS, alcoholism, and addiction, and they include both Tilleraas's own thinking and quoted material from others. In Part Two, which constitutes the bulk of the book, individuals with AIDS, AIDS-related complex, or human immunovirus tell their stories of childhood abuse, addiction, despair, and recovery.

Analysis: This is a long and somewhat repetitive book. So many of these stories carry the same themes of tragic childhood, of young people both spiritually and physically abandoned by and estranged from their family, and of self-destructive and antisocial behavior, that the reader may become overwhelmed. The explicit narratives can appall and shock, as evidence mounts of what human beings sometimes do to each other and to themselves. The work would be best recommended to mature readers, who might want to dip selectively into the chapters rather than attempt to cover the whole book.

■ Ulene, Art. *Safe Sex in a Dangerous World: Understanding and Coping with the Threat of AIDS.* Vintage, 1987. 108pp. (0-394-75625-8) Reading Level: Grades 7–12. (BL 1 S87; KLIATT S87; VLS O87)
Disability: AIDS; AIDS-related complex (ARC)

Ulene, the "family physician" on NBC's "Today" show, is an obstetrician/gynecologist. His primary consultant was Michael S. Gottlieb, a founder of the American Fund for AIDS research. Ulene has dedicated his book to all the men, women, and children who have battled the disease and to the people who care for them. The book speaks personally to readers primarily to instruct them on how to avoid contracting the AIDS virus and secondarily what to do if already infected. A few diagrams and many tables amplify the text.

The introductory discussion of the problematic expression "safe sex" is a theme that is elaborated on throughout the book. The way the AIDS virus attacks the body's T cells is explained in the first chapter. The four stages of the natural course of the disease are given: acute infection, silent infection, AIDS-related complex, AIDS. The spread of the virus in the United States is traced: in 75 percent of the cases through semen and in 20 percent through exchange of blood.

Surgeon General Koop's admonition to use condoms is quoted. Ulene analyzes the failure rate of condoms and concludes that, for 100 percent protection from AIDS, one must abstain from sexual activity or have a safe partner (with whom any sexual behavior is therefore safe). In between these options, there is a gradient of risks that are explored at length. Specific advice follows on how to have "almost safe sex," through judicious choice of partners and through recommended practices and procedures. Six types of possible physical sexual interactions between men and women or between men are covered. (Lesbianism is not specifically mentioned.) For each activity, such as, for example, vaginal receptive intercourse with an infected partner, the biological mechanism involved in the transmission of the virus is explained, its relative risk assessed, and helpful precautions delineated.

The steps involved in AIDS testing and various related issues are covered in the fifth chapter. Under the headings "The Best You Can Do for Yourself" and "The Best You Can Do for Others" (pp. 86–87), explicit recommendations are made for those who test positive for the AIDS virus. Counseling and support services available to people with AIDS are listed. Ulene learned from a survey that not all advice given by such agencies was appropriate or correct, however.

Analysis: The figures in any book on AIDS are already out of date, as Ulene anticipated. In March 1991, the estimate of the number of people worldwide who are infected by AIDS is 3 million, with a predicted doubling of that number within the decade. That increase underscores the author's contentions that it is a dangerous world and that people need to take pains to protect themselves against this deadly disease.

The specific mechanisms of sexual contact and transmission of AIDS are made more precise in this work than in many of the works on the subject for young people. For readers who are ready for this level of explicitness, this is a superb book. It is clearly and simply written, well organized, and humane. It should be on the shelf of every high school library in the country.

In changing the focus of AIDS prevention from "safe sex" to "safe partners" or abstinence, Ulene has cut through much of the confusion that has attended efforts to educate people on the subject. While moralists will applaud his strong case for abstinence, this is made on the basis of survival. He is equally evenhanded about various sexual practices, and he does not discuss such issues as premarital sex, contraception, or homosexuality. He does mention the advisability of an infected woman's practicing birth control, and the possibility of aborting a child she might conceive. He stresses a compassionate attitude toward those infected with AIDS, that they can be treated like everyone else, except with respect to sexual behavior.

■ White, Ryan, and Ann Marie Cunningham. *Ryan White: My Own Story.* Illus. Dial, 1991. 277pp. (0-8037-0977-3) Reading Level: Grades 7–12. (BL 1 F91; SLJ Je91)
Disability: AIDS

Ryan White was born in Kokomo, Indiana, in 1971. His severe hemophilia was discovered within three days; in the following years, he was treated with Factor VIII, a blood product derived from the blood of thousands of donors that provides the clotting factor lacking in hemophiliacs. In December 1984, at 13, he came down with an illness eventually diagnosed as pneomocystis pneumonia; he had contracted AIDS from contaminated blood in Factor VIII. His parents had divorced some years earlier, his father separating himself from the family almost completely; his mother's second marriage had also ended in divorce, but Ryan's stepfather remained a close friend. Ryan had a younger sister.

Ryan became a nationally known figure some months later, when he tried to return to his school in Kokomo. His mother brought suit against the company that had made the contaminated blood product, a reporter interviewed her, and everyone in the town learned of his illness. Although the state health commissioner had ordered the school to admit Ryan and had announced guidelines for schools with students like him, the school insisted that he be taught at home via a telephone hookup. At church, fellow congregants asked the family to take either the front pew or the last one, so that everyone else could know their location and stay away; they were treated as untouchable by friends and neighbors. Ugly rumors circulated about actions that people feared would spread the disease, including Ryan's spitting on vegetables in the grocery store.

When the school was forced to readmit Ryan, a group called the Concerned Citizens and Parents of Children Attending Western School Corporation sued the family, the county health officer, and the school. A court order forced Ryan's admission again, but it was a difficult time; other students refused to have anything to do with him and were actively hostile. Eventually, Ryan's mother decided to move the family to Cicero, Indiana, a small community on a lake. In contrast to Kokomo, here they were welcomed by neighbors, other teenagers, and the whole school; to prepare for Ryan, the faculty and students engaged in a two-week "crash course on AIDS," and then the school undertook to educate the community.

With national press attention, Ryan became a public figure. He appeared on television shows, traveled around the country, was befriended by media celebrities like Michael Jordan and Elton John, testified before the President's Commission on AIDS in 1988, and spoke at the annual convention of the National Education Association. A movie was made about Ryan's and the family's experiences in Kokomo. Despite bouts of illness, Ryan was able to live a fairly normal teenager's life for a time, but eventually his health began to deteriorate more dramatically. He went to California in March 1990, where he made public appearances and met President and Mrs. Reagan, but he then became so ill that his mother tried unsuccessfully to get him treated in a Los Angeles hospital. They flew back to Riley Children's Hospital in Indianapolis, where Ryan had been treated since the discovery of his AIDS; surgery was performed to put him on a ventilator, but he never regained consciousness and died on April 8, 1990.

The book concludes with an epilogue describing Ryan's last days and his funeral, which was attended by 1,500 people, including Elton John, First Lady Barbara Bush, Michael Jordan, and Phil Donahue. Jordan's poem about Ryan and Elton John's eulogy follow. Ryan's testimony before the President's Commission on AIDS is reprinted. There are several pages of questions and answers about AIDS and a list of resources, including three videotapes made for children and teenagers by Ryan, the names of national AIDS organizations, and information about other materials.

There are many photographs, both black and white and color.

Analysis: Accounts of the lives of people who, like Ryan, have contracted AIDS unwittingly through measures designed to save them are particularly poignant. Ryan and his family exhibited determination and courage, and their legal battles and the subsequent attention they received have certainly influenced the way the public now views the disease. Ryan's written voice sounds natural for the most part—the voice of a youngster who wanted above all else to be normal. Not an intellectual or particularly introspective boy, he loved clothes and cars and other accoutrements of contemporary teenage life; one reviewer pointed to the family's preoccupation with material possessions and celebrities.

Many young people who read this book will probably hear a voice that sounds like their own. They may also learn something about what it is like to be faced with both a serious lifelong disability and then a fatal illness, and to experience ostracism because of ignorance and fear. And, finally, they will learn about the current state of our knowledge of the causes and treatment of AIDS.

■ Whitmore, George. *Someone Was Here: Profiles in the AIDS Epidemic.* New American Library, 1988. 211pp. (0-45-30060-19) Reading Level: Grades 10–12. (LJ J188; NYTBR 10 Ap88; PW 26 F88) *Disability:* AIDS

The narrative of this book covers a three-year period (1985–87) in the lives and deaths of people with AIDS, and AIDS-related illnesses. The first story describes a group of gay young men who had migrated to New York to begin a career in business, fashion, and the like. The author came to know these people very well as they coped with the downward cycle of sickness, treatment, health, and sickness again that defines the course of the disease. The second story is about a gay Chicano drifter who had left family and school as a young adolescent. When he became very ill, his mother took him back into his family in Colorado, where he eventually suffered a painful death.

The setting of the third section is in the South Bronx section of New

York in a public hospital that serves the poorest of the poor. Many of the patients treated there have contracted AIDS through the use of dirty needles for intravenous injection of drugs. Others were infected by sexual partners, and the babies by their mothers when they were born. The hospital is portrayed as under siege, partly from the sheer weight of bureaucracy and to some extent by a public policy of willful or thoughtless neglect of the afflicted population, who are desperate, needy, and often unpleasant. The efforts of stalwart medical personnel, chaplains, and parents serve to alleviate somewhat the suffering of the dying and those close to them.

The author discusses the disproportionate percentage of young blacks and Hispanics in New York who are drug abusers, are HIV positive, or have AIDS already. He discusses the very high rate of infection among the prison population as well.

In an epilogue, the author confesses that he began this book after he, a young gay man himself, had been diagnosed as HIV positive and almost certain to get AIDS. Throughout the book he points out the element of denial both by those at risk for the disease and by those in its early stages. In the end, he felt that this writing project itself represented an aspect of his own denial mechanism, as he attempted to distance himself from his own reality.

Analysis: A great deal of information about the AIDS epidemic is skillfully interwoven in the discourse without destroying the momentum of the drama. The work devotes more attention to the plight of the poor, homeless, and minority populations than do most books about people with AIDS. All of the sufferers are presented with compassion and acceptance, and the health care workers, in the main, are portrayed as heroes. This book is a real "downer," up to and including the forthright disclosure by the author in the epilogue.

ORTHOPEDIC/NEUROLOGICAL DISABILITIES

■ Addams, Jane. *Twenty Years at Hull-House.* Foreword by Henry Steele Comager. Illus. by Norma Hamilton. New American Library, 1961. 320pp. (0-451-51955-8) Reading Level: Grades 7–12.
Disability: Scoliosis

The founder of the first settlement house in the slums of Chicago, Illinois, chronicles her life from her earliest recollections through her first twenty years in a career dedicated to the initiation of the settlement movement in the United States and to the pursuit of social justice. Subsequent to the events in this book, Jane Addams became the first president of the Women's International League for Peace and Freedom and cowinner of the Nobel Peace Prize for 1931.

Jane Addams was born in the pastoral community of Cedarville in northern Illinois, where her father, a man of quiet rectitude, was a well-to-do merchant. Her mother died in Jane's infancy, leaving her father to raise "an ugly, pigeon-toed little girl whose crooked back obliged her to walk with her head very much upon one side" (p. 23). Abraham Lincoln died when Jane was 4 years old, an event that she remembers moved her father to tears.

In the 1870s, at age 17, Addams went to Rockville Seminary, often referred to as the Mount Holyoke of the West, where she gained a classical education and was urged toward missionary service. She represented her college as orator in an intercollegiate oratorical contest. "Women certainly did lose the first place and stood fifth, exactly in the dreary middle . . ." (p. 53), she wrote. A fellow student, the later famous William Jennings Bryan, took a prior place, in prophetic anticipation of his cross of gold speech.

At the end of college, Addams determined to study medicine and "live with the poor." She went to Women's Medical College in Philadelphia for six months, but her spinal problem grew worse, and she had to spend the next six months in bed, foregoing medical studies. She attributed a lack of energy and a lingering melancholy to her disability, which periodically brought her usually active life to an abrupt end for weeks at a time.

In the tradition of her older siblings, she went to Europe for two years of cultural enrichment. What impressed her, however, were the "submerged tenth," the near-starving poor in newly industrialized England and on the continent. Her struggle to achieve autonomy and purpose as an adult was intimately connected with her need to address the brutal suffering she describes in the desperate working conditions of match makers in London and in a brewery in Saxe-Coburg.

At 28, Addams finally decided on her life work: the establishment of a settlement house amid the sweatshops and slums of Chicago. The author describes the reciprocal work, study, and sociability between Addams and her many followers in the communal living arrangement, with a succession of poor young and old members of union grant groups and industrial workers. Countless anecdotes, sad or amusing, bring to life the bustling environs of Hull House.

In ten years at Hull House, Addams and other residents effected social change in many cases. For example, they led a coalition to legislate and oversee labor laws. They fostered the women's union movement in order to alleviate some of the terrible working conditions, such as long hours and dangerous working conditions, which had resulted from uncontrolled industrialization.

Analysis: Although the style of writing is more ornate than that to which young people of today are accustomed, Addams' thoughts and descriptions contain the directness, lucidity, and simplicity that might be compared to those of her great hero, Lincoln. Her deep human insights are illustrated by personal examples, and she draws equal wisdom from important men like Tolstoy and from the humblest of immigrants in her neighborhood. Her story, although told in the first person, is astonishingly selfless. She does not introspect on her motivations, and only in passing does she address the occasional long bouts of illness associated with her disability. Yet the reader really gets a sense of knowing this great woman, who was known as Saint Jane throughout the world in her lifetime.

The book gives a vivid picture of an early tumultuous historical time, although the deeper struggles, involving prejudice, abuse of power, and minority rights, seem timely today. While Addams' basic tenets remained constant, she considered all sides of an argument from the human perspectives of her many associates.

■ Backus, Jim, and Henny Backus. *Backus Strikes Back.* Illus. Stein & Day, 1984. 124pp. (0-8128-2962-X) Reading Level: Grades 10–12. (KR 15 My84; LATBR 26 Ag84)
Disability: Basal ganglia disease

Jim Backus, the Hollywood actor best known nationally as the voice of the cartoon character Mr. Magoo, and his wife, Henny, tell the incredible story of Jim's years of illness during most of which he was professionally active. As he describes it, his body stopped listening to him. He could not, at times, control practically any one or certain ones of the parts of his body. The obvious neurological symptoms were first diagnosed as Parkinson's disease and treated with L-dopa, whose side effects proved to be as problematic as the illness itself. Later, Backus learned that he had basal ganglia disease, which eventually began to heal, thus proving conclusively that he did not, in fact, have Parkinson's.

Analysis: Backus has a terrific sense of humor, as does his wife, and the text, while dealing with a serious subject, never stays serious for very long. Teenage readers should enjoy the humor and appreciate that it is the voice of Mr. Magoo speaking. Highly recommended.

■ Bergman, Thomas. *Going Places: Children Living with Cerebral Palsy.* Photographs by Thomas Bergman. Gareth Stevens, 1991. 48pp. (0-8368-0199-7) Reading Level: Grades K–4.
Disability: Cerebral palsy; Hearing impairment

In this most recent book in the Don't Turn Away series, Thomas Bergman describes in words and black-and-white photographs the life of Mathias, a 6-year-old Swedish boy whom he followed for six months. Mathias was born three months premature and was diagnosed as having cerebral palsy at 8 months old. When he was 2, his parents learned that he had almost no hearing. He did not crawl until he was 5, is unable to walk, and has difficulty standing and holding his head straight; his right arm is often bent. His family speaks to him in sign language; Mathias can say a few words, but sign language is hard for him because he cannot use both hands.

Bergman shows him at home, at the doctor's, working with his physical and speech therapists, and practicing on the computer with a teacher. He has an electric wheel chair, which his mother says has changed his life by giving him new independence of movement; once a week he goes to a class where children practice wheelchair skills. Four days a week he attends preschool, where some of the children also have hearing disabilities, but none has cerebral palsy and the rest have no disabilities. The decision about his next school will be difficult to make; he does not yet sign well enough to enter a school for deaf children, as he would like. Mathias also rides horseback, and on Sundays he and other children with disabilities go swimming with their families. After swimming, Mathias's father takes him and his little sister to a McDonald's for hamburgers.

The book concludes with several pages of information about Mathias's condition. Questions children might ask are posed and answered; projects to help readers understand cerebral palsy are suggested; and a list of organizations dealing with disabilities, a bibliography of children's books, a glossary, and an index complete the book.

Analysis: Like the other books in this fine series, *Going Places* is informative and sensitively written. Mathias is a very appealing little boy, cheerful and expressive, who responds to his many activities with enthusiasm and zest. He does not appear to experience frustration or discouragement, but both text and pictures show how hard he works to make progress. His family, teachers, and therapists are encouraging and supportive, and the book concludes, "Mathias is very proud of all the new things he has learned. 'We have learned a lot, too,' his father says. 'We are very grateful for that. And we are very proud of Mathias.' " The format of the book is appealing, with generous margins and expressive photographs on every page; the text is clear, and the choice of present tense gives immediacy to the descriptions. This is a book to be recommended to parents and teachers of primary school children.

■ Brickner, Richard P. *My Second Twenty Years: An Unexpected Life.* Basic Books, 1976. 198pp. (0-465-04773-4) Reading Level: Grades 10–12. (BL 15 O76; LJ1 S76; NYTBR 12 S76.)
Disability: Quadriplegia

Richard Brickner is a writer and a teaching faculty member. He wrote this remarkable and compelling book at the age of 40 about his "second twenty years," so designating them because at the age of 20, he broke his neck in an automobile accident. He "lay for a while, precariously, on the furthest rim of existence" (page 3); then in essence he got on with his life.

In the mid 1950s, opportunities for those in wheelchairs were considerably more restricted than they are now; for example, access problems were not even a conscious public or private consideration then. Brickner, with dogged determination, went on to finish his education, work for a time for a New York publishing house, and finally become a writer and a teacher. In the book, he tells how he made a place for himself, both professionally and personally, in a basically inhospitable world. As he does so, he also draws on his life experiences prior to the accident, including his sexual relationships with women from his teens to the present, about which he is candid and open.

Analysis: As a writer, Brickner is both very serious and introspective and also very humorous. He is always very literate. Recommended for teens who are mature and capable of high-level reading.

■ Burns, Kay. *Our Mom.* Illus. Franklin Watts, 1989. 48pp. (0-531-10677-2) Reading Level: Grades K–4. (BCCB J189; BL 1 My89; SLJ Je89)
Disability: Paraplegia

The author has been a paraplegic since 1968 as the result of an accident. Her book, told in the group voice of her four children, explains in text and black-and-white photographs how she manages without assistance such daily routines as dressing, bathing, shopping, driving, and enjoying activities with her youngsters.

Analysis: Both words and photos succeed in portraying a woman with disabilities who leads a full, active life. The book would be stronger, however, if the text, straightforward and clear though it is, were not quite so pedestrian. Although a note about the author at the end gives information about the cause of Burns' paralysis, it appears in small type and is probably not intended for young readers, who, without explanation from an adult, might well wonder why Mom cannot use her legs. Furthermore, mention of the father/husband, also mentioned in this note, is totally absent from the body of the text. In sum, this is a book that can certainly be useful and informative but that falls short of being distinguished.

■ Callahan, John. *Don't Worry, He Won't Get Far on Foot.* Illus. by John Callahan. Vintage, 1990. 217pp. (0-569-72824-4) Reading Level: Grades 7–12. (PW 9 Mr90)
Disability: Quadriplegia; Alcoholism

Callahan quips, "Yes, quads wish they were paras, paras wish they were able-bodied, and the able-bodied wish they were Jane Fonda" (p. 72). He begins his story, "On the last day I walked" (p. 1)—a walk to the liquor store on a bright Los Angeles afternoon, in hopes of forestalling the pangs of withdrawal from his drunk the night before. He was redheaded, six-foot-three, and 21 years old. He had come to town from Oregon to find a job. He was ashamed as he sucked relief from the half pint of tequila, opened even before he reached his boarding house. He drank all day and continued into the evening at a party. He picked up a friend to go driving. The man mistook "a Con Edison pole for an exit, and had run into it at 90 miles per hour" (p. 21), severing Callahan's spine in the neck area.

Callahan recaps his life before the accident: He was born in 1951, an illegitimate Catholic baby. He was adopted by a loving religious couple who proceeded to have five biological children as well. During his adolescence, he began feeling like a guilty outcast because of the circumstances of his birth, because he eschewed sports, and because he loved the Russian literature that was inexplicably in the family library and that he read through insomniac nights. At his grandmother's wake, when he was 12 years old, he discovered gin. He drank until he passed out. He lived a life of carousing throughout high school and beyond. His outrageous pranks and pastimes masked the deep depression that coexisted with his humorous outlook on life.

Callahan's early recuperation from his accident took place in the intensive care unit of a public hospital. Here he was strapped, in traction, in a circle bed. Although sedated, he experienced pain, despair, and disbelief. After six weeks, he was transferred to Rancho Los Amigos, "one of the largest and most advanced rehabilitation centers in the world" (p. 67). There he had bone transplanted to reinforce his neck—the same procedure that his doctor had done for George Wallace. Interspersed throughout the book is a great deal of information about the rehabilitation of patients with spinal cord injury, including discussion of sensitive subjects such as the management of urination and of sexuality.

Even in the grueling rehab setting, his drinking and pranks continued. While sunning in only a towel, he got the urge to buy a six-pack at a

7-Eleven a half hour away by wheelchair. His towel caught in his chair wheel, stranding him in the middle of the road's grass lane divider. He waited ages stark naked until a passerby took pity on him.

After six months, he was discharged and began to live with the help of attendant care. He was finally persuaded by his family to move back to Oregon and did go back to school, but he also made friends and allies who abetted him in becoming hopelessly alcoholic. Then, after 14 years of dodging emotional stress by drinking, he felt the physical sensation of a hand patting him on the back. He began his recovery through the twelve steps of the Alcoholics Anonymous program.

At long last, Callahan was freed to develop his considerable talent for cartooning. He has since sold his work to major magazines and newspapers. Chapter 10 consists of ten tongue-in-cheek, copiously illustrated rules, headed "How to Relate to Handicapped People." It ends with a "far-out" test for the reader.

The last chapter describes in detail Callahan's typical day 16 years after his accident. After three hours of preparation, he is ready to explore the environs of downtown Portland, lunch with a girlfriend, and talk with his publisher. In the evening, he draws his world in iconoclastic cartoons, delighting in people's strong reactions, whether positive or negative. He writes, "My life certainly has a black side, but in other ways it's almost charmed. I always knew it would be. It's really satisfying in quite a wonderful way" (p. 217).

Analysis: The role of alcohol and drug abuse as a cause of and response to disability is often overlooked in the popular literature. This firsthand account is instructive and relays an important message. The author also gives a detailed and unvarnished picture of the hour-by-hour demands that the disability of quadriplegia imposes. Callahan's constant verbal clowning leavens this sobering information.

This book is irreverently and outrageously humorous. The jokes are at the expense of the medical establishment, the disability movement, religion, and the American Civil Liberties Union. The deceptively crude and ghoulish line drawings illustrate perfectly the black humor of the text. Street language is used to describe bodily functions and disabled people. At the same time, Callahan depicts poignantly the physical and psychological agonies and tragedies that he and his friends have endured. He is never hurtful or self-pitying. He comes across as a funny, honest, and deeply courageous man.

■ Carling, Finn. *And Yet We Are Human.* Trans. by C. Van O. Bruyn. Illus. Arno, 1980. 133pp. (0-405-13100-3) Reading Level: Grades 10–12. *Disability:* Cerebral palsy

This volume is part of the Arno Press collection The Physically Handicapped in Society. It also includes *Kierkegaard: The Cripple,* by Theodor Haecker, which is reviewed separately. Carling's autobiographical account was conceived in 1951 and published in 1962. He realized that in the course of his writing, he would have to come to final terms with the cerebral palsy that had prevented him from walking until he was 15 years old.

Carling was born in 1925, the last of three boys in a family residing in a rural setting outside Oslo, Norway. He had a pleasant childhood despite his severe disability and was educated in a small progressive school that followed the principles of Rudolph Steiner. It was not until he was a young man that he became aware that as a cripple he could be frightening and repugnant to others and that he must act the role and know his place.

In his teens, he worried about both earning a living and whether he could ever marry. At 20, he went to the University of Oslo. He yearned for "contact on equal grounds," and generally found it with his fellow students. He volunteered to talk to new students about the anatomy of the nervous system as a way to overcome his shyness and as a first step toward the talks and lectures on the psychology of disability that he would give later. He went on to become a professional writer of novels and plays and attributes this calling, in part, to his need to create a simpler, easier world than his actual one.

In a series of recollections and metaphors, he tells the story of his life. His reminiscences are often painful. The lessons learned usually relate to his relationship to others as a person who is different. When he first had sex with a young woman who found him attractive, he felt reborn and the "equal of men." At that time, his trembling lessened, his strength increased, and he felt that a miracle had occurred—"the miracle of breaking through the wall between me and life" (p. 114). He mentions his eventual marriage but no details of its circumstances.

In the last chapter, he tells of an old man from Iceland who had been told at age 12 that he had a disease that would totally cripple him. Desperate and afraid, he went out on the desolate heath, where he had a transforming experience he took to be a visitation from God. The boy's fear left him, and, in the end, he was not afflicted. Carling, however, has an absurdist view of life, rather than such a faith. He deeply believes that all share in the inexhaustible power of life that allows us to feel at one with ourselves and with all beings.

Analysis: This short book offers a series of very personal reflections on a life, rather than a conventional autobiography. Carling's prose is spare when he expresses his thoughts, but he evokes exquisitely the scenery of his native land in his various stories.

There is no indication that this work is a translation. American readers might object to the liberal use of the word "cripple," which we are inclined to find pejorative. But, since Carling is speaking of himself, the use is his prerogative.

■ Cole, Harry A., and Martha M. Jablow. *One in a Million.* Little, Brown, 1990. 27̂pp. (0-316-15117-3) Reading Level: Grades 10–12. (BL 15 F90) *Disability:* Cerebrovascular disease; Coma; Stroke

Jacqueline Cole was 43 years old in March 1986 when she suffered a massive stroke that flooded her brain with blood. The story of her illness, her 47-day coma, and her seemingly miraculous recovery is told by her husband, a Presbyterian minister with extensive experience in counseling.

The Coles were married in 1977; the couple had met when Harry Cole took a part-time job at the Maryland Department of Education, where Jackie worked. It was the first marriage for Harry and the third for Jacqueline, who already had four children whom she was raising alone and whom her new husband adopted. Though they loved each other, the marriage was not always serene; they were going through a particularly rough time in 1986.

Jacqueline was at home with her three younger children—two college students and one in high school—when struck by a violent headache. She realized that she was having a stroke, and one of the last things she said before losing consciousness was addressed to her daughter: "Oh, Christina, I don't want to live this way." For the next 47 days, she lay in a deep coma, in what is termed a persistent vegetative state. She had pneumonia, which required insertion of a drainage tube; her breathing was maintained by a respirator, she had a tracheostomy, and she was fed through a nasogastric tube. Once an active, vibrant, compelling woman, she had gone beyond the reach of all who loved her. Her medical prognosis was extremely poor and her principal physician put her chances of waking up as "probably on the order of one in a hundred thousand or one in a million."

As the weeks dragged on, Jacqueline's husband, children, and sister began to feel that the merciful course would be to disconnect her from the life support systems. A thoughtful and deeply religious man, Harry Cole felt that by releasing his wife, by letting her go, he would enable her to go home to God. Jacqueline had watched her own mother drag through a debilitating illness before her death and had said on many occasions that she herself would not want to be kept alive as a vegetable; her exclamation to her daughter on the morning of her stroke reinforced those previous statements. After much soul-searching and with the full support of the family, Harry Cole sought permission from a judge to remove the respirator tube; to their surprise, the judge refused. A few days later, Harry Cole was making arrangements to move his wife from Maryland General Hospital to a nursing home. While he and an old friend were standing at Jackie's bedside, she opened her eyes, looked at her husband, and smiled. It was an astounding return, completely unexpected by all the medical personnel.

Over the following months, Jacqueline Cole made a slow recovery. Once the hospital had done for her everything that was possible with its facilities and staff, she was moved to a rehabilitation hospital; after she went home, she continued to go to a day program. Gradually, she recovered most of her physical mobility; restoring her short-term memory was more difficult, and she also experienced some disorientation. At first, the relationship between husband and wife was more like that between parent and child, with Jacqueline dependent on Harry for nearly everything. They have moved toward a more equal relationship, although she still is not able to drive. She has not gone back to her old job, but has done volunteer work and at the time of the writing of this book was working two days a week in the day care center at Harry Cole's church.

Analysis: This is a long book, with a detailed discussion of the medical ethics and religious philosophy involved in the questions raised by a case such as Jacqueline Cole's. In the last chapter, Harry Cole offers guidelines for others confronted by the same dilemma as the one he faced. It is a dilemma that has become much more commonplace in recent years, as medical technology advances so as to permit the survival of patients who would previously have died soon after the episode that caused their coma. The account of Jackie's illness takes up about two thirds of the book and becomes rather tedious at times; the section on her rehabilitation is less detailed. Nevertheless, there are gripping moments, particularly the description of Jackie's awakening. This is thus a book for able high school readers and especially for those interested in the ethical as well as the medical aspects of the case.

■ Corbet, Barry. *Options: Spinal Cord Injuries and the Future.* 5th ed. Illus. Hirschfeld, 1986. 151pp. Reading Level: Grades 10–12.
Disability: Quadriplegia; Paraplegia

Barry Corbet, a young, athletic filmmaker, sustained a spinal cord injury in a helicopter crash in 1968. He describes himself as a model patient, cooperative and cheerful. The same day that he left the hospital, he undertook a solo shopping expedition driving his new, hand-controlled car. He returned to work the same week, "fully rehabilitated. . . . A sixty-day wonder. Everybody loves a winner." However, Corbet goes on to admit that despite the fact that people admire the way he has responded to his injury and are sure that he has all the answers, "I never did know what was going on, never did have the answers. . . . What characterizes those years is not happiness or unhappiness but change" (p. 3).

The title of the book, *Options,* signifies the author's belief that no matter how limited people in wheelchairs may at first feel their lives are, they do have a large number of choices to exercise in the process of living a full and active life.

Analysis: Corbet is interviewer, narrator, compiler, and, with others, photographer for this outstanding book. He weaves together the stories of the lives of 56 individuals with spinal cord injuries with whom he has spoken extensively. His focus is on their everyday lives, especially on how they feel about themselves and how they have learned to deal with the changes that their injuries have brought to their life. Interspersed among the essays are brief sections containing outstanding quotations from the interviews and describing matters of interest in the life of people in wheelchairs. The tone of most of the book is upbeat yet realistic. The realities of depression and suicide are considered, as are those concerning marriage and childbirth.

■ Cross, Helen Reeder. **The Real Tom Thumb.** Illus. by Stephen Gammel. Four Winds, 1980. 92pp. (0-590-07606-X) Reading Level: Grades 4–6. (BCCB Mr81; BL 1 F81; SLJ S81)
Disability: Short stature

Cross tells the life story of Charles Sherwood Stratton, born in Connecticut in 1838, who became famous (and rich) as Tom Thumb, the protégé of Phineas Taylor Barnum.

Like many people of short stature, Charles Stratton was an average-sized baby but failed to experience normal growth; at 4, when Barnum met him, he looked like a 2-year-old. The showman recognized the potential of the bright, engaging child as a drawing card for his American Museum and took him on as a performer and exhibit. They did phenomenally well, toured Europe as well as the United States, and even met Queen Victoria. The boy grew so little and so slowly that at 19 he weighted 29 pounds and was 30 inches tall. Barnum introduced Tom Thumb to Lavinia Bump, also a person of short stature, and gave them an elegant, elaborate wedding. Tom alternated periods of retirement with returns to the stage. At one point, he and Vinnie toured the world with Lavinia's sister, also a midget, and another small person called Commodore Nutt. Tom Thumb died in 1883, at the age of 45.

A note from the author at the end of the book discusses her sources and tells the reader about the Barnum Museum, in Tom Thumb's birthplace (Bridgeport, Connecticut), and Grace Church, in New York, where Tom Thumb and Lavinia were married.

Analysis: Stories of small people attract us both in folktales and in real life (for example, many cultures have traditional tales of tiny characters who may delight in mischief and do brave deeds). The author presents Charles Stratton as a thoroughly attractive person, much loved by his family, who, in large part because of his association with Barnum, surmounted the disabilities of his situation and turned them quite literally into gold. Barnum too is seen as an essentially good-hearted person who used his "bit of hokum," as he called it, judiciously to enhance his presentations and bring people entertainment they could enjoy.

The author has elected to use invented dialogue, which may bother some adult readers but will probably not deter youngsters. For the most part, this conversation is believable. Each chapter is headed with a full-page pencil drawing by Stephen Gammel, showing Stratton from childhood to middle age. There are also reproductions of contemporary prints and photographs.

The Real Tom Thumb could be recommended to youngsters who like biography, to those who are intrigued by details of Stratton's life as Tom Thumb, and to children who are themselves of short stature or who may know such people. The author does not speculate as to the causes of Stratton's failure to grow normally, which in any case would probably not have been known in the mid-nineteenth century. Parents and teachers could help young readers find answers in other sources and might recommend such titles as Susan Kuklin's *Thinking Big.*

■ Daly, Ida, and Hazel Flagler Begeman. *Adventure in a Wheelchair: Pioneering for the Handicapped.* Illus. Whitmore, 1973. 79pp. (0-87426-031-0) Reading Level: Grades 10–12.
Disability: Muscular dystrophy

In a foreword, the coauthor, who is Daly's sister, recaps the many accomplishments of her younger sibling. The book is written in the first person. Daly was one of six children born to a homesteading family in 1901. When she was 4 years old, she began to lose strength through a puzzling illness that was diagnosed many years later as progressive muscular dystrophy. Nevertheless, she led a relatively normal and happy life until she was 14, after which she could no longer climb the stairs of her school to class. Because of such architectural barriers, it took her 12 years to complete high school.

Finally enrolled in college, Daly pursued her hobby, painting, that she had enjoyed for years. She used both hands and a free-arm movement powered by muscles in her shoulder and back to produce the floral designs and landscapes bought by many friends. One painting was awarded first prize at the Western Washington State Fair Exhibit. The Great Depression forced Daly to leave college, but she became manager of a four-unit apartment house she would later purchase near the University of Washington in Seattle. At this time she began to use a wheelchair, receiving help with daily living from a tenant in exchange for reduced rent. She continued to attend art classes and to paint, often finding subjects right outside her window.

In 1944, she met a pharmacist, Frank Daly, who became a friend and then her husband for 14 years until his death. Her art activities came to a close as her muscles progressively deteriorated, but she and her husband then traveled widely with adaptations he devised to make her safe and comfortable in their car. They eventually covered 9,500 miles across eight states and Mexico.

Daly became a crusader for organizations of handicapped people, which they themselves managed. She helped establish the Seattle Handicapped Center, an arts and crafts and recreational facility. One of her projects, the Center Park Apartments for the Handicapped, became a reality in 1969. The first of its kind in the country, it offered disabled people a place to live independently without architectural barriers. She took in a "residential janitor" after her beloved husband died.

Daly went to Europe under the People-to-People Program inaugurated by President Eisenhower. She came back by way of Washington, D.C., whose inaccessibility motivated her to lobby against barriers. Her increasing inability to dial the telephone led to a new instrument devised by engineers from the phone company, which served her for 15 years. She edited a club paper, typing first by mouth, then with her "flippers," a ball-bearing arm-support device attached to her wheelchair.

In her 70s, with many awards to her credit, Daly became director and resident in the newly built Seattle Handicapped Center. A last chapter tells how she has countered depression in her life—chiefly by not thinking about herself but by concentrating on the needs of others.

Analysis: Daly's joie de vivre is infectious and puts to shame those of us who take for granted such pleasures as observing scenery from a car or dialing a friend on the telephone. Interspersed in the chapters are a number of black-and-white photographs showing her as a pretty, cheerful person engaging in activities in the various stages of her life.

This book puts the disability movement in historical perspective. Much current thinking was either in its infancy or nonexistent when Daly first began struggling with her physical problems. Some terms and practices she mentions are by now outmoded or controversial, for example, calling people "the handicapped," or segregating disabled people in separate housing. However, Daly emerges as an important and courageous contributor to the betterment of disabled persons in this very readable account.

■ Davidson, Donald, and Jesse Outlar. **Caught Short.** Illus. Atheneum, 1972. 177pp. (o.p.) Reading Level: Grades 10–12. (KR 15 My72; LJ Jl72; PW 26 Je72)
Disability: Short stature

At the time he wrote this book, Donald Davidson, then 47 years old, had worked for the Braves—the National League baseball team—for 36 years in three different cities: Boston, Milwaukee, and Atlanta. He started as a batboy and ultimately became assistant to the president of the organization.

Davidson begins his story at the 1971 New York Baseball Writers' Dinner, where he was receiving a prestigious award. He then relates the story of his childhood and his 35 years in baseball, during which he came into close contact with all the greats of that era. Davidson had sleeping sickness at the age of 6. At that time he was exactly 4 feet tall. He never grew another inch. He talks candidly about his height, of which Ted Williams, in the introduction, says, "Don Davidson has turned what to some might be a physical impairment into a powerful part of his immense personality. He may be small in stature, but his character, reputation, and abilities are all enormous" (pp. xi–xii).

Analysis: The book is more about baseball than about Davidson's disability, though he deals with it as situations occur. Anyone interested in baseball or in the history of the sport would enjoy reading it for these aspects alone. In addition, Davidson's story is a wonderful example of how a person with a disability is just that, a person first, who happens to have an impairment or disability as one aspect of her or his life. Recommended for high school age readers and for baseball fans of any age.

■ deMille, Agnes. **Reprieve: A Memoir.** Foreword and Notes by Fred Plum, M.D. Illus. Doubleday, 1981. 288pp. (0-385-15721-5) Reading Level: Grades 10–12. (NYTBR 27 S81; PW 7 Ag81)
Disability: Stroke; Hemiplegia; Heart attack

Agnes deMille has written ten books related to her long career as a ballet dancer and foremost American choreographer. In 1975, when she was 66 years old, she suffered a massive cerebral hemorrhage that initially left her blinded and speechless, as well as permanently paralyzed on her right side.

This terrible event occurred one hour before the opening performance at her cherished Heritage Dance Theater, for which she was to have been the narrator.

Part one of her book chronicles a patient's-eye view of her first long hospitalization, through which she remained precariously close to death. Interspersed throughout the entire narrative are brief notes from a medical perspective written by her neurologist in order to clarify the physical problems and the procedures that were necessitated by her condition. Finally, although not even half well, she was sent home to the care of her ever-solicitous and patient husband. She later experienced a serious heart attack.

Part two is the story of deMille's "rebirth" as she began painfully to relearn the activities of daily living. She writes, "Many people have said, 'How difficult for you. How much more difficult than for anyone else: How cruel because you are a dancer.' This, of course, is nonsense. The experience is difficult. It is final and it's lasting. But it's easier precisely because I was a dancer. I have submitted to physical discipline the whole of my life. I have learned to obey" (p. 86). Independently negotiating a trip to the bathroom proved as big a challenge to her as her dancing triumphs had been. Perhaps her most important attainment was a new peace of mind that came with a regained appreciation of the minutiae of life that she had experienced as a child. In addition, during the crisis of her illness, her son and husband, long estranged, achieved a loving reconciliation. And yet, she felt herself grow suddenly old on her son's wedding day, when she was unable to dance with him. The story ends with the successful execution of the long-delayed dance performance, complete with her narration. As she took her bow, deMille was able, for the first time since her stroke, to raise her right hand as she acknowledged the thundering applause.

Analysis: This witty, sensitive book portrays a woman who seems ageless rather than old. Her practical admonitions to disabled people and to those who interact with them have relevance beyond any particular impairment. Her simple depiction of what it is like to be paralyzed and dependent is powerful, showing unflinching honesty without a trace of self-pity. The description of the course of her physical and psychological rehabilitation reflects her skill as a choreographer and teacher. DeMille's philosophy of life, to do the very best you can, is inspiringly illustrated in this lovely memoir.

■ Drimmer, Frederick. *The Elephant Man.* Illus. Putnam, 1985. 143pp. (0-399-21262-0) Reading Level: Grades 7–12. (BL 15 Ja86; BCCB D85; SLJ F86)
Disability: Neurofibromatosis

Drimmer has written what he calls a fictionalized biography of the life of Joseph Merrick, made famous as "the elephant man." Merrick was befriended and treated by the young English surgeon Frederick Treves, who discovered him in a freak show. Treves wrote about his patient in his reminiscences; other accounts include *The True History of the Elephant Man,* by Dr. Michael Howell and Peter Ford, Ashley Montagu's *The Elephant Man: A Study in Human Dignity,* and Bernard Pomerance's play, also called *The Elephant Man.*

Merrick, who was born in Leicester in 1862, suffered from an extreme case of neurofibromatosis, a genetic disease for which there is still no cure. His mother believed that his condition was caused by her having been terribly frightened by an elephant during her pregnancy, a belief held at that time both by medical people and by the general public. The first symptoms of the disease appeared before the child was 2, with a swelling in his mouth; other increasingly disabling deformities followed. Only one arm and hand escaped; the rest of his body was grotesquely enlarged and distorted by growths on the bones and skin.

Merrick's mother died while he was still a child, and his boyhood and youth were marked by suffering and deprivation. While he was still relatively mobile, he worked in a cigar factory and peddled goods from door to door. He also spent time in the workhouse. His situation improved when he was taken up by sideshow operators, but some time after Treves' first meeting with him, he was abandoned by his manager in Brussels; he found his way back to London and collapsed in the railroad station with Treves' card in his hand. The surgeon had him taken to London Hospital for treatment; arrangements were eventually made for him to live in a private basement apartment in the hospital.

Treves remained his physician and his friend. Merrick's fame spread, and he attracted patrons and visitors, including the actress Madge Kendal and the Prince and Princess of Wales. Merrick died in 1890, probably of suffocation caused when he fell asleep in a prone position rather than with his heavy head propped up. His skeleton, casts of his head and limbs, and the cap and mask he wore to hide his face can all be seen at London Hospital Medical College.

Drimmer includes black-and-white photographs, an afterword discussing both Merrick and his disease, and a selected bibliography.

Analysis: Drimmer tells Joseph Merrick's story with skill and sympathy, acknowledging that he has added incidents, details, and dialogue to the recorded facts. The result is a readable book, well suited to junior and senior high school readers. In life, Merrick's sweet nature, dignity, and intelligence were able to penetrate the horrifyingly distorted body that imprisoned him; even his speech was impeded, and only his eyes could convey expression, but once those who met him overcame their initial reaction, they were attracted to him as Treves had been. Similarly, the reader comes to know Merrick as a person, beyond his freakish physical condition.

■ English, Jennifer. *My Mommy's Special.* Illus. Regensteiner, 1985. 32pp. (0-51-60386-13) Reading Level: Grades K–4. (SLJ Mr86)
Disability: Multiple sclerosis

Jennifer English wrote this book when she was about 7 years old, apparently after a teacher had her class write stories and make books. Jennifer's mother has multiple sclerosis and uses a wheelchair. Black-and-white photographs and text describe their days together, going back to the time when Jennifer was a toddler. They are a team, Jennifer writes, and enjoy working together, doing the grocery shopping, reading, and playing. When Jennifer started school, she worried about her mother and thought, "Who will play with her?" but a friend keeps her company. "Now you see that my mommy is just like your mommy, except that she has to sit in that chair. The next time you see somebody sitting in a wheelchair, you can think of my mommy and me, and remember that they are not so different after all. If they are like my mommy, they are very special."

Analysis: Jennifer appears to be a very attractive and engaging little girl, and her mother too is very photogenic (she was once crowned Miss Wheelchair Virginia). The book emphasizes ways in which the mother functions as an active, involved person and especially as a parent, as well as the close cooperative relationship between the two. Multiple sclerosis is not mentioned until an afterword gives details about Jennifer's birth date, hobbies, etc.; young readers are almost certain to wonder about this early on, so the information might have been better placed. Although Jennifer also lives with her stepfather, he does not appear in these pages, so that mother and daughter seem to be managing everything alone.

Children who are interested in this subject might want to look at *Our Mom,* by Kay Burns, and compare the two. They might also want to talk about whether Jennifer wrote this book on her own or whether she had help.

■ Feinberg, Barbara Silberdick. *Franklin D. Roosevelt: Gallant President.* Illus. Lothrop, Lee & Shepard, 1981. 94pp. (0-688-00434-2) Reading Level: Grades 4–6. (BL 15 Je81; KR 1 Je81; SLJ D81)
Disability: Poliomyelitis

This is a brief, readable biography of Franklin Roosevelt, covering his entire life from birth to death. It is heavily illustrated with interesting, well-selected black-and-white photographs.

Approximately six pages treat the onset of polio, the way Roosevelt dealt with it, and the way he returned to politics as soon as possible. There are a very realistic drawing of the iron braces that he wore "to stand and take a few steps by himself" (p. 41), a picture of him bathing at Warm Springs with others who have polio (p. 43), and, later in the book, a picture of him in a wheelchair (page 87). The treatment of his disability in these pages is factual, straightforward, and unsentimental.

Analysis: There are two limitations to the work. The seriousness of polio as a life-threatening illness is not explained. Children will see it as something that took away the use of Roosevelt's legs, but they will not learn anything about the disease beyond this. Since this generation of young readers is unlikely to know much about polio, a few pages of explanation about its physical and social consequences during the years that it was rampant would have been helpful. In addition, the effect of polio on FDR's life is never mentioned—except for the picture of him in a wheelchair—outside the six pages in which his illness and recovery are narrated. Some integration of the results of the lasting effects of the illness, rather than treating it as an isolated episode, would have also been helpful. The picture of Roosevelt in a wheelchair accomplishes this aim toward the end of the book, of course, but some integration of the disability into other parts of the text would have added to the quality of the book as a treatment of disability. However, it is still an excellent book and highly recommended for young readers.

■ Fishman, Steve. *A Bomb in the Brain: A Heroic Tale of Science, Surgery and Survival.* Macmillan, 1988. 318 pp. (0-684-18706-X) Reading Level: Grades 10–12. (LJ 1 N88; NYTBR 27 N88)
Disability: Epilepsy; Seizures

Twenty-cight-year-old Fishman was a journalist, covering the events in Nicaragua during the war. Very suddenly, he experienced the onset of terrible pain and a vision impairment that signaled a brain hemorrhage. However, this correct diagnosis was achieved only when he went back to New York University Medical Center and after a computerized axial tomography scan of his brain by a neuroradiologist. By his third night back in the United States, he learned from a neurologist that he must undergo brain surgery to prevent another attack.

As the events unfold, the author describes in journal form his innermost feelings at the time. He also recaps the evolution of diagnosis and treatment of his brain pathology in the course of the narrative. The reader is introduced to the talented and eccentric medical personnel who cared for Fishman and his fellow patients. The account is written in the present tense giving a sense of immediacy to each stage of the ordeal. However, the author had the benefit of hindsight, because he spent the year after his convalescence reading about neurosurgery, interviewing hospital personnel, and observing the workings of the operating room.

Although Fishman had the support of loving parents and his long-term girlfriend, he felt fearful and alone. He likened the role of the dependent, helpless patients in a modern hospital to that of prisoners.

Surgeons were successful in removing the congenital malformation in the brain that had caused his original hemorrhage, and he gradually recovered his vision. He was prescribed phenytoin (Dilantin), an anticonvulsant medication, as a precaution for a year after his surgery. Gradually the dose was reduced, and he felt that he could finally put the whole episode behind him. At that point he experienced his first seizure. The abnormal firing of brain cells that signal an attack seems to have been the result of surgical scarring in the region of his operation. He was told he could anticipate treating this symptom for the rest of his life.

Although Fishman was actually to have only five or six seizures a year, he was emotionally distraught at becoming one of the 2.5 million people in the United States who have epilepsy. His illness seemed to become an obsession, and he could not seem to get on with his life. His relationship with the young woman who had seen him through his crisis ended. He still lived in the same small, unrefurbished apartment he had before his illness. He interviewed some cohorts from his hospital unit and found that they, too, were having problems in their personal lives.

On the positive side, Fishman worked on this book. Further, he joined a support group for people with epilepsy that was most helpful. He did find employment and was beginning to date again. In the end, his attitude was hopeful.

Analysis: This book gives an exciting and graphic look at a field on the forefront of modern medicine. The narrative moves skillfully back and forth from the subjective view of the patient to the professional perspective. Fishman can be commended for his honesty in relating events, even when they are not flattering to himself or others. He is not heroic, and he does not seem to have been improved by adversity. He appeared developmentally to be a late adolescent before and after his ordeal. Many of the people with disabilities described in the volume are extraordinary—Fishman comes across as a common man beset by an uncommon problem. It is easy to relate to him and to sympathize with him.

■ Freedman, Russell. *Franklin Delano Roosevelt.* Illus. Clarion, 1990. 200pp. (0-89919-379-X) Reading Level: Grades 7–12. (BL 15 O90; PW 4 Ja90; SLJ D90)
Disability: Poliomyelitis

Russell Freedman is the author of many books for young people, including *Lincoln: A Photobiography,* which was awarded the prestigious Newbery Medal in 1988. Here he tells the story of the life of Franklin Delano Roosevelt, who, born to wealth and privilege and raised as a cherished only child, became the president who promoted social legislation that has had a profound effect on American society. In 1921, at the age of 39, Roosevelt came down with poliomyelitis while the family was vacationing at Campobello Island in Canada. The illness affected his legs, and despite persistent efforts to regain their use through exercise, Roosevelt was never able to walk without braces and assistance from a crutch, a cane, or a strong arm.

Freedman describes the reactions of Roosevelt's family and friends to his illness and subsequent disability; his mother wanted him to retire from political life. His wife, Eleanor—who up until this time had often been dominated by her mother-in-law—urged him to return to his active political career. This was the course he followed. He refused to spend time in self-pity or vain regrets and went on to become governor of New York in 1929 and president of the United States in 1932. When he found that swimming was helpful, he visited Warm Springs, Georgia, bought the resort, and turned it into a center for study and treatment of polio.

Freedman writes that Roosevelt "was such a dynamic president that people forgot he could not stand up without help. Sitting at his desk, he gave the appearance of great physical strength. Through constant exercise, he developed massive shoulders, muscular arms, and a powerful chest. Jack Dempsey, the boxing champion, said that FDR had the "most impressive shoulder muscles he had ever seen" (p. 2). He was almost never pictured with a cane, crutch, or wheelchair; his big, handsome head, famous flashing smile, and charismatic personality, combined with his vigorous leadership and the many innovations and accomplishment of his political life, all presented him as a man of action—far from the invalid country squire his mother may have imagined. His death in 1945, just before the end of the European phase of World War II, wrenched the whole world.

Freedman has illustrated his text with many black-and-white photographs. At the end of the book, the reader will find a short section called "Places to Visit," a collection of more photos, an annotated bibliography, and an index.

Analysis: Roosevelt's life remains fascinating no matter how often the story is told. Freedman has done an excellent job of presenting FDR as a person, husband, father, politician, and leader, but he does not attempt to make him a saint. He includes discussion of Roosevelt's affair with Lucy Mercer and its effect on Eleanor and on their marriage; he describes the attempt to pack the Supreme Court; he discusses briefly the criticism that Roosevelt did not do all he could have done to rescue Jews and others persecuted by the Nazis. Occasionally, the author's choice of words seems out of keeping with current sensitivity when writing about people with disabilities—for example, using the terms "afflicted" and "crippled." Nevertheless, young readers will find much information, well written and attractively presented, and teachers and parents may find themselves reminded of the many far-reaching accomplishments of this man whom Frances Perkins, his secretary of labor (and the first woman to be given a Cabinet post) described as "a great man—not merely a President, but a man who . . . will be loved as a symbol of hope and social justice long after his generation and his works have passed away" (p. 5).

■ Friedman, Marcia. *The Story of Josh.* Praeger, 1974. 281pp. (0-275-19960-6) Reading Level: Grades 10–12. (KR 1 Ag74; LV 1 N74; PW 9 S74)
Disability: Brain tumors

This story was written by Josh's mother at his request, liberally interspersed with transcriptions of tapes that he made in the last year of his life.

Josh was born in 1951 and had a relatively uneventful upper-middle-class life with his parents, who were real estate brokers, and his younger brother. When he was about 8 years old, he had dizzy spells, and at 16, a convulsive seizure. He began taking phenytoin and had few seizures after that. At 20, when he was at college, he had tremors and vision problems, which proved to be caused by a tumor in the left hemisphere of the brain. A brain operation was scheduled, and Josh's prognosis seemed hopeful. Unfortunately, the 12-hour operation uncovered a malignant growth, too extensive to be completely excised. The surgeon cried when he told the parents the news.

The main part of the book is an account of the year of Josh's dying. He had a relapse and new surgery as well as cobalt treatments before the long, partial recuperation could begin. The operations had left Josh with residual brain damage causing specific communication problems; for example, he retained the ability to write but had lost the ability to read. The young man went from a brief and desperate attempt at suicide to a deepening appreciation of living as fully as possible each day that remained to him. After his treatments, a deterioration is noticeable in his language, but his meaning comes through in teenage vernacular. His subjective description of aphasia and the dilemmas occasioned by his selective brain damage give his condition a reality that would be hard to achieve otherwise.

Life gradually slipped away. Josh's loss of mental ability and stamina resulted in loss of companionship. His days were a holding action of personal chores, reading lessons, and family activities before the inevitable, painful demise. Josh died in his 22nd year after a 13-month illness.

Analysis: The author intersperses quotes, such as the following, to reflect her philosophy: "As a drop of water in the sea, as a grain of sand on the shore, are man's few days in eternity. The good things in life last for limited days" (Apocryphe, Ben Sira 18:10, 41:13). Josh's tapes have the quality of stream of consciousness. They are colloquial and ring true as the thoughts of a suffering young person. They contrast well with the more formal language of his mother and her more intellectualized perception of the events and more idealized view.

Friedman provides deep insights by both example and analysis into the challenge for parents, siblings, friends, and dying patients themselves as abilities wane, options become fewer, and financial resources and energy are drained. She is honest about her mistakes and ambivalences, but her intelligence, patience, and love of her family prevail. This is a totally believable book, which may be enlightening to some and offer validation to others who have endured similar experiences.

■ Gaffney, Timothy. *Jerrold Petrofsky: Biomedical Pioneer.* Illus. Childrens Pr., 1984. 111pp. (0-516-03201-1) Reading Level: Grades 7–9. (BL 15 S84; SLJ O84)
Disability: Spinal cord injury

Jerrold Petrofsky is executive director of the National Center for Rehabilitation Engineering at Wright State University in Dayton, Ohio, as well as a professor of biomedical engineering. The story begins with an experiment with Nan Davis, a girl with paraplegia. Electrical stimulation of her muscles enabled her to walk "six impossible steps on paralyzed legs" (p. 12).

The next chapter traces Petrofsky's years as a precocious child who was always interested in applied science. In 1969, by then in college, he was introduced to the nascent computer age when he took on the job of repairing one of the first microcomputers. At the same time, he began to study physiology, and eventually his two interests merged. His work continued in collaboration with a colleague who was both a physician and an engineer. The research on spinal cord injury was initially carried out on animals. The first human subject was a youth who had become quadriplegic in a swimming accident six years before.

The story switches to Nan Davis's life as a young athlete and runner on her high school team. The night of her high school graduation, her boyfriend ran his car over an embankment, resulting in Nan's broken neck and back. Nan began taking college courses at Wayne State, which is totally accessible for wheelchairs. She became an enthusiastic volunteer in the biomedical engineering laboratory. First she was wired to a bicycle so that her legs could exercise and their strength be restored. Such "active physical therapy" (p. 61) tended to improve the general health of people with cord injuries. Nan Davis also propelled a wired tricycle, the "Zap Mobile." Finally, with much national and international fanfare, she took her first steps. Later she walked at her college graduation. A quadriplegic young woman followed her example, and both young women experimented with voluntary control of microcomputer systems.

In 1982, a commercial company, Therapeutic Technologies, Inc., was formed to make and sell Petrofsky's devices. He continues to develop and refine his inventions.

The book closes with thumbnail biographies of the book's most prominent characters, a chronology, and an index.

Analysis: Scientific explanations are presented clearly and simply as needed to advance the story. A simple experiment for the reader is suggested at one point. The descriptions of Petrofsky's many interests and hobbies, past and present, serve to make him an appealing figure for young people. His disabled volunteers come alive in the text and in full-page black-and-white photographs. The book captures well the excitement of the interaction between these college students and biomedical engineers.

■ Gallagher, Hugh Gregory. *FDR's Splendid Deception.* Illus. Dodd, 1985. 350pp. (0-395-08521-0) Reading Level: Grades 10–12. (BL 15 Ap85; KR 1 Ap85; SLJ S85)
Disability: Poliomyelitis; Paraplegia

As he explains in the preface, the author, like Franklin Delano Roosevelt, contracted polio as an adult; paraplegic like the former president, he used a wheelchair ever after. Most biographers of the famous, four-times elected president have treated his illness as one episode, rather than as an ongoing influence that permeated his entire life. This biography, in contrast, examined FDR through the prism of disability and focuses, perhaps as a first, on his enormous accomplishments in the disability community.

At 39, FDR, with a family of five children, was leading the happy patrician life to which he had been born. In late summer in 1921, he was suddenly struck by polio. For seven years after, he doggedly underwent a rehabilitation process that, in the end, resulted in his ability to stand for short periods of time and to walk haltingly with braces when steadied by a strong helper.

In the course of his rehabilitation, he tried the springs at a fading resort in Warm Springs, Georgia. He decided to buy the property to develop a treatment center for the many postpolio patients who desperately needed attention beyond the merely medical and set up a foundation that in part financed his ambitious undertaking. He evolved, from his own personal experience, many of the revolutionary principles of therapy and rehabilitation that are still espoused today. His efforts culminated in sponsorship of research for a vaccine that finally eradicated polio in the United States.

Meanwhile, with great support from his wife, Eleanor, and his Democratic Party associates, FDR managed to prevent the derailing of a promising political career. This effort included considerable subterfuge to hide his massive infirmity from the public. The book covers political campaigns and conventions, and it climaxes with FDR's three years and four months as commander in chief in the conduct of World War II. All of the diplomatic and political events are examined with an eye to the management and concealment of the president's disability. The book includes anecdotes and quotations from many people who were part of the drama. Historic photographs are interspersed as well.

The charismatic Roosevelt dominated everyday life in his freewheeling circle of family and friends. He is described as a paradoxical personality, at once deeply isolated and lonely and yet surrounded by adoring men and women from whom he demanded absolute fealty. The observation by Supreme Court Justice Oliver Wendell Holmes about FDR is amply illustrated: a "second rate intellect, first rate temperament (p. 167)."

Many references and an extensive bibliography are included.

Analysis: Gallagher, who has published several other books, worked 30 years on this study. Despite his scholarly research, his prose is not pedantic and is therefore most readable. It is surely encouraging to the disability movement that the "splendid deception" has been unmasked. Further, as the author notes, FDR seems a far more admirable person as we become familiar with the full extent of his suffering and struggles.

Some of the speculations may miss the mark, as, for example, in the case of FDR's early affair with Lucy Mercer. This had resulted in a threat of divorce from Eleanor and ultimately culminated with his agreeing, in 1918, to give up Mercer and forgo all claims to conjugal privileges. Yet Gallagher unconvincingly argues that this relationship was not sexual, albeit deeply loving and abiding. When he extrapolates in terms of the many effects of paraplegia, he seems on firmer ground. He makes a strong case for the view that FDR suffered severe depression and postpolio syndrome during the last months of his life.

■ Gino, Carol. *Rusty's Story.* Bantam, 1985. 342pp. (0-553-25351-1)
Reading Level: Grades 10–12. (LJ Ja86; PW 29 N85; SLJ O86)
Disability: Epilepsy

Carol Gino is a nurse. At the time she met Rusty, Carol was the divorced
mother of two young children and had just started a new job at a nursing
home. Rusty was a teenager who worked at the nursing home as an aide.
She had a uniquely caring and compassionate way of dealing with the
elderly or terminally ill patients that immediately caught Carol's attention.
The two became close friends, and Rusty eventually moved in with Carol
and her children.

Rusty had a form of epilepsy that was both severe and hard to diagnose
and treat. Some years earlier, she had also been declared mentally ill and
confined to an institution where she was treated in an abysmal manner.
She had been seizure free for some time, but eventually seizures of increasing intensity began again and along with them signs of mental illness that
ultimately, after a long, tortuous series of emergencies, hospitalizations,
tests, and near-death experiences, proved to be caused by the medication
she was taking to control the seizures.

Gino, who is a professional writer as well as a nurse, tells Rusty's story
in a compassionate, detailed narrative that reads like a novel. Her insights
into the psychological trauma that both she and Rusty endured during this
time are both keen and thoughtful. She reflects deeply on the motivation
and behavior of medical and mental health professionals, including her
own. Eventually the two women resumed reasonably uneventful lives after
Rusty's seizures stabilized. Carol remarried, and Rusty left the family but
lived nearby.

Analysis: Highly recommended for its good writing, interesting story,
and insights into human behavior, this book is also recommended for its
portrayal of strong, independent women and its view of the world beyond
the stereotypical nuclear family.

■ Goldman, Raymond Leslie. *Even the Night.* Macmillan, 1947. 196 pp.
(o.p.) Reading Level: Grades 7–12. (BL N47; LJ A47)
Disability: Poliomyelitis; Deafness; Diabetes

Professional author Raymond Goldman's earliest recollections dated
from 1899, when at 4 years of age, he was stricken with the poliomyelitis
that would paralyze his legs for life. When he was nearly 6, he regained his
ability to crawl, and the act of will, joy, and power he experienced at that
moment became a metaphor for facing the many extraordinary challenges
and setbacks that life would offer him. He eventually mastered walking on
his "broomstick legs" and became a good swimmer and boxer by develop-

ing the upper half of his body. In adolescence, he began a descent into deafness, due to hereditary osteomyelitis. In his 30s, his beautiful young wife of two years died of cancer, leaving him with a small child. At that time he developed severe diabetes.

Throughout the account of his personal suffering, Goldman also describes his warm family, his continuing education for his writing career, and his adventures with many and diverse friends. Always he seeks to develop a philosophy of life and a religion to give meaning to the joys, sorrows, and struggles he encounters.

His writing has included screenplays for Hollywood movies, some mystery stories, and a certain number of works directed toward inspiring others who have faced difficult problems.

As a result of his physical differences, as well as being Jewish in a primarily gentile world, he ultimately felt completely unfettered by any group allegiances. As the book ends, he is celebrating his 50th birthday with his new wife, little son, and loving family.

Analysis: This is an old book, with historical import for those interested in the popular literary scene of the 1930s. The direct, honest, and often humorous writing seems fresh and relevant even today. Goldman's love of life and of people keep the book upbeat, even when he describes really painful situations. His humility and sense of humor save the book from being preachy.

■ Goshen-Gottstein, Esther. ***Recalled to Life: The Story of a Coma.*** Yale Univ. Pr., 1990. 208 pp. (0-300-04473-9) Reading Level: Grades 10–12. (BL A90)
Disability: Coma

Esther Goshen-Gottstein is a clinical psychologist with a practice in psychotherapy; she was born in Germany, grew up in England, and lives in Israel. Her husband, Moshe Goshen-Gottstein, also German born, is an Israeli scholar of philology and linguistics. In June 1985 he had triple bypass surgery at Hadassah Hospital in Jerusalem to correct a condition caused by dangerously narrowed coronary arteries; at the time, he was overweight, had diabetes and high blood pressure, and had experienced angina pectoris. Complications probably caused by a mitral valve leak required that he go back on the heart-lung machine twice while still in the operating room; he probably also had an undetected heart attack during the surgery. Forty-eight hours after the surgery, he was still unconscious. Then, on the third day, he had to have another operation, because a large blood clot had formed in his chest. Following this operation, his coma deepened and it was feared that decreased blood flow to his brain, with consequent inadequate oxygen, had caused the coma and possible brain damage. He was able to breathe on his own, but this was about the only hopeful sign, and doctors were pessimistic.

Goshen-Gottstein's family refused to resign themselves to his remaining in his deep vegetative state. Through her mother's physician in London, Esther Goshen-Gottstein obtained a drug called Nootropil, which was administered with Parentrovite, a compound of vitamins B and C and which had been used to stimulate comatose patients. Over the following weeks and months, Esther, her grown sons, and other family members spent hours at Moshe's bedside, talking to him as if he could hear them. Slowly, he made some progress: he opened one eye and then the other, moved arms and legs, shooed away a fly, made sounds, whispered nonsense syllables and eventually words. Twelve weeks after surgery, he was able to give correct responses, use Hebrew, German, and English appropriately, read a sentence in German, and take a first step. He was very angry at this point and was aggressive and violent both in his actions and in his language. Then, four months after the onset of the coma, he emerged, "not," says the author, "with a bang but with a whimper. It was a seamless transition. We hardly realized that the great event for which we had so eagerly hoped and prayed had appeared at long last, unaccompanied by thunder and lightning." She comments that for the family, his reawakening "is associated with the reemergence of his humor. It was crude at first, but who cared?"

Moshe Goshen-Gottstein's convalescence was arduous. Gradually, his anger—which had been directed chiefly against his wife—diminished, and his faculties and abilities returned. He was able to go home for weekends and then permanently; he attended a day hospital three times a week until he himself decided to stop going. He resumed his place in the family as husband, father, and grandfather and picked up his active professional life as a world expert in his field. At his son's wedding in March 1986, he gave a 20-minute speech and danced with the bride. He and his wife traveled in the summer of 1986, and that fall, 11 months after his release from the hospital, he resumed his full teaching load. Some reminders of his perilous physical crisis remain as the book ends: he is less extroverted and more passive, more dependent on family members, more forgetful, less able to perform mathematical calculations; his vocal chords were damaged by the tube he had to have for many weeks, and eventually he had voice therapy; he also had a "dropped foot." However, writes his wife, "With his tenacity, will, and drive for independence, Moshe has succeeded in returning to a meaningful and creative life, after battling against incredible odds—and against what seemed to be a hopeless state of neurological devastation."

In an epilogue, Esther Goshen-Gottstein speculates about possible causes of her husband's recovery, when all medical signs seemed to predict a dramatically different outcome. Perhaps, she says, there have been more cases of emergence from coma than we know of; maybe it was the continual stimulation determinedly provided by family and friends, maybe the unconventional medication helped, perhaps it was a lucky spontaneous recovery, maybe it was the intervention of God. The Goshen-Gottstein sons are deeply religious, and Moshe Goshen-Gottstein himself is a practicing Jew.

Moshe Goshen-Gottstein has written a postscript. Two appendixes by Esther Goshen-Gottstein follow: "Child Development and Recovery from Coma," in which the author compares her husband's recovery to the developmental steps observed in infants and toddlers, and "Advice to Those in a Similar Situation," with a short bibliography of selected titles. Their friend, Dr. Rodney Falk, a cardiologist, has contributed a third appendix, called "Unexplained Recovery from a Persistent Vegetative State: A Physician's Viewpoint." The foreword is by Oliver Sacks, well known as the author of *The Man Who Mistook His Wife for a Hat* and *Awakenings* (both reviewed in this volume).

A Hebrew edition of the book appeared in 1988. Some changes and additions have been made to the English edition.

Analysis: This is a fascinating account of recovery from an ominous medical crisis. As a psychologist, Esther Goshen-Gottstein is able to observe her husband's illness and its aftermath with the background of professional knowledge and insight. Though she suffered no less anguish than anyone else in a similar situation, she was able to bring a certain detachment to the experience. Thus, when her husband raged against her, calling her a bad wife, when he uttered blasphemous curses, she understood the causes of his fury and rode out his angry storms. In his own postscript, Moshe Goshen-Gottstein says that he is ashamed to read of his behavior, of which he retained no memory.

The author's organization of material is sometimes confusing. There are chapters on such subjects as speech and movement, in which the narrative moves back and forth across the chronology of recovery. An appendix giving a time line is helpful, but the reader may very well not discover this until the book is finished. However, this is a minor defect.

Moshe Goshen-Gottstein is 59 when he has the surgery, and thus it might be supposed that most high school students would not be attracted to the subject. However, the interest in coma raised by the movie version of *Awakenings* may very well lead readers to *Recalled to Life*.

■ Haecker, Theodor. *Kierkegaard: The Cripple.* Trans. by C. Van O. Bruyn. Illus. Arno, 1980. 53pp. (0-405-13100-3) Reading Level: Grades 10–12.
Disability: Hunchbacked persons

This volume is part of the Arno Press collection The Physically Handi-capped in Society. It also includes *And Yet We Are Human,* by Finn Carling, which is reviewed separately.

An introduction to Haecker's essay was written by A. Dru. In it he talks of the author's admiration for Kierkegaard, the great religious philoso-pher of nineteenth-century Denmark, with whom he shared a strong Christian belief. Haecker, who died in 1945, was Catholic, but he had a lifelong interest in Kierkegaard, who was a Danish Lutheran. Dru tells a story about an earlier German scholar, Rikard Magnussen, from one of his books on Kierkegaard. Magnussen wanted to support the erection of a public monument to celebrate the centenary of the philosopher's birth. He went to an 80-year-old nephew, who did not support the idea, and who said, "But don't you know what he was like? Soren Kierkegaard was hunchbacked (p. viii)." This fact had been glossed over by his uncle's supporters and future historians. It is only ambiguously evident in the accompanying drawings in the present text.

In 1838, when Kierkegaard was 25, at precisely 10:30 in the morning, he had a religious revelation, after which he lost all doubt about the existence of God, father of Jesus, and that He is love. Haecker discusses the significance of this experience and also the effect of his deformity on the evolution of his religious thought. He is persuaded that his deformity was the "thorn in the flesh" and the individual cross to which Kierkegaard referred in his writings. He suggests that it figured prominently in signifi-cant turning points of his life and that it was pivotal in relation to his thought. At age 25, Kierkegaard broke off his yearlong engagement to young Regine Olsen. Haecker attributes this to the young man's melan-choly. Actually, Kierkegaard spoke of this relationship on his deathbed, when he was 42. In his will, he named Regine, who had since married, as his inheritor.

Haecker proceeds to explore Kierkegaard's metaphysics, which he cri-tiques in terms of his own Catholicism. He talks of paradox and the absurd. He suggests that a deformed and isolated person might be particu-larly vulnerable to demonic powers, as was Shakespeare's hunchbacked Richard III.

Analysis: This work is presumably translated from German. The philo-sophical discussions make for heavy reading for those not versed in Chris-tian metaphysics. Haecker critiques the thought of a person raised in the Lutheran Church and Nicene creed in terms of his own Catholic theology. While he adulates Kierkegaard as Denmark's greatest man, his essay is at least as much about his own thought system as that of his subject. He assumes a greater knowledge of Kierkegaard than most American readers possess. The introduction was helpful in putting the essay in perspective.

■ Heller, Joseph, and Speed Vogel. *No Laughing Matter.* Putnam, 1986.
335 pp. (0-399-13086-1) Reading Level: Grades 10–12. (BL 15 D85; LJ
1 My86; NYTBR 16 F86)
Disability: Guillain-Barré syndrome

Joseph Heller, author of *Catch-22* and other well-known novels, and his
friend Speed Vogel together have written an account of Heller's encounter
in 1981 with Guillain-Barré syndrome that is at once both light and
humorous and also deadly serious. Heller, middle-aged, successful, in top
physical condition, and living the good life in New York, was suddenly,
with no warning, rendered unable to control his swallowing mechanism
and his limbs.

His internist made an amazingly accurate telephone diagnosis of Guillain-Barré syndrome and personally escorted Heller to the hospital. For a
time, Heller was on a respirator and in intensive care, and at first he was
totally unable to move. After several months in the hospital and several
more in the Rusk Institute for rehabilitation training, he had recovered
sufficiently to go home, with the help of a full-time nurse and his friend
Speed. Both of the men alternate in telling the story of their lives together
during this period. Their accounts are often hilarious, and even the more
grim aspects of the disease are dealt with in a matter-of-fact way.

Analysis: Despite the fact that the story deals with a middle-aged adult,
teenagers who are good readers should find the book to be fast paced,
funny, and entertaining, as well as instructive and thoughtful. Highly
recommended for mature teens.

■ Howell, Allen R., and B. Carleen Loveland. *Call Me Dad.* Exceptional Success Associates, 1990, © 1988. 152pp. Reading Level: Grades
10–12.
Disability: Quadriplegia; Birth defects

This is a paradoxical book, simple yet profound, moving yet straightforward, imaginative yet true, sentimental yet tough. It is the story of Randy
Howell, son of one of the two authors. Born a quadriplegic because of
multiple birth defects involving muscles and nerves but not the spinal
cord, Randy was expected to die almost immediately. He lived, and,
eventually, thrived, the oldest child in a family of eight, living in Utah,
where his father is director of risk management at Brigham Young University.

Randy attended elementary school with nondisabled children and junior high school as a special education student. At the age of 18, he was
graduated from junior high school, according to the usual practice for
special education students, and this was expected to be his terminal educa-

tion, even though he had no mental disabilities. However, he applied for special admission to a high school in Salt Lake City, from which he was also graduated. He then went on to earn a college degree.

Randy lived most of his life on his stomach, a position that gave him maximum body flexibility. As a youngster, he was pulled around on a series of red wagons by his siblings and playmates. In elementary school, he lay on a special desk, constructed for him by his father. Later on, he managed to have a car specially modified so that he could drive it in his usual horizontal position. He loved books, computers, chess, and all kinds of social activities.

He met and married a woman named Lynn, and they moved from Utah to California, where they became the parents of a son, Roy. When Roy was 5, Randy became ill. The diagnosis was a swift, terminal cancer of the stomach, so he and his family returned to Utah, where he died shortly thereafter at the age of 35.

In *Call Me Dad,* Randy's life story is not told so prosaically as it has just been recounted above. Rather, the authors tell it using a series of sometimes poetic vignettes, from the viewpoint of various people in Randy's life, including Randy himself. These vignettes are labeled either by the speaker's name or by other labels, such as "Earth Father," "Earth Mother," "Heavenly Father," "Time Marker," "Mother Alone," and "Halo Wisdom," to name only a few. The latter recurs frequently and speaks from a religious/philosophical viewpoint.

Analysis: The book is gripping and deeply moving. It is a testament to infinite human capabilities and to the centrality of the family in human society. Highly recommended for high school readers, it may also appeal to mature junior high school students as well.

■ Jewell, Geri, and Stewart Weiner. *Geri.* Morrow, 1984. 250pp. (0-688-02452-1) Reading Level: Grades 7–12. (KR 15 N83; PW 25 N83; SLJ Ag84)
Disability: Cerebral palsy; Hearing loss

The story opens with an account of an ill-fated pregnancy and the premature birth of Olga Jewell's third child. The birth was a bloody mess. The little girl was baptized in the hospital chapel, because doctors thought she would not survive. She did survive, but by 6 months of age, she was showing abnormal muscle patterns that her mother recognized as cerebral palsy. The doctors in Buffalo, New York, would not listen to Olga. This precipitated the family's decision to move to a new life in California.

Olga's diagnosis was confirmed, and she enrolled her daughter for nursery school and therapy. By age 3, Geri was still not crawling alone.

The family, now with a new baby girl, could barely make ends meet. When Geri was 7, the family made one of their many moves, this one to the suburbs of Orange County. Geri was desperate for acceptance, but on the first day, the neighborhood kids ambushed her and took her wagon. This was the first time she felt truly different from other people. She was eventually enrolled in a school for physically handicapped children. It was right next to a "normal" school, but the children were forbidden to cross into each other's territory. Obstreperous Geri did, of course, only to be chased back by a host of teachers and children. In special education, she had more therapy than instruction. She loved speech therapy, which was necessary because she had a hearing problem as well as an unsteady gait and flailing arms. She was a tomboy who was fearless physically. "I just love it when somebody tells me I can't do something physical. It turns on my juices" (p. 130).

In sixth grade, Geri was mainstreamed in "Regularland" for summer school. She learned that other kids had fears and insecurities also, only on her it showed. Back in special education, she admitted to her teacher that she wanted to be an actress. She was allowed to write and act in a school play. Once off to a partially mainstreamed high school, she writes, "I was a blob. I walked like a drunk, I was deaf as a haddock, and I had all the personality and maturity of an eleven-year-old" (p. 154). She was not accepted by her peers in regular education, who nicknamed her "Ortho." Her one date during high school was to a drive-in; she was driven there by a disabled boy who managed to rip the speaker off the pole and cause a huge commotion. Later, they drove away with hamburgers, fries, and milk shakes falling from the roof of the car. Geri laughed so hard that she soaked the seat of her date's mother's car.

Geri kept her dream of being a comedian like Carol Burnett so that she could have attention and acceptance. Near the end of high school, she was employed by Goodwill Industries for three months in order to be evaluated. She earned 1 percent of the minimum wage. She felt as if she were in prison and at the end of the road. Against everyone's better judgment, Geri enrolled in theater classes in the community college, still immature and still craving attention.

In the fall, she, like Alice in Wonderland, gulped from the bottle that said, "DRINK ME," and "things would never be the same again" (p. 217). Her van driver took her and a blind man to participate in amateur night at the Comedy Store, and her handicap routine was a big success. Her career really took off when she lied her way into her first television performance at the 1980 United Cerebral Palsy telethon. She was soon discovered by TV producer Norman Lear and has had a recurring role on the NBC show "Facts of Life." She has been on talk shows and featured in magazines, not just as a comic, but as an advocate "on behalf of all the people who have the same goods that I do and are dying to deliver them" (p. 250).

Analysis: Jewell comes across as a spunky, irreverent, and truly funny young woman. She lacks self-pity but says up front that cerebral palsy are the two ugliest words in the English language, where "your brain's relationship with your muscles is on the rocks" (p. 55). "It's just that because our lights aren't on, nobody thinks we're home" (p. 55). The book is easy and entertaining reading. Jewell, with the participation of Weiner, writes with warmth and candor.

■ Jones, Tristan. *Outward Leg.* Hearst Marine, 1985. 286pp. (0-688-04308-9) Reading Level: Grades 10–12. (BL 30 Mr86; KR 15 Ap86) *Disability:* Amputations

Tristan Jones, veteran sailor, adventurer, and author of several books about his seafaring journeys, spent seven years ashore after having his left leg amputated. Then, at the age of 59, he decided to attempt, in a plan he called Operation Star, to sail around the world as a way to inspire others with disabilities and to prove to himself that he could still accomplish this daunting task.

In San Diego to give a fund-raising lecture about his plans, he found a sailboat that was perfectly suited to his physical requirements, a 36-foot trimaran. It became *Outward Leg,* and on it, with only one crew member, Jones set sail for a voyage around the world.

In the book, Jones takes the reader on the first half of that voyage from San Diego to Central America, through the Panama Canal to Colombia, Venezuela, Aruba, and the Dominican Republic. From there he sailed up the east coast of the United States to New York, and from there to London, where he had first become a sailor 30 years earlier. At the end of the story, he is reviewing maps of Europe for the next part of his voyage.

Analysis: Jones' writing style is colorful and picturesque. One can easily visualize the verbal pictures that he paints. His descriptions and perceptions of people and places are vivid and real. His account of the pain and misery that preceded his leg amputation and ultimate postoperative adjustment is likewise keen and sometimes brutally realistic. He refers to himself, for example, as a one-legged cripple, yet his behavior does not match the image.

Teens should enjoy this as a good adventure story in which the central character's disability plays a pivotal yet minor role.

■ Kaufman, Curt, and Gita Kaufman. *Rajesh*. Illus. by Curt Kaufman. Atheneum, 1985. 32pp. (0-689-31074-9) Reading Level: Grades 1–3. (BCCB O85; SLJ Mr86)
Disability: Congenital amputations

The young narrator, Rajesh, was missing both legs and one hand at birth. His story opens as he dresses for his first day of kindergarten in Public School 166. A large black-and-white photo shows him pulling his long trousers over artificial legs. In school, after his initial anxieties about acceptance are allayed, he explains to his classmates how his prostheses have enabled him to stop using a wheelchair. At one point, the class discusses the many advantages of human differences. When the days grow warm, Rajesh feels comfortable playing outside in the spray with the others, dressed only in his bathing suit and plastic legs. He ends his account, happy that he can do almost anything the others can do, and he is proud to be himself.

Analysis: Gita Kaufman was actually Rajesh's kindergarten teacher. Her husband, Curt Kaufman, is a professional photographer whose delightful pictures include winsome close-ups of Indian-looking Rajesh and his classmates of many races. The front and back inside covers are decorated with portraits of each of them.

The simple and straightforward narrative is presented in large print. The discussion of human differences seems a little muddled, but the illogic probably would not bother young children. This book delivers its dual message very well. That is, it fully acknowledges the handicap that a disability imposes, but it relegates that difference to small consequence relative to the attractiveness and accomplishments of the story's young protagonist.

■ Kittredge, Mary. *Jane Addams: Social Worker*. Illus. Chelsea House, 1988. 111pp. (1-55546-636-2) Reading Level: Grades 7–9. (BL 15 Je88; KR 1 My88)
Disability: Tuberculosis of the spine

This book is one of 50 in the collection American Women of Achievement, which remembers women, past and contemporary, who have been prominent in the arts, sciences, sports, politics, and government. Matina S. Horner, of Radcliffe College, has contributed an introduction, in which she stresses the need to redress the historical bias toward males that was prevalent until only recently.

Jane Addams was the founder and leader of the settlement movement in the United States. In addition, she was a world-renowned leader in the peace movement. Her most significant disability, warranting her inclusion in this collection, was tuberculosis of the spine, which left her in early childhood with a curved back and a pigeon-toed walk. In her 20s she suffered severe back pain and depression, causing her to drop out of medical school after one semester. She then had a major operation on her spine, after which she lay on her back for six months. For another year she wore an uncomfortable corset of leather, steel, and whalebone. She completed her recuperation by going abroad. During her European trip, she discarded her brace and regained her health.

The story begins in 1888, when Addams, then 27, was on her second trip to Europe and attending a bullfight in Spain. Shortly after that exhilarating, yet cruel experience, she crystallized her aim to set up a settlement house for the many immigrants working in Chicago, a crowded, industrialized city.

The reader is then taken back to Addams' early, financially privileged life in Rockport, Illinois. Her lively participation in the Rockford Seminary for young women, her matriculation at the men's school (Beloit College), and her brief foray in medical school are viewed as steps on the way to her destiny, "to become someone" (Ch. 3).

Addams invested much of her personal wealth in her Hull House, where her upper-class volunteers chose to live among the poor. With indefatigable energy, she started a kindergarten, opened the first public playground, and established a women's cooperative residence for factory workers. She arranged two-week summer vacations for poorhouse residents, in addition to plays, cultural clubs, and a folk museum at Hull House. She involved herself personally with all of the needy people in the neighborhood. She led the fight for child labor laws, honest city government, and the first juvenile court in the nation. Unlike most of her class, she was evenhanded toward the union movement. She became a strong advocate for the welfare of black people, who she felt suffered many of the same problems as new immigrants. Addams wrote some highly praised books, and her autobiography is still in print today.

When she visited Russian author Leo Tolstoy at his home, she was deeply influenced by his views on pacifism and the possibility of international peace. She urged the United States to take the role of peacemaker at the onset of World War I. She never lost her fervor for peace, even when it made her extremely unpopular. She worked earnestly for the Women's International League for Peace until her death. She won the Nobel Peace Prize in 1931, when she was 71 years old.

A list of books for further reading, a chronology of Addams' life, and an index close the book.

Analysis: Kittredge has furnished a lively, fact-filled account about the preeminent social worker. The quotations and anecdotes she has selected bring Addams to life. The struggles against poverty, injustice, and war seem especially relevant today. Fortunately, the author does not overly dwell on attitudes toward the role of women in society. Rather, she lets the facts speak for themselves.

The prose is straightforward. A few difficult words are defined in brackets. The black-and-white photographs with text, liberally displayed throughout the book, are treasures.

■ Knight, Harold V. *To Get Up, First Fall Down*. Illus. Roberts Rinehart, 1986. 181pp. (0-911797-18-1) Reading Level: Grades 10–12. *Disability:* Cerebral palsy; Athetosis

Knight was 77 years old at the time his memoir was published. He had made a precarious living as a free-lance writer and has written five other books, including a textbook on the Constitution. He marketed a popular political column on state government in Colorado. The introduction to this book contains an interview by a television anchorman with the Colorado governor and state treasurer during a United Cerebral Palsy Association telethon in 1983. The men discussed Knight, their colleague, who impressed them as having accomplished much despite his cerebral palsy.

Knight opens with a description of his not unhappy early childhood near the turn of the century. His school years began in Salina, Kansas, where his father was a college professor. He was the only child with a disability in his elementary school classes. Although he always had difficulty walking, talking, and grasping, his parents did not really know what was wrong with him, and he received no treatment until he saw Dr. Earl Carlson (see "Born That Way" in *Accept Me as I Am,* 1985) in his late 20s. His personality was overemotional and sometimes depressive. He writes, "See how I stumble—and how I mumble, and Oh! How I grumble!" (p. 5).

With the advent of World War I, Knight helped his family to farm. When he was 12, the family moved to Jamestown, North Dakota, where he would spend the next 25 winters. He began writing in high school and won several contests. With his eye on journalism as a career, he was awarded a scholarship to Jamestown College, where his father taught. Fifty-seven years later, he received an honorary degree from that institution.

Graduating in 1929, at the start of the Great Depression, Knight had difficulty finding a job. Because he had learned to drive, he was finally hired to sell subscriptions of the local paper to farmers, often in exchange for chickens. His career was launched as he wrote about the Farmers' Union, labor politics, and the stormy North Dakota politics of the hard depression years, when drought also plagued the Midwest. He interviewed the Socialist candidate who ran for president against Franklin Roosevelt. Thirty years later he hosted him again in his capacity as part-time executive director of the Colorado American Civil Liberties Union.

Knight describes many perilous times, often associated with lack of acceptance due to his disability. When he was 50, he entered his second (but first happy) marriage, to a grade school teacher. He had a new measure of happiness and financial security until his wife's death 20 years later. He wrote this book in a hospitable retirement home in San Diego. At the end of the story he is still a reformer and still getting up after he falls down. He wants to live until the year 2000, when cerebral palsy among newborns is predicted to be rare.

The book concludes with his "best poem," for which a talented "foster granddaughter" is composing music. A few black-and-white snapshots are included.

Analysis: Knight comes across as a quirky, irrepressible person, who has not, in his own words, lost his wits in his old age. The book reads like a diary, with the spunky writer careening through a long and eventful life. He has had an unwavering espousal of Christianity, the disability movement, and liberal causes.

The author displays little self-pity or denial with respect to his substantial disability. He honestly, and often humorously, describes his bumptious, volatile personality. Typically, he wonders if cerebral palsy affected it, but he never blames his impairment for his shortcomings.

■ Kriegel, Leonard. *Falling into Life: Essays.* North Point, 1991. 195pp. (0-86547-458-3) Reading Level: Grades 10–12. (KR 15 D90)
Disability: Poliomyelitis

In his introduction (and repeated in every essay), Kriegel writes that he was struck down by polio virus at age 11 in 1944. In 1965, as a young writer with a wife and young son, he had an idyllic stint at the University of Leiden as a Fulbright scholar. During the course of that year he went to Paris without his family to deliver a lecture. Alone there, as a tall man in full leg braces and crutches, he realized the rage that he felt, and still feels, over the disease that left him crippled. In middle age, he has written essays in an attempt to come to grips with his rage, his loss, his pride, and his love. Many of these pieces have been previously published in various literary magazines.

Kriegel is the son of Eastern European immigrants, raised in New York, where he still lives. He was enrolled in religious school when he was 8, and has always had a close, if somewhat ambivalent, tie to Judaism. He loves big cars (actually easier for him to maneuver) and weight lifting.

The first essay bears the book's title. In it, Kriegel recounts his rehabilitation from near death at the New York State Reconstruction Home, where he received therapy with 21 other young boys. Nine months after his arrival, he was fitted with hip braces and crutches. He was terrified of learning to fall on the padded exercise mats. Finally he did it. "There you go! And there it is," said his therapist (p. 13). Thus he learned to "fall into life. . . . I could let go, I could fall, and best of all, I could get up" (p. 15).

Thirty-eight years later, when Kriegel could no longer pull up from a simple fall, he confronted his own mortality. Several more essays recall his growing up. He contrasts his thinking with that of fellow college students of the '50s and '60s. He attributes the roots of his creative inner life to years of recuperation, when "fantasy carried me through long, tedious afternoons and empty nights" (p. 42). He fantasized, for example, that he was a triumphant Jewish athlete like the boxer and war hero Barney Ross, whom he once met.

Kriegel faces the subject of disability from a very personal perspective in the piece "Claiming the Self—The Cripple as American Man." He deplores being defined from the outside by a society that acknowledges the disabled people's presence, but not their reality. Further essays develop the relationship of his writing career (he has published numerous books and articles) to that chance event—infection by a virus—that changed his life so radically. In middle age, he began to use a wheelchair. He contrasts wheeling in tolerant San Francisco with Paris, where he experienced condescending attitudes that he attributed to the European sense of authority. Then he writes of the ambivalent view of the cripple in Western literature, as embodied in Shakespeare's *Richard III* and in Melville's *Moby Dick*. He feels akin to Einhorn, the "Survivor Cripple" described in Saul Bellow's novel *The Adventures of Augie March.*

Analysis: In this collection of essays, the mature writer seems always in touch with his boyhood self, first healthy, then transformed by polio virus. The essays address, over and over, his quest for self-identity and creation of self. Each can be read on its own, and all are relevant to this volume, because the serious disability that has formed, informed, and plagued the author pervades the entire book. He might be criticized for using the word "cripple," but he feels this is an honest word for a cruel and unrelenting affliction.

The prose is beautifully crafted, with sentence after sentence that reads like aphorisms. The musings are often personal and self-critical. The author's numerous literary illustrations could be daunting for some young readers, yet his interesting insights could inspire the uninitiated to explore such writers as Mark Twain or Franz Kafka.

■ Kriegel, Leonard. *The Long Walk Home.* Appleton-Century, 1964. 213pp. (o.p.) Reading Level: Grades 10–12. (BS1 My64; Nat 21 S64) *Disability:* Paraplegia; Poliomyelitis

This book was written at the beginning of Kriegel's career as a professional writer and teacher. His story begins during the fateful summer when he was 11 years old. He went on a bus to a camp for poor New York boys—his first time away from his home in the Bronx. He made friends with a boy named Jerry, and the two shared the same cabin. A few days before their scheduled departure, Jerry became terribly sick and went to the infirmary. His friend Leonard soon followed him. After a night of pain and paralysis, the boys were taken to the hospital by ambulance. Jerry choked to death that night. The polio virus paralyzed Kriegel's legs.

When the sickness subsided, he was sent to the New York State Reconstruction Home, "The Rock," where he would spend the next two years. He describes life on the boys' ward, where the patients were terrified in their helplessness and segregation from "the outside." He found delightful freedom when he finally graduated from his bed to a wheelchair. The boys often perpetrated pranks on each other, some funny, some cruel, as if reclaiming some power over their lives. Once, in chairs, they stormed the candy store in the small town nearby, in simulation of the attacks they saw in weekly Western movies. Kriegel was dismissed from a Boy Scout troop for cursing. He kissed his first girl.

A year after entering The Rock, he was fitted for braces and crutches by the man who had fitted the later-to-be-president, Franklin Delano Roosevelt, for his prosthesis. FDR was Kriegel's role model and ideal. He had his bar mitzvah in braces and fine clothes in a synagogue near the institution. He was by now terrified of impending dismissal from the sheltered ward, where being crippled was the norm. The day inexorably came, and his beloved friends saw him off in an ambulance to his home, two years after he had left for camp.

Kriegel encountered ignorant and curious people who shamed him with their patronizing attentions upon his homecoming, and he agonized about his sexual potential, a subject never broached during his rehabilitation. He had a lonely home instruction one hour each morning. He watched the world go by from his apartment window, but he "was out of it, out of it all" (p. 141). Grossly overweight, he retreated to fantasy, TV, and the weekly movie.

Not until four years later, at 16, did he finally face the reality that he was a cripple. He wept bitter tears of self-pity, then, in rage, determined that "I would show them. I would show them all. . . . It was another beginning. And I was ready" (p. 152). He began a rigorous course of exercise for the upper body, and his excess fat dropped away. He became friends with a group of boys who taught him that he was not so different from others.

Kriegel had never been in a high school classroom, so it was with trepidation that he enrolled in Hunter College. He became immersed in literature, through which he continued to seek his identity. In his freshman year, he met a girl who would later become his wife, over the strenuous objections of her parents. "From the first time we went out together, she filed the teeth of my public rage and crippled the myth of my cripple" (p. 192). He declared his war with polio over, and his self won, in his senior college year.

Analysis: Kriegel's writing talent is evident in this sensitive and personal account. He paints a wrenching picture of institutional life, contrasted with a delightful description of the Bronx of long ago, where so many European immigrants had come to seek a new life. The steps in his coming-of-age, which he delineates so poignantly, are typical but rendered stark against the ravages of the polio virus. His boy's hopes and fears have universal truth to them.

The segregation and isolation that Kriegel experienced seem, in hindsight, unnecessary and inhumane. In light of present laws and enlightened medical practice, it can be hoped that this kind of treatment is a thing of the past.

■ Kuklin, Susan. *Thinking Big: The Story of a Young Dwarf.* Illus. by Susan Kuklin. Lothrop, Lee & Shepard, 1986. Unp. (LB 0-688-05826-4) Reading Level: Grades K–4. (BCCB My86; CBRS My86; PW 30 My86)
Disability: Achondroplastic dwarfism

Jaime Osborn is an 8-year-old achondroplastic dwarf, who lives with her normal-sized parents and 5-year-old brother. Many aspects of her life are common to middle-class American children; she rides her bike, goes to school, plays with her friends, sells Girl Scout cookies. Yet as this book shows, in text and photographs, the physical characteristics of her dwarfism require continual adaptation. The acts of going up and down stairs, ringing doorbells, reaching food in the refrigerator, sitting in a classroom, opening containers, and getting new clothes all present a challenge to Jaime and her family. Her physical condition is monitored by a specialist. The Osborns are members of Little People of America, which offers social occasions, information, and support for dwarfs, midgets, and their families.

The epilogue gives additional information about Jaime's dwarfism and her parents' response and decisions and discusses possible aspects of her future.

Analysis: This is a fine book. The text is well written, and the explanations are clear. Kuklin shows us a remarkably outgoing, friendly little girl, very comfortable with herself and her size. She is good at art and reading and has a well-developed sense of humor. Yet the author does not omit the darker side of Jaime's life, for example, her difficulty in standing or walking for a long time, her frequent falls, the gym and playground activities that she cannot participate in, and the name-calling that she has had to learn to deal with. Jaime's parents are succeeding in bringing up a little girl who can internalize the motto of the Little People of America and "think big."

This book is recommended for all children in the age group and certainly for youngsters who themselves are dwarfs or midgets or know someone who has this condition. If used in a classroom, it could spark a fruitful discussion on differences and similarities and on creative adaptation.

■ Landau, Elaine. *Alzheimer's Disease.* Illus. Franklin Watts, 1987. 67pp. (LB 0-531-10376-5) Reading Level: Grades 7–12. (BL 15 D87; SBF My88; SLJ N87)
Disability: Alzheimer's disease

Using examples of patient histories and the words of the relatives (mostly young people) of Alzheimer's patients, Landau presents a realistic picture of this devastating disease. She discusses the form of the illness and its usual symptoms, making the point that thus far medical science has been unable either to predict the condition or to stop its progress once it has attacked. She writes about the role of the family in caring for the affected person in addition to the decisions that relatives must make about living arrangements, stressing that it is important to do this at onset if possible, so that the patient can participate in the discussions. The two final chapters deal with nursing home care and death. There are a bibliography and an index. Black-and-white photographs of Alzheimer's patients, their families, and their caregivers illustrate the text.

Analysis: This is one title in the series called First Books, published by Watts, which deals with medical matters. Landau, who has training as a writer and librarian, has written a straightforward, clear book about a baffling and tragic disease. The accounts by family members read a little too smoothly to sound completely authentic, especially those by the youngest contributors; perhaps Landau supplied editorial shaping. Nevertheless, this could offer valuable information to youngsters, some of whom may know or be related to older people with Alzheimer's. The last personal account is hopeful despite the fact that it describes the death of the young writer's grandmother, for it includes the wise words spoken to Landau by a nurse in the home where her grandmother died: "You know, your grandmother may be dead, but I don't think of her as gone. I see her sweetness in your smile and your caring. A part of her continues to live on in the best part of you. Your challenge is to let your grandmother's real legacy survive through all the good things you achieve.' "

■ McDonald, Steven, Patti Ann McDonald, and E. J. Kahn III. *The Steven McDonald Story*. Illus. Donald I. Fine, 1989. 270pp. (1-55611-133-9) Reading Level: Grades 7–12. (BL 15 S89; KR 15 My89; LJ J189; NYTBR 30 J189)
Disability: Quadriplegia

In July 1986 Steven McDonald, a young New York policeman, was in Central Park with a fellow officer, looking for boys suspected of stealing bikes. They split up, and McDonald saw three who fit the description. One had a suspicious bulge under his pant cuff, and, when McDonald bent to investigate, another boy shot him. The bullet entered his spine below the second vertebra, and he became paralyzed from the neck down, with feeling only in his head. At first, even his survival was in doubt. Steven and Patti McDonald had been married less than a year, and Patti was pregnant. Their son Conor was born the following January.

The brutal shooting of an attractive young officer attracted immediate media attention. Both the McDonalds are Catholic, and John Cardinal O'Connor, Archbishop of New York, visited the hospital regularly and conducted services for the family. Mayor Koch was another visitor. There were press conferences and newspaper articles. After nine months in Bellevue, with only limited improvement, McDonald was transferred to Craig Hospital in Englewood, Colorado, for a period of intensive training and therapy designed to make him as independent as possible. Gradually, he was able to do without his ventilator for periods of time, to use his voice again, and to sit up; he learned to use his mouth, to breathe with a mouthstick so as to drive his motorized wheelchair, and to write with a pen and a computer. Back in New York, a house bought for him was being extensively remodeled to fit his needs, and a special van was purchased. Before his return, Patti McDonald went on a pilgrimage to Lourdes, Rome, and Medjugorje, Yugoslavia. In November, Steven McDonald returned from Colorado to his new home, his family, and a new life, with nurses round the clock and the realization that, unless some dramatic medical breakthrough was achieved, he would be immobile and physically dependent for the rest of his life.

The text is illustrated with many black-and-white photographs.

Analysis: The authors have chosen to present their story in a narrative that moves back and forth in time and is told by different voices. Sections of text are headed with date and place, but Steven and Patti McDonald are not identified as narrators, although others, such as the mayor, are. All the voices have a certain similarity, probably because they have been edited by the third writer, E. J. Kahn III, a professional.

The McDonalds do not disguise their pain, periods of despair, and regret for what can now never be. Sustained by their close family and friends, Steven's colleagues in the police force, their joy in their son, and their firm religious faith, they struggle to find a way to live as fully as possible. In an epilogue, Steven McDonald asks his readers to do everything possible to act responsibly in the fight against crime. "Pick up the phone when you witness a crime," he writes. "Call the police. If you don't want to give your name, call just the same, and tell the police that you're calling for Steven McDonald.

"Then, and only then, will I be able to know that my time in this wheelchair will be spent as a worthwhile sacrifice, not as a life sentence."

Although the book is long, competent middle school and high school readers should not find it difficult, and many will be attracted by this account of a young couple whose lives change in a fraction of a second and who must learn to face dramatically altered circumstances.

■ Mahanes, Frances F. *A Child's Courage, A Doctor's Devotion: Triumph over Head Trauma.* Illus. Betterway, 1985. 157pp. (0-932620-49-3) Reading Level: Grades 7–12. (KLIATT W86)
Disability: Head trauma

On an icy day in February 1984, Frances Mahanes was driving her three children home from school in Waynesboro, Virginia. They had an accident on a mountain road, injuring two of the children seriously; Mahanes's 15-year-old daughter, Dea, sustained a ruptured spleen; 9-year-old Michael was in a coma as the result of severe head trauma. In subsequent weeks, Dea recuperated steadily in the hospital and at home. Michael underwent brain surgery to repair a cerebrospinal fluid leak, progressed to a semicoma, and at last, exactly eight weeks after the accident, emerged from the coma completely. He was treated first in the University of Virginia Hospital and then at Children's Rehabilitation Center. His recovery has been remarkable, and, although there were still effects of the accident at the time his mother wrote this book, by the fall of 1984 he was carrying a full program in school and taking part in sports and other activities. Throughout Michael's months of treatment and rehabilitation, his primary doctor, and the one in whom his parents placed their hope and trust, was a 28-year-old resident in neurology, Dr. Karen Roos, who has written the foreword.

In an appendix, Mahanes gives information about the National Head Injury Foundation, NHIF state associations, and support groups, with names and addresses, as well as a list of training centers. She includes sources of information on prevention of accidental trauma. She also has written a brief description of head injury, with a glossary of medical terms. Black-and-white photographs record Michael's progress.

Analysis: Mahanes has described her family's ordeal in specific detail, and the reader can follow Michael's case closely. Unfortunately, the book is marred by the author's tendency to overwrite. Perhaps she is herself a person who lives at this keyed-up level, but the high pitch of the prose may distract readers. There is no doubt that she looks on Dr. Roos as the savior of her son, and her portrayal of Roos's devotion and involvement is certainly believable. Mahanes does best as a writer in the brief appendix, when she concentrates on offering to her readers the most helpful information she can gather. One odd omission is that, although in the section on prevention of accidents she discusses wearing seat belts, in narrating the details of her family's accident, she does not mention whether they had their belts on.

Young people who have experienced trauma, either themselves or through someone they know, and those considering a career in the medical profession would probably find the book of interest.

■ Mairs, Nancy. *Carnal Acts.* HarperCollins, 1990. 161pp. (0-06-016494-8) Reading Level: Grades 10–12. (KR 1 J190; NYTBR 2 S90) *Disability:* Multiple sclerosis

Nancy Mairs is the author of a book of poetry, a memoir, and a collection of essays preceding *Carnal Acts.* She has also written the "Hers" column for the *New York Times,* where some of the essays in this book first appeared; she has included a short story as well. In her early 40s at the time of publication of *Carnal Acts,* she had had multiple sclerosis for 17 years. She writes about the effect of her illness on her life, her writing, her family, her relationships, her thinking. In addition to her multiple sclerosis, she and her husband have had to deal with his two operations for melanoma. Her condition is seldom absent either from her mind or from her work. In the title essay, she writes about the early stages, when she had a "foot drop" and a limp so minor that she could still wear high heels; then her deteriorating condition required a cane, a brace, and ultimately a motorized scooter. "Challenge: An Exploration" describes how she ventured to California alone to teach in a writing program and then moves to a consideration of language as she examines the phrase "physically challenged." The final piece is about the trip she and her husband made to Zaire to visit their daughter who was serving in the Peace Corps there—a difficult journey even for able-bodied people. As she leaves Africa, she thinks to herself, "What if I'd never come? . . . How could I bear never to have seen this? . . . this is the only way I know to live as a woman with multiple sclerosis," she continues, "not to listen to the ominous questions of Lufthansa agents but to hear instead the confidence . . . of the daughter who believes that you're sure what you want to do, of the husband who says you can manage together, of yourself, in whose pronouncement that 'you never know what you can do until you have to do it' hides the stronger, even more enabling message: 'If you decide you *have* to do something, you'll do it.' "

Analysis: Mairs is clearly a woman of great courage, determination, and honesty. She does not flinch from facing the hard facts; multiple sclerosis is a cruel disease, gradually robbing a person of mobility, independence, and freedom, affecting relationships and career, altering the structure of life at almost every turn. The essay *"I'm Afraid, I'm Afraid, I'm Afraid"* begins with the fear of flying alone that limits the options of an elderly acquaintance and then describes the fears Mairs lives with and the way she tries to acknowledge and use them. Without preaching or self-pity or the pretense that suffering ennobles, Mairs has written compellingly of her disease and the way she lives with it.

■ Mairs, Nancy. *Plain Text: Essays.* Univ. of Arizona Pr., 1986. 154pp. (o.p.) Reading Level: Grades 10–12. (NYTBR 27 Ap86; WRB Ag86) *Disability:* Multiple sclerosis; Depression

The author was 28 when she began tripping and dropping things. She had just entered graduate school, and her condition was misdiagnosed as a brain tumor. Only a year and a half later was it recognized as multiple sclerosis (MS), which, in her case, followed a slow and steady debilitating course.

Ten years later, Mairs began the dozen essays that compose the book. By that time, she walked with the aid of a brace and cane, and she used an Amigo, an electric scooter, for negotiating distances. Her left hand had been weakened, and she was experiencing more involvement on her right side. Nonetheless, she was teaching, had written prize-winning poetry, and was an active wife and mother.

In most of the essays, the reader is reminded to a greater or lesser degree of the author's incapacity. "On Being a Cripple" confronts the reality of living with a serious disability head-on. "People—crippled or not—wince at the word 'cripple,' as they do not at 'handicapped' or 'disabled.' Perhaps I want them to wince. I want them to see me as a tough customer, one to whom the fates/gods/viruses have not been kind, but who can face the brutal truth of her existence squarely. As a cripple, I swagger" (p. 9). In "Being a Scientific Booby," she touches tangentially on her disability in a rumination inspired by her daughter's deft dissection of the chicken that she herself is not able to prepare.

In the course of the essays, Mairs reviews her entire life, which, she thought, was rather ordinary from the outside. Her father died in an accident when she was 4. She remembers having always been melancholic, introverted, passionate, and self-doubting on the inside, while quite competent and successful on the outside. This discontinuity of realities that she experienced led to bouts of depression, several suicide attempts, and the prolonged hospitalization described in "On Living Behind Bars."

Analysis: Through these essays a picture emerges of a sensitive woman, who, though ill, is still functioning creatively and still struggling for her place in a patriarchal world. The writer Hilma Wolitzer portrays Mairs' work as "original, nervy, and memorable. She writes like a poet, and like a survivor." The essays are witty and most readable; the uncommon spin of the ideas is arresting and thought provoking.

Mairs does not reveal herself as an angry feminist or as an angry (as she calls herself) cripple. She writes, "A friend who also has MS startled me once by asking, 'Do you ever say to yourself, "Why me, Lord?"' 'No, Michael, I don't,' I told him, 'because whenever I try, the only response I can think of is "Why not?"'" Her exquisitely articulated, unsentimental philosophy offers a refreshing and helpful outlook to those struggling with the changes and losses that life brings.

■ Marx, Joseph Laurance. *Keep Trying: A Practical Book for the Handicapped by a Polio Victim.* Harper & Row, 1974. 203pp. (0-06-012827-5) Reading Level: Grades 10–12. (BL 15 My74; KR 1 F74; LJ J174) *Disability:* Poliomyelitis

A professional writer, Joseph Marx had polio in 1913, when he was 3½ years old. The disease affected his legs and, although a series of operations over the years greatly improved his mobility, he was left with a marked disability. Despite this, he has led an active life; he can drive a car and fly an airplane, has traveled, has had a number of different kinds of jobs, has married twice, and has four daughters. His book is a series of chapters addressed to others with disabilities. Know yourself, he advises, and feel proud of yourself; learn how to deal with pain and how to respond to the pity of others; develop your motivation. He writes about medical professionals, hospitals, and rehabilitation. An addendum talks about the effect of the Salk and Sabin vaccines and the necessity of seeing that every child is immunized lest an epidemic return. A bibliography and an index complete the book.

Analysis: Written nearly 20 years ago, Marx's book is in some respects out of date. For example, the reader may be brought up short by a reference to hospital rooms costing as much as $100 a day! The tone is serious and admonishing, which may discourage some readers. Nevertheless, it gives a picture of polio and its treatment in the first half of this century; in addition, the author's suggestions about how to conduct one's life with a disability can still be helpful.

■ Noakes, Vivien. *Edward Lear: The Life of a Wanderer.* Illus. Ariel Books, London, BBC, 1985. 304pp. (Paper 0-563-20-3870) Reading Level: Grades 10–12. (Pun 23 Ja80; TES 21 D79)
Disability: Epilepsy; Seizures

This book was first published in 1968 and was revised in two subsequent printings. It is the only comprehensive biography of the Victorian artist, musician, and well-known writer of nonsense verse. The book's sections describe events in Lear's life in a detailed chronology, with many references to his letters and diaries, beginning with his birth in 1812 as the twentieth child in a London stockbroker's family.

When he was 5 or 6, he had his first attack of epilepsy—"The Demon," he called it. His seizures were to occur almost daily for the rest of his life, and we are told that they caused him endless worry. Because he experienced a warning aura, he was able to prepare for the attacks and so to keep them unknown outside his most immediate family. He developed a lifestyle that allowed him to distance himself from intimate relationship and hence to protect his secret.

Lear's childhood was marred by the exigencies of his financially unstable family and the early death of his exhausted mother. His virtual abandonment by his parents was compensated for by his much older, fun-loving sister, Ann, and his other sisters, who nurtured and tutored him.

Lear became familiar with the emerging English romantic poets of the day, of whom Byron (also, incidentally, epileptic) was his favorite. He began formal schooling at age 11, the year Lord Byron drowned. His sister had taught him painting, and when he was 15, he was introduced to the works of Turner. No longer supported by his aged father, he resolved to earn his living as a painter, which he did in precarious fashion for the rest of his life.

He drew almost anything for anyone: He published ornithological drawings of the parrot family. He contributed to *Illustrations of British Ornithology,* by Prideaux Selby. He was even summoned to give Queen Victoria twelve art lessons. As his reputation flourished, he began to illustrate published verses, including those of Tennyson. In his lifelong, extensive travels, he painted vast numbers of watercolors and oils.

Lear liked to create his own "Nonsenses," which allowed him to express his exuberant, original view of life. He published five books of the nonsense genre that he invented. He set his and other verses to music and would entertain his many hosts by singing and playing the piano. During his lifetime, Lewis Carroll contributed *Alice in Wonderland* to this new form.

Much of the book is devoted to Lear's far-flung travels: to Albania, Greece, the Holy Land, and finally India, where he would avoid the damp English winters and eke out a living with his art. Only at the end of his life did he buy properties and settle in San Remo. He died in 1888 at 76.

Lear constantly toyed with the idea of marrying a very compatible friend, but he did not want to share with her the burden of his epilepsy. Actually, the author suggests that Lear was homosexual and had an unfulfilled longing for several of his close friends. Said his friend Lord Derby, "But he has been out at elbows all his life, so will remain to the last" (p. 174).

A chronology of Lear's travels, a bibliography of his works, notes about the text, and an index conclude the book. Pen drawings by Lear and photos of his art and his friends are interspersed in the text.

Analysis: This book brings to life Victorian upper-class society as it existed in England and in pockets throughout Europe and the British Empire. Lear comes across as a delightful eccentric. Noakes stresses Lear's loneliness and sadness, to which the epilepsy contributed. Nevertheless, Lear hobnobbed freely with the famous artists and poets of the day, always found sponsorship for his travels and his work, and had many friends. The author seems to have a more tragic view than her evidence documents. Perhaps she has held back some of Lear's more personal reflections. Overall, she has supported the view of Lear's friend Congreve, who eulogized him as "a man of versatile and original genius, with great gifts, one of the most interesting, affectionate, and lovable characters it has been my good fortune to know and love" (p. 216).

The book is interspersed with Lear's own comical line drawings, as well as some black-and-white photographs illustrating periods of his life.

■ Nolan, Christopher. *Under the Eye of the Clock.* Preface by John Carey. St. Martin's, 1987. 163pp. (0-312-01266-7) Reading Level: Grades 7–12. (NYTBR 13 Mr88; SLJ N88; TLS 31 J187)
Disability: Cerebral palsy; Quadriplegia; Nonverbal persona

Twenty-one-year-old Nolan had already published a book of poems before undertaking this picaresque book of poetic prose that richly describes the events of his unusual life. "Weaned by pummelled blows to his conscious babbling cries, he now wrote the gilded story of his survival in an alien, silent, lock-jawed world" (p. 31). In the first person, as Joe Meehan, he writes of family life with his mother, father, and younger sister in Ireland.

Joe's cerebral palsy at birth left him with four paralyzed, uncontrollable limbs. He could move his eyes, nod, and laugh but could not speak. He types with a head stick, his head steadied by his mother, Nora.

Early in the book, Joe (like the author) makes the transition from a remedial clinic school to a coed, interdenominational comprehensive school populated with able-bodied students. His father drives him "under the eye of the school's clock" to his new experience. The hero has a keen concentration and a sense of adventure that help him to absorb the richness of his surroundings. He attends classes in history, Irish, music, and geography in his new school. His father tells stories and recites poems. Joe's publications eventually gave him a voice and made him a celebrity. "Access to the normal man's world came through Joseph's breakthrough to written creative musing" (p. 3).

The book recounts adventures at school, at home, and, finally, during a semester at Trinity College. Events surrounding the success of the book of poems, *Dam-Burst of Dreams,* are chronicled. The bittersweet quality of Joe's life is always apparent, but the only complete downer in the story involves a feature in an American magazine in which an interviewer hinted that he was a fraud and that his poems were ghostwritten. His mother comforted him saying, "It's too early in your life to have had to confront someone like him" (p. 107). Over this episode he mentally defied his God but ended by seeking absolution.

The preface was written by author John Carey.

Analysis: This story uses a stream-of-consciousness style accompanied by rich imagery and much poetic wordplay. The insistent voice of the body-trapped boy rings true, and the striking dualities in the book are noted by Carey: the detachment of the writer from himself and his condition and the adult perspective contrasting with that of a child. The book has been well received on both sides of the Atlantic and has become a best seller.

■ Phifer, Kate Gilbert. *Growing Up Small: A Handbook for Short People.* Illus. Paul S. Eriksson, 1979. 214 pp. (0-8397-3136-1) Reading Level: Grades 7–12.
Disability: Dwarfism; Achondroplastic dwarfism; Turner's syndrome

The author of this handbook is 4 feet, 9 inches tall. When she complained of her height problems to an officer of Little People of America, who is an achondroplastic dwarf, he said, "To compare you to me is like comparing a man with a limp to a man with both legs amputated" (p. 4). Nevertheless, Phifer's short stature and that of her two daughters have impelled her to learn about the condition and to write for parents and others so as to improve the lot of short people.

A popular record, Randy Newman's "Short People," was released in 1977. It brought in a host of complaints, but, Phifer writes, it did bring people of short stature to the world's attention.

In the book's first chapter, Phifer speaks somewhat humorously of all the pitfalls and prejudices facing the very short child. In her case, for example, because she was stocky and had red hair, she was nicknamed "Fireplug." She makes a distinction between the very short people, like herself, who are extremes on the normal curve, and the disproportional dwarfs and midgets, who have some kind of abnormality. She pleads for the social tolerance that will allow small people to grow mentally and emotionally.

Subsequent chapters cover in some depth how the body grows, genetics pertinent to growth, cell processes, hormones, and bone development. Normal and abnormal height differences are explained in relation to these body functions. Chapter 7 is devoted to little people and to their organization, Little People of America. Many members, in all walks of life, are described. Phifer concludes the discussion, observing, "For the rest of us, even short people like me, let's not concern ourselves so much with how a little person reaches the bank teller's window, but instead be more concerned about how a little person can become a bank teller" (p. 159).

Phifer evokes the painful years endured by adolescents with delayed or abnormal growth patterns. She has hard-won advice for parents, small people, and their peers to help the different youngster to achieve a sense of self-esteem and to foster healthy relationships. She draws on experiences of many parents and short-statured children.

The last chapter is a personal statement by the author concerning her own diminutive size. Black-and-white photographs portray her accomplishing various tasks at home and driving in her specially adjusted car. She offers advice on apparel selection for males and females. A number of lists include "Sports for Talls and/or Bigs" and "Sports for Shorts and Others" (p. 193). She closes with an exhortation to small people to strive to be the best they can.

An appendix lists several organizations, including the Human Growth Foundation. The book is indexed.

Analysis: Phifer has attended workshops and parent discussions and talked with professionals and short-statured people to enhance her first-hand knowledge about growing up small. Although her own insights and experiences are sprinkled throughout the work, it is more a didactic handbook than a personal story. However, there is much information and support for all undersized people that will also serve to demystify the condition for everyone else as well. This well-written book is a welcome addition to the scanty collection available on this common exceptionality.

■ Powers, Mary Ellen. *Our Teacher's in a Wheelchair.* Illus. Whitman, 1986. Unp. (0-8075-6240-8) Reading Level: Grades 1–3. (SBF J/F87; SLJ D86)
Disability: Paraplegia; Brain damage

The book's simple narrative tells about Brian Hanson, a young man who teaches in an urban day care center. Hanson was head injured in a college game of lacrosse, and he has used a wheelchair ever since. Among the large and numerous black-and-white photographs are pictures of a lacrosse team and ambulance personnel taking on an injured person. Other pictures and text depict Hanson at home, in the community, and at work. The book portrays the disabilities, consequent adjustments, and accomplishments of a warm and effective teacher. The children's initial trepidations upon meeting Hanson, and some of his own sensitivities are discussed. The last page pictures Hanson with four of his happy little charges.
    Analysis: Fortunately, the text of this book, unlike its title, emphasizes what the hero does and how he does it, rather than focusing on being "in a wheelchair." Most of the fine photographs are also action shots suggesting mutuality between the teacher and his students. The matter-of-fact style of the writing is balanced by the exuberance that is evident in the pictures.

■ Prall, Jo. *My Sister's Special.* Illus. by Linda Gray. Childrens Pr., 1985. 31pp. (0-516-03862-1) Reading Level: Grades 1–3. (SLJ Mr86)
Disability: Cerebral palsy; Mental retardation

In this book, a boy about 7 or 8 describes family life with his disabled younger sister, Angie. He explains that Angie is brain damaged due to an illness shortly after her birth; her legs and arms are paralyzed, and she is unable to speak. Full-page black-and-white photographs display a smiling youngster in her wheelchair enjoying family activities, such as a story her brother reads to her. Angie's switch-operated language board is explained. She is shown in her special school bus with a lift for her chair. The narrator remarks on people who stare at his sister; he also says she gives very wet kisses. He concludes that he does not mind, because she is "someone very special."
    Analysis: This simple, honest narrative is buttressed by quite effective

and realistic black-and-white photographs. It avoids being cloying or patronizing. One poignant photo in the story consists of a scene in a shopping mall, when a bystander is momentarily staring at Angie, the mom looks ahead with a somewhat forbearing expression, and the brother looks over at her face with a tentative smile, across his oblivious sister in her chair. The text and photos describing the communication board and the specially adapted bus are particularly instructive for young children.

■ Puller, Lewis B., Jr. *Fortunate Son: An Autobiography.* Grove-Weiden-feld, 1991. 389 pp. (0-8021-1218-8) Reading Level: Grades 7–12. (NY 26 Ag91)
Disability: Amputations

Lewis Puller Jr. had a twin sister and an older brother. His father, the outspoken Lieutenant General "Chesty" Puller, was the most decorated marine in the history of the corps. He served in five wars and was retired at the end of the Korean war at age 57.

In Part One, Puller describes his boyhood. Life on the base and, later, in Saluda, South Carolina, was filled with mostly happy boyhood adventures. He and his father were avid hunters, and he was given a 22-caliber single-shot rifle on his sixth birthday. He writes of his family's expectations even at age six: "I had first begun to grasp the concept of battlefield glory and with it sensed a commitment to a calling over which I would be powerless" (p. 5).

Lewis Puller left undergraduate life at William and Mary College to join the Marine Corps against the backdrop of the Vietnam war. Like many of his social class and conservative background, he had little understanding of the cause he was volunteering to fight for. When he graduated from the rigorous officers' training school, his father pinned on his lieutenant's bars. That same year, he fell in love with Toddy. When she became pregnant, they had a hasty wedding before he was to go to Vietnam.

The green officer was assigned a platoon of very young men, mostly white and lower middle class. Together they endured rains, terrible heat, and interminable forays through the jungles and rice paddies of Vietnam. His troops suffered ambush, booby traps, and mortar fire in terrain where the local residents could be friend or foe and, even if the former, were not above bilking their American liberators. The platoon suffered casualties through wounds, disease, and psychic breakdown. When Puller had been platoon leader for almost three months, he turned to flee some North Vietnam troops in a skirmish. He was booby-trapped by a howitzer that vaporized most of both his legs and took off his left hand, right thumb, and little finger. He writes, "I knew that I had finished serving my time in the hell of Vietnam" (p. 157). He felt that he had let his platoon down and failed to prove himself worthy of his father's name. Close to death, he was returned to Washington in the fall of 1968.

The second half of the book concerns Puller's long haul back to health and sanity. He endured almost two years of hospitalization and numerous operations on his stumps and hands. The birth of his son, Lewis Burwell Puller III, gave him the moral boost to begin his struggle for personal independence. Ultimately he realized that ambulation would not be possible and that he would be in a wheelchair. He learned to drive with hand controls. In 1970, he was accepted by William and Mary's law school on a total disability stipend. Toddy became pregnant with their daughter.

Puller became increasingly dismayed at the discrepancy between the antiwar and complacent mood of the country and the sacrifices asked of the troops in Vietnam. He was disillusioned by the hypocritical utterances and maneuvers of the politicians in charge. The Watergate hearings increased his feeling of disenchantment. In school he found accessibility lacking for his wheelchair. He felt lonely and out of place with people who had not been in combat.

After graduation, Puller pursued a number of activities, but at age 36 he became powerless to control his ever heavier drinking. He was treated for suicidal depression. He went through detoxification and therapy at the time the Vietnam Memorial was being debated and built. In an epilogue, he describes a poignant meeting at the memorial with Soviet veterans from the Afghanistan war. Puller has made his separate peace and come to terms with his war experience.

Analysis: Puller's descriptions of the war and his rehabilitation are detailed and vivid. He brings to life the images of his family and his friends. His doubts about the profession for which he trained and the war that he fought are not at all pontifical or strident. This straightforward and honest book is a worthy addition to the literature about the Vietnam conflict.

■ Rabin, Roni. *Six Parts Love: One Family's Battle with Lou Gehrig's Disease.* Scribner, 1985. 224pp. (0-684-18281-5) Reading Level: Grades 10–12. (KR 15 My85; LJ 1 Je85; PW 10 My85)
Disability: Amyotrophic lateral sclerosis

David Rabin, a 45-year-old physician trained as a neurologist but now an expert in endocrinology, found himself developing certain physical symptoms at an unusually rapid pace that he quickly recognized as amyotrophic lateral sclerosis (ALS). After a neurologist confirmed these suspicions, Rabin was very angry but also very determined that he would fight the disease and attempt to live a full, normal life as long as he could. He succeeded for five years, at the end of which time he died, and he was active and working for nearly this entire period.

Roni Rabin, author of this book, is David's daughter. Shortly after he became ill, she decided to chronicle his and the family's struggle. David himself wrote the preface and coauthored the appendix. The preface is introductory in nature; the appendix is very practical, offering advice to ALS patients on how to exercise; how to deal with weakness of the limbs, eating problems, breathing problems, and communication problems by using such devices as talking books, a computer, and a page-turner; and how to adapt to physical limitations as ALS progresses farther.

Analysis: This is a down-to-earth, pragmatic book; nonetheless, it is emotionally charged just beneath the surface because of the matter-of-fact way that this family is coping with illness, tragedy, and impending death. Recommended for high-school-aged readers.

■ Robinson, Ray. *Iron Horse: Lou Gehrig in His Time.* Illus. Norton, 1990. 300pp. (0-393-02857-7) Reading Level: Grades 9–12. (BL J190; LJ J190; PW 15 Je90)
Disability: Amyotrophic lateral sclerosis

An outstanding, definitive biography of Lou Gehrig, and the only thorough, contemporary analysis of his life and times, this detailed treatment, well researched and well written, will undoubtedly stand as the central account and interpretation of his story for many years to come. Its only rival, Frank Graham's *A Quiet Hero,* is more anecdotal, less detailed, and more subjective, all due mainly to the fact that it was written closer to the time that Gehrig lived.

Gehrig, nicknamed the Iron Horse for the number of consecutive games he played for the New York Yankees baseball team, died in 1941 after a two-year struggle with amyotrophic lateral sclerosis (ALS), a relatively rare and always fatal neurological disorder, thereafter commonly known as Lou Gehrig's disease. The bulk of the book is about Gehrig's development as a baseball player and about the world of the major leagues in the 1920s and 1930s. It is must reading for baseball and sports buffs.

Analysis: While the work would appeal only to mature high school students and those who have some curiosity about recent American social history, it is included in this bibliography, first because it is a truly excellent book, and second because its final segment, approximately the last 50 of its 300 pages, treats Gehrig's early symptoms, diagnosis, and deterioration from ALS. Gehrig carried on the last two years of his life with dignity and determination, often unable to control his once finely tuned athletic body and feeling tired and ill most of the time. Retired from baseball, he served as parole commissioner of the City of New York and made a serious effort to turn around the lives of young men in trouble with the law. A legendary figure since his death, he has earned a permanent place in twentieth-century U.S. history.

■ Roy, Ron. *Move Over, Wheelchairs Coming Through.* Illus. by Rosmarie Haushen. Clarion, 1985. 83pp. (0-89-919-24-91) Reading Level: Grades 4–6. (BCCB Je85; SLJ S85; VYA Ag85)
Disability: Arthrogryposis; Hemolymphangioma; Cerebral palsy; Spina bifida; Muscular dystrophy

The book's text and photographs present seven physically disabled, mentally normal boys and girls between the ages of 9 and 19, who use a wheelchair. The author spent months getting to know the youngsters and their families, and the chapters devoted to each of them include direct quotes and many personal anecdotes. The latter include narratives of accidents involving a spill from a wheelchair and a runaway chair. Some of the young people are attending special classes, some are mainstreamed, and one young adult is in the job market. The last chapter, entitled "A Few More Facts," gives additional details about the specific impairments of the various boys and girls in the book: arthrogryposis, hemolymphangioma, cerebral palsy, spina bifida, and muscular dystrophy. A brief appendix lists further reading. It is followed by an index.

The pictures show the seven actively participating at school, in the neighborhood, and at home. Special adaptations, such as a head stick used for typing, a ramp for aiming a bowling ball, and a hydraulic lift on a public bus, are clearly displayed and discussed in the text.

Analysis: The author faces squarely both the many problems confronting people who have such severe disabilities and their consequences for families and friends as well. The various youngsters have undergone multiple operations, physical degeneration, or struggles with speechlessness and paralysis. Formidable architectural barriers are described, as are the many ways these are coped with. A common theme involves social rejection or misunderstanding in terms of people who stare, shun, or underestimate their intelligence and ability. The book is explicit over issues that are often avoided in books for younger children. For example, it is explained how a child with a urinary bypass manages toileting. The book exudes realistic optimism, and the subjects do the kinds of happy things that all children like to do, such as playing games, feeding the baby, and picnicking in the park.

The work is clearly and sensitively written. It is both entertaining and informative. The numerous pictures are exceptional and self-explanatory enough to be suitable for children unable to read the text.

■ Rushing, Phillip. *Empty Sleeves.* Zondervan, 1984. 156pp. (0-310-28820-7) Reading Level: Grades 7–12. (BL 1 N84; LJ 15 O84; VYA F85) *Disability:* Amputations

For approximately 25 years after the events of his story, the author has been a social worker, administrator, and pastor. He has been active in the civil rights movement, in politics, and in community agencies. He is a family man. His story is divided between a "before" and "after." The introduction opens, "There's a gigantic stripe running right through the middle of my life, separating it into those two parts, like the double line down the middle of a road" (p. 11).

Phillip, called "Bud Doggy," after an impressive redneck, was raised until he was 8 by his grandparents prior to World War II. His Grand-daddy Forty-Four was so named because he had stood off a white man who put a .44 pistol in his face. Forty-Four, grandson of a slave brought from Africa, worked for "the Man" on a large cotton plantation in the Mississippi Delta. When he died, Rushing was taken from the impover-ished, yet secure rural life to join his parents and seven siblings in a town in "The Valley."

With Forty-Four's blood coursing through his veins, Bud Doggy be-came a daring and somewhat defiant adolescent, his emotions inflamed by a growing understanding of the evils of racial segregation. By the time he was 13, he was a field hand doing a man's work, since he had outgrown the program at the one-room school into which three plantations fed 150 black children. He became a tale spinner and joke teller, who even had some clandestine friendships with "poor white folk."

At Christmastime in 1947, the cotton and grain harvests having been good, all the plantation folks had money in their pockets. Sixteen-year-old Bud Doggy and his best friend, Bubba, were happily ambling along the road on their way to court young women. Bud Doggy spied a silver wire lying across the road. "I closed my hand around the wire, and when I did, the fiery gates of hell broke loose and my life was changed forever" (p. 59). The live wire had burned his arms and killed Bubba when he went to help his friend.

Horrified and guilt ridden, Bud Doggy wanted to die also, but he was saved by an endless round of painful operations and skin grafts that left him armless. Finally back home, he learned how to take care of himself, and he read copiously while his family toiled in the fields. At 17, he was still full of despair and decided to end his life by jumping off a high bridge.

Once on the bridge, he experienced a vision and spoke with God. Transformed, he said, "And nothin' but me can stop me now. 'Cause I know who I is, why I'se here, and what I gotta do . . . I'se a son of God, and that makes me a real somebody" (p. 86).

Opportunities began to come his way. He left his family, friends, and girlfriend to attend Saint's School. As the first plantation boy in his class, he determined to lose his valley dialect. The school's formidable headmistress featured her armless prodigy at many money-raising events. This exploitation caused a strain and helped persuade Rushing to move on to the Southern Christian Institute at Edward, Mississippi, and then to Stillman College in West Tuscaloosa. At the age of 26, he was fitted with artificial arms, which served him well. He left for good the subjugation of plantation life as he proceeded to Lexington Seminary. He felt that his liberation had been made possible by the burning wire and the grace of God.

Analysis: The narrative in this book is written in a straightforward, personal style. Conversations from the plantation are recorded in black dialect. Vivid descriptions reveal a cohesive group who suffered yet lived richly within the confines of poverty and segregation. The discussion of their sexual and religious mores is subtle and informative. The rural country of the Deep South is evoked in its lushness and beauty.

While Rushing's faith emerges as the primary focus of his life, he is honest about his religious hypocrisies and pridefulness in pursuit of success and self-esteem.

Rushing makes no comment about the late age at which he was fitted for prostheses. It could be speculated that a white person in similar circumstances would have received help much sooner.

■ Sachs, Albie. **Running to Maputo.** HarperCollins, 1990. 215pp. (0-06-016468-9) Reading Level: Grades 10–12. (BL I S90; KR I J190; LJ Ag90) *Disability:* Amputations

Albie Sachs is an attorney, born in Cape Town's Jewish community, who has devoted his life to working against the South African system of apartheid. A member of the African National Congress, he was jailed in 1963 and forced into exile in 1966. After earning a Ph.D. from the University of Sussex in England, he moved to Mozambique in 1977 to teach law and direct research. He continued his antiapartheid political activity.

In 1988, on his way to the beach for some jogging, Sachs opened his car door and was blasted 30 feet into the air by a bomb planted in his car by an ultrarightist hit squad. He lost consciousness so rapidly that he never heard the blast but was so badly injured that he was expected to die.

Miraculously, he lived, but with the loss of his right arm and the sight in one eye.

In this book he writes about the details of his long, slow, painful recovery, both physically and emotionally. In addition, for the first time, this man who had spent his entire life thinking about others had of necessity to think about himself both in the physical sense and in the emotional and spiritual sense as he pondered the meaning of humanity. Finally, seven months later, he managed to recover sufficiently to run on the beach. At the time of the writing of this book, he was both director of the South Africa Constitution Studies Center at the Institute of Commonwealth Studies in London and a member of the Constitutional and Legal departments of the African National Congress but with hopes, expressed at the end of the book, to return to South Africa with Nelson Mandela and run on the beach with him.

Analysis: Highly recommended for teenage readers, who will enjoy the writer's heroic courage and his dedication to a cause as well as his skillful, vivid writing style.

■ Sandness, Grace Layton. **Brimming Over.** Illus. Mini-World, 1979. 303pp. (Paper 0-931323-01-0) Reading Level: Grades 7–12. *Disability:* Quadriplegia; Poliomyelitis

This autobiography was typed by mouth stick 25 years after the author contracted polio in 1950. The facts are essentially correct, although writer's liberty has been taken in the reproduction of some quoted dialogue, and some names have been changed.

Sandness was home on summer break after her freshman year at college, when she contracted a particularly virulent case of the disease, which almost killed her. The virus destroyed all use of her arms and legs, and it impaired her breathing so much that she was completely dependent on an iron lung until the following Christmas. After a long recuperation she was returned to her loving family's home.

The next months found her wrestling to come to grips with her many losses: lack of energy, lost ability to play the piano, confinement to a wheelchair, and total dependency for personal care. Eventually, she was able to breathe on her own during the day and to control a powered wheelchair with one foot.

During the days at home, she learned to draw by mouth and developed a successful greeting card business aptly named "Gracenotes." For Christmas cards, she composed religious messages that expressed her deep Christian faith. She was designated North Dakota's Artist of the Year in 1956, and later she was featured in Erling Rolfsrud's *Extraordinary North Dakotans.*

When one of her brothers left for military service, she learned to use his ham radio, clicking out Morse code with a mouth device. She met Dave Sandness through the ham radio. Against the better judgment of most of the people around her, she agreed to marry this young man who was courting her. The travails experienced by the young couple as they pursued school and job entry were not different in kind from those of others, but they were certainly exaggerated by Grace's immobility and occasional hospitalizations. Indeed, they were forced to leave one small town where Dave was teaching school, because their relationship could not be tolerated.

Once Dave had a steady job, they bought a modest house and adopted their first child, a very young, disabled Korean girl. By the end of the story, they had eight children from various countries and of different races, ages, and physical conditions. The growing family careened from place to place as Dave completed education as a psychologist and found employment.

Grace's health was problematic, and at one stage she precariously existed, back in the iron lung, scarcely able to think right due to oxygen deprivation. She was admitted to the famous postpolio hospital, Ranchos Los Amigos, where a hole was cut in her windpipe to connect it directly to the breathing aid she would now have to live with henceforth.

The couple's worst struggle centered on the half-black, sullen, and defiant Korean girl whom they adopted as a teenager. Kim began to destroy the cohesiveness of the family with her domineering and bullying ways. She had bouts with drugs, detention, and truancy. She moved out to her own apartment and became a single parent. Sandness began her book during this time of parent-child confrontation, and she struggled to conquer her own negative feelings toward her sixth adoptee. Both she and Dave were ecstatic over their granddaughter, and they watched Kim grow through the experience of motherhood, but they also feared for the baby because of Kim's jealousy and explosive temper.

An epilogue to the book describes what happened when Kim read the first printed edition of her mother's book. She was moved to tears and came to her mother to apologize for all the wrongs she had caused. The two finally forged a mutual understanding and a new bond of love.

The Sandnesses' latest project has been Crossroads, an adoption agency established to help link families with foreign and special children, some with handicaps. Grace became an adoption counselor in the next stage of her life.

Analysis: The accomplishments and fortitude of both the author and her husband may be humbling to readers. Few people have suffered losses as severe as those of Grace Sandness, and few spouses would elect to set up a home together with a completely paralyzed person, much less assemble a polyglot household of needy adopted children, all under stringent financial circumstances. And yet these people emerge as unassuming and modest, determined to lead ordinary lives in a Christian context. The greatest anger expressed in the book is toward the mindless racism that their multihued brood sometimes attracted.

The life of this couple is filled with children, friends, and relatives of their children, as well as beloved household pets. As the anecdotes are recounted, it is sometimes difficult to keep the names and characters straight, even with some helpful, accompanying black-and-white photographs. However, this detracts little from the enjoyable narrative.

■ Sayers, William F. *Don't Die on My Shift.* Major, 1977. 236pp. (0-89041-161-1) Reading Level: Grades 10–12.
Disability: Poliomyelitis

In 1952, William Sayers, a young New York bank clerk, collapsed in the street, suddenly ill and unconscious. Weeks later, he awoke in a hospital full of people sick with and often dying from polio. He was critically ill for a long time, as were most of the patients. One evening, unable to sleep, he heard a nurse at the nearby station say, "I hope that one doesn't die on my shift." As he listened further, he realized that the staff was discussing him.

Sayers recounts his 16 unbelievable years in this long-term-care facility for patients with polio. Since the patients were kept together in large, open rooms with many beds, there was no privacy. He witnessed the breakup of engagements and marriages, as well partners decided they could not remain committed to ill ones. Sayers's own young wife quickly divorced him. He witnessed many deaths and chronic suffering. Both surrounded by and a participant in horrendous physical pain, lonliness, abandonment, boredom and alienation, Sayers is still able to take an ironic, darkly humorous view of his world. Earthy, wisecracking characters parade through the pages, all with names like Clarinet, Truck Driver, Gorilla, Slavic, Witch, and Green Eyes. Some are patients, some staff, some volunteers. He portrays the medical staff, by and large, as crude, cruel, careless, and nasty, lacking in warmth, empathy, and concern for patients.

While Sayers was hospitalized, both of his parents died, and he was left alone. Sometime in 1966 or 1967, a 30ish volunteer, Hazel Eyes, became his friend. She encouraged him to pursue a writing career, and after many manuscript rejections, he finally received an acceptance and a check. It arrived in 1968, on the very day that he was leaving the hospital permanently to marry Hazel Eyes and live with her in a Queens, New York, apartment.

A postscript to the book tells readers that Sayers has weaned himself from his chest respirator and now uses a positive pressure machine that pumps air into a hose held in the corner of his mouth. He is a free-lance writer who has published stories and articles in more than 60 newspapers and magazines. He and his wife, Ann (Hazel Eyes), moved to Buffalo, New York, where he has continued his writing. He uses an electric typewriter by striking the keys with a stick clenched in his teeth.

Analysis: Teenage readers should like the gritty realism, blunt language, and ironic humor that characterize this book. Its style and themes are contemporary, its narrative moves quickly, and its descriptive passages are vivid, gripping, and often painful.

■ Schommer, Nancy. *Stopping Scoliosis.* Illus. Doubleday, 1987. 183pp. (0-385-23386-8) Reading Level: Grades 7–12. (BL 15 S87; KR 15 Ag87, PW 21 Ag87)
Disability: Scoliosis

Similar to some of the books reviewed in the chapter on AIDS that deal with both the disease and the people who have it, this excellent book on scoliosis gives extensive information on the disorder. Although it does not emphasize primarily the people who have scoliosis, a number of case histories are interspersed throughout the various chapters.

Scoliosis is a relatively hidden disorder that affects numbers of youngsters, particularly but not exclusively girls, and, if untreated, remains with them for the rest of their life. Although pediatricians and school health personnel have now begun to do routine spinal checks to detect early symptoms of scoliosis, books like this one offer an important supplement by making comprehensive information widely available in school and public libraries. The author—editorial director of a communications firm and writer of articles for popular magazines—herself has scoliosis, which was not detected and treated until she was in college. By such time, surgical procedures, such as those that she had, are usually necessary.

Analysis: The book has five chapters, the first one of which defines and explains scoliosis with the help of a number of drawings and photographs. Following are three chapters on detection and treatment, including both nonsurgical and surgical alternatives, and a final chapter on the search for the cause of the disorder. Three appendixes list a bibliography of recommended readings, scoliosis organizations, and scoliosis specialists. A bibliography and an index conclude the volume.

■ Scott, Toni Lee. *A Kind of Loving.* Illus. World, 1970. 205pp. (o.p.) Reading Level: Grades 7–12. (BS 1 O70; KR 15 Ap70; LJ J170)
Disability: Amputations

The book's prologue recounts the motorcycle accident that changed 19-year-old Toni Scott's life forever, ten days after her second marriage began. Her leg was terribly mangled, and she was not to leave the hospital for 20 months after she was admitted. Scott still had her leg when she went to her mother's cottage on Malibu. However, it was so dysfunctional that she decided to have the subsequent operations that resulted in an above-the-knee amputation when she was just 21. After recovery, she insisted on driving herself home from the hospital. Soon she went to the beach with her crutches.

Scott details her upbringing in several homes and in a convent while her mother, deserted by her father, struggled to provide for her daughter. She always knew she wanted to be a singer, so she began to associate with musicians who helped her learn her craft and break into the business. At 14, lying about her age, she auditioned and sang in the famed Venetian Room of San Francisco's Fairmont Hotel.

After the accident, she had sued the driver of the car that hit her friend's motorcycle and dragged her under the wheels, but the jury ruled against her. Too poor even to afford an artificial leg, she declared bankruptcy to pay for her 39 operations. Auditioning at one club, she overheard the owner say, "Sure she sings good, but what do I need with a freak?" (p. 64). Next, she was hired for a television program that showed her only above the waist. She was seen by the manufacturer of a new kind of prosthesis, which was made for her in exchange for the publicity she could give. She walked out of the maker's office on two legs, in high-heeled shoes!

The story follows both Scott's formidable career as a vocalist and her quest for personal fulfillment up to the time she wrote the book at age 33. Scott chronicles many deep friendships, including one with James Dean, and some harrowing misadventures. For example, she was inadvertently involved in a robbery ring, although she was exonerated in the course of a highly publicized trial. Her first love was always music, and her career took off when she went on the road with Scobey's Frisco Jazz Band. Between gigs, Scobey packed her leg with his trumpet. Scott also was able to establish a foundation to help amputees (often children who became dear to her), so as to regain a feeling of self-worth and hope. By the end of the book, she has successfully fused the professional and personal aspects of her life as a singer with a cause.

Analysis: Scott, with editing help from Curt Gentry, gives an inside view of the entertainment world that is very different from its outward appearance of glamour and glitter. With considerable humor, she describes years of hard work, uncertain earnings, depressions, and ill health. Her adventures include exposure to criminal activities and deceptions by colleagues and friends. She is introspective and modest about herself, often humorously deprecating. However, she also comes across as a very talented, generous, and tough lady who is a wonderful example to others facing physical adversity. Her style is chatty, and her anecdotes about celebrities are fun, particularly if their names are familiar to the reader.

■ Shebar, Sharon. *Franklin D. Roosevelt and the New Deal.* Illus. by Gary Lippincott. Barron's, 1987. 168pp. (Paper 0-8120-3916-5) Reading Level: Grades 4–9.
Disability: Poliomyelitis

Shebar follows Roosevelt from his birth and childhood as a privileged, much loved child through the chief episodes of his life, with emphasis on his political career. Several chapters describe his illness in mid-life, his convalescence at Warm Springs, and his return to active public life. Eleven years after he was struck by polio, he became president and then led his country through the Great Depression and World War II. A glossary, a list of topics for discussion, a bibliography, a map of Europe of 1939, and an index complete the book.

Analysis: The author manages to cover many of the salient points in Roosevelt's full and unusual career. Young readers should gain a valuable picture of the events that have shaped present society, as well as a sense of Roosevelt's personality and his great courage in adversity. A criticism might be made of the illustrations, which are obviously drawn from photographs, leaving one to wonder why the editor did not simply use the photos instead. Despite these comments, however, it is a book that can be recommended; it might lead youngsters to more reading on Roosevelt, on the history of the period, and perhaps on polio as a scourge that has been largely conquered.

■ Shyne, Kevin. *The Man Who Dropped from the Sky.* Illus. Messner, 1982. 63pp. (0-671-44164-7) Reading Level: Grades 4–9. (BL 15 Ja83; IBCB 58 83; SLJ F83; VYA Je83)
Disability: Orthopedic injury

Roger Reynolds began skydiving when was 17 years old. By the time he enlisted in the army after high school and volunteered for Jump School, he had already made more than 100 jumps as a civilian. After ranger school, he was chosen to be a member of the elite Golden Knights, the Army Exhibition Parachute Team. A year later, on his 959th jump, his first parachute did not open properly and his second tangled in the first. He dropped 2,800 feet and hit the ground at 85 miles an hour, landing on the lawn of a doctor's home. The fall broke all the major bones in his left side, and he spent months in the hospital. When the bone graft in his shin refused to heal, he secretly used the doctors' hospital library to read about the subject. Deciding that he needed to improve the blood circulation in his leg, he sneaked off to the army gym and exercised. The graft healed. When the therapist told him that his left elbow was permanently locked, he devised his own exercise program.

Reynolds had thought he would never want to jump again, but after he got out of the hospital, a friend persuaded him to overcome his fear, and he jumped successfully and with his old exhilaration. He entered college, planning to study medicine with the goal of being an orthopedic surgeon. He still walked with a cane but embarked on a program of jogging and exercise; in 1978, four years after his accident, he ran the 26.2 miles of the Boston Marathon.

Black-and-white photographs illustrate the text.

Analysis: Kevin Shyne is a free-lance writer who became a friend of Reynolds' while writing an article. In the brief introduction, he summarizes Roger Reynolds' accident and survival; in unadorned prose, the following chapters detail the events of Reynolds' life. Reynolds comes across as a young man of great physical courage, endurance, and determination. While not everyone is able to achieve such victories over disabilities, he provides a useful example of a person who took an active part in his treatment. He is quoted as saying that, whereas some people advise that one should "set realistic goals and go after them," he does not: "I aim for the moon. So even if I miss, I'm still going to land pretty high."

■ Sienkiewiecz-Mercer, Ruth, and Steven Kaplan. *I Raise My Eyes to Say Yes.* Houghton, 1989. 225pp. (0-395-46109-X) Reading Level: Grades 7–12. (KR 15 Je89; NYT 30 S89; NYTBR 22 O89)
Disability: Cerebral palsy; Quadriplegia; Meningitis

Kaplan, now a lawyer, begins the book with a description of his collaboration with his nonverbal coauthor. The book was developed from 1979 to 1985 in 2,000 hours of communication by means of a spelling board, yes-no answers to questions through facial gestures, and a repertoire of sounds. Now, for the first time, Ruth's story could have a voice. The few key words she spelled are listed before each chapter.

Ruth was born physically normal in 1950, but she acquired quadriplegia as an infant from what was thought to be a meningitis infection. She spent her early years alternating stays in private rehabilitation facilities with living with her loving family. She made no physical or psychological improvement in the institutions and was consequently labeled mentally retarded. When she was 12, her mother could no longer handle her care, so her parents reluctantly committed her to the free, public state hospital for the retarded.

Ruth spent her first days in her new home in isolation, flat on her back and in diapers. Most of the residents were mentally deficient and exhibited many bizarre behaviors. However, Ruth's first bed mate and some others through the years were as alert as she was. They evolved a form of communication based on the few sounds and gestures they could muster.

Many of the chapters describe life in a cold, overcrowded, and unresponsive institution on a ward for the severely disabled. Little triumphs are noted, such as the time a sensitive attendant first moved her from lying flat on her back to a sitting position in a chair bed so that she could see more than the ceiling. Soon after this, attendants began to realize that she laughed at their jokes, and, finally, that she raised her eyes to say yes.

A real breakthrough came when the Communication Resource Center was set up at the institution. There, researchers developed the first communication boards and spelling systems for a few residents with specific communication disorders. Further, the trend toward deinstitutionalization enabled the author and other higher-functioning residents to move to apartments in the community, assisted by personal care attendants. Eventually, Sienkiewicz married an old friend and former coresident, and they set up housekeeping together.

At the time of the book's completion, the couple was struggling to manage on very little money and experienced, as well, lack of adequate programming in their lives. However, the two frequently speak as advocates for severely disabled people, and they are working toward the goal of total deinstitutionalization of this population.

Analysis: Kaplan has accomplished a prodigious task in terms of time and imagination to wrest the story of Sienkiewicz-Mercer from a lively, understanding mind, which is otherwise deficient in the area of expressive communication; he addresses his methodology and its limitations up front and at length. He has apparently had a real meeting of the mind with a long-suffering victim of the institutional system.

This book gives a very realistic portrayal of the tedium of institutional residents' empty days and their powerlessness in the decisions that determine their life. The worst sins by bureaucracy become painfully evident. The policy of deinstitutionalization seems overdue for those who have been doubly incarcerated—once by their crippled bodies and again by society. The ramifications wrought by the technical development of communication systems for disabled people are personalized and made vivid in this fine account.

■ Smith, Elizabeth Simpson. *A Service Dog Goes to School: The Story of a Dog Trained to Help the Disabled.* Illus. by Steven Petruccio. Morrow, 1988. 65pp. (LB 0-688-07648-3) Reading Level: Grades 1–6. (BL 1 Ja89; SLJ Ja89)
Disability: Spinal defect; Paralysis

Licorice, a black Labrador retriever, has been trained as a service dog to assist a boy paralyzed from the waist down as the result of a spinal birth defect. The book describes the dog's background and first weeks in a kennel, where she is given various tests to judge her abilities. The text then covers the months spent in the home of a young puppy trainer followed by six months of intensive schooling before Licorice is matched with Scott and they finish their training together. Licorice can now help Scott live more independently. She can pull his wheelchair and get his clothes out of the drawer; in a store she can lift from the counter the items Scott has chosen and give the salesperson Scott's money; she sits by his desk in the classroom, takes him through the cafeteria line, and teams up with him to play frisbee with the other children.

The book is illustrated with black-and-white drawings. It concludes with "A Special Message" about interacting with disabled people and their service dogs, a "Partial List of Service Dog Training Schools or Organizations," and an index.

Analysis: This is a book filled with information clearly presented, which could be of interest to the general reader, to young animal lovers, and to children who themselves have disabilities. The illustrations are detailed but somewhat wooden, as if they were copied from photographs. Neither the catalog material nor the text itself indicates whether this is a true story; it would have more impact if it were presented as nonfiction. Despite these caveats, it is useful because, although there are books on dogs trained to help blind and deaf people, there is not much published information on this type of service dog.

■ Stehele, Bernard. *Incurably Romantic.* Illus. Temple Univ. Pr., 1985. 243pp. (0-87722-307-6) Reading Level: Grades 7–12. (LJ S85; PW 7 Je85)
Disability: Severely physically disabled

This book provides portraits, both in black-and-white pictures and in brief prose commentaries, about love relationships between people when one or both of the couple are severely physically disabled. The writing is done from the perspective of residents of Inglis House, known at that time as the Philadelphia Home for Incurables—hence the title, *Incurably Romantic.*

The author had originally come from a local community college to teach an English composition course, but his interest in the commitments and experiences of the residents led to the three-year-long book project. Relationships of all kinds are portrayed, from long-standing marriage to a remembered crush on a nurse. One unmarried young woman has a baby.

Intergenerational, interracial, and interfaith friendships are common. The sincerity, simplicity, and joy in the prose of various speakers contrast with the pictures of their painfully distorted and malfunctioning bodies.

By the completion of the book, Inglis House had undergone a formal change of designation to the Philadelphia Home for Physically Disabled Persons, a change in part due to pressure from the residents.

A scholarly, six-page afterword by sociologist Joseph W. Schneider concludes the book. Schneider discusses public attitudes with regard to the severely disabled population. He speculates about institutional policy toward sexuality, right to privacy, and social enrichment.

Analysis: The simply stated commentaries make easy reading, and the ideas are relevant to young as well as older people exploring relationships. For example, when Gail, 24, was recorded speaking about her difficulties with 31-year-old Gregory, she says, "Biggest problem? Attitudes, my attitude. He tells me things—I don't listen. I want to do what I want to do—when I want to do it. He doesn't like that. So we argue. Then he gets mad and goes home. So then we start all over again the next day." (p. 42).

In the writing, there is very little emphasis on disabilities themselves, and often the specific physical problems of the residents are not mentioned. However, the extent of the disabilities is in stark evidence in such pictures as a person strapped into an electric wheelchair, a partner feeding another with a mouth-held spoon, distorted and wasted limbs and faces, and a hand-powered van with a lift.

The afterword, rather heavy reading, tries to explain the significance of this work and is somewhat critical of its limited scope. The book's message has to do with the essence of humanness—communication and caring even under the most difficult of life's circumstances. It is provocative and probably will impress various readers very differently, depending on their own particular personality and circumstances.

■ Van Etten, Angela Muir. **Dwarfs Don't Live in Doll Houses.** Adaptive Living, 1988. 256pp. (0-945727-80-1) Reading Level: Grades 7–12. *Disability:* Dwarfism; Larsen's syndrome

The author begins her life story by describing the difficult birth that made her survival problematic for the first two years of her life. "This is one that should never been born," whispered the director of nursing. Angela Muir had a rare type of dwarfism, Larsen's syndrome, which includes, besides characteristic short stature, thumbs and knees that do not bend and dislocated joints. Even so, she walked before she was a year old.

She describes her early homecoming from the medical institution to her warm and sensible New Zealand family. They treated their eldest and smallest offspring as normally as possible. Angela was always a good student and generally enjoyed her school years. As an adult, she attained the height of 3 feet, 6 inches.

Muir was admitted to law school in 1972. She practiced law for five years in New Zealand. She was then awarded a Winston Churchill Fellowship to come to the United States to meet members of the disability movement, including the Little People of America (LPA). From the book's acknowledgments readers learn that she married Robert Van Etten, who has served as national president of the LPA.

Much of the book is organized according to themes, such as "Dating Desires as a Teen-ager" and "Adaptations as a Way of Life." All of Muir's reflections are punctuated with anecdotes, some painful, but most humorous, that illustrate her points.

Analysis: Muir's straightforward prose includes many one-liners and a healthy dose of cynicism regarding the wisdom and attitudes of normal-sized people. In general, the book is upbeat, funny, and optimistic. With illuminating candor, it gives a dwarf's-eye view of the world.

■ Vaughn, Ruth. *Accept Me as I Am.* Nazarene, 1981. 72pp. (o.p.)
Reading Level: Grades 10–12.
Disability: Quadriplegia

Burrell Leatherwood was one of five boys in his family. At 15, he broke his neck in a diving accident and was not expected to live. He had no feeling or movement below his neck but survived the first critical days as well as some difficult surgery.

Burrell's mother carried on a constant dialogue with God, not understanding how He could have allowed this tragedy to happen in such a religious family. She kept reminding herself that it was God's will, not hers, that was to be done.

Burrell, always encouraged by his mother, was fitted with a neck brace, and he learned to sit again. He made a conscious decision to participate in therapy and was sent to the Portland Rehabilitation Center, 40 miles away from his home. He learned to hold up his head without the brace, to feed himself, and to type. He made his first visit home five months after his accident. Finally back home for good, Burrell had to adjust to traveling to school in a van with an attendant. He completed his junior and senior years of high school.

The family moved to Yukon, Oklahoma, where he was able to attend the state college, taken by an attendant from the nursing home where he lived. Then the nursing home canceled its commitment to young disabled people, and it looked as if Burrell's college career was finished.

Through her accustomed persistence, his mother arranged an interview at Bethany Nazarene College. Though Burrell was depressed and doubtful, "his mother was joyful and exuberant . . . like a will-o-the-wisp standing on tiptoe as she told him that this could be God's way to answer their prayer" (p. 47). As described in the prologue, the boy was accepted warmly. He was carried to inaccessible classes by willing classmates. He wrote his class notes by mouth. The concern and friendship extended to him contrasted with the years he had been ignored on the uncaring state college campus. Good in his studies, he qualified to be a tutor and also a counselor for students with problems.

Burrell received a B.A. degree in psychology, in his wheelchair, next to the rest of his class. In the audience, his mother was filled with gratitude. He was to add a B.S. degree in computer science in 1981.

Analysis: Burrell emerges as a plucky kid who kept trying despite setbacks and self-doubts. The way he was treated at Bethany Nazarene College, where he was given help and made to feel like one of the rest, could be a model for all students. One could hope that colleges will be able to make architectural modifications to their buildings so as to eventually obviate the need for so many "Chariot Carriers" for wheelchairs.

At worst, this book is gushy about religion. The reader might wonder, when Vaughn writes about Burrell's flailing arm missing one of the knobs on the wheel of his chair, banging into a wall, and requiring a friend to Band-Aid his bloody elbow, why this "is another of those gifts from God" (p. 57). However, the book demonstrates the power of deep faith both to help a family deal with a catastrophic experience and to influence young people to act humanely toward one another.

■ Verheyden-Hilliard, Mary Ellen. *Scientist and Teacher, Anne Barrett Swanson.* Illus. by Holly Meeker Rom. Equity Institute, 1988. 31pp. (0-932469-16-7) Reading Level: Grades 1–6. (BL 15 F89; SLJ Ap89) *Disability:* Osteogenesis imperfecta

Anne Barrett was born in Coal City, Illinois, in 1948 and was immediately diagnosed as having osteogenesis imperfecta, a condition in which the bones are so weak that they break easily, and subsequent growth is stunted. One doctor advised her parents to institutionalize her, apparently believing that her brain as well as her bones were affected, but her parents heeded a second doctor and brought her home. On her many visits to the hospital to have broken bones attended to, Anne was introduced to the lab and, deciding that exciting things went on there, made up her mind to become a scientist.

Anne was not only an outstanding student but also a gifted pianist who could have made a career in music. Instead, despite discouragement from some colleges, whose officials believed she was too short to do laboratory work, she studied science at Northern Illinois University. She married a fellow student, and they both went on to earn doctorates at the University of Wisconsin; Anne's degree is in biochemistry. She did research on cancer and taught on the college level, becoming department head; one year, she was invited to work at the National Science Foundation in Washington. In a quote at the end of the book, she encourages youngsters to consider a career in science.

Analysis: This short book tells its story in simple language printed in large type; each two-page spread is illustrated with black-and-white drawings that are not particularly distinguished. The author has chosen to emphasize only the positive elements in the subject's life; although difficulties in being accepted as a science student are mentioned, readers are told only that "Anne had a hard time at first" and thus do not gain a real sense of what these rebuffs meant to her. Nevertheless, although this is not an outstanding example of juvenile biography, it could interest young readers who are just beginning to read in this genre.

■ Waugh, Eileen. *No Man Is an Island: A Biography of Peter Spencer.* Triton, 1970. 196pp. (0-363-00025-9) Reading Level: Grades 10–12. *Disability:* Paraplegia

Peter Spencer, a young fighter pilot with the Royal Air Force during World War II, was injured in a runway collision between a plane and a truck in which he was riding in 1945 six weeks before the end of the war. Thrown from the truck, he broke his neck. He injured his left arm, leaving it permanently paralyzed; his right arm was injured so badly that it had to be amputated at the shoulder.

While hospitalized, he overheard a conversation about "people like that" usually dying from depression and finally realized that he was the subject of the conversation. In fact, he did suffer from some depression, but the recollection of that conversation and the help of family and friends lifted him out of it. Although his girlfriend drifted away from him after he failed to regain the use of his paralyzed arm, he eventually met and married June Lynette—a singer and actress—and they had two children, who are now grown.

He taught speech for a time but eventually became a proficient foot and mouth artist. A skilled public speaker, he became active in his town's political life and also in causes to assist people with disabilities. Spencer faced attitudes ranging from pity to rudeness about his disability and all the frustrations inherent in being unable to do so much of what he had once taken for granted, such as playing the piano. The book is an account of how he dealt with these challenges and his ultimate successes at meeting them.

Analysis: Although Spencer was, at the time of the writing of this book, a middle-aged man, the book does not have a middle-aged feeling. He was approximately 20 when he lost the use of his arms, and the entire book retains a youthful atmosphere. Teenagers who are mature readers should not be put off by the beginning of the story in the mid-1940s or its ending in the late 1960s. Nor should they be put off by the British language usage, which, although obvious, does not get in the way of the story. Waugh is a skilled writer who has produced a book that manages to transcend potential problems with time, place, and language. It is not recommended for younger or less talented readers.

6

BOOKS DEALING WITH SENSORY
PROBLEMS

For the young child, human variation is a fact of life,
even when it comes to handicapped children.
— William C. Morse, in *The Handicapped in*
Literature (1980 Eli Bower, ed.)

He has seen but half the universe who has never been
shown the house of pain.
— Ralph Waldo Emerson

The titles here are classified in three sections: Deaf-Blind, Hearing Impairments, and Visual Impairments. Citations are alphabetical by author within each section.

DEAF-BLIND

■ Adler, David A. *A Picture Book of Helen Keller.* Illus. by John and Alexandra Wallner. Holiday House, 1990. Unp. (0-8234-0818-3) Reading Level: PS–3.
Disability: Deaf-blind

The author has written several books in the Picture Book Biography series for very young readers and listeners. Here, with minimal text, he gives some of the salient details in the life of his famous subject, with almost twice as many pages devoted to her early life as to her adulthood. Adler describes Keller's early illness and subsequent loss of sight and hearing, her frustration and untamed behavior, and the radical changes effected by

Anne Sullivan Macy; he touches on Keller's education at Radcliffe, her writing and public appearances, and her work both for the American Foundation for the Blind and for soldiers wounded in World War II. Blocks of type are set in the double-page illustrations, which the book's artists have done in line and watercolor. The final page lists important dates in Keller's life.

Analysis: Writing with simple clarity, Adler gives young children what will probably be their first acquaintance with Helen Keller. The illustrations, though lively and colorful, are much less successful, especially for those who know Keller through photographs. There seems little resemblance between her beautiful, expressive face and the person depicted here; for example, her eyes, which were actually open though unseeing, are represented in most of the illustrations by squinty lines. Nevertheless, parents, teachers, and librarians can use this book to introduce young children to Keller's life of remarkable courage and achievement, although they might want to show the photographs that appear in many other biographies.

■ Hunter, Nigel. *Helen Keller.* Illus. by Richard Hook. Bookwright, 1986. 32pp. (0-531-18031-X) Reading Level: Grades 2–6. (CBRS My86; SL D85; SLJ Ag86)
Disability: Deaf-blind

Hunter begins with a short summary section called "A Life of Achievement" and then moves back to Helen Keller's birth, following the main events of her life chronologically. He recounts such familiar stories as the moment at the pump when the child Helen understood the relationship between thing and word, describes the deeply distressing controversy over Helen's authorship of "The Frost King" (written when she was 11), and summarizes her education and her life's accomplishments. The book is illustrated with photographs and colored drawings. It concludes with a chronology of dates and events, a glossary, a short list of suggested readings, and an index.

Analysis: The first edition of this guide (*Accept Me as I Am,* 1985) annotates five books about Helen Keller, including Joseph Lash's biography for adults, as well as a biography of Anne Sullivan Macy, but none is more recent than 1980. Actually, although the facts are familiar, each book is done with a different viewpoint. Here, the author has chosen to give an overview of Keller's whole life, without concentrating on any particular phase. Except when discussing "The Frost King," he scarcely alludes to difficulties or discouragement, presenting Keller as unfailingly courageous, happy, and sunny tempered; this was probably the persona that she showed the world in her public appearances. A teacher might build a stimulating class project out of a comparison of biographies of Keller. It remains strikingly clear that no matter what the stance of the biographer, what she or he chooses to emphasize, Keller had a remarkable life, and she has become almost an icon for our age.

■ Kudlinski, Kathleen V. *Helen Keller: A Light for the Blind.* Illus. by Donna Diamond. Viking, 1989. 58pp. (0-670-82460-7) Reading Level: Grades 4–6. (BL 15 F90; HB J189; SLJ Ap90)
Disability: Deaf-blind

Helen Keller's story is so well-known that it hardly needs to be summarized. Kudlinski's book covers Keller's whole life, from her illness at a year and a half to her death at 87 in 1968. The author describes the child's initial anger and unmanageable behavior, the famous scene with Annie Sullivan at the water pump, and Keller's subsequent amazing intellectual growth. She touches on the accusation of plagiarism, made when Helen was 12 and Mr. Anagnos, director of the Perkins School for the Blind, had published her story called "The Frost King" in the school yearbook; the story was later traced to a book that had been read to her three years earlier, which her conscious mind no longer remembered.

After Helen left Perkins, her education continued at private schools and Radcliffe College. Then came the long years of writing, travel, and public appearances and her work with the American Foundation for the Blind and with blinded soldiers during World War II. Anne Sullivan Macy was always at her side until Macy's death in 1936. Polly Thomson became Keller's companion until she herself died in 1960. Helen Keller, who had always been an optimist, could look back and say, "My life has been a wonder-tale of kind people who helped me to light the path of the handicapped."

Analysis: In a brief postscript, the author writes about the effort she had to make to understand "Helen, the person," who lived in a world that Kudlinski herself could never enter. She had to remember "Helen's plea that we 'forget she is deaf and blind and think of her as an ordinary woman.' . . . I had imagined Helen's mind to be different from mine simply because her senses were." In fact, Kudlinski does a good job of capturing the essence of this remarkable story in a relatively short book written in a way that makes it accessible and attractive to young readers. She makes occasional reference to the way in which Anne Sullivan controlled what entered Keller's dark and silent world and influenced even the way Keller smiled and carried herself. Yet there is no doubt here about Keller's strength of character and the effect her life has had on the world. This biography is a worthwhile addition to the many books on Keller available to young readers.

Diamond's soft drawings, while they do not always resemble closely the photographic images we have of Keller and Sullivan, are pleasant and unobtrusive.

■ Man, John. *The Survival of Jan Little.* Illus. Viking, 1987. 342pp. (0-670-81514-4) Reading Level: Grades 10–12. (BL 15 Mr87; LJ 1 F87; PW 23 Ja87)
Disability: Retinitis pigmentosa

Jan Little was 28 when she arrived in San Cristobal, Mexico, from the United States to make a new life for her small daughter, Becca, and herself. Already, she was hard of hearing and legally blind, symptoms of her progressive disease. However, she was eager for new experiences and harbored a secret dream of homesteading. She married eccentric Harry, who came to be known in San Cristobal as "the jungle tyrant," the man who thought he was Jesus.

The first third of the book chronicles not only the couple's strange relationship but also a rich and full family life, conducted for ten years in the pristine wilderness. When Jan's daughter was 15, loggers and home-steaders came in to destroy the jungle, so the family, with Jan now com-pletely blind and going deaf, went into the northern Brazilian interior to find another creek and mountain. Again, after many hardships, they established a homestead in the Amazon, in a mountainous region up the river, overlooking a vast mountain range, days away from their nearest neighbors.

On New Year's Day, 1980, the little family began a descent into illness. In the middle of a terrifying storm, young Becca died as she and Harry wandered, weakened and dazed, looking for their cabin in the dark. Then Jan and Harry settled down to wait their end as well. During this time, Jan had a spiritual vision and decided that she was "going to try for it." She and Harry struggled against malaria, weakness, and starvation for several months. Finally, emaciated, Harry died. A recovering Jan dragged his body into the jungle, to be cleaned to the bones by jungle creatures just as she had done earlier for her daughter.

Grief finally gave away to action, as blind and deaf Jan planned for her survival. She began marking with rags, poles, and typewriter ribbons the trails she must take for food and water. She learned to chop wood and clear land with a machete by feel. By burning Braille papers, she finally made a fire in order to have her first hot meal in two months. She settled down to learning Portuguese from the Brazilian Ministry of Education

Braille magazine, anticipating her need to communicate with the Indians who had promised to come by boat in the spring.

Her eventual return to the United States was fraught with problems, as Brazilian police were suspicious that the homesteaders were actually hoarding gold, or smuggling, or working for the CIA. Finally, Jan returned to her elderly parents. Her total blindness was diagnosed to be the result of cataracts, so operations restored her tunnel vision and gave her limited independence.

The author learned of Jan's story, which led to a television documentary on the BBC. The filming enabled Jan to fulfill her dream of returning to Homestead Hill, the burial ground of her daughter and husband. The book ends with Jan's oration at a simple but eloquent funeral service at the grave site.

Analysis: This book is written in simple, journalistic prose by a Time-Life reporter. It reads like fiction but would most likely not be accepted as such because of sounding too improbable. Even if the heroine of the story had not been so disabled, her situation and her adventures would be notable. Her very eccentric, resourceful family were truly modern pioneers, looking in the far reaches of the wilderness for the hard, independent life-style that would have been more common in the United States several hundred years ago.

The account is detailed and colorful and gives a sense of immediacy to Jan's incredible feats of endurance and courage. In a time when it is being debated in the newspapers whether a blind man can sail a boat alone (one has in fact sailed partway across the Atlantic), this account adds overwhelming evidence of disabled people's ability to live fully and creatively.

■ Tames, Richard. *Helen Keller.* Illus. Franklin Watts, 1989. 32pp. (0-531-10764-7) Reading Level: Grades 4–6. (BL 1 N89)
Disability: Deaf-blind

In short chapters, the author describes some of the chief events in the life of world-famous Helen Keller. Alternating with this narrative are pages, printed against a pale lavender background, that give information on such subjects as the Bell telephone and its inventor, the Irish potato famine, the Braille system, and Franklin D. Roosevelt. Each two-page spread is illustrated with black-and-white photographs or, in one case, a drawing; the text is printed in large type. At the end, the author invites readers to "find out more" and gives a short bibliography; a list of important dates; the addresses of the Royal National Institute for the Blind, American Foundation for the Blind, and Perkins School for the Blind; a short glossary; and an index.

Analysis: This book, one of a new series called Lifetimes, is an attractive and somewhat different presentation of the familiar story of a remarkable woman. The inclusion of ancillary material gives an added dimension to the biography; the many illustrations, large clear type, and readable style should make it a good choice for elementary school students who might also want to look at some of the many other studies of Keller's life available in libraries.

■ Wepman, Dennis. *Helen Keller.* Illus. Chelsea House, 1987. 110pp. (1-55546-662-1) Reading Level: Grades 5–10. (BL Ag87; SLJ S87) *Disability:* Deaf-blind

The author, Dennis Wepman, is a professor of English at Queens College and a writer on such subjects as linguistics, popular culture, and sociology. Matina Horner, former president of Radcliffe College, has written an essay called "Remember the Ladies" (after Abigail Adams' famous words written to John Adams at the Continental Congress) in which she talks about the women's movement and about the power and place of biography. Opening with Keller's hard-won admission to Radcliffe in 1900, Wepman goes back to the beginning of her life and her devastating illness at the age of 19 months; the rest of the story follows in chronological order. This biography is one in the American Women of Achievement series.

The book is illustrated with many black-and-white photographs, and the text includes passages from Keller's own writing. A short list of suggested further reading, a chronology, and an index complete the text.

Analysis: Wepman's biography tells Keller's story with grace and clarity. The opening paragraph, however, contains one puzzling sentence: Writing about the highly qualified students who applied to Radcliffe College, the author remarks that in contrast, "Keller had never been to any school at all." In fact, as he later states, she had attended both a special school for deaf children in New York and a regular college-preparatory school in Cambridge. This inconsistency aside, the book is absorbing and moving; older readers may be familiar with the details of Keller's biography, but the story of this remarkable life and vibrant personality remains powerful through many retellings.

■ Yoken, Carol. *Living with Deaf-Blindness: Nine Profiles.* National Academy of Gallaudet College, 1979. 175pp. (0-934336-00-8) Reading Level: Grades 10–12. (RSR Ap82) *Disability:* Usher's syndrome; Retinitis pigmentosa; Marfan's syndrome

The purported goal of this work is to inform students who are preparing for entry into one of the helping professions about the disability group that constitutes deaf-blindness. The book focuses on circumstances in the lives of nine white adults, each of whom was interviewed by the author with the assistance of other interpreters in whatever mode of communication was effective. Interviews lasted from several days to a full week. The age of the individuals was between 23 and 71. Their educational level varied from completion of sixth grade to an earned doctorate. They came from many different regions of the country. One was born abroad. Four had severe sensory losses from birth.

The opening chapter is written in the hardscrabble southern dialect spoken by a man who spent his teenage years and early 20s in and out of prison, until a motorcycle accident caused his deaf-blindness. The second account describes a man born with Usher's syndrome, who felt himself slowly abandoned by the deaf community as he gradually lost his vision. The third person interviewed was a clinical psychologist of Sicilian background who received all of his higher education after the onset of his blindness, while he still retained his hearing. The next case was a 37-year-old woman who has had vision and hearing problems since girlhood, apparently associated with Marfan's syndrome. She works in an advisory group to Seattle's mayor on programs serving disabled citizens.

The fifth chapter describes a 47-year-old bachelor congenitally afflicted in areas of vision and hearing. He turned to religion when a church of the deaf was established in his city. The next chapter deals with the childhood of a young man with Usher's syndrome who was educated in the deaf division of the state school for deaf and blind children and in Gallaudet College. The seventh report is transcribed in the dialect of a Latvian woman who lived through the Russian revolution and two world wars and as a deaf refugee in the United States since 1951. She worked as a key-puncher until her lonely retirement. Another deaf-blind woman had deaf-blind sisters. At 43, she married a man who had been totally deaf-blind for 42 years. The last profile portrays a man with a full-blown delusional system involving "Radar Mind Research," who is nonetheless able to work productively and to function in the community.

A final chapter offers conclusions based on the nine profiles. All of the subjects expressed isolation, dependence, anger, and resentment. This seemed largely due to the inevitable reduction in communication ability that is inherent in their condition. The author sees some of the coping mechanisms as implying "a remarkable human resilience in responding to adversity" (p. 160). In every case, the people interviewed articulated the desire to work and love. The last paragraphs admonish society to better accommodate disability to reduce the handicapping implications of deaf-blindness. An appendix describes the procedures used in arranging the interviews.

Analysis: Yoken has skillfully and patiently drawn out the nine interviewees, attending to their wishes for privacy. The dialect in several chapters enhances the uniqueness of those particular profiles. The loneliness, frustration, and misunderstandings engendered by double sensory deprivation become painfully obvious. The author's respect and liking for each of the individuals come through. The forbearance, honesty, and good will that she encountered attest to the fortitude of the human spirit. Perhaps this work will lead to a more enlightened view of deaf-blindness, particularly from Usher's syndrome, on the part of the deaf community.

HEARING IMPAIRMENTS

■ Adler, David A. *Thomas Alva Edison: Great Inventor.* Illus. by Lyle Miller. Holiday, 1990. 48pp. (0-8234-0820-5) Reading Level: Grades 1–6.
Disability: Deafness

In this volume of the First Biography series, Adler tells the story of Edison's life. The first chapter emphasizes the questioning mind and early experiments that characterized Edison's childhood. The next two chapters describe some of the familiar events of Edison's boyhood, including the famous incident of the train conductor who pulled him aboard by his ears; Edison ascribed his deafness to this moment, but Adler, like most other biographers, points out that the disability was more likely caused by childhood scarlet fever and recurrent ear infections. The remaining four chapters cover Edison's mature career and his many inventions that shape our lives today.

A list of important dates precedes the text, and there is an index. Large black-and-white drawings illustrate every two-page spread.

Analysis: This is an attractive biography for children in elementary school. The large format, generous margins, many illustrations, and clear, well-leaded type make it visually inviting for young readers; the text itself is clear and well written.

■ Albronda, Mildred. *The Magic Lantern Man: Theophilus Hope d'Estrella.* Illus. California School for the Deaf, 1985. 140pp. (o.p.) Reading Level: Grades 10–12.
Disability: Deafness

Albronda continues her biographical and historical treatment of famous deaf American artists from the California School for the Deaf with this biography of Theophilus Hope d'Estrella, the well-known California photographer. In an earlier work, reviewed in *Accept Me as I Am* (Bowker, 1985), she has also chronicled the life of the famous California sculptor Douglas Tilden. Unlike Tilden, who was d'Estrella's fellow student at the California School for the Deaf and his lifelong friend, d'Estrella came from an impoverished background and was orphaned at the age of 5. He became a residential student at the California School for the Deaf, where he achieved great success, and then attended Berkeley for three years to study science. However, his interest in the graphic arts and photography led him into careers as both a teacher and a practitioner of art and photography.

Analysis: D'Estrella took many striking black-and-white photographs, especially of the San Francisco area and of students at the School for the Deaf, with which he had a lifelong association as a teacher when he was not engaged in other artistic endeavors. The reproduction of many of his photographs is a highlight of the book. While a scholarly and factual treatment, the text is quite readable and should prove interesting to mature teens with an interest in either deafness or the fine arts.

■ Ancona, George, and Mary Beth Miller. *Handtalk Zoo.* Illus. by George Ancona. Four Winds, 1989. Unp. (0-02-700801-0) Reading Level: Grades PS–6. (BL 1 O89; HB N/D89; SLJ O89)
Disability: Deafness

Using words, color photographs, signs, and finger spelling, this book presents animals and children at the zoo, translating the written English words into the language of hearing-impaired people. A zebra is a horse with stripes, the sign for lion shows a child baring her teeth and gesturing toward her head to indicate a mane, a girl crooks her finger over her nose to signify parrot. Other words are included, for example, "lunch time" followed by a list of foods, and simple sentences are also illustrated. Domestic animals found in the Children's Zoo are shown, as are the expected lion, tiger, monkey, and the like. The front endpapers show the children at the zoo, asking when it opens; the back endpapers picture the children saying, "So long!" on one side and finger spelling for the letters of the alphabet on the other.

Analysis: Using bright-colored photographs, attractive and expressive faces, and an appealing collection of animals, the authors show a cheerful group of youngsters on an outing to the zoo. There is no plot or narrative line, except for the movement implied by entrance and exit, the succession of animals, the mention of noontime and food, and the discovery of one child hanging on ropes like a monkey. Format, design, and type of information vary from page to page, so that the book never becomes a dull catalog of terms and signs. Readers with full hearing capability should find the information accessible and easy to assimilate, and children with hearing disabilities will see themselves and their experiences reflected. This would be a good choice for school and public libraries.

■ Bergman, Thomas. *Finding a Common Language: Children Living with Deafness.* Photographs by Thomas Bergman. Gareth Stevens, 1989. 48pp. (1-55532-916-0) Reading Level: Grades K–4. (BCCB F90; BL 15 Ja90; KR 1 N89)
Disability: Deafness

In text and black-and-white photographs, Thomas Bergman describes the life of a 6-year-old Swedish girl, Lina (Caroline), who, like her older brother, has been deaf since birth; their parents, however, are not deaf. Lina attends a nursery school for hearing-impaired children and next year will be going to first grade in a school for deaf youngsters. She is shown in good moods and bad (but mostly good), doing carpentry, having speech therapy, being fitted for new hearing aids, attending a play at the Silent Theatre, going on a class trip to the country, swimming with a deaf friend, and playing with the little girl with full hearing capability who is her best friend.

The book is ample in format, and each page has a large illustration. The last pages are devoted to the questions that children ask about deafness and the answers to their queries, an explanation of signing, suggestions for simulating deafness, a list of places to write to for more information, a short bibliography, and a glossary.

Analysis: Bergman has written and illustrated an attractive, informative book. Lina is a most appealing little girl, with an expressive face that Bergman has captured in a variety of moods and responses. While not minimizing the effects of hearing loss, the author-photographer demonstrates the many ways in which a deaf child is like a hearing one. The other children are similarly animated and attractive. Lina's brother Marcus does not appear until late in the book, but their companionship is indicated in these two pages; the two are united in disobedience, riding their bikes on the main road despite their parents' injunction.

Even though the text is well written, it sometimes does not describe the photograph under which it is placed. For example, the children are shown at lunch with something flat on their plates (perhaps an omelet), but the text talks about soup. However, this is a minor flaw in an otherwise excellent book that should absorb young readers, whatever their own hearing ability or their acquaintance with hearing-impaired people.

■ Blackwood, Alan. **Beethoven.** Illus. by Richard Hook. Bookwright, 1987. 32pp. (0-531-18131-6) Reading Level: Grades 4–6. (BL 15 D87) *Disability:* Deafness

This biography is one in a series called Great Lives, published simultaneously in England and the United States. The illustrations on each page—color photographs and drawings as well as black-and-white prints—and the text together take readers through the composer's life. Beethoven began to have acute trouble with his hearing when he was about 30, suffering from buzzing noises in his head and increasing deafness; however, as is well-known, he continued to write the music that has distinguished him as one of the world's greatest composers.

The final pages contain a chronology of Beethoven's life, a glossary, a short bibliography suggesting other books about the composer and music, and an index.

Analysis: The author writes simply and yet eloquently, compressing the life story into a short text with grace and style. The large type and abundant illustrations should make the book attractive to young readers, and it would be a good read-aloud for children not yet able to manage all of the words on their own.

■ Bowe, Frank. **Changing the Rules.** Illus. T.J., 1986. 204pp. (0-932666-30-2) Reading Level: Grades 10–12. (JVIB N87; VR Ja88) *Disability:* Deafness

Frank Bowe, teacher of children and adults who are deaf, researcher, and activist for the rights of the disabled, has written a fast-paced autobiography. He details the influence that his severe hearing impairment, caused by an early childhood illness, has had on his life and how he learned to adapt within the hearing world, particularly by learning to lip-read. Beyond this training, he had no special education designed for deaf students until he enrolled in a master's degree program at Gallaudet College.

"Mainstreamed" long before the term had meaning in the education of children with disabilities, Bowe learned quickly how to deal with the cruelties of some of his peers and also with the coldness and lack of empathy among those in the medical profession.

A good student and bound for college, he considered Gallaudet but rejected it in favor of Western Maryland College, where he majored in English. Afterward, unable to follow his first career choice of journalism because of the necessity of listening to great amounts of information, he went to Gallaudet for a master's degree in the education of deaf persons. Here he first learned to sign. Work on a Ph.D. at New York University led him into the thick of the disability rights movement that was just gaining momentum at that time.

Analysis: Bowe's story should appeal to teens. It is fast moving, clear, and vivid. He comes through as dedicated, energetic, and likable. From childhood he is determined and purposeful. Although he certainly does not portray himself in a heroic light, teens should admire his social conscience, which extends to all types of civil rights. Recommended for high-school-level readers.

■ Brearley, Sue. *Talk to Me.* Photographs by Jenny Matthews. A&C Black, 1989. 25pp. (0-7136-3192-9) Reading Level: Grades K–4. (SL My90)
Disability: Hearing impairment; Speech impairment

Using large, full-color photographs on every page along with short passages of text, author and photographer present children who are learning a variety of ways to communicate. They discuss lip reading and sign language, speech therapy, computers, and symbol boards. The children pictured have various disabilities—not only deafness but also difficulty in speaking clearly and in making language express thoughts. Some youngsters appear to have cerebral palsy, and another has Down's syndrome, although these terms are not used. The book concludes with a list of pertinent associations in England, Australia, and New Zealand and a chart illustrating the finger alphabet.

Analysis: This is an attractive book for young readers. Appealing children are shown in a school setting, both indoors and outdoors. Unobtrusively, the text emphasizes communication and the desire to share thoughts and feelings, and it makes the point that this communication can take place through various kinds of "talking." In the final pages, Brearley addresses her listener/reader directly, asking, "Do you know someone who doesn't speak? If you do, she probably wants to talk to you. Are you letting her talk? Do you know how she talks?"

This is a book that can be shared in a group setting in a classroom or library or in side-by-side reading at home. Children might well ask questions about the causes of the disabilities described, and then adults can guide them to finding further information.

■ Buranelli, Vincent. *Thomas Alva Edison.* Illus. Silver Burdett, 1989. 133pp. (0-382-09522-7) Reading Level: Grades 4–9. (CBRS F90; HB Ja90; SBF My90; SLJ J190; SLJ Ag90)
Disability: Deafness

The author of this biography has written books on history and biography as well as Hardy Boy stories and has coauthored an encyclopedia of espionage. He begins this work with Edison's famous saying that "Genius is one percent inspiration and ninety-nine percent perspiration." Edison's life as an inventor was characterized by his persistence even in the face of disappointing results. Buranelli takes Edison from his boyhood in Ohio and Michigan through the long years of experimentation and invention to his death at 84: "He was born in 1847 into a world of gaslights and still photography. He departed in 1931 from a world transformed by electric lights, motion pictures, and the phonograph. He himself worked this transformation with his inventions."

As is well-known, Edison became deaf as a boy, probably as a result of scarlet fever and ear infections. This disability was never a major problem for him, although Buranelli does refer to its effect as Edison grew older and less able to follow conversations. His second wife, Mina, helped him in social situations. Buranelli writes, "He was so accustomed to her voice that he could comprehend what she was saying when other people's voices failed to register with him. So, when she saw he was in trouble, she would repeat the words in a manner he could understand. They became so adept at communicating in this way that some persons who talked to Edison in the company of his wife scarcely realized she was interpreting for him."

The book is illustrated with black-and-white photographs. At the end are a list of important dates, a bibliography, and an index.

Analysis: Buranelli has written a clear, comprehensive biography, well suited to readers in the middle grades. The many details and anecdotes bring the subject to life, but the author has wisely refrained from including invented dialogue. Although there are many books on Edison, this one is a notable addition to the list.

■ Cousins, Margaret. *The Story of Thomas Alva Edison.* Illus. Random, 1981. 160pp. (Paper 0-394-84883-7) Reading Level: Grades 4–9. (BL 1 Mr66; CR Ag83; LJ 15 Ap66)
Disability: Deafness

The author takes the famous inventor from his birth in a small Ohio town in 1847 to his death at 84 in 1931. As a child, Edison was bright and inquisitive. Except for a few months in a school, he was educated at home by his mother; to a large extent, he was self-educated, his investigations and study fueled by his seemingly inexhaustible curiosity, energy, and capacity for hard work. As a youngster, he began contributing to the family income by peddling candy and fruit on the train that ran between Port Huron and Detroit. He lost much of his hearing while still a boy, probably as the result of scarlet fever. The condition was no doubt made worse by the two episodes so often recounted: the box on the ears given by the conductor when the experiment he was conducting in the baggage car caused a fire and the time when he was late for the train and was pulled aboard by a trainman who grabbed him by the ears. Cousins writes that Edison's loss of hearing "has been diagnosed as arthritis of the small bones of the ear."

Seldom dismayed by failures and setbacks, Edison did not view deafness as a disability and is reported to have said that his lack of hearing contributed to his ability to concentrate. Cousins quotes him as saying: "Think of all the nonsense I haven't had to listen to by not being able to hear it." One of the world's great inventors, Edison affected dramatically the course of modern life.

The biography is illustrated with black-and-white photographs and drawings; there is an index.

Analysis: Cousins, a professional editor and author, has written a readable, accessible biography. She draws a sharply focused portrait of a remarkable man, with clear descriptions of many of his inventions. Although originally published more than 25 years ago, the book holds up well and would be enjoyed by elementary and middle school students.

■ Egan, Louise. *Thomas Edison: The Great American Inventor.* Illus. by Frank Riccio. Childrens Pr., 1987. 165pp. (Paper 0-8120-3922-X) Reading Level: Grades 5–9. (SBF S88; SE Ap88)
Disability: Deafness

This full-length biography takes Edison from the age of 3 in 1850 to his death in 1931. Those years saw tremendous changes in the way people lived and worked; many of the developments were the result of Edison's prodigious series of inventions. As the subtitle indicates, these are the focus of Egan's book and are described in considerable detail. Edison's hearing disability was probably the result of scarlet fever in childhood and of the well-known incident in which the boy Tom, with a pile of newspapers, was running after the train on which he worked and was pulled aboard by the trainman who grabbed him by the ears. According to this biographer, the disability was not a hindrance and even gave him privacy, shutting out the noisy distractions of the world.

The text is illustrated with black-and-white drawings. At the end of the book are a glossary, a list of topics for discussion, a brief bibliography, and an index.

Analysis: Egan tells Edison's story with a lively, enthusiastic style. There is heavy use of invented dialogue, distracting perhaps to the adult reader but probably not to a young one. Edison's inventions are described in considerable detail and would be especially interesting to readers with an inventive bent and scientific curiosity. The author successfully conveys a sense of the enormous changes that took place in Edison's lifetime, many of which were of course the result of his inventions. For some reason, World War I is never mentioned, which may seem odd. The illustrations are uneven in quality, some appearing almost grotesque in their heavy use of cross-hatching. There are occasional references to Edison's hearing deficit, but the disability is not dwelt on, just as he himself did not give it much attention.

■ Forecki, Marcia Calhoun. **Speak to Me.** Gallaudet, 1985. 143pp. (Paper 0-913580-95-3) Reading Level: Grades 7–12. (BL J185; LJ 1 Jn85)
Disability: Deafness

Forecki became a single parent when she was asked by her husband to leave home with their little boy, who was only 1½ years old. Bereft, she returned to her parents' home. Everyone in the family but his mother realized that little Charley was not responding to sound. Finally, the young mother was forced to acknowledge a professional diagnosis of deafness for her lively but silent child.

The author had at one time been a Spanish teacher and had an interest in languages. She and her sister-in-law enrolled in a sign language class that emphasized "total communication." When Charley was 2, Forecki enrolled him in a class for hearing-impaired children. She also enrolled herself in the John Tracey Clinic home course for parents.

In general, she felt inept and frustrated in her attempts to meet her child's needs. She humorously describes her ten attempts to play the "surprise box" game, in which Charley was encouraged to learn words and signs for new toys. He did not behave in the manner described in the game's directions but cheerfully grabbed the new toy and ran each time. She shares her agonies in trying to communicate with such a young deaf child: "Have you ever tried to persuade a child to settle for Spaghettios when it's Noodle Roni on which she has set her breaking heart?" (p. 59).

Forecki realized that she was receiving much support from her family and from competent professionals. She was finally rewarded for her own efforts when her son had been in school almost a year. He spontaneously signed "water" to his mother, and she was overjoyed that real communication between them had begun. Later she decided that the little boy needed the full-time preschool environment that the Iowa School for the Deaf provided. She packed up the two of them and moved to a new town, and eventually to a new job for her.

Many humorous and embarrassing encounters are chronicled, in which she mediates with Charley in the hearing and deaf worlds. She describes her gaffes in misinterpreting the signs of deaf people. She acknowledges that she will never fully understand her deaf son, but she is able to look forward in eager anticipation to their future.

By the end of the book, Charley is enrolled in residential school during the week. His speech is not yet very intelligible, but he and his mother communicate with increasing success in sign language.

Analysis: On the book jacket a parent commented that the author was like an Erma Bombeck with a deaf child. Indeed, Forecki writes in hyperbole and mixes wit with poignancy. At times her humor seems forced or off the mark, but typically her candid, self-deprecating style makes for pleasant easy reading. She renders most palatable and informative the otherwise serious story of a single parent struggling to raise a deaf preschooler. She comes across as a loving, enterprising mother, and she shares her hard-won insights, to the general reader's distinct advantage.

■ Greenberg, Judith E., and Carin Bea Feldman. **What Is the Sign for Friend?** Illus. by Gayle Rothschild. Franklin Watts, 1985. 31pp. (LB 0-531-04939-6) Reading Level: Grades K–4. (BL 15 My85; CBRS My85; SLJ S85) *Disability:* Deafness

Shane, a boy of about 8, was born deaf and wears hearing aids. Text and black-and-white photographs describe his life, both those aspects that are common to many children—eating pizza, playing soccer, having a good friend, watching television, going to school—and those that are peculiar to his disability. Each spread has one or two drawings showing signs for words, with arrows and dotted lines that indicate how the signs are made. Shane goes to school with hearing children and has both hearing and deaf friends, spending some time in special classes but most of the day in mainstreamed classes. A speech therapist helps Shane learn to talk, and an interpreter stands beside his classroom teacher. Shane and his best friend ride bikes, swim, and play soccer, and, when Shane can't hear, Mitchell tells him what to do.

Analysis: Writer and photographer together present Shane as a lively, active boy with many interests. The well-written text makes clear some of the ways in which Shane's experience differs from that of hearing children. He loves to read but finds writing sentences difficult; his friends sometimes cannot understand his speech; he cannot hear the splash of water in the swimming pool and often does not catch everything on television; when he removes his hearing aids and goes to bed, his world is silent. Yet there is no implication that these differences diminish Shane.

This is an excellent book and would be a good choice both for family reading and for sharing in a mainstreamed classroom.

■ Greene, Carol. *Ludwig van Beethoven: Musical Pioneer.* Illus. by Steve Dobson. Childrens Pr., 1989. 45pp. (0-516-04208-4) Reading Level: Grades 1–6. (SLJ My90)
Disability: Deafness

The book begins with a five-sentence introduction to this story of Beethoven's stormy and productive life. Chapter One chronicles the sad boyhood of the great composer in Bonn, Germany, where his tyrannical father taught him music but ridiculed his attempts at composition. The narrative follows Beethoven to Vienna, Austria, where he studied with Joseph Haydn, achieved eventual wide acclaim, and died in 1827. In Chapters Three, Four, and Five, the musician's despair over his worsening deafness runs counterpoint to his deepening commitment to his music and to the development of his prodigious power in composition.

A brief chronology recaps the story. An index paginates the copious illustrations, which appear on every double page, many with captions. They range from photographs to etchings and drawings.

Analysis: This large type book, part of the publisher's A Rookie Biography series, is written in short, simple sentences. Yet, many pertinent facts are included, commitment and feelings are dealt with, and some famous anecdotes about Beethoven are told. The musician's faults, as well as his genius, are apparent. The reading level is low, but the content is not juvenile. The illustrations are well chosen to enhance the events described, and many are beautiful in their own right.

■ Greene, Carol. *Thomas Alva Edison: Bringer of Light.* Illus. Childrens Pr., 1985. 128pp. (0-516-03213-5) Reading Level: Grades 4–9.
Disability: Deafness

This is one of a series of 18 People of Distinction biographies offered for young readers. The book contains many anecdotes about Edison's childhood, illustrating his curiosity and his pranks. For example, the story is told about his attempt, when he was 6, to burn autumn leaves in a barn, resulting in the barn's burning down. His hearing loss is attributed to many ear infections, which were a result of his fragile health as a youngster. At 12, he entered the work world, selling newspapers on a railroad line.

In part because he had difficulty hearing voices, young "Al" began practicing the telegraph. He happened to save the life of the 3-year-old son of the stationmaster, who would have been hit by a boxcar; the man rewarded him by teaching him to become a telegraph operator. At 16, Edison wandered about, getting jobs here and there while doing experiments on the side.

By age 24, Edison determined to be a full-time inventor. He courted young Mary Stillwell, who worked at Western Union, where he was also employed to set up stock ticker tapes. He said his deafness helped him, in that it excused him for "getting quite a little closer to her than I would have dared . . . to hear what she said" (p. 43).

The book continues chronicling Edison's prodigious output of inventions, the establishment of his laboratory in Menlo Park, New Jersey, and the efforts that culminated in his patent for the electric light bulb, filed in 1879. His financial problems and competition with other inventors and businessmen are documented.

Edison's wife died of typhoid fever when she was 29. He was devastated but would eventually marry Mina Miller, a beauty from Akron, Ohio. He had taught her Morse code during their courtship, and he tapped his proposal of marriage into her palm. The careers of his children are mentioned briefly.

The book ends with the later successes and failures of the indefatigable inventor. Into his old age, he thought up new ideas and collaborated with others, including his dear friend Henry Ford. A chronology lists some major events in Edison's life and in the world from his birth in 1847 to his death in 1931. An index follows.

Analysis: The material covering Edison's life and work is so plentiful that the various children's books about him tend to supplement rather than repeat each other. This title is particularly well written and quite complete in its coverage. Edison's business dealings are emphasized, whereas his important inventions are only generally explained. The continuing effects of his disability are not ignored in the story. Perhaps the greatest strength of the book lies in its rich portrayal of Edison's forceful personality, from his childhood through old age. The rich collection of black-and-white photographs tend to highlight this aspect.

■ Groce, Nora Ellen. *Everyone Here Spoke Sign Language: Hereditary Deafness in Martha's Vineyard.* Harvard Univ. Pr., 1985. 169pp. (0-674-27040-1) Reading Level: Grades 10–12. (CLE 23 F86)
Disability: Deafness

For over two and a half centuries, the isolated island communities on Martha's Vineyard had a strikingly high incidence of inherited deafness within their white population. Groce's interest in this phenomenon brought her to the island to interview a core group of some 50 old-timers about their recollections of the several hundred deaf people they had known or heard about. The author also delved into various archives to verify the oral histories and to learn more about the island's past.

It transpired that for most of the nineteenth century and beyond, almost everyone on the Vineyard was bilingual for sign language and English. Furthermore, the interviewees did not perceive this as a peculiar situation. They showed a largely unconscious, complete acceptance of deaf people. Apparently, the deaf themselves regarded their disability as a nuisance, but nevertheless they were completely integrated into all community activities and intermarried freely with hearing people. All the children picked up "deaf and dumb" early, although they did not necessarily learn the manual alphabet. Even hearing people often communicated with each other in sign.

Groce traces the history of Martha's Vineyard from its settlement by Native Americans 4,000 years ago until today; this group still plays an important role in island life. The first settlement by Europeans consisted of a group of farmers who came from Watertown, Massachusetts, in 1644. The island's farming capabilities were depleted by the end of the Revolution, so its men took to the sea for whaling, sealing, and hauling of cargo. A somewhat isolated town, Chilmark continued to be home to sheep farmers. It had the largest deaf population. By the beginning of the twentieth century, tourism had replaced other industries in the island's economy, but the descendants of the old Vineyard families still remain, and they make up the majority of the year-round population.

One informant in her 80s remembered that a "professor from Boston" (actually the great inventor Alexander Graham Bell) came to talk to her mother about Vineyard deafness long before her birth. Bell was interested in the hereditary aspect, but he was not familiar with Mendelian principles and never understood that a recessive trait for one specific cause of hearing impairment was at work here. Groce finally tracked down Bell's copious notes in storage in a warehouse of the library of the Alexander Graham Bell Foundation in Washington.

The type of deafness propagated in the Vineyard communities was nonspecific and was not associated with any abnormalities except profound hearing loss. Eighty-two percent of children born deaf had hearing parents. Presumably the deaf offspring were all related to a deaf fisherman, Jonathan Lambert, who settled on the island in 1694, and to other settlers of that time who must have been carriers of the trait. Two of Lambert's seven children were born deaf. This group of people had come from isolated parishes in the Kentish Weald in England, a region where deafness was common.

There is evidence that hearing people learned a locally used sign language in the 1630s, and Groce speculates that this was the language brought to the Vineyard. The deaf population on the island peaked at 45 in the 1840s. Later, deaf children would be sent to residential schools on the mainland, where they would meet partners outside their gene pool. Hearing people intermarried with new arrivals to the island, further diminishing the propagation of deafness. The last deaf islander died in 1952.

The author concludes, "The most important lesson to be learned from Martha's Vineyard is that disabled people can be full and useful members of a community if the community makes an effort to include them. The society must be willing to change slightly to adapt to all" (p. 108).

Analysis: This story highlights an interesting corner of the United States, where, by chance, a natural experiment on integration of deaf and hearing people lasted over a century. Besides the history of a bygone age, the author gives an instructive discourse on deafness. Her facts and speculations are thoroughly discussed and referenced in 33 pages of appendixes and notes. The extensive bibliography and index would be useful to historians. The narrative itself is clearly organized and well written.

■ Kisor, Henry. *What's That Pig Outdoors? A Memoir of Deafness.* Hill & Wang, 1990. 270pp. (0-8090-9689-7) Reading Level: Grades 10–12. (BL 15 Mr90; LJ 15 Ap90; PW 6 Ap90)
Disability: Deafness

In 1944, when he was almost 3½ years old, Henry Kisor had a critical illness, which was probably actually two illnesses, meningitis and encephalitis. When he began to recover, the doctor realized that he was deaf, his auditory nerves destroyed by the fever. He had been a verbally precocious child, but now, although he began to read lips in rudimentary fashion, he also stopped speaking.

As his parents searched for ways to educate him, his mother saw an ad that led them to a gifted, eccentric teacher named Miss Doris Mirrielees, who believed that "All deaf children could enjoy lives as full and productive as those of their hearing peers, if only they could acquire the gift of language—the *whole* gift, not a small part of it—as soon as possible" (p. 25). She had developed a method that urged parents to begin teaching their deaf children to read in babyhood so that they would hear with their eyes; speech and lipreading could come later. She had produced manuals so that parents could follow her method on their own, and Kisor's parents began to work with the Mirrielees lessons; some months later, the child had an experience similar to Helen Keller's famous moment at the pump, a breakthrough in which he recognized the connection between written and spoken language. He began to speak again. When he entered a regular class in public kindergarten, he was already reading and was ahead of most of his contemporaries.

Although he had speech instruction along the way, Kisor's entire education took place with hearing classmates. His parents always believed that only he could discover his limits, rather than be confined by limits imposed by others, and the best of his teachers shared this belief. Accommodations were made when necessary (for example, sitting in the front row so that he could see the teacher's lips or studying the chapter ahead of time so that he could follow the class work better), but for the most part, his academic experience was not very different from that of students with normal hearing.

Kisor participated in sports, worked on the high school newspaper, had friends, and dated. In adolescence, however, he became self-conscious about his different speech, an unease that has been with him most of his life, though much abated in middle age. He graduated from Trinity College, earned a master's degree from the Medill School of Journalism at Northwestern University, and became a newspaperman, at first in Wilmington, then on the Chicago *Daily News,* and last on the Chicago *Sun-Times.* He worked first as a copy editor—a job well suited to a deaf person, because it usually does not involve telephoning—and then as a book editor. He has been successful in his work and has also taught at Medill, is happily married to a hearing woman and has two sons, and has conquered the alcohol dependence that grew out of both the newspaperman's hard-drinking style and his shyness in large gatherings. Periodically, he goes to speech therapists so that his speech will not deteriorate and become unintelligible.

In addition to telling his own story, Kisor discusses oralism, sign language, and total communication, as well as controversies surrounding the mainstreaming of hearing-impaired children. He writes about devices that have made the lives of deaf people much less isolated; for example, the TDD for telephone communication, the use of computers (also for communication), and closed-captioned television.

The book's foreword has been written by Walker Percy, whose deaf daughter was, like Kisor, brought up in the speaking world and who is an oralist.

Analysis: As a professional newspaperman, Kisor writes with style and clarity, though some may quarrel occasionally with his choice of words; for example, he speaks of those who *suffer* from various conditions and calls loss of hearing and of sight *our afflictions,* but these are minor caveats. He is pleased with his life and proud of his accomplishments, but he tells his story with a wry honesty and often with humor, avoiding indulging himself in self-congratulation. His views on the education of deaf children and on deaf culture may be controversial to some, but he avoids polemics and rejects rigid orthodoxies. He fears movements, programs, and philosophies that divide people—the hearing from the deaf, the oralists from the signers, those who use signed English from the ones who use American Sign Language—and takes his motto from E. M. Forster's famous phrase "Only connect!"

This is an absorbing book, one of the few accounts about deafness written by a deaf person, and its interest is certainly not limited to those seeking information about this impairment. Youngsters will be attracted by Kisor's account of his growing up, particularly of his adolescence, and readers with an interest in the world of newspaper writing will enjoy the descriptions of his work.

■ Kudlinski, Kathleen V. *Juliette Gordon Low: America's First Girl Scout.* Illus. by Sheila Hamanaka. Viking, 1988. 55pp. (0-670-82208-6) Reading Level: Grades 4–6. (BCCB O88; BL 15 N 88; SLJ Ja89)
Disability: Deafness

A biography in The Women of Our Time series, this book follows Juliette Gordon Low from her birth in Savannah, Georgia, in 1860 until her death in 1927. She was born into a well-to-do southern family, but her mother was from the North. Deprivation during the Civil War and a severe illness when she was 4 affected Low's health but not her energy and enjoyment of life. However, she developed a severe hearing loss, first in one ear, when she insisted that the doctor treat an earache with silver nitrate, and then in the second ear, when a grain of rice thrown at her wedding lodged in her ear and caused infection.

Low married a very wealthy Englishman and lived in England until her husband's death. There she met Sir Robert Baden-Powell, founder of the Boy Scouts; his sister had started Girl Guides. Childless, Low had now found a way to channel her energies and her interests in young people. She founded troops of Girl Guides in Scotland and England and then established the Girl Scout movement in the United States. Her hearing deficit had frightened her originally, but she learned to adapt to it and even to use it. When she herself told jokes and initiated discussion, she did not have to strain to hear others, and when she asked someone to do something—for example, to take on the leadership of her English Girl Guides troop—she never heard the answer "no." She used an ear trumpet to augment her residual hearing.

The book is arranged in six short chapters and is illustrated with black-and-white drawings.

Analysis: Kudlinski has succeeded in integrating many details into her text and has avoiding fictionalizing; there is little direct dialogue. The author explains in a postscript that she drew material from Low's letters and what her friends and family had written about her. Low's deafness is not central to the story but is not ignored; Kudlinski mentions Low's initial distress when she became nearly deaf after her wedding, but she does not go into detail. A curious omission occurs when the author identifies the illness that struck Low when she was 4 as "brain fever" but does not speculate as to what it might be called today. The illustrations are not always satisfactory: the text describes Low as a child with a "pointed face" and "sharp little freckled nose," but the picture on the facing page shows a girl with a round face, cheeks almost swollen.

This is an adequate, if not outstanding, biography of a forceful, influential woman that will be of particular interest both to elementary school girls who are in scouting and to youngsters who themselves have a hearing impairment.

■ Lampton, Christopher. *Thomas Alva Edison.* Illus. Franklin Watts, 1988. 96pp. (0-531-10491-5) Reading Level: Grades 4–9. (BL 15 Mr88; SBF Mr89; SLJ Ap88)
Disability: Deafness

This is a First Book biography, one of eight in the series. The hardback cover shows a photograph of Edison holding an early electric light bulb. Pages of illustrations, usually black-and-white photos, alternate with the text.

In the introduction, "The Man Who Changed the World," young readers are invited to imagine the world as it was when Edison was born, in 1847—a world without the modern forms of transportation and communication or the vast utilization of electricity. The latter was the area of Edison's greatest contributions.

Eight chapters chronicle the inventor's life, from his boyhood in Milan, Ohio, to his death 84 years later. Edison's early troubles with authority and in school are discussed. "My father thought I was stupid, and I almost decided I must be a dunce," he said many years later (pp. 14–15). Scarlet fever, contracted when he was 7, affected his hearing and rendered him almost completely deaf in old age. At age 12 he went to work selling newspapers on a railroad train, where he maintained a laboratory in the baggage car, until one of his experiments caused a fire. He turned his attention to the telegraph at age 15. His eccentric personality earned him the nickname "The Looney."

In his 20s, Edison became a full-time inventor, and his career began to soar. He eventually opened the world's first "invention factory" in Menlo Park, New Jersey, where he greatly improved Bell's telephone and invented the phonograph. A chapter is devoted to his invention of the light bulb and the forerunner of the vacuum tube, as well as his consequent foundation of the electric power industry. His demonstration power plant in New York was the ancestor of today's Consolidated Edison. His "current wars" with George Westinghouse are mentioned, the latter rightly backing alternating current for power supply. Edison's last great invention was the motion picture, probably in collaboration with a young assistant, Dickson.

At the height of his success, his 29-year-old wife died of typhoid fever, leaving him with three children. Soon he married again and moved his work to a larger laboratory in West Orange, New Jersey. In later life, he became a great friend of the younger Henry Ford. He was feted by dignitaries the world over and adulated by the nation.

Footnotes, a list of recommended readings, and an index close the book.

Analysis: The author, in a clear and informal style, addresses readers directly to explain such things as the operation of the telegraph, telephone, and phonograph. Once Edison's adult years have been covered, the story concentrates on his career rather than on the personal details of his life. His disability is discussed at the beginning of the book and is never mentioned again.

The attractive illustrations are helpful, both by showing the specific inventions and by re-creating the feeling of a bygone time.

■ Lane, Harlan. *When the Mind Hears: A History of the Deaf.* Illus. Random, 1984. 537pp. (0-394-50878-5) Reading Level: Grades 10–12. (AHR D85; NYTBR 21 O84; LJ 15 O84)
Disability: Deafness; Deaf-blind

In the foreword, the author states that this book is a study in the anatomy of prejudice. Deaf people, he contends, use a language of manual signs that has been designated by linguists as a language system comparable to spoken language systems. A sign language, such as American Sign Language, will be learned naturally by young deaf children if they are exposed to it. This history of the deaf portrays the struggles of a linguistic minority to have the same rights and respect that other groups enjoy.

The story is based on roughly 2,000 sources and 1,200 reference notes, which are cited in the 120-page appendix.

The first part of the narrative is written in the voice of the deaf Frenchman Laurent Clerc, who was a central figure in deaf education. In eighteenth-century France—the Age of Enlightenment—language was considered the hallmark of humanity and necessary for salvation. Hence there was great interest in the pioneer teachers of the deaf, such as Pereire and the Abbé de l'Eppé, who endeavored to teach deaf children to speak. Sign was considered an inferior method of communication by many hearing deaf educators. The controversy still flourishing today over oralism (speech) versus manualism (sign) is explored at length in historical context in Clerc's narrative and later in the book.

Clerc was introduced to Jean-Marc-Gaspard Itard, who had undertaken the education of the foundling known as the wild boy of Aveyron. Itard applied his methods of special education to the "semi deaf," and they were later tried by his colleague, Sequin, with mentally retarded individuals. Long after Itard had given up on his wild boy, he continued medical experiments (most detrimental) on the boys in the Parisian school for the deaf where Clerc resided. Itard himself vacillated in his opinions concerning the relative merits of speech and sign.

The American experience becomes foremost in Chapter Seven, when Thomas Gallaudet began to tutor deafened young Alice Cogswell. As Gallaudet investigated the field of deaf education, Clerc, now residing in the New World, became his collaborator and eventually his lifelong friend. An entire chapter, "Concerning Women," focuses on four notable deaf women of the day, including Clerc's wife. Attitudes prevalent in nineteenth-century America toward women in general and toward disability are discussed at length. Clerc advocated instruction in sign for deaf-blind individuals, such as Laura Bridgeman, as well as for the deaf. However, Bridgeman's teacher, Horace Mann, lent his considerable political influence toward the oralist cause.

Finally, the narrative shifts to the voice of the author, a 46-year-old psychologist with a present perspective. He continues the history of American deaf education: In two thirds of the network of schools that Clerc had established before his death in 1869, the oral approach was ultimately adopted. Alexander Graham Bell and his deaf wife were active in promulgating oral/aural education, and in part their interest motivated Bell's invention of the telephone. Bell also promoted the eugenic movement in the name of social Darwinism with regard to intermarriage among deaf people. Gallaudet's son Edward became an advocate of manual communication and was in open and eventually hostile disagreement with Bell. During the Civil War, Edward founded Gallaudet College.

Analysis: Lane feels that the struggle of deaf persons for dignity and the right to learn and use their own language is not over to this day. His book is an effective polemic supporting his point of view. He is ever the crusader battling for the authenticity of manual language systems. He provides a rich historical setting in which he embeds the interesting stories of deaf and deaf blind individuals.

Lane is a very popular writer of books in the disability field. However, his fact-packed and detailed prose is apt to limit his accessibility to rather sophisticated readers. In addition, he has fashioned the first third of his history in the rather stilted style of an eighteenth-century narrator. Readers who have the fortitude and patience to tackle this long book will receive an unusual and extensive education.

■ Lane, Leonard G., and Ivey B. Pittle, eds. *A Handful of Stories: Thirty-seven Stories by Deaf Storytellers.* Transliterated from the Deaf Storytellers Videotape Series, Roslyn Rosen, Project Coordinator, and Bernard Bragg, Program Coordinator. Illus. Gallaudet, 1981. 118pp. (0-913580-77-5) Reading Level: Grades 7–12.
Disability: Deafness

Bernard Bragg, the dynamic actor and mime, who is deaf, coordinated a project for Gallaudet College, which resulted in the production of the Deaf Storytellers Videotape Series. This book is a transliteration of the first group of stories in this video series, all of which were taped in sign language.

The storytellers are 16 adults, who have been deaf since birth or a very young age. A photograph of each storyteller accompanied by a brief biography appears at the beginning of the book. The stories they tell are based on their experiences as persons with hearing impairments. Some are humorous, some are poignant, and others illustrate the misconceptions that hearing people harbor about deaf people or the types of discrimination that deaf people regularly encounter.

Analysis: This is a unique book, especially useful to those persons who are interested in the deaf community and in sign language. It is especially relevant to hearing persons who are studying sign language to help them to understand the connections and correlations among signs, words, and meaning. Two pages at the conclusion give activities that one could carry out if using the book as a text with a class.

■ Mintz, Penny. *Thomas Edison: Inventing the Future.* Illus. Fawcett, 1989. 120pp. (0-449-90378-8) Reading Level: Grades 4–9. (KLIATT Ap90; SLJ Je90)
Disability: Deafness

One of the titles in the Great Lives series, this biography begins not with Edison's birth in 1847 but with his invention of the phonograph 30 years later. The chapter ends with a paragraph on the inventor's perseverance and hard work: "No matter how long it took, once something caught Edison's interest, he wouldn't stop until he found the answer. Even as a boy, there was no end to the things he had to know about. Young Thomas Edison was the most curious child anyone had ever known." These statements lead into a description of Edison's childhood and boyhood and, in subsequent chapters, an account of his life and career, including the famous incident that Edison believed precipitated his deafness. Like other contemporary biographers, Mintz notes that doctors believe it was scarlet fever and untreated ear infections that caused the disability.

Edison married his first wife, Mary Stilwell, in 1871; she died in 1884, at the age of 29, leaving three young children. Unlike other biographers who write for younger children, Mintz alludes to Mary's years of unhappiness and poor health. Edison was so involved in his work that he was often inattentive to the needs of his family. Mary put on an enormous amount of weight and in the last summer of her life suffered from headaches, dizziness, and irrational behavior. Although Edison later told his daughter that her mother had died of typhoid fever, the cause was more likely a brain tumor—a condition that, Mintz says, Edison "had trouble accepting." A year and a half later, Edison married Mina Miller. He was 38 and she was 20; this marriage seems to have been much happier than the first.

There are black-and-white photographs. A short list of suggested books about Edison appears on the last page.

Analysis: Mintz's biography is detailed and well written, with much information about Edison's scientific work and the enormous contributions he made to the world. The publishers have indicated that the book is for middle school readers, but fourth- and fifth-grade students might enjoy dipping into it or hearing it read aloud.

■ Padden, Carol, and Tom Humphries. *Deaf in America: Voices from a Culture.* Illus. Harvard Univ. Pr., 1988. 134pp. (0-674-19423-3) Reading Level: Grades 10–12. (BL 15 S88; KR 15 J188; NYTBR 26 Mr89) *Disability:* Deafness

In their introduction, the authors state, "The traditional way of writing about Deaf people is to focus on the fact of their condition—that they do not hear—and to interpret all other aspects of their lives as consequences of this fact." Rather than follow this pattern, Padden and Humphries concentrate on the culture created by the deaf—their life, "their art and performances, their everyday talk, their shared myths, and the lessons they teach one another" (Introduction, p. 1).

Padden grew up with deaf parents, a deaf older brother, and other relatives who were deaf; Humphries became deaf as a child. Both have written about the language of deaf people. The authors distinguish between "deaf," which they use to mean the physical condition, and "Deaf," when they are "referring to a particular group of deaf people who share a language—American Sign Language (ASL)—and a culture" (p. 2). This distinction was first made by James Woodward in 1972.

In subsequent chapters, Padden and Humphries explore how deaf children learn that there are both deaf and hearing people in the world, and they describe ways in which deaf people interpret their experience. They discuss the languages used by the Deaf and the rather recent recognition that sign is not a crude approximation of speech but a rich and fully developed language. Descriptions of performances by deaf artists are illustrated by line drawings. Throughout, they draw both on their own experience and on the accounts of others, both published and informally related. A long bibliography and an index complete the book.

Analysis: This is a complex and sophisticated study, which could be of interest to mature, able readers. Padden and Humphries offer—as they set out to do—a view and analysis of Deaf culture quite different from the more usual book on the deaf. Although much of the book is probably beyond both the ability and the interest of younger readers, Chapter 6, "The Meaning of Sound," might well be read by a more general audience. Here, Padden and Humphries deal with what they call a "widespread misconception among hearing people . . . that Deaf people live in a world without sound" (p. 91). They describe the games invented by deaf children in residential schools to make noises and vibrations that they could hear and feel. They also recount amusing stories told to them by deaf people who remembered how they had dealt with sounds inaudible to themselves but that created social situations (e.g., the sounds of bodily functions).

■ Pelta, Kathy. *Alexander Graham Bell.* Illus. Silver Burdett, 1989. 137pp. (0-382-09529-4) Reading Level: Grades 4–9. (CBRS F90; HB Ja90; SBF My90)
Disability: Deafness

Alexander Graham Bell was born in Edinburgh in 1847. His father and grandfather were speech teachers, and his mother was deaf; despite this disability, she was a competent pianist, and Alexander inherited her talent. He began his teaching career at 16, as an instructor of music and speech. His father, Melville Bell, devised a method, which he called Visible Speech, of representing every vocal sound with a symbol. At 21, Alexander used this system to teach young deaf girls. Not long afterward, the family moved to Canada in search of a healthier climate; Alexander's two brothers had died of tuberculosis, and the parents worried about their remaining son. Eventually, Alexander Bell went to Boston, where he continued to teach deaf students as well as "Vocal Physiology and Elocution" at Boston University. In 1873, a 16-year-old young woman named Mabel Hubbard came to him as a private pupil; she had been completely deaf since contracting scarlet fever at the age of 5 but had been brought up in a speaking environment, had gone to a regular school, and had studied in

Germany; however, her parents felt she needed to learn to speak more clearly. She and Bell fell in love and were married in 1877.

In the meantime, Bell was carrying out the research and experiments that were to lead to the telephone. He continued experimenting and inventing until the end of his life, sometimes in response to needs and emergencies. For example, after President Garfield was shot by an assassin, Bell produced a needle probe to find the bullet; although the president died before it was used, it became a valuable tool for doctors. When his wife bore a premature baby who had severe breathing problems and died, Bell invented a "vacuum jacket" similar to the later iron lung. Like the Hubbards, Bell was convinced that the oral method of teaching deaf children could prevent their being isolated from the hearing segment of society, and he argued against the use of sign language.

One of the most important events of Bell's life in terms of its consequences was not an invention at all but his meeting with 6-year-old Helen Keller and her father. Keller had come to consult Bell about his daughter's education, and Bell's advice led him to both the Perkins Institute and Annie Sullivan, Helen's teacher, who was to give her the key to language, understanding, and expression. Another contribution to deaf people was the founding of the Volta Bureau—now the Alexander Graham Bell Association for the Deaf—as a source of information about deaf people and deafness.

Bell died in 1922, aged 75.

Black-and-white photographs illustrate the text. A chronology of Bell's life, a bibliography, and an index complete the book.

Analysis: Pelta has written a lively, absorbing account of Alexander Graham Bell's energetic life and career. She includes the difficult parts as well as the triumphs; for example, Bell suffered from sick headaches when under stress, he had a hard time financially in the early days, and he had to deal with court fights over his telephone patents.

Young readers interested in invention and science, as well as in methods of teaching speech to deaf people, will find this a rewarding book.

■ Pittle, Ivey B., and Roslyn Rosen, eds. *Another Handful of Stories: Thirty-seven Stories by Deaf Storytellers.* Transliterated from the Deaf Storytellers Videotape Series, Roslyn Rosen, Project Coordinator, and Barbara Kannapell, Program Coordinator. Gallaudet, 1984. 124pp. (0-913580-86-4) Reading Level: Grades 10–12.
Disability: Deafness

A follow-up to *A Handful of Stories,* edited by Leonard G. Lane and Ivey B. Pittle, this volume continues in a similar vein. It presents 37 stories, told by 24 storytellers who are deaf. Each storyteller is introduced in the beginning of the book with a photograph and a one-page biography. Thirty-seven stories, originally told by these persons in sign language on videotape, are presented after the section of biographical material. Unlike *A Handful of Stories,* however, this volume includes some original, creative tales in addition to true stories based on the life of the storytellers. One story, for example, "The Sonic Boom of 1994," tells what happened in 1994 when a giant sonic boom made everyone in the United States deaf.

Analysis: This is an entertaining as well as didactic volume and is recommended reading. Both books may be used with or without the videotapes upon which they are based.

■ Robinson, Kathy. *Children of Silence: The Story of My Daughters' Triumph over Deafness.* Dutton, 1990. 189pp. (0-525-24663-0) Reading Level: Grades 10–12. (AntR Sp90)
Disability: Deafness

The Robinsons live in England. When their older daughter Sarah was 2½, Kathy Robinson took her for an evaluation of her hearing; Sarah had had a hearing test as a baby, which did not reveal any abnormality, but the Robinsons were concerned because their daughter was not speaking. Now they were told that Sarah had a significant hearing loss due to nerve deafness, and they were stunned and appalled. "I had lost Sarah," writes Robinson. "Lost the Sarah I knew. Sarah was *deaf!*"

In her book, Robinson describes the next years. She was determined that Sarah would learn to speak; she wanted her to be integrated into the speaking world, not into the culture of the deaf. At first she was distressed by the appurtenances and requirements of deafness—the clumsy hearing aid with a big box worn on the child's chest, the speech of deaf people, the special schools. Helped by an excellent teacher who visited their home every week, Robinson worked to make Sarah understand what speech is for, to give her the skills she needed to name the world, to express feelings, to ask questions, to understand stories, and to process information and sensations. It was not easy. Sarah was a strong-willed, determined child, and her very determination often placed her in opposition to her parents as they struggled to teach her and socialize her. Descriptions of some episodes are reminiscent of Anne Sullivan Macy's early battles with Helen Keller.

The Robinson's second daughter, Joanne, was 15 months younger than Sarah. She was a much easier child, but when she was a toddler, Robinson began to worry that this daughter, too, was not hearing everything. Testing revealed that Joanne also had a hearing loss, less severe than Sarah's but still significant. Both Robinsons had a recessive gene for the disability, and their children had a one in four chance of inheriting it. This news was a terrible blow. Though she writes, "Any remaining vestige of confidence in myself as a mother had been swept away with Joanne's diagnosis," Robinson began to work with Joanne as well as with Sarah. The specialist had told her that whatever she put into the effort, she would get back; the home teacher gave her the techniques, strength, and encouragement to persevere. In addition to her concerns about her daughters, she also had to deal with anxiety attacks herself; these ended 18 months after the diagnosis of Sarah's deafness.

Sarah went to an ordinary nursery school and then at age 4 to a school for the deaf. Robinson felt that her daughter could not get the language stimulation she needed there, and eventually she was able to persuade the educational authorities to permit a transfer to a "partial hearing unit" in an ordinary school, where the children were mainstreamed for some activities. At about the same time, both children were fitted with radio-telemetry hearing aids that greatly improved both their ability to hear and the ease with which others could communicate; as Robinson explains, this device worked on the same principle as a walkie-talkie. Sarah also got a better ear mold, made by the same company that produced the radio-telemetry aids and superior to the one issued by the National Health Service. When it was time for her to go to school, Joanne entered an infant class for normal children, where, although she was the youngest child, she was ahead of the others; her teacher reported that she had "remarkable comprehension" and that "she's a fluent reader, her number work is excellent, and her written work is very good." Then Sarah was allowed to transfer to the local school, and by the end of the book, first she and then Joanne enter the Comprehensive School (similar to American middle and high schools), on a par with their age mates and fully accepted.

In an epilogue, Robinson explains that in the process of writing this book, she had "discovered that many of the services established to support and aid our children often work *against* their development." She began to write, give talks, and speak on radio and television and to campaign for early diagnosis of hearing loss. In this final section, she comments on her own opinions and on what she learned from research and the evidence of others. In brief sections, she discusses late diagnosis and the importance of early detection, causes of deafness, hearing aids, and total communication. She includes a list of addresses useful to American readers.

Analysis: Although she describes herself as indolent by nature, Kathy Robinson comes across as a woman of great determination who bent all her energies and skills to giving her daughters the gift of language. With the help of professionals and family, she found the ways to reach her children and to bring them into the world of the hearing. She wanted them to grow up with an image of themselves as "working, competing, playing and cooperating, not as different people, unequal people, or even hearing-impaired people, but as Sarah and Joanne." This is the picture the reader is left with at the end of the book.

Robinson is not a professional writer, and the text would have benefited from more editing (for example, in the use of commas to set off names in dialogue or in the distinction between "infer" and "imply"). It should probably be explained to young readers that the Robinsons are English, for this is not immediately evident. It would have been helpful too to know the time period Robinson is describing, because medical and educational practices evolve; the English edition of the book was published in 1987. These caveats notwithstanding, this is a book that could be recommended to parents and teachers of deaf children and to high school students with hearing impairments as well as to those of normal hearing with an interest in the subject.

■ Sidransky, Ruth. *In Silence: Growing Up Hearing in a Deaf World.* Illus. St. Martin's, 1990. 335pp. (0-312-04589-1) Reading Level: Grades 10–12. (PW 31 Ag90)
Disability: Deafness

This memoir of her childhood with deaf parents was written by the author when she was middle-aged and after her parents' death. She learned sign as her first and only language until she went off to public school in Brooklyn, where the family lived with many other recent Jewish immigrants to the United States. Throughout the book, she attempts to render sign in a written dialogue for the reader, although she acknowledges that it can be only an awkward translation of the beautiful body language spoken by her beloved parents and deaf relatives. Speaking of her mother, she writes, "In time I did learn [English], but the vibrant language of her hands was not matched by oral speech—not ever, not then, not now" (p. 40).

Sidransky was aware of her strange existence between two worlds, while she was a part of neither. "Once I entered our apartment, the door closed on the hearing world. My voice became the voice of my hands and I became a deaf little girl with ears that could hear" (p. 26).

After a brief initial placement in a class for retarded children, 5-year-old Ruth began to learn to attend to the sound of English. At the principal's request, her parents bought her a radio so as to bring sound into her otherwise silent home. She developed other sensitivities as well. "I listened to the inner voices of people, aware of their unspoken words. I could hear what I could see" (p. 49). By the time she was 8, she was in a class of gifted children, using the public library and exploring the world of literature. The book follows her progress into college days, where she met the man she would eventually marry.

Sidransky's father, Benjamin, had lost his hearing and, temporarily, his vision from spinal meningitis, contracted at age 2. In school, he was placed in a class for "hard-of-hearing" children, who were punished if they communicated with their hands. When he was 12, he was introduced to signing children from a school for the deaf. For the first time in his life, he was able to talk to people. He left school early and earned a precarious living during the Great Depression by working long hours as an upholsterer. He had a great sense of fun and was adored by his children.

Sidransky's mother, Miriam, was congenitally deaf, as were several of her siblings. Her grandparents brought their family to Ellis Island from Russia. They settled on the East Side of New York among many other immigrants. Miriam was stifled by the oral approach then used at the Lexington School for the Deaf. She left school after eighth grade to do assembly work to help support her family.

In loving detail, Sidransky chronicles the lives of her parents. They were sometimes misunderstood or mistreated because of their deafness, but more often they found joy and richness in their life. In many ways, Sidransky was the parent of her parents—interpreting and mediating for them in the hearing world. As such, she was alone and unprotected. Thus, when the local grocer sexually abused her, she felt that she had nowhere to turn for help. The book ends in the near past, when first her father, then her mother, died, surrounded by the family.

Analysis: This poetic memoir evokes a time long past, when Eastern European Jews struggled for assimilation and survival as new immigrants in a harsh economic climate. In turn, the author's unique childhood has enabled her to illuminate a culture within that culture, the world of the deaf. She is exquisitely sensitive to the subtleties of her several languages and to the pain of difference for her parents and for herself. As she describes the awakening of her own identity, she is revealed as a talented and imaginative person, ever grateful for the love and gifts bestowed by her parents. Although readers learn that she has a family, little mention is made of the adult life of this interesting woman. Perhaps that will be another book.

■ Tidyman, Ernest. *Dummy.* Little, Brown, 1974. 277pp. (o.p.) Reading Level: Grades 10–12. (LJ 15 My74; NYRB 21 Mr74; NW 13 My74) *Disability:* Congenital deafness

This book describes both the events surrounding two murders and the subsequent trials of a 20-year-old deaf man who had grown up on the

South Side of Chicago. The presiding judge is quoted as saying, "There is probably no other case like it in the annals of Anglo-Saxon law" (p. 264).

Donald Lang was born to a poor black woman whose husband abandoned her and his five children. This son was profoundly deaf at an early age from undetermined causes. He was excluded from most special education services, although his mother did seek help. Donald never learned sign, the manual language of the deaf, nor any written or spoken English. Nonetheless, he had street smarts, was strong and willing, and as a young adult he maintained a job as a freight handler. He lived with some of his siblings, and he was well liked by fellow workers. He satisfied his strong sexual drive by soliciting prostitutes, whom he picked up in the local bar. He was known to everyone as The Dummy.

In 1965, a young prostitute was murdered, and Lang was the last one seen with her. He pantomimed her stabbing to the police, but he did not seem to understand that they were charging him with the crime. A deaf lawyer, Lowell J. Meyers, agreed to defend Lang. Meyers was the son of economically comfortable deaf parents. He had encountered prejudice and other barriers because of his deafness, and he had an abiding interest in advocating for disabled people.

Lang was sent to a hospital for the criminally insane, to several state schools for the retarded, and to a number of experts for psychological testing. He was usually a tractable, cooperative resident, but he could not be taught sign. After five years, the indictment of murder was quashed for lack of evidence. After his release from custody, Lang went back to his old neighborhood and his old life-style.

Then another prostitute was murdered under similar circumstances to the first, and again the evidence pointed to Lang. Meyers defended him skillfully, but this time the jury found him guilty of murder. It was speculated that the victims may have tried to rob or rebuff him, because he was not a violent man except when frustrated sexually.

By the end of the book, Lang was confined to Cook County Jail in Chicago, because no regular prison seemed appropriate and he might be a danger to female residents in a state hospital. He received a little instruction in sign and was, as always, a hard worker at the jobs assigned to him.

Analysis: This is an engrossing, albeit sad story, written by a well-known writer of screenplays and other popular works. It highlights the negative consequences of the social neglect and indifference that too often are the plight of poor, minority, and disabled people. The care and attention that Lang received from the legal and special education professions came too late to help him or to prevent the tragedies he probably instigated.

An intriguing character in the story is the deaf lawyer who defended

Lang. The book might have been more balanced if his life had been more fully explored and his character presented in greater detail. The juxtaposition of the two deaf people, the one highly competent and the other a complete social outcast, lends an ironic twist to this bizarre case.

■ Toole, Darlene K. *Successful Deaf Americans.* Illus. Dormac, 1981. 79pp. (o.p.) Reading Level: Grades 4–6.
Disability: Deafness

A collection of brief biographies of eight Americans who are deaf and who have successful careers, this text emphasizes the life of ordinary people in an interesting career rather than the few who are in extraordinary positions or in the public eye. The people involved are a skier, a dentist, an actress, a teacher, a government worker, a manufacturer and distributor of teletype equipment for deaf persons, a TV news reporter, and a deaf activist who works within an organization that acts on behalf of the welfare of persons who are deaf.

Analysis: Recommended for both hearing and hearing-impaired upper-level elementary school children as representing good role models.

■ Toward, Lilias M. *Mabel Bell: Alexander's Silent Partner.* Illus. Metheun, 1984. 220pp. (0-458-98090-0) Reading Level: Grades 10–12. (BIC Ap85; Quill&Q F85)
Disability: Deafness

Mabel Hubbard was born in 1857, the daughter of a distinguished family in Cambridge, Massachusetts. When she was 5, she became deaf as the result of scarlet fever. At this time, there was little education for hearing-impaired children, and that little took place in asylums; people without hearing were described by terms like "deaf mute" and "deaf and dumb," and they were cut off from communication with the larger world. Mabel's parents were determined that their daughter would have a different life. They had been advised that deaf children could not be taught to speak, even if they had talked before the hearing loss; nevertheless, the Hubbards, particularly Mrs. Hubbard, and Mabel's governess succeeded in maintaining her speech and understanding so well that four years later, Mabel entered the same private school that her sisters went to. Later she traveled in Europe and studied in Vienna. Meanwhile, her father was instrumental in founding the Clarke Institution for the Deaf in Northampton, Massachusetts, an oral school where children learned to speak and to lip-read. Mabel herself was a proficient lip-reader.

Alexander Graham Bell came from a family that had studied and taught speech for three generations. His mother was partially deaf and his father developed a system called visible speech, using symbols to show how positions of the tongue and lips produced different sounds. Born in Scotland, Alexander taught in London, emigrated with his family to Canada, and went to Boston, where he taught people with speech defects and teachers of the deaf and pursued his interest in inventions. The Hubbards met him and sent Mabel to him so that she could improve her speech. Although at first Bell seemed middle-aged to Mabel (he was in fact ten years older), the couple fell in love and married in 1877.

Brilliant, sometimes unworldly, a bit eccentric, and passionate in pursuing his ideas and inventions, Bell was not the easiest of husbands, and his wife did not conceal from him or others in the family her occasional irritation at some of his habits. Yet they were otherwise well matched, and they remained devoted to each other through difficulties, separations, and sorrow. Their first years were uncertain financially, but they soon became prosperous and were able to lead a very comfortable life, with homes in Washington and a large estate in Nova Scotia.

Described as a creative listener, Mabel Bell was bright, energetic, and intellectually curious; her husband often discussed his scientific work with her, and sometimes she made useful practical suggestions. The Bells produced four children—two sons, who died at birth, and two daughters, both of whom married distinguished men. Mabel Bell's interests included the women's club that she formed in their tiny community in Nova Scotia, painting and gardening, and Montessori education; she was influential in establishing the first Montessori school in Canada and another in Washington.

Lilias Toward has made extensive use of the Bell papers, particularly the letters of Alexander and Mabel, in writing this biography. Although Mabel lived completely in the hearing world and there is little reference to her disability, there are moments when the difficulties it caused her became apparent. When her older daughter was about 3, Mabel wrote to her own mother that Elsie must already notice a difference for Elsie talked so little to her and so much to others. "I know she is fonder of me than anyone else but she does not talk to me as she does to others— from what her nursemaid says, she must be full of childish prattle and pretty dictatorial ways—all of which I see nothing as she talks so indistinctly, hardly moving her lips." She found it difficult to share Alexander Bell's interest in the heredity of deafness and the education of deaf children. Toward the end of her life, she wrote to her son-in-law about her "life-long desire to forget or at least ignore—the fact that I am not quite as other people." She had kept her daughters "from association—and therefore possible interest and sympathy—with the deaf. Above all things I was antagonistic to my husband's efforts to keep up his association with the deaf and to continue his teaching of them." Looking back, she recognized the many contributions made by both her father and her husband to improving the lives of hearing-impaired people and felt that her earlier antipathy arose from her desire not to be part of a group identified by their defect. "When I was young and struggling for a foothold in the society of my natural equals, I could not be nice to other deaf people. It was a case of self-preservation."

Black-and-white photographs show the family and their homes. There is a short bibliography.

Analysis: Lilias Toward has written an absorbing biography of a remarkable woman that is also the story of a remarkable marriage. She has included considerable discussion of Alexander Bell's scientific work and inventions. Extensive use of quoted material from the Bell correspondence gives the text immediacy and authenticity; both Mabel and Alexander were fluent, sometimes eloquent writers, and their voices make their world poignantly alive. The author shares the view of the Hubbards and of Mabel Bell herself that the best education of deaf children is the one that teaches them to speak and lip-read. Indeed, when Mabel was a child, everyone in the household was instructed not to respond if she attempted to communicate with signs. Readers will have to look elsewhere for discussion of the long battle between the oralist school of thought and those who advocated sign language.

This is a book that can be recommended to able high school readers, whether or not they have a prior interest in such subjects as the education of deaf people, inventions, or the story of an outstanding woman married to a much more famous man.

■ Verheyden-Hilliard, Mary Ellen. *Scientist and Physician, Judith Pachciarz.* Illus. by Linda Stanier. Equity Institute, 1988. 31pp. (0-932469-13-2) Reading Level: Grades 2–4. (BL 15 F89; SLJ Ap89)
Disability: Deafness

Judith Pachciarz became deaf after contracting encephalomeningitis at the age of 2 in 1943. Through her mother's efforts, a class for deaf children was started in a school 40 miles from their home in Illinois, and the now-3-year-old child was enrolled. At 6, she entered a regular classroom, though she still had special education in reading lips and in speaking. She went on to become the first deaf graduate of the University of Illinois, but her desire to be a doctor was thwarted when she was refused entrance by medical schools; she got a doctorate in microbiology instead. Much later, she was finally admitted to medical school, and she graduated in 1983, the first profoundly deaf woman to have earned both a Ph.D. and an M.D.

Analysis: An American Women in Science biography, this short book gives not only the facts of Pachciarz's disability and career but also little anecdotes from her childhood, and it mentions her current avocations. The style is simple and straightforward and the type large; pleasant pencil drawings appear on every spread. The book would be a good choice for young readers, no matter what their gender, physical condition, or academic interests.

■ Walker, Lou Ann. *Amy, The Story of a Deaf Child.* Photographs by Michael Abramson. Lodestar, 1985. Unp. (0-525-67145-5) Reading Level: Grades K–4. (BCCB S85; BL 15 N85; SLJ O85)
Disability: Deafness

Walker, herself the hearing child of deaf parents, writes this book in Amy's voice. Amy is 11, a deaf child with deaf parents and a hearing brother. Text and black-and-white photographs tell about her life at home and at school, with family, friends, and teachers. She is the only deaf child in her school. At one time, she had an interpreter, provided after her parents went to court to ask that she have the same opportunities as hearing youngsters. Since the Supreme Court reversed the decision of the lower courts, Amy has had to manage without one, although of course work was easier for her with such help. An afterword in Walker's voice says that Amy and her family have since moved to a different community, where the school district, recognizing the difficulties Amy was having, has hired interpreters to help her in three subjects. Amy's life includes adaptive measures used by hearing-impaired people, such as hearing aids, the TTY (teletypewriter) for telephone communication, lipreading, and lights instead of bells and buzzers. Amy has speech therapy and uses sign language. The book includes three pages of photographs of Amy signing words. There is a list of resources.

Analysis: Amy is presented in both photographs and text as a lively, energetic, cheerful youngster, happily comfortable in her life. Friendly and outgoing, she has both hearing and deaf friends and seems able to move well in both worlds. Perhaps the fact that her parents are also deaf has contributed to her ease. Walker does not discuss the cause of Amy's impairment, but one assumes that it is genetic.

Although there are already a number of books available about deaf children, this is a worthy addition to the group. Amy's voice has an authentic ring, the photographs and general design are attractive, and the information is conveyed deftly. The book can be recommended for school and public library collections, for hearing and hearing-impaired readers alike, and for individual reading and classroom discussion.

■ Walker, Lou Ann. *A Loss for Words: The Story of Deafness in a Family.* Harper & Row, 1986. 208pp. (0-06-091425-4) Reading Level: Grades 7–12. (BL 15 S86; KR 15 J186; NYTBR 5 O86)
Disability: Deafness

Lou Ann Walker grew up as the oldest of three hearing daughters of deaf parents. From her earliest years, even as a preschooler, she acted as interpreter for her mother and father, helping them negotiate in the hearing world. She opens with a description of the long trip from Indiana to Massachusetts, as her parents drove her to Harvard, where she would spend her last two undergraduate years. Then, moving backward and forward, she examines her family history and particularly the experience of her parents as deaf children, as adults, as a couple, and as parents. Her mother lost her hearing at the age of 13½ months, as the result of spinal meningitis. Her father became deaf as a 2-month-old infant, after a high fever; his oldest brother was also deaf, from an undetermined cause.

Walker looks at educational practices for deaf children, at the controversy between the oral and manual schools of thought, and at societal attitudes toward deaf people. She describes her family's life and the many ways in which deafness affected activities and relationships. At the same time, she pictures the ordinary aspects of the Walker household and of her own growing up.

Analysis: Lou Ann Walker has written a moving and compelling book. She concludes the prologue by characterizing her parents as "two ordinary people in extraordinary circumstances" and then says, "I started out writing about my parents. I learned a tremendous amount about life. And I ended up finding out about myself." Similarly, the reader will learn a great deal about what it was like to grow up as deaf children in the 1930s and '40s, what it was like to live with parents who could never hear your voice or speak to your teacher, how a young child acquires the maturity to be a parent's guide and bridge to the hearing world, and what it was like for Walker and her sisters simply to grow up in the middle class and the Midwest. *A Loss for Words* should be easily accessible to middle school and high school readers and is highly recommended. Walker has also written a fine book for younger children called *Amy, The Story of a Deaf Child.*

VISUAL IMPAIRMENTS

■ Alexander, Sally Hobart. *Mom Can't See.* Photographs by George Ancona. Macmillan, 1990. Unp. (0-02-700401-5) Reading Level: Grades K–4. (BCCB N90; CBRS O90; SLJ N90)
Disability: Blindness

Sally Alexander became blind at the age of 26 as the result of rupturing blood vessels in her eyes. In this book, her 9-year-old daughter, Leslie, is the narrator, talking about what it is like to have a mother who is blind. When Leslie was an infant, her mother could distinguish her from other babies by her big feet and the sound of her gurgles. "I still make noise for Mom," says Leslie, "especially when Joel [her older brother] silently teases me. If I screech, Mom comes to the rescue." Leslie talks about the adaptations her mother makes: her guide dog, Marit, her Braille recipes and labels in the kitchen, the Braille picture books she read her children when they were younger. The family camps and bikes together (Leslie's parents ride a tandem), Leslie's mother can play baseball by throwing the ball into the air and hitting it, and she and Leslie swim together and play duets on the piano. Leslie's mother makes mistakes, too, that are result of her blindness; some are funny, like spraying furniture polish on the ironing, and some are embarrassing, like continuing to talk to someone who has moved away or hugging the wrong man at the airport. Sometimes, Leslie can use her mother's disability to her own advantage—reading past bedtime if her father is not home to see or sneaking cookies, though the smell of chocolate chips betrays her. Leslie helps her mother when sight is important, and she understands how her mother uses other senses like touch and hearing to know her children and their activities and to express her love.

The black-and-white photographs are by George Ancona, author and/or photographer of more than 50 children's books.

Analysis: This is an outstanding book: moving, funny, informative, and extremely well written. Alexander weaves her material together skillfully: for example, the big feet that identified her newborn infant for her are mentioned again on the last page as characteristic of her 9-year-old daughter; a paragraph about Marit's harness is followed by one about the harness and leash Leslie wore as a toddler so that her mother could keep track of her. The overall tone is bright, happy, and energetic, but the text includes mention of the negative aspects of blindness—the stares and questions of strangers and most of all, the wistful note struck when the children wish that their mother could see their athletic exploits or magnificent natural sights "too wonderful to describe." "I wish she could see me, too," says Leslie. "Mom says she'd love to get a little peek at me or Joel or Dad. Since she can't, she says she takes a double share of touching and hearing us."

Every spread is illustrated with Ancona's striking photographs, showing a handsome, spirited, courageous mother and her equally handsome and spirited daughter.

■ Bergman, Thomas. *Seeing in Special Ways: Children Living with Blindness.* Photographs by Thomas Bergman. Gareth Stevens, 1989. 54pp. (1-55532-915-2) Reading Level: Grades 2–6. (BCCB F90; BL 15 Ja90; KR 1 N89)
Disability: Blindness

Originally published in Swedish in 1976, this book has a different format from others in the Don't Turn Away series. In his introduction, Bergman explains that the children he presents here are students at the Tomteboda School for the Blind, a residential school in Stockholm. "I felt hesitant at first about photographing children with impaired sight who would never be able to see or approve my pictures," he writes but also goes on to say that the children were quite willing to be photographed and that talking with them and watching them taught him new ways of seeing.

The children are between the ages of 7 and 11; two are girls, seven are boys; one is black. Some can distinguish light and dark and make out colors; some have been blind since birth, others lost their sight when very young. The text is a conversation between each child and Bergman, in which the author asks each of them questions about what they would most like to do, how they are treated by other children, whether they wish they could see, what they suggest to improve life for blind people, and what they can do that sighted children cannot. Most pages have photographs, and the children are shown playing together, observing the world through their fingertips, using Braille blocks and a Braille machine, and demonstrating skill at pouring milk.

As in the other books in this series, the concluding pages give more information about blindness, with suggestions for how to help a blind person and activities that will give an idea about what it feels like to be blind. There is an index.

Analysis: Bergman's technique of presenting his and the children's conversations gives the speakers character and voice; this text and the compelling black-and-white photographs make the youngsters vivid, lively, and appealing. While there is a certain amount of repetition, since Bergman asked some of the same questions of each child, the children come across as vigorous individuals, cheerful and active, despite the wistful statements by most that they wish there were schools for blind children all over the country so that they would not have to live away from home. For young readers, *Seeing in Special Ways* is a good addition to other books about blindness.

■ Bernstein, Jane. ***Loving Rachel: A Family's Journey from Grief.*** Little, Brown, 1988. 279pp. (0-316-09204-5) Reading Level: Grades 10–12. (NYTBR 20 Ag89; PW 2 Je89)
Disability: Optic nerve hypoplasia

When Jane Bernstein's second daughter, Rachel, was about 2 months old, Jane and her husband acknowledged to each other that something was wrong with this beautiful, placid, fat infant, who slept so much and seemed so "good." The specialists they consulted told them the baby had optic nerve hypoplasia, failure of the optic nerve to develop completely. Rachel appeared to be blind, but since visual development continues until 9 months, it was not possible to predict accurately whether she would have any vision. The cause of the condition was unknown, and it was also unclear whether there would be other problems involving brain malfunction.

Bernstein and her husband, Paul Glynn, reacted differently, and their ways of coping and not coping varied. At times it seemed that the strain would pull them so far apart that their marriage would disintegrate. Their 4-year-old daughter accepted her baby sister, disability and all, with unworried calm but was buffeted by the emotional storms of the household. Bernstein found help and comfort in the social worker who visited them at home and in the infant stimulation program at the Children's Specialized Hospital in New Jersey, near their home.

In an incident in a restaurant, when they were serving Rachel kidney beans on her high chair tray, the parents suddenly realized that she saw the beans before she grasped them. However, her motor and verbal development were delayed. An EEG at 9 months revealed abnormalities, but the specialist, who said he was "confounded and frustrated" by these results, could not predict whether Rachel would have seizures and "whether the damage is confined to the optic nerve." In fact, Rachel did develop seizures, which increased in severity; she was put on a course of ACTH— adrenocorticotropic hormone—which her parents learned to inject. A harsh medicine, it reduced Rachel to a sick, miserable baby who was wretchedly uncomfortable and could not be comforted. When at last the treatment was over, the parents waited for the baby's body to heal and watched anxiously for improvement.

Ultimately, there was improvement. Rachel learned to walk and to talk, though her speech was often characterized by perseveration. She had some vision. Seizures returned but were treated by other medications. Her fine motor and cognitive skills were delayed. At 3 she entered a special preschool. Then the social worker told Bernstein about an optometrist who was very successful in working with children who had low vision; after tests to measure her visual acuity, this doctor prescribed prismatic glasses, which made it possible for Rachel to use her area of vision much more successfully and with much less distortion of her body and gait and less strain.

Bernstein ends her book in 1987, when Rachel is 4. She summarizes her daughter's accomplishments and limitations and describes the ways in which she herself has changed: "I am with you, Rachel," she writes. "These last four years have prepared me. I have learned to introduce you to the world, and to be proud of you in the face of pity or ridicule. I have grown to love you so deeply that I can truly say that I can no longer imagine my life without you" (p. 279).

Analysis: This is an absorbing, moving book. Bernstein is a professional, published writer with a gift for catching the moment, the scene, the emotion, in words. She is clear-sighted and honest and has not flinched at revealing her own flaws, weaknesses, and unworthy thoughts and actions nor at describing the misunderstandings and additional sufferings that she and her husband inflicted on each other as they struggled with the pain of Rachel's blindness and other damage. She is particularly adept at picturing children, those in Rachel's infant stimulation group and preschool class as well as her own daughters.

Loving Rachel could be recommended not only to students and parents with a particular interest in this rare condition but also to general readers.

■ Birch, Beverley. *Louis Braille.* Illus. Gareth Stevens, 1989. 68pp. (0-836-80097-4) Reading Level: Grades 5–9. (BL 1 Ap90; BW F90)
Disability: Blindness

The author begins the biography with a description of young Louis Braille, still only 14 years old, working night after night in the dormitory of his Paris school to develop the system of writing that has come to bear his name. Birch then goes back to Braille's childhood in the village of Coupvray. Here in 1812, when no one was watching, the 3-year-old got hold of an awl or knife used by his saddler and harnessmaker father and injured his eye; infection set in and spread to the other eye, and the child gradually lost his sight. Bright and dexterous, he attracted the attention first of the parish priest and then of the new schoolmaster; unlike most blind children of the time, he was permitted to go to school, where he learned rapidly. When he was 10, his father took him to a school for blind children in Paris, and here he spent the rest of his life—as student, teacher, and inventor.

The system of writing that Braille devised is based on the alphabet of dots and dashes developed by an army captain for nighttime transmission of messages. Until that time, the only books for blind people used embossed letters; huge in size, inherently clumsy, they depended on a system clearly inferior to the one developed by the young Braille, but it took many years before Braille was adopted officially even by his own school, let alone by other institutions. France adopted Braille in 1854, the United States not until 1917.

Damp, crowded, unsavory conditions in the old school building and in the surrounding neighborhood affected Braille's health; the first signs of tuberculosis appeared when he was in his 20s; he died at 43. Accounts of his life describe him as eager, gentle, passionate, and dedicated.

This biography is illustrated by reproductions, photographs, and drawings. The final pages contain information about blindness, a list of organizations and places to visit, a bibliography for young readers, a glossary of terms, a chronology, and an index.

Analysis: This is a first-rate biography. Birch is a skillful and expressive writer with the ability to convey a great deal of information in a short space without weighing down the reader (the book is only 68 pages long). Braille and his world come alive, and the magnitude of his achievement is made clear. The illustrations, drawings, and full-color reproductions are well chosen to depict Braille's environment; photographs, most in full color, show such items as Braille's watch and set of dominoes as well as pages embossed with the letters that preceded his system and the dots that he developed. There are also photographs of modern-day scenes.

This book is highly recommended as the best current biography of a remarkable man whose invention changed the lives and opportunities of all blind people.

■ Butler, Beverly. *Maggie by My Side.* Illus. Putnam, 1987. 96pp. (LB 0-399-21696-0) Reading Level: Grades 4–12. (BCCB J187; BL Ag87; SLJ Ag87)
Disability: Blindness

Beverly Butler, a writer and a teacher of creative writing, lost her sight when she was 14, as the result of glaucoma. She begins her book with the sudden and unexpected death of her golden retriever guide dog, Una. Before Una, there had been three other guide dogs: a Doberman pinscher and two German shepherds. There are a number of guide dog schools in the United States, and she had gotten her training and her dogs at Pathfinder in Detroit, AA in Wisconsin, Pilot Dogs in Columbus, Ohio, and Guiding Eyes for the Blind in Yorktown Heights, New York. She decides to return to Pilot Dogs and to ask for a German shepherd.

Most of the book describes her two weeks of retraining with Maggie and their experiences together when they go home to Wisconsin. Maggie is different in temperament from Una, in part because of generic differences in the two breeds. She is a strong-minded dog, and the two undergo a period of trying each other out before they become truly a harmonious pair. Butler includes some information on the history of dog guides as well as descriptions of the training process. Black-and-white photographs illustrate the text.

Analysis: Butler writes smoothly and professionally, giving a readable account of the process by which she and her dog learn to know and trust each other. Readers gain a picture of life without sight from the senses she emphasizes in her descriptions as well as from the incidents chosen to illustrate her training with Maggie and their subsequent months together. The last chapter includes accounts of occasions when people—a fellow-traveler in the bus station, a headwaiter, a restaurant manager—objected to the presence of Butler's guide dog; she explains both to objectors and to readers that the law permits a guide dog to go with its owner in all public places.

The easy readability of the text makes this an appropriate choice for middle school children, but the book might also be enjoyed by older students; readers of any age might want to seek out other books on the training and use of guide dogs.

■ de Montalembert, Hugues. *Eclipse: A Nightmare.* Trans. by David Noakes. Viking, 1985. 244pp. (Paper 0-670-44437-5) Reading Level: Grades 10–12. (BL 1 O85; BS Mr86; KR 1 S85)
Disability: Blindness

In 1978, the 35-year-old French author, an artist, was the victim of a mugging by two drug-crazed men in his New York apartment. They were so enraged because he had so little money that they threw acid onto his face and into his eyes. He began this book in his native language as a journal during the following several months he spent in the hospital. In several operations, his eyelids were sewn together over his burned eyeballs, and he was finally released full of "the fear and mental anguish of those who, like me, have been stabbed in the heart of life" (p. 57). He lived in a sublet apartment and attended the Lighthouse, a rehabilitation center for the blind, for the next ten months. He learned orientation and mobility, Braille, and typing.

Montalembert had traveled widely in Africa, Asia, and the Americas and was well connected. He had coauthored a ten-page article in the *New York Times* magazine on the practice of voodoo in Harlem. He derived solace from a voodoo deity throughout this story. A Russian girl who had danced for George Balanchine now entered his life in a great, but doomed, love affair. She encouraged him to seek further medical opinions about his eyes, and he eventually sought help from a famous ophthalmologist in Barcelona, Spain. However, a preliminary operation revealed that his eyes had atrophied too much for the surgery upon which he had built his hopes.

In despair, Montalembert returned to the island in Java, where he had lived seven years earlier and where his now estranged love was visiting. He stayed eight months there and gradually came to terms with the new life he was destined to live. The book ends with a poetic statement of hope.

Analysis: The book's prose is often poetic and metaphorical, particularly in the parts written in the South Seas, where the author went for reconciliation and peace. It is also replete with hard-edged humor. For example, when an attendee of a Lighthouse lecture says he has become a much better person since being blind, Montalembert shouts, "Cut off your legs; you'll be even better!" (p. 79). Only a blind Hindu laughs, and the two mavericks leave together. Reflecting more thoughtfully, he adds, "Loss of sight is a mechanical accident, not a state of grace or an event fraught with spiritual consequences" (p. 79).

Unlike most people, the author is not much constrained by financial need. Many of his friends and acquaintances the world over lead an opulent life. Yet he sees through pretense, and he abhors our inhumanity. He views his attackers as victims of evil, in this case slavery and racism, rather than evil themselves.

■ Eldridge, Leslie, comp. *R Is for Reading.* Library Service to Blind and Physically Handicapped Children, 1985. 192pp. (0-844-40467-5) Reading Level: Grades 10–12. (BL 1 F86; LQ Ap86)
Disability: Visual impairment

Eldridge's book is a collection of interviews she conducted with children who have visual disabilities and with their mothers. She also talked to special education teachers as well as classroom teachers and teachers-in-training, child counselors, reading specialists, and librarians. She was specifically interested in investigating the effectiveness of services to the blind and physically handicapped children in the United States and in gathering ideas about how teaching programs and services for visually impaired children can be improved. The people she interviewed are located in widely distant parts of the country, including California, Georgia, Hawaii, Louisiana, New Jersey, and Pennsylvania. The text is organized by the category of person speaking (e.g., children and mothers, child development specialists, or librarians). There is a conclusion with recommendations for the future.

Analysis: Although this is clearly an adult book, and one most specifically directed toward readers whose personal and/or professional life involves them with visually impaired children and young people, high school students with an interest in the subject would find it stimulating and informative. The first section, in which children and mothers speak, is particularly accessible to nonprofessionals. No fathers are represented, which seems a curious omission. The format and arrangement of the material are attractive. Although the book does not include a bibliography, which would have been useful, interested readers could find articles and books written by the professionals interviewed. Many of these people are critical of existing programs and services, and they make specific suggestions about change.

■ Emert, Phyllis Raybin. *Guide Dogs.* Illus. Crestwood, 1985. 47pp. (0-89686-282-8) Reading Level: Grades 4–6. (RT My86; SLJ Ag86)
Disability: Blindness

The first chapter of this book for younger readers tells the story of Morris Frank, the blind insurance agent who in 1927 learned about the use of guide dogs in Europe and founded the first training school for them in the United States. The rest of the book explains the selection, training, use, and care of guide dogs.

Analysis: Attractively bound and illustrated with both color and black-and-white photographs, the story is told clearly and simply. As well as telling the story of Morris and Buddy, it also provides a good general introduction to the history and use of guide dogs. In addition to being read silently by individuals, this book would also be useful in a classroom situation for reading aloud, in which case it could be used with those grades below 4.

■ Hickford, Jessie. *I Never Walked Alone.* Illus. St. Martin's, 1977. 125pp. (o.p.) Reading Level: Grades 10–12.
Disability: Blindness

Jessie Hickford, a schoolteacher, became blind at the age of 52. She acquired a guide dog and set about becoming independent. She wrote a book about this experience entitled *Eyes at my Feet.* This book is a sequel. It begins with Miss Hickford and Prudence—her dog—adjusting to changes in their life. Aware that Prudence is now 7 and slowing down physically, Miss Hickford set about building an addition to her house so that she would have a first-floor apartment designed for her unique needs while a friend and her two grown children would inhabit the remainder of the house.

Miss Hickford describes the various experiences of her daily life with Prudence, such as increasing difficulties with mobility as her town began various urban renewal and expansion projects, as well as various adventures in traveling on buses and trains. When Prudence became 12, her arthritis, generally slower reflexes, and lessened strength became impediments to her mobility, efficiency, personal comfort, and safety, so Miss Hickford retired Prudence to pet status, with the help of her housemates, and went off to train a new dog, Dorothy.

Analysis: Miss Hickford is a remarkably independent and tough woman. Her narrative and description are factual and detailed. Readers who are at all interested in either the life-style of the blind or in animals will be intrigued by the details of this book. Although Miss Hickford clearly speaks as a middle-aged person, some teenage readers should find her story appealing.

■ Kang, Young Woo. *A Light in My Heart.* John Knox, 1987. 80pp. (0-8042-0921-9) Reading Level: Grades 7–12.
Disability: Blindness

Kang's story is summarized in an introduction written by Elsie Griffith McNeill, one of his American benefactors. The rest of the book is in the author's voice.

Young Woo Kang was born in 1944 in a small village near Seoul, South Korea, the eldest son of a farmer. During the Korean war, the entire village was destroyed, so the family went to Seoul. Kang's father died when the boy was 13. A year later, Kang was hit in the eye by a soccer ball, and he gradually lost his sight, despite operations and other medical treatments. His mother then died of a stroke, followed by his overworked, 18-year-old older sister. Thus, Kang was the head of his family, yet unable to support his younger brother and sister.

Blind people, considered unlucky in Korea, usually became fortune tellers or masseurs, but Kang dreamed of going to college. He went to the Rehabilitation Center for the Blind of Korea to learn Braille and typing and then on to the Seoul School for the Blind. Like a gift from heaven, an American couple, the McNeills, agreed to pay his tuition and living expenses for nine years, enabling him to graduate from Yonsei University, which is Christian and noted for its English instruction.

While preparing for college admission, Kang met Kyoung Sook Suk, a college freshman who became his reader, then his "sister," and eventually his wife. When he was finally permitted to take his entrance examinations, he excelled. He matriculated in Yonsei University's Department of Education, where he once again entered the world of the sighted. He overcame many obstacles, the worst being ignorance and prejudice, to become a top student with many friends. Meanwhile, Kyoung Suk went to the United States for a year to study rehabilitation of the blind. After the two received their college degrees, they were married in front of 300 people.

Kang was awarded a Rotary scholarship to study the education of the visually impaired at the University of Pittsburgh in Pennsylvania. From the first, a cadre of students and volunteers helped him with English and with his studies. Kyoung "stayed as close as my shadow" (p. 50), he writes. He finally learned independent mobility skills just before the birth of their first son. In 1976, he earned his doctoral degree, guided in the commencement procession by his wife.

Kang was the first blind Korean Ph.D. in history. However, efforts to obtain a job in Korea were for naught, despite recommendations of his competence from many professionals. The family was financially bereft and supported by friends. A second son was born at this difficult time. Just as the couple were about to open a small grocery store, Kang got a teaching position in Gary, Indiana. He has been the U.S.-based associate dean of Taegu University in Korea, teaching and speaking for colleges and schools in both countries.

The closing chapter is a reflection by Kang on his blindness. A postscript gratefully recognizes Rotary International and its foundation.

Analysis: This book provides a glimpse of a culture and a way of thinking very different from our own. Kang is inclined to emphasize form and appearance, rather than substance. So, for example, he details his grades and degrees but never mentions the subject matter or outcome of his dissertation research. He recognizes in thanks many people who might not be of interest to those outside the rehabilitation field. He is strong in his Christian faith, convinced that every event in his life was planned by God. He is at his best when he describes his thoughts on disability and his often brave and original attempts to gain acceptance for himself and other disabled people, both in his native land and in America.

■ Keeler, Stephen. *Louis Braille.* Illus. by Richard Hook. Bookwright, 1986. 43pp. (0-531-18071-9) Reading Level: Grades 4–6. (BCCB D86; SLJ F87) *Disability:* Blindness

This book is one in the Great Lives series, which comprises at least 12 other books about notables as diverse as Shakespeare and Elvis Presley.

The story begins with Louis Braille's birth in 1809 to the family of a saddle maker in a small town near Paris. An accident with a knife in the saddle shop precipitated the boy's total blindness by the time he was 5. Eventually, a priest enrolled him in his small school, and Louis excelled, relying on listening skills and his excellent memory.

When he was 10, he journeyed with his father to Paris to begin his lifelong association with the National Institute for Blind Youth. The founder of the school, Valentin Hauy, had devised a system of large, embossed letters that could be read by blind readers. This process was, however, very slow and cumbersome. A French army officer, Barbier, came to the school to demonstrate his invention, "night writing," consisting of dots and dashes punched into paper tape, for silent communication on the battlefield.

Braille resolved to improve upon this promising system, eventually developing the six-dot, embossed notation reading and writing system that is used by blind people worldwide today. Braille, an accomplished pianist and organist, adapted his system to music notation as well.

The governors of the school, all sighted, opposed Braille's new system and actually banned it. They even fired a principal when they discovered that he had produced textbooks in the "dot" system. Braille had become a teacher in the institution, so he could secretly teach his students. By 1835, fatigued with overwork, he became ill with tuberculosis. Two days after his 43rd birthday, he died.

Six months after, the Braille code was adopted by the National Institute as its official reading and writing system. Eight years later, it was brought to the United States, as well as to England. In 1952, Braille's body was taken from his home town of Coupvray to join the heroes buried in the Pantheon in Paris.

A glossary summarizes the important dates in Braille's life and defines some important terms. Several other books about blind people are listed. A page-long index follows.

Analysis: This colorfully illustrated book, in simple language, recapitulates the events in Braille's life. His writing system is lucidly described. Unfortunately, the eventual development of the mathematics code is not mentioned. The book reads less like a story than a young person's history text. As such, it is a good one, giving a clear account of the breakthrough that the Braille system was for blind people. The obtuseness, or worse, of those who opposed Braille and who actually burned all Braille books upon his death is treated with unjustified evenhandedness and without explanation. Nevertheless, this book fills what has been a serious gap in children's biography.

■ Kuklin, Susan. *Mine for a Year.* Illus. by Susan Kuklin. Coward, 1984.
76pp. (0-698-20603-7) Reading Level: Grades 4–9. (BCCB J184; NYTBR
1 J184; SLJ O84)
Disability: Blindness

George, the narrator of this story, is a 12-year-old boy who lives in the
country with his foster mother and a number of foster brothers and a birth
brother. The boys belong to the 4-H club and participate in Puppy Power,
a 4-H program that places young dogs with families for their first year of
life before they are trained as guide dogs. George is given a black Labrador pup named Doug, his first, and the book follows them together
through the year. These initial experiences in a household, with a master,
and in training classes, lay the groundwork for the dog's later intensive
education. Doug and George are both in a sense foster children. In addition, George wears glasses, has had three operations on his eyes for
cataracts, and fears that he will have to have more surgery, so the exercises
designed to help young trainers understand what it feels like to be blind
have particular poignancy for him. After he is told that he will not need
another operation, George says, "At first I trained Doug with the idea that
someday I would be repaid for my effort when I needed a dog guide. Now
things had changed. I trained Doug so that I would help someone in need.
I didn't care about being paid back. My love for Doug and his devotion
in return were enough." The book concludes with George's painful fare-
well to Doug, followed by his meeting with his new puppy; the final
paragraph describes how George is invited to watch Doug perform before
he is assigned to his blind master. The text is illustrated with many black-
and-white photographs taken by Susan Kuklin in New Jersey.

Analysis: Kuklin has successfully combined the conveying of detailed
information with a personal story. Although the text is much smoother
and more sophisticated than most 12-year-olds would write, the voice
sounds authentic. The reader shares George's anticipation, excitement,
worries, pain, and satisfactions. George's story and the dominant theme
are successfully integrated, and the points of connection are made clear
without being labored. The book is attractively designed, with clear, well-
leaded type, wide margins, and plentiful illustrations. It would make a
good addition to either a public or school library collection, for both
general and reference reading.

■ Little, Jean. *Little by Little: A Writer's Education.* Illus. Viking, 1988.
233pp. (0-670-81649-3) Reading Level: Grades 4–9. (BCCB J188; BL
J188; HB S/O88;)
Disability: Strabismus; Nystagmus; Corneal opacities; Eccentric pupils

Jean Little is an accomplished writer for children. The heroine of her first book, *Mine for Keeps* (1964), has cerebral palsy, and characters in subsequent novels have other disabilities. In *Little by Little,* she opens with a scene from her early childhood in Taiwan, when her playmate taunts her and says that she cannot be allowed to climb the banyan tree because she has "bad eyes"; her mother settles the argument by saying that Jean does indeed have bad eyes but that she can climb the tree. Her visual problems were probably caused by an infection her mother had during pregnancy. The corneas were scarred, and the iris stuck to the cornea in places. Her pupils were off center and could not fuse images; she looked through one eye at a time, her vision was limited, and she had to hold a book right up to her face in order to read. Seeing the writing on the blackboard was extremely difficult, unless the teacher wrote with broad strokes using special chalk. In addition, her eyes were crossed, and other children frequently teased her and called her names. Little's physician parents brought her up to recognize and deal with her disabilities but not to be limited by them and not to indulge in self-pity.

Little describes her growing up in Taiwan and Canada, her school experiences, her childhood life as a reader and a spinner of tales, and her beginnings as a writer. Her father not only encouraged his daughter to become a writer, but he also coached her and edited her work; she often resented his suggestions and the changes he made, sometimes without consulting her. When she was first published, with two poems appearing in a weekly magazine, he wrote a fan letter to the magazine under a pseudonym. Little was furious when she realized what he had done. "I did not fully forgive him until after his death," she writes. "I did not begin to see how endearing it was of him until I was thirty. I did not tell the story in public until I was forty-five. My fond father was the kind of parent every aspiring writer should be lucky enough to have" (p. 182).

The book ends with the acceptance of *Mine for Keeps* by Little, Brown and the award of the Little, Brown Canadian Children's Book Award.

Analysis: Just as Little has refused to allow her visual disability to circumscribe her life, here the physical condition of her eyes is just one part of the story. She is also writing about family relationships, about going to both special and mainstream classrooms, about being a hungry outsider, about friendships, and about becoming a writer. The same could be said of her fiction, which avoids polemics and didacticism; her books have been popular with young readers for 25 years, and deservedly so.

At the end of this book, Little writes a particularly poignant chapter describing how she became a teacher of children with motor handicaps. She found that "these were deprived children, not because they were not loved, but because they had largely been kept indoors due to their handicaps"—a situation that Little proceeded to remedy. Then, "[r]emembering how I had never found a cross-eyed heroine in a book, I decided to search for books about children with motor handicaps"—not because she wanted to limit her students' reading but because she wanted them to know books that reflected their experience. She found characters with motor handicaps, but they nearly always experienced complete recovery (e.g., Clara in *Heidi* and Colin in *The Secret Garden*).

> Why couldn't there be a happy ending without a miracle cure? Why wasn't there a story with a child in it who resembled the kids I taught?
> Somebody should write one, I thought.
> It did not yet cross my mind that that somebody might be me. [p. 225]

Youngsters who have enjoyed reading Jean Little's fiction will be attracted to this book; it will certainly appeal to children with physical and/or social difficulties. Little never preaches or lectures; rather, she informs us through her descriptions and observations. Her remarks about her relationship with her father might certainly help young readers gain a little perspective on their own struggles with their parents. She describes scenes and moments vividly, often with humor and with attractive self-mockery and honesty. Black-and-white photographs show Little and her family. A book to be recommended.

■ Mehta, Ved. *The Stolen Light: Continents of Exile.* Illus. Norton, 1989. 462pp. (0-393-0-26329) Reading Level: Grades 10–12. (NYTBR Mr89) *Disability:* Blindness

Some of the sixth installment of Mehta's multivolume autobiography has appeared in the *New Yorker* magazine, where Mehta has been a staff writer since he was 26. This segment covers his days at Pomona College in California, the subject of his youthful autobiography, *Face to Face* (Little, 1957). Mehta was blinded by infection in his native India when he was 3 years old. He was sent to a school for the blind in his country and was eventually to complete a high school education at the Arkansas School for the Blind.

Mehta writes in characteristic lavish detail of his struggle to fit in at a coed college in an alien culture. In addition, he had to contend with financial insecurity as his father, exiled and retired, endeavored to find funds to pay for his education. At one point, he hoped to go on to Harvard College, but he was thwarted by bureaucratic and financial tangles. Eventually, he rose to the top of his class and was accepted for graduate studies at Oxford University.

Mehta experienced his first love for a coed nicknamed Johnnie. His feelings of loneliness and difference were heightened. His knowledge of sexuality was sketchy at best, and he could find no books translated into Braille to enlighten him. Indeed, he could not even find a reader to read an assigned book, D. H. Lawrence's *Women in Love,* so he had to drop a particular English class. He was to meet Johnnie again, 30 years later, for a long conversation.

The book includes sections of Mehta's college journal, as well as his father Daddyji's diary and that of a friend, Mrs. Clyde.

Analysis: This story of the author's adolescent quest to find a place in the world incorporates his youthful memoirs with the perspective of a fulfilled, mature man of almost 60. The descriptions of his adolescent yearnings and many adventures are fun to read. His pluck and determination are inspiring.

As always, Mehta meanders through anecdotes, evocative images, and old memories with such perceptiveness and lucidity that he seems to have a second sight. The lengthy style and elegant prose demand both a patient and able reader.

■ Moore, Virginia Blanck. **Seeing Eye Wife.** Chilton, 1960. 177pp. (o.p.)
Reading Level: Grades 10–12.
Disability: Blindness; Burns

Virginia Blanck was badly burned as a young child in the 1920s. She sustained noticeable facial scars and irregularities that resulted in her being treated as somewhat of an outcast. When she went to college, she was even required to live in a room by herself and sit at a dining hall table with two students who were blind. Her association with one of these students turned into a paid reader's job and a lifelong friendship; it also led her to a career with an agency in Des Moines, Iowa, that worked with persons who are blind.

Virginia had always vowed that she would never marry a blind man because she had observed that the blind spouse often seemed to develop a dependent, passive relationship when her or his partner was sighted. Nevertheless, she met Bob Moore, and after nearly 30 years as a single person never seriously involved with a man, she was ready to marry Bob within a few weeks.

Though this story is about Virginia's life with Bob, her own life prior to meeting Bob certainly prepared her for dealing with disability and difference. Shortly before she met Bob, she had undergone additional plastic surgery that by this time was much improved over her many earlier operations, and her facial appearance was also much improved. Nevertheless, she still carried some physical scars as well as permanent emotional scars from the many years that she had been shunned and treated as different.

Analysis: The work is Virginia's story of her life with Bob. The story is notable and still readable for several reasons. First, it is one of the few books written by the nondisabled spouse of a person who is blind. Second, the couple's social attitudes toward disability in general and blindness in particular are far ahead of the era about which Virginia writes. Third, although on occasion some of its references are dated, this book is, 31 years after its publication, still fresh in tone and honest in its description of the life of a person who is blind. Virginia recounts some incredible stories about the actions and words of people who encountered Bob in public.

With few opportunities for social life, Virginia had read widely and thought deeply about disability and difference and the minority status that it creates. All this aside, the book is not without humor. The title is Virginia's wry comment on the fact that when Bob married her he decided to give up his young guide dog whom he had been using for only a year. As it was, he could use the dog only on weekends, because taking him to the factories where Bob went to try to place blind workers proved to be difficult and distracting to his main purpose for being there. Now that he was to marry Virginia, he would not use the dog enough on weekends to keep him trained. Therefore, Virginia dubbed herself the Seeing Eye Wife. Recommended for mature teen readers.

■ Ryder, Stephanie. *Blind Jack.* Illus. Houghton, 1961. 145pp. (o.p.)
Reading Level: Grades 4–12. (BL 15 My61; NYTBR 26 Mr61)
Disability: Blindness

The British author adopted a pitiful jackdaw who had been found blinded and half dead by a person standing in the queue at the fish market. Jackdaws as a species are highly social, but this wounded one was feeble, stunned, and starving. Ryder nursed him to health and began a rehabilitation program based on developing his other senses and a trust in her. She gave lessons in balance, locomotion, and direction. Blind Jack learned to respond to his name and to fly again, using a light brush of his head on the ceiling to judge his height. When he inadvertently flew into the river, he was able to save his own life by swimming to shore. Ryder reports many observations and experiments, even the unsuccessful introduction of a prospective mate. At the end of the story, Jack had lived for three years in the Ryder household of children, ducks, budgerigars, doves, and a physician husband and was still going strong.

Analysis: Blind Jack is a delightful story with keen insights into bird behavior. The author immediately puts her reader into the mind-set of the bird. "We can never fully imagine what blindness must mean to a bird." By doing this herself, she is able to devise an environment where Jack can learn and explore. Her techniques are very much like those one would use with a blind child. Indeed, by the end of this delightful story, Blind Jack has become like a person to us. The black-and-white photos are a welcome addition to the book.

■ Swenson, John. *Stevie Wonder.* Illus. Harper & Row, 1986. 160pp. (0-06-097067-7) Reading Level: Grades 10–12. (BL 15 F89)
Disability: Blindness

One of a large number of Stevie Wonder biographies, this book is a chronological account of Wonder's life, written for adults but certainly accessible to teens. Detailed and factual, it narrates Wonder's life from his birth in Saginaw, Michigan, in 1950 through his rapid rise as a Motown artist in the early 1960s, and up to his present-day work.

Analysis: The emphasis here is on his work; Stevie Wonder fans will definitely enjoy this aspect. Conversely, those who are more interested in his personal life and/or his disability and the ways that it has influenced him will find these aspects somewhat buried, but present, nevertheless. Stevie Wonder the Musician is definitely paramount in this work. His blindness, however, is discussed from the very first page, and it is brought into the text when it has some bearing on the topic under discussion. This treatment is quite appropriate in its emphasis on the person rather than on the disability.

Liberally illustrated with black-and-white photographs, the text concludes with a 13-page discography, which is also heavily illustrated.

7

BOOKS DEALING WITH COGNITIVE
AND BEHAVIOR PROBLEMS

> *It [The Settlement] must be grounded in a philoso-*
> *phy whose foundation is on the solidarity of the*
> *human race—a philosophy which will not waver when*
> *the race happens to be represented by a drunken*
> *woman or an idiot boy.*
>
> —Jane Addams

> *"Well, where DO the Mermaids stand? All the*
> *"Mermaids"—all those who are different, who do*
> *not fit the norm and who do not accept the available*
> *boxes and pigeonholes?*
> *"Answer that question and you can build a school,*
> *a nation, or a world on it."*
>
> Robert Fulghum

Titles here are classified under three headings:

Emotional Disturbances, in which such disabilities as autism, posttraumatic stress syndrome, and mental illness are portrayed.

Learning Disabilities, in which dyslexia and other specific learning problems are discussed.

Mental Retardation, including people with Down's syndrome, fetal alcohol syndrome, and developmental disabilities.

Annotations are alphabetical by author within each section.

259

EMOTIONAL DISTURBANCES

■ Allen, Carol. *Tea with Demons*. Morrow, 1985. 335pp. (0-688-05093-X)
Reading Level: Grades 10–12. (BS D85; KR Je85; PW 12 Jl85)
Disability: Mental illness; Schizophrenia

Carol Allen was a 30-year-old Philadelphia housewife and part-time philosophy instructor. From a solid Midwestern family, she had the ideal
home for an educated woman of the mid-70s: two children, a boy and a
girl who were 1 and 3 years old; a handsome, achievement-oriented husband who was a college professor; a part-time career; a circle of couples
as friends; good health; and good looks. Quite suddenly, for no apparent
reason, she began to suffer panic attacks, uncontrollable, racing, obsessive
thoughts, vague but persistent fears of something unknown, and bizarre
dreams. At first, she isolated these symptoms by totally submerging them
when in the presence of others, but eventually they began to affect her
behavior. Her husband attempted to be understanding and agreed, somewhat reluctantly, that she should undergo psychotherapy.

Allen found a therapist, Dr. Herbert S. Lustig, whose office was near
her home and with whom she established an immediate rapport. Her
therapy was progressing well; within six months, however, her marriage
disintegrated, and she found herself facing all the problems of a single
parent, including a very limited income. Nevertheless, her therapy continued to be positive, until an incident occurred involving a sexual relationship between a close friend and the friend's psychotherapist, which Dr.
Lustig investigated and deemed a lie on the part of the friend. This pushed
Allen over the edge into madness, as she calls it.

Dr. Lustig, in his comments at the end of the book, declines to label the
illness, lest readers should attempt self-diagnosis; however, for the purpose of indexing this title, we have identified it as schizophrenia. Hospitalized for a period of time, Allen eventually recovered and has resumed her
life's activities, including the rearing of her children and a new career.

Analysis: Allen writes very well. She uses vivid, descriptive language
and strong, definite narrative. She has been able to step back and objec-
tively write about what happened during this period of her life. She is
highly analytical, no doubt the effect of her training as a philosopher.
Highly recommended for high-school-aged readers.

■ Anderson, Luleen S. *Sunday Came Early This Week*. Schenkman, 1982.
129pp. (0-07073-575-6) Reading Level: Grades 7–12.
Disability: Emotional disturbance

The author is a clinical psychologist, who at the time of the writing of this book was coordinator of psychological services for the public schools in Quincy, Massachusetts. In her introduction, she explains that she has specialized in "the treatment of suicidal and severely disturbed adolescents." Here she tells the story of a 17-year-old young woman, whom she calls Becky, and her therapist, whom she calls Amanda Adams. Becky and her parents have been referred by their pediatrician, whose note reads, "I fear this girl has psychotic episodes and poses a high suicidal risk." Using accounts of the therapy sessions and the letters Becky sends to Dr. Adams as well as her journals and diaries, Anderson describes the difficult journey toward health and stability.

The brilliant only child of older parents, Becky has many severe problems. Her father is passive and distant, her mother undemonstrative and critical, and she feels estranged and completely out of harmony with them. Torn by contradictory impulses, she both rebels against her parents and attempts to fulfill their high academic expectations. Her social life is also unsatisfactory. A psychotic episode in which she throws a dart gun at Dr. Adams and injures her eye seems to be a turning point for Becky. They work together for nine months before she goes away to college, and though there is another breakdown there, with a severe eating disorder, Dr. Adams is able to arrange for further therapy. The book ends with Becky's achievement of a degree of stability and understanding.

Analysis: As is often the case with emotional disorders, Becky's story presents emotions and problems that are experienced by many people but that in her are raised to a feverish, unmanageable pitch. By focusing on a young woman who is unusually bright, articulate, and introspective, Anderson draws a vivid portrait of pain and rage that are eventually replaced by a movement toward understanding and acceptance. She also makes clear the dilemma faced by the therapist, who must decide at certain points whether Becky's illness and frantic state of mind call for hospitalization or whether such a move would have a negative effect on her recovery. The issue becomes most pressing immediately after Becky injures the therapist, runs from the office, and is not discovered until hours later; Dr. Adams' superior expects that hospitalization will follow without question, but she holds off, and this proves to be the best choice.

Anderson has apparently written widely for both professional and general audiences. Although of course the focus here is on an extreme situation, this book could help both parents and their adolescent children to achieve a better understanding of the often turbulent emotions and complex parent-child relationships that frequently mark the teenage years.

■ Ashton, Ian B. *Autistic Children: One Way Through: The Doucecroft School Approach.* Illus. Souvenir, 1987. 205pp. (0-285-65040-8) Reading Level: Grades 10–12. (BBN Ap87)
Disability: Autism

The author's aunt had been a neighbor of an autistic boy. This young acquaintance inspired Ashton to write an essay on autism as part of his college finals. He went on to teach French in a "tough school" in Manchester but finally was assigned to a class of slow learners. He loved this work, so he went back for a full-year course in special education. His dream was to open a residential school for autistic children, because the educational system in England had little to offer them at the time.

On a Monday in May 1977, his goal was fulfilled, as his new school in Kelvedon, Colchester, reached deadline day. It was called Doucecroft, meaning sweet dwelling place, or home. As the first of five charges was delivered to the school by a driver bloodied by a deep scratch on his neck, the staff was "into a place which, unbeknown to everyone at the time, was about to erupt into what could only be described as a total disaster area" (p. 50). The children were nonverbal, self-destructive, and unsocialized. At first, they traumatized both the day and night staffs.

With persistence, the workers were able to begin to enter the autistic children's world, manipulating them into more acceptable and socialized behavior. Ingenious individualized therapies were applied. For example, when all else failed with an 11-year-old head banger, Ashton deliberately banged the child's head to the floor and told him to continue the behavior. At that, the boy said his first word, "No," and ceased head banging for good. Ashton added a nursery unit in the belief that the school could be more helpful to younger children and also spare their parents years of coping alone.

Near the end of the book, several parents offer their perspective on caring for an autistic child. All express gratitude for the Doucecroft School, but most are concerned about their children's future. In the final chapter, Ashton discusses the arduousness of fund raising and of making physical improvements in his school. He suffered a heart attack and had heart surgery at age 34. "I no longer rush about like a demented lemming," he avows (p. 202). In 1983, Ashton was instrumental in establishing a Life Care Center for autistic school leavers.

The text is supplemented by black-and-white photographs showing the children and staff in various activities.

Analysis: Ashton provides a joyful romp through his school. He obviously adores his young charges and sees their bizarre behaviors as interesting challenges. His successes and failures alike are recounted with a delightful rustic humor. His north country vernacular includes such words as chuffed, diddycoys, scoffered, and chuntering, but in general the prose is easy reading.

■ Bartocci, Barbara. *My Angry Son: Sometimes Love Is Not Enough.* Donald I. Fine, 1985. 269pp. (0-917657-16-0) Reading Level: Grades 7–12. (BL 15 My85; LJ Jl85; PW 12 Ap85)
Disability: Emotional disturbance

Barbara Bartocci was a young Navy wife with three children, when her husband, a pilot, was killed in Vietnam. John Bartocci, the angry son of the title, was 7 years old. His father's death, John writes in the preface, "nearly destroyed" the family. Unable to express his grief or even to believe that his father would never return, full of rage because he felt abandoned, the youngster acted out his disturbance in increasingly disruptive and violent ways. When his mother remarried, the boy's angry behavior continued, until, at 13, he was sent to a special Boys' Home. Eventually, after much suffering and many destructive episodes, therapy helped the family heal itself. In an afterword, Barbara Bartocci's second husband summarizes their story and tells readers where they all are: John and his older sister have graduated from college, his younger brother is still in school, and John is working to become a writer.

Analysis: The author, who works in advertising, writes in a fluent, professional style. She is able to describe intensely personal and painful events and thoughts with apparent honesty and directness. Obviously, she could not have recalled all the conversations recorded here in such precise detail, but this method gives her account the readability of fiction. She has written the story not only of a profoundly troubled son but also of a second marriage strained almost beyond bearing. Young readers who have themselves experienced great loss might gain understanding from this book, as might those whose families have undergone great change and restructuring. The eventual happy resolution of problems and the repatterning of behavior are made believable and heartening in this account.

■ Callahan, Mary. *Fighting for Tony.* Illus. Simon & Schuster, 1987. 172pp. (Paper 0-671-6326-5) Reading Level: Grades 7–12. (BL 15 S87 KR 1 Jl87; LJ 15 S87)
Disability: Autism

The author, a registered nurse, tells the story of her son, who at 2 was diagnosed as an autistic child. A beautiful, apparently normal baby at birth, at 1 week Tony began to have periods of screaming that grew increasingly longer and more difficult to manage. In other ways, he seemed to be developing appropriately, and his parents tried desperately to find ordinary causes for his extraordinary crying. As he grew, he appeared to exhibit many of the classic characteristics of autism, such as ritualism, self-stimulating behavior, echoing of words rather than real processing of language, and self-isolation. Callahan put him into preschool programs for special children but also formed with her friends a mothers' group in which Tony was the only child with a disability. When Tony was 17 months old, his baby sister was born. Eventually, the strain and the anger both felt drove Callahan and her husband apart, and they divorced, although he remained in his children's lives, taking them to his apartment on weekends.

While accepting her son's impairment, Callahan continued to read widely about autism and to try different approaches. When she tested various foods, Tony appeared to react violently to milk, so, although medical personnel discounted such an allergy as a cause of his behavior, she substituted soy milk in his diet. Gradually, Tony became less difficult and began to emerge from his unreachable state, thanks in large part to his little sister, who, says Callahan, took him with her through her own stages of development. Callahan and her husband remarried, and the family began to move toward normalcy.

At Tony's 5-year-old evaluation at the Programs for Children, the doctor told the boy's parents that his original diagnosis was wrong, that he was not autistic. However, Tony still had deficits. For example, he had auditory processing problems, but Callahan was able to help him work through these with what she calls her amateur speech-therapy sessions at home. Preschool testing indicated difficulties with visual processing as well, but Callahan insisted that they try a regular classroom before putting Tony into special education. He entered kindergarten with his little sister, a year later than usual, and in the epilogue Callahan describes him as a normal second-grader.

An episode at 5½, when Tony had been given two cartons of milk by a teacher and exhibited a dramatic regression to autisticlike behavior, convinced Callahan that cow's milk had been the culprit from the beginning, ingested through her breast milk. When she told this story to an allergist, he said, "Some people think it's possible for the brain to swell as a result of an allergy, just like bronchial tubes swell in asthma and sinuses swell in hay fever. They think it can mimic retardation, autism or hyperactivity." The doctor had never seen such a case and did not believe in the theory, though he did say that if the condition existed, it was very rare and that Tony might be one of no more than 50 cases in the country.

In the epilogue, Callahan briefly discusses research into possible causes of autism and urges parents to be active in seeking information and help for their children. She recommends sources such as the National Society for Autistic Children and the Institute for Child Behavior Research. She also gives a reading list of books she herself found especially helpful and a short list of references.

Analysis: Unlike some books by parents or others who write about finding a solution to medical problems that has escaped the professionals, Callahan is never polemical. She has written a very readable and engrossing account of one family's experience with a devastating condition; although she seems to have almost total recall of many conversations, an unlikely feat of memory, this is not a major detraction. Callahan does not shrink from describing unattractive, even destructive, attitudes and actions in herself and her husband. She says honestly that she and her family have been very lucky: "Of the 100,000 or so children in this country diagnosed as autistic, only a handful recover completely, and a dozen or so more are able to function well in spite of their symptoms. Tony is one of the very fortunate few because we accidentally fell upon the cause of his autistic symptoms in our trial-and-error attempt to improve our situation. I know we haven't found the cure for autism, but I do believe we may have found a solution for a small subgroup of people diagnosed as autistic" (p. 166).

The black-and-white photographs show an exceptionally attractive family. In the early pictures, Tony is crying or self-absorbed; in the last ones, he is bouyant, smiling, and engaged with the outside world.

This book would be of special interest to readers who know or are related to an autistic child and to those who are considering the field of special education, as well as to people concerned with food allergies and their effects.

■ Christopher, William, and Barbara Christopher. *Mixed Blessings.* Illus. Abingdon, 1989. 224pp. (0-687-27084-7) Reading Level: Grades 9–12. (KLIATT S90; LJ 1 Je89)
Disability: Autism

William Christopher, the actor who played Father Mulcahy on "M*A*S*H," and Barbara Christopher, an artist and his wife, have coauthored this book about the second of their two adopted sons, Ned, who was obviously different from infancy and whose behavior eventually was diagnosed as autistic. During the years that William Christopher was acting on "M*A*S*H," he was also intensely involved in efforts to help Ned. His and Barbara's attempts to improve Ned's situation led them to a large number of medical facilities and various programs for exceptional children, including the controversial Doman-Delacato program, which appeared at first to be promising but ultimately did not work out.

Ned lived with his family until he was 13, when his aggressive behavior became so severe that for everyone's safety and emotional well-being, it became essential to place him in a residential treatment facility. The first facility was too limited in various ways, but the second one, operated by the Devereux Foundation, has proved to be effective, although the Christophers had to enlist the services of several specialists before a program that worked for Ned could be established.

The Christophers have dedicated an enormous amount of their time and financial resources, far beyond the reach of many people, to help Ned. Their love and devotion to him shine through in each page of the book. Barbara Christopher has worked into the text various letters that she and other family members, including Ned himself, wrote over the years, both to each other and to the various organizations and professionals who worked with Ned.

Analysis: Both William and Barbara alternately tell the story with a natural flow from one narrator to the other that is not easy to achieve. They have kept detailed information about Ned's progress and his various regressions, as well as about the different diagnoses and treatments over the years. This information constitutes a valuable history of the evolution of the psychological and medical beliefs about and treatments of autism over the past two decades as well as a thoughtful, unhurried examination of the various practical approaches that help in dealing with an autistic child. Highly recommended for high school readers and for anyone who comes into contact with persons who are autistic.

■ Dinner, Sherry H. *Nothing to Be Ashamed Of: Growing Up with Mental Illness in Your Family.* Lothrop, Lee & Shepard, 1989. 212pp. (LB 0-688-08493-1) Reading Level: Grades 7–12. (BCCB Mr89; BL 1 Je89; KR Ap89; SLJ Ap89)
Disability: Mental illness

Addressing her young readers directly, Dr. Dinner, a psychologist, begins by examining the subject of mental illness and distinguishing its manifestations from behaviors that fall within the so-called normal range. After a chapter devoted to reactions to living with a mentally ill person, she goes on to chapters that discuss six conditions: schizophrenia, mood disorders, anxiety disorders, posttraumatic stress disorder, Alzheimer's disease, and eating disorders. Profiles and histories of individuals and families illustrate the illnesses and are presented from the point of view of the well youngster. Final chapters discuss the work of mental health professionals and the assistance they can offer, things that young people can do to help themselves cope as successfully as possible, and ways in which they can help their families. The book concludes with an appendix of support groups, a glossary, references, and an index.

Analysis: Dinner presents complex material clearly, keeping her audience always in mind and frequently addressing young readers. Her tone is empathic but not sentimental, her suggestions practical and realistic. While she describes the various treatments available for these serious illnesses, she recognizes that complete cures are often not possible; she offers help to young readers who must learn to live with mental illness in the family, who must accept the situation whatever the outcome of treatment, and who must develop a healthy life. Though her subtitle makes it clear that she is writing for a particular population, the book can be read by a much wider group. Youngsters interested in the subject of mental illness, those who have known it through friends or more distant relatives, and those considering a career in the mental health professions might all want to read it as well. Therefore it is a good choice for a school library or young adult collection in a public facility.

■ Flach, Frederic. *Rickie: With Recollections by Rickie Flach Hartman.* Ballantine, 1990. 275pp. (0-449-90349-9) Reading Level: Grades 10–12. (BL 1 Mr90; LJ 15 F90; NYTBR 11 Mr90)
Disability: Depression

The author was a successful practicing psychiatrist, when his eldest daughter, 13-year-old Rickie, was hospitalized for a sudden descent into depression and aberrant behavior. At the same time, Flach's own seemingly perfect marriage broke up, and he experienced doubt in his own erstwhile strong Catholic faith.

Part One of the book describes Rickie's torments and her self-destructive behavior on the hospital unit. Part Two carries on with the three years in which Rickie underwent intensive psychotherapy, pharmacotherapy, electroshock therapy, and milieu therapy at various times. Throughout the book, she contributes her perspective in italicized sections, and some of her poems are quoted.

Rickie was in both private and public hospitals, receiving the best and the worst they had to offer. She would swing from appropriate patient behavior to such self-destructive or aggressive acts that one doctor suggested she should be lobotomized. Her father experienced his own agony. Even though he was a psychiatrist with many well-meaning professional friends, he never actually determined the exact diagnosis of his daughter's problem.

Part Three sees Flach take a primary role in Rickie's therapy after she had been ill for ten years. A developmental optometrist discovered a long-neglected vision problem. Rickie underwent vitamin therapy and began to work with a rehabilitation counselor. At this time, her father realized that when Rickie was 13, she had, in quick succession, lost her beloved grandfather, almost drowned, witnessed the incipient dissolution of her parents' marriage, and suffered a major humiliation in her convent school. He began to wonder if her bizarre symptoms had been learned from the older, sicker patients with whom she had been forcibly incarcerated.

In the end, Rickie's resilience seemed to win out. She recovered, earned a high school equivalency diploma, got a job, married, and had a child. Her extraordinary experiences gave her a toughness, a faith, and an empathy that were appreciated by her family and her many friends.

Analysis: The concomitant perspectives of father and daughter are a unique contribution. Here is a father doing the very best he can as he sees it; here is a young girl drawn perhaps unnecessarily into a psychiatric system with its attendant horrors and miseries. And yet Rickie managed to manipulate and frustrate that system in a manner that invited much of the treatment she received.

Flach has written a number of books accessible to the layman. His style is forthright. He honestly acknowledges his doubts and mistakes, but he expresses also a belief in the healing power of faith and love.

■ Gordon, Sol. *When Living Hurts.* Illus. Union of American Hebrew Congregations, 1985. 127pp. (0-8074-0310-5) Reading Level: Grades 7–12. (PsyT S86; SLJ Ag86; VYA Ag86)
Disability: Depression

Sol Gordon is a clinical psychologist who has earned a place in the disability field as an author and lecturer particularly concerned with sexuality. He states that he was a lonely and sometimes depressed youngster, much like those he is reaching out to in this book.

The first subject dealt with is suicide. About 6,000 young people kill themselves every year, a rate that has tripled in the past 30 years. In addition, several hundred thousand more young people make serious suicide attempts each year. Gordon gives advice both to the suicidal person and to the friends of that person in order to help avert this tragedy. He also discusses concerns about sexuality, religion, and parental relations. He takes pains to distinguish between irrational guilt and anger and that which propels people to be better. He acknowledges that one's life and circumstances can be miserable and unfair, but he offers advice on what to do and what to think so as to improve a bad situation. He stresses self-forgiveness, compassion, and tolerance. He says living well is the ultimate revenge.

Boldface and large print frequently highlight important points. For example, Gordon writes, "THE CRUCIAL PART TO UNDERSTAND

IS THAT SUICIDAL INTENT IS ALWAYS TEMPORARY. IT CAN BE REVERSED" (p. 19). The text is occasionally humorous: "They [teenagers] don't realize that the first experience of sex is usually grim (almost no girl will have an orgasm—the boy gets his three days later when he tells the guys about it)" (p. 61). Interspersed in the text are relevant quotes from other books and articles. Several pages with brief messages asking parents for help are intended to be cut out of the book. Gordon closes the book by asking readers to write to him and possibly to contribute to the next edition of the book. An appendix lists crisis intervention and suicide prevention hot lines nationwide and in Canada.

Analysis: Gordon's tolerance of various sexual practices, such as masturbation and homosexuality, may seem extreme to some. However, he is a fervent advocate of personal responsibility and compassion in human relationships. To illustrate, he takes the position that, "It's o.k. to have thoughts of sexual seduction, but it's not o.k. to exploit someone" (p. 62).

The simple but powerful messages in this book are delivered without pomposity or preachiness. Many causes of teenage depression are explored, including having a disability. In fact, it would seem that almost any reader could identify with some of the burning questions and concerns that are covered. The approach is eclectic and nonthreatening enough to warrant use with disturbed as well as better adjusted youngsters. The black-and-white photographs and drawings depict nature. They are probably intended to be uplifting, and they might be used in meditation.

■ Grandin, Temple, and Margaret M. Scariano. *Emergence: Labeled Autistic.* Arena, 1986. 182pp. (Paper 0-87879-524-3) Reading Level: Grades 7–12. (LATBR 4 My86; LJ 15 My86; PsyT N86)
Disability: Autism

Temple Grandin was diagnosed as an autistic child while still very young. Unlike many such youngsters, she was able to go to a school for normal students. In the introduction, she says that she is proof that, though many might not believe it possible, "the characteristics of autism can be modified and controlled." At the time she wrote this book, she was "a successful livestock handling equipment designer, one of very few in the world," an active professional person finishing work for a doctorate in animal science.

Emergence describes Grandin's life from her first memories. She is able to remember which stimuli and situations distressed her and which gave her comfort. While still in high school, she visited an aunt who had a cattle ranch in Arizona. She was fascinated by the squeeze chute used to restrain the animals while they were being attended to; eventually she designed a similar squeeze machine for herself, finding that being in it calmed her and that "the effect was both stimulating and relaxing at the same time." Though she was held by a mechanical device, she remained in control. Eventually, this interest led her to her life's work in animal science.

The text includes letters describing Grandin, which were written to her doctors by her mother; a chapter called "Autistics and the Real World," which contains advice and suggestions for parents and professionals; a diagnostic checklist for behavior-disturbed children from the Institute for Child Behavior Research in San Diego; a selective bibliography; and a Technical Appendix with information for parents, teachers, and professionals. The foreword was written by Dr. Bernard Rimland of the Institute for Child Behavior Research, and the preface by one of Grandin's teachers.

Analysis: This is an unusual book, perhaps the only published account of autism written by an autistic person. One of the characteristics of this condition is that it seems to wall the affected person off, making her or him unreachable; in addition, autistic people are not usually able to communicate easily. Thus Grandin's descriptions of her reactions and her view of the world make fascinating reading. Her mother seems to have had great understanding and patience; she mentions her father only occasionally. In his foreword, Dr. Rimland writes that few autistic people achieve the high level of education and competence that Grandin has reached, but he is convinced that she is indeed, as he says, "a recovered (or recovering) autistic." Clearly, her disability was not as severe as that of many others with this condition.

Though written for an adult audience, this account could be read by youngsters in middle school and by older readers as well.

■ Greenfeld, Josh. *A Client Called Noah.* Holt, 1986. 371pp. (0-8050-0085-2) Reading Level: Grades 10–12. (BL 15 N86; NYTBR 15 F87; Time 9 F87)
Disability: Mental illness

A follow-up to *A Child Called Noah* and *A Place for Noah,* this latest entry further chronicles the life of Noah Greenfeld, son of Hollywood writer Josh Greenfeld. Beginning in 1977, when Noah is 11 and on the brink of adolescence, this book, written in journal form, relates the life of Noah and that of his family: Josh and Foumi, his parents, and Karl, his brother. Noah's behavior and his psychological development have not changed greatly since the last book. He is still nonverbal, with intelligence and behavior ranging under that expected of a 3-year-old. His family, determined to care for him, is nearly pulled apart. Josh develops health problems, Foumi is tense; Karl is not doing well in school and also begins experimenting with drugs.

The family decides that it is time for Noah to go away to school. After great traumas, they find a school, which seems to suit and which will accept Noah. Soon, however, the family finds that Noah is having trouble at the school and that the trauma of keeping him there is even greater. So he comes home and is enrolled in a day program. His development and behavior really remain the same. Ultimately, in 1984, when he is just 18, the Greenfelds find a supervised group home where Noah can live, and the family's life begins to approximate something normal.

Analysis: Must reading for fans of the first two Noah books, this latest entry is also readable if one is unfamiliar with the earlier volumes. Teenagers should find it appealing, interesting, and in some cases, thought provoking.

■ Haas, Scott. *Hearing Voices: The Notes of a Psychology Intern.* Dutton, 1990. 193pp. (0-525-24899-4) Reading Level: Grades 10–12. (BL 15 S90; KR 15 J190)
Disability: Mental illness

The author relates his experiences as an intern in clinical psychology at Commonwealth Mental Health Institute/Harvard Medical School. His narrative/descriptive account is frank, graphic, and detailed. In the beginning, Haas was awkward and frightened, never having worked in a hospital environment or having dealt with really ill patients. He conducted his first intake interviews with a security guard present, lest the patients should become uncontrolled and violent. As time went by, however, he adapted rapidly; his relationship to the patients, as well as the staff, and his ability to diagnose and give therapy, went through a quick transformation. By the end of the year, he is clearly a seasoned professional. His attitude toward the patients has transformed from a "them" to an "us" approach.

Analysis: The story begins slowly, but if the reader forbears for a few short pages, it picks up and continues to move more rapidly, reflecting perhaps the author's strangeness and nervousness at the beginning of his internship and his relative comfort as it progressed. Mature high school readers should enjoy this book. They should also find it beneficial. It is important both for its reflection of the attitude that mentally ill persons are not, after all, so different from the rest of us, and for its insights into the world and the mind of a mental health professional. Highly recommended.

■ Hayden, Torey L. *Just Another Kid.* Avon, 1988. 411pp. (0-399-13303-8)
Reading Level: Grades 10–12. (LJ 15 My88; NYTBR 6 My88)
Disability: Emotional disturbance; Learning disabilities

In this latest book recounting her interactions with emotionally troubled
youngsters, teacher/author Hayden treats one school year in a self-con-
tained special education classroom for six "E.D." (emotionally disturbed)
students. Two sisters and a boy had been war traumatized and orphaned
by the troubles in Northern Ireland; two had been severely sexually and
physically abused. The last, 7-year-old Leslie, was mute, not toilet trained,
and completely controlling, day and night, of her parents' life at home. As
in other Hayden books (see *Accept Me as I Am,* 1985), the chapters
chronicle the day-by-day operation of the class, dramatizing the triumphs
and setbacks of the kids as they interact with their loving, ingenious, and
infinitely patient teacher.

The person who inspired the title of the book was Ladbrooke, the
beautiful, imperious mother of young Leslie. She was an unemployed
physicist who had become increasingly addicted to alcohol. In the fall,
Hayden engaged in several power struggles with Ladbrooke and her husband, he a famous artist. The unlikely resolution of these encounters was
that Ladbrooke became a volunteer aide in the class, adding an extra pair
of hands that Torey (as everyone called her) desperately needed. It transpired that much of Ladbrooke's self-destructive and inept behavior was
a reaction to an unrecognized learning disability that manifested as a
significant problem with verbal expression, particularly when she was
under stress. So Ladbrooke began the year as "just another kid" in
Torey's class, as needy and vulnerable as the children. Her personal struggle involved conquering her drinking problem, mothering her child more
effectively, and changing (eventually ending) an unhealthy relationship
with her husband.

A brief epilogue, written five years after, supplies a follow-up to that
eventful school year. Torey and Ladbrooke have remained friends—each
with a new husband, new babies, and a new career. An update on each of
the children reveals that most of them have continued to make progress
and have the possibility of happy future lives.

Analysis: Fans of Torey Hayden should not be disappointed by the
latest offering. Her fine sense of humor, tender descriptions, and crisp
narrative make for delightful, fast reading. She engages the reader to care
with her about her worrisome charges. She is not pedantic or self-con-
gratulatory, yet she gives a dramatic demonstration of the power of love
and understanding to change children's lives.

■ Kasha, Al, and Joel Hirschhorn. *Reaching the Morning After.* Illus.
Thomas Nelson, 1986. 192pp. (0-8407-5509-0) Reading Level: Grades
9–12. (LJ 1 My86)
Disability: Agoraphobia

In a prologue, Kasha describes his receipt of the Academy Award for Best
Song, from the film *Poseidon Adventure.* His triumph was short-lived,
however, for the next day he had an anxiety attack that presaged the
agoraphobia that would make him a prisoner in his own home.

Part One of the book is a recounting of the childhood of Alfred and his
older brother, Larry. Their brutal, alcoholic father and conniving, seduc-
tive mother had a combination barber shop and beauty parlor in Brooklyn. The family shared an impoverished apartment above the store. Their
mother pushed the boys to become famous in show business, ostensively
to rescue her from her violent husband. Alfred tended to overeat to
compensate for his father's abuse and his mother's selfish, conditional love
for her children.

Alfred Kasha had small parts in Broadway shows and in films from an
early age. He sang in temple and in school productions. Despite his
agonizing home life, he enjoyed school, fell in love, and learned about
music. Early one morning, when he was 20, his father attacked him with
a mop handle and knife, and the two had their first all-out fight. Years of
rage surfaced as he fought his father bloody, battered, and semiconscious.
He left home for good and entered the precarious music business to begin
his life's "ultimate seduction," songwriting.

Part Two chronicles Al Kasha's rise in his profession as he began
working with great writers and performers in the recording and film
industries. His success was ensured when Elvis Presley cut a record of a
song written by him and his friend and collaborator, joint author Joel
Hirschhorn. He had slipped into a brief and unhappy marriage and had
occasional anxiety attacks. His brother, Larry, became an eminent producer, and he won the Tony Award.

The Kasha boys' financial success enabled them to indulge their mother
in mink and opening nights, but she never abandoned her husband or her
old apartment. To the end of her life, she seemed to favor her elder son
and to hold him up as a role model for "L'Alfred," as she called him. She
objected to Alfred's eventual marriage to a non-Jew, even though his
beloved Ceil converted to Judaism.

Al Kasha went off to Hollywood for a bright career as an executive and
songwriter. His daughter was born, and he "had it all." Still, he fought his
lifelong insomnia and weight gains with ever-increasing doses of pills. The

crisis came when his father, on a first visit to Beverly Hills, roughly slapped his 5-year-old granddaughter for inadvertently hitting him on the leg with a mop handle. Kasha became a frazzled recluse, panicking if he left his house or even saw people. His father and mother ultimately died of cancer.

Finally Kasha sought help and joined a group for agoraphobics. He left his family briefly and, alone, had a religious experience that ushered in the beginning of his psychic healing. He has become a strong supporter of victims of child abuse and of agoraphobia. He is particularly a spokesman for males, who are in a minority among those striving to overcome phobias. The book concludes with a list of emergency centers for abused and phobic people.

Analysis: This book offers an interesting glimpse into the songwriter's phrenetic world. However, someone not acquainted with this group and their work might have welcomed more complete descriptions of the people involved, or possibly less name dropping. Kasha also skillfully re-creates a family where love and hate have inextricably meshed parents and children in a neurotic bind.

The black-and-white photos of the attractive family belie the dark dynamics operating below the surface. The author speaks in sincere and fervent tones about his conversion to Christianity. An irony seems apparent—that he was the abused son of an intensely bigoted Jewish father, for whom a son's conversion would have seemed the worst revenge.

■ Kirkland, Gelsey. *Dancing on My Grave: An Autobiography.* Illus. Doubleday, 1986. 286pp. (0-385-19964-3) Reading Level: Grades 10–12. (LATBR 12 O86; PW 29 Ag86; TB 5 O86)
Disability: Mental illness; Eating disorders

Kirkland recounts her years as one of the ballet world's leading dancers and her eventual plunge to the depths of illness and despair. She first endured several bouts of eating disorders, which gave way to severe cocaine addiction. The eventual end results of drug abuse were severe brain seizures, temporary but severe symptoms of mental illness, the near-loss of her fabulous dancing career, and, finally, the near-loss of her life.

The dance world refused to acknowledge Kirkland's addiction, always skirting the issue to protect her privacy by chastising her for inappropriate professional behavior rather than for the cause of this behavior. Mental health professionals, including those in a hospital to which she committed herself for a period of time, likewise did not deal with the addiction and its causes, but rather, tried to place other labels on her and to assess blame and guilt to Kirkland and her mother, while never dealing with the drug addiction itself. Kirkland finally pulled herself out of the depths, with the help of Greg Lawrence, himself a recovering addict, whom she eventually married.

Analysis: Gelsey Kirkland's autobiography is at times an engrossing story populated with the famous names of New York's glittering world of ballet and at other times a complex, dense, introspective examination of our contemporary culture's convoluted, distorted values, particularly about mind and body, that have led to the current excesses in alcohol, drugs, diet, and related obsessive-compulsive disorders. This book is highly recommended for mature upper-level high school students who are good readers.

■ Lee, Essie E., and Richard Wortman. *Down Is Not Out: Teenagers and Depression.* Messner, 1986. 95pp. (0-671-52613-8) Reading Level: Grades 7–9. (BL 1 Mr86; SBF Ja87; SLJ My86)
Disability: Emotional disturbance

Essie Lee is a professor of community health education and has worked with the problem of drug addiction, as well as having gained experience in counseling and education. Richard Wortman has a specialty in adolescent psychiatry. The authors discuss the definition of depression and its causes, symptoms, effects, and treatment. Profiles of young people experiencing different kinds of depression are interwoven in the text, with attention paid to what the authors call "normal moodiness," reactive depression, mild but chronic depression, and severe depression. The last chapter considers assessment and various courses of treatment. The book ends with a bibliography, a short list of suggested fiction and nonfiction, and an index.

Analysis: Lee and Wortman present their material clearly and realistically. While never minimizing the pain of depression or its dangers, their calm tone and their factual description of the types of the illness offer reassurance. Parents, teachers, and young people themselves should find helpful such sections as "What to Look For" as they try to determine whether a depression is potentially life threatening or mild and transitory as they seek appropriate treatment.

■ Marek, Elizabeth. *The Children at Santa Clara.* Viking, 1987. 177pp. (0-670-81509-8) Reading Level: Grades 7–12. (NYTBR 5 Ap87; SLJ S87; VYA 15 Ag87)
Disability: Emotional disturbance

Twenty-year-old Marek dropped out of Harvard College, where she had experienced a lack of identity or purpose in her life. The present story begins with her arrival in a poor southwestern town in order to take a volunteer job in a residential treatment center in a more remote area on the outskirts. Her charges were to be eight or so seriously disturbed preteens and teens and a few violent or disruptive day students from a neighboring foster care facility, where the young residents generally attended public school.

Each of the subsequent chapters focuses on the individual children, whose backgrounds and personalities are very different, but who are alike in having been scarred by and surviving horrendous events in their short lives: one had witnessed the murder of a parent; another, the suicide of a parent; two siblings in an otherwise well-functioning, large family were incarcerated in a small closet for seven years; another abused teen had been abandoned. Daily life in the therapeutic milieu is described through many calamities as well as humorous incidents that reveal the gradual psychological healing, at least to some extent, of the troubled and troubling youngsters.

Marek finds her place among the sensitive and patient staff. By the end of the year, she has been promoted from volunteer to fellow worker. She has grown in strength and personal insight, which enable her to return to student life. As for the children of Santa Clara (a fictionalized name), their futures are precarious but hopeful to some degree.

Analysis: This fast-moving book is written with compassion but avoids sentimentality. The author is not sensationalistic or judgmental about the devastated charges she has come to love, and she describes their fractious and unlovable behavior as well as their winsomeness with an even hand.

One piece seemed to be lacking in the account: The staff were shown to have deep insights into the youngsters' psyches, and they made prodigious efforts to accommodate the deep needs of each of their charges, even in the face of hostility and violence. The book was unclear as to how they became so wise and skilled or how Marek in turn learned so much. In fact, the nominal leader of the whole enterprise was usually missing, or less than helpful when present. However, this is small objection to an easy-to-read, entertaining, and heartwarming book.

■ North, Carol. *Welcome, Silence: My Triumph over Schizophrenia.* Simon & Schuster, 1987. 316pp. (0-671-52834-3) Reading Level: Grades 10–12. (LATBR 7 Je87; LJ 15 Je87; PW 1 My87)
Disability: Schizophrenia

At the time of the writing of this book, Carol North was a resident in psychiatry at Washington University, having graduated from that institution's medical school in 1983. She had reached this point of professional accomplishment despite an eight-year battle with schizophrenia.

North goes back to her early childhood, beginning with a fire in her home when she was 6, an event that created many fears in her. She had many other fears as a youngster and also began to hear the voices that would torment her for so long. Her parents took her to a psychologist and to the family doctor, but the chief result was that she learned to cover up for herself; it did not occur to her that other people may hear voices too, and she decided that discussing the phenomenon was taboo, like discussing bodily functions. Other symptoms followed: altered visual perceptions that she calls interference patterns, belief in parallel dimensions existing in a plane of reality distinct from the one on earth, mysterious apparitions such as a figure she believed to be that of Jesus, and the conviction that other people—her mother, for instance—could read her mind. On a number of occasions, beginning in adolescence, the voices enticed her to come to "the other side," where her confusion would end and all would become clear; several times she came close to suicide.

She went off to college, and at first all seemed well. She was glad to be away from home, she studied hard, she had a boyfriend, and the voices were so much in the background that at first she mistook them for the conversation of others. Before long, however, her fears were back, and though she gave up both pot and liquor in an effort to exorcise them, they increasingly controlled her life. Soon she was hospitalized in the university's psychiatric hospital. The subsequent months and years were a roller coaster of intensely hard work, sleep deprivation, psychotic disturbances, and medical treatments, including periods of hospitalization. She was extremely sensitive to medication, and it proved almost impossible to find drugs that would control her symptoms without causing severe side effects. Nevertheless, she graduated from college and entered medical school at the same university. In her second year, her illness became so acute that she had to drop out, an eventuality she had dreaded and fought, but she stayed in the same town, supporting herself by working part-time for her psychiatrist, Dr. Hemingway, and typing lecture notes for former classmates.

At this point, both her parents and a former boyfriend saw a television program that described a new treatment for schizophrenia developed by doctors in Kentucky who were using kidney dialysis on their patients with what they claimed to be a two-thirds rate of cure. North's doctor was aware of the work in Kentucky but had been reluctant to raise hopes before more definitive results were in; dialysis treatment is complicated and risky. North's condition continued to deteriorate, and, urged on by the voices that told her to be ready for "the Change," she was to prepare at the right moment to jump off a high building; the voices promised that this would enable her to cross to the Other Side, where she would be "enlightened" and that then she would return to her body and to the world ready to finish medical school and to "enlighten mankind."

The situation had clearly become desperate. Dr. Hemingway had applied for a grant to carry out a dialysis research project and when it was awarded, North became the first patient to try the procedure. The first two treatments were painful and unpleasant and seemed to effect only almost imperceptible changes. However, before the third treatment, she awoke one morning to a deafening silence. The voices that had mumbled and chattered and shouted since her childhood were gone, she was no longer burdened by psychotic delusions, and she seemed to see the world with a new clarity. Her doctors and of course her parents were all excited and delighted, and even one habitually skeptical doctor was convinced. However, the medical school refused to reinstate her as a student; she applied to twenty others, subsequently transferring to Washington University— apparently the only institution willing to take a chance. On her psychiatric rotation, she treated schizophrenic patients, and when one asked her if she heard voices too and remarked that North seemed able to understand and help her more than any other doctor she had had, North decided to become a psychiatrist.

Her doctor was not able to achieve the same success with dialysis of four other patients, and a conversation between Dr. Hemingway and a colleague raises the possibility that North was not truly schizophrenic; they agree that she was not typical. North writes, "To date, no careful studies have been published that report dialysis to be conclusively effective as a treatment for schizophrenia, at least so far as I know. Only further research will determine why dialysis works for some schizophrenics and not others."

Analysis: North has described her tortured experience in painful, descriptive detail. In the preface she explains that she has used her diary and called on the "recollections and perspectives of events" of others who knew her; she also was given access to her medical records. She explains further that she has reconstructed dialogue to present as close as possible what people said, and, though the resulting conversations often have a rather stilted formality, they do work convincingly. At times, the piling up of recurring psychotic experiences may begin to seem tedious, but the reader is impelled forward by the promise that this is the story of a person who has been cured and a curiosity to know how this came about. Despite her years of suffering, North is free of self-pity. Even before her cure, she accomplished a great deal under often difficult circumstances, but she does not indulge in self-congratulation. Nor does she appear to harbor anger; the treatments she had to undergo were sometimes nearly as harrowing as her illness, and she describes the treatments and her physical and emotional reactions to them at the time, but it is the power of those descriptions rather than any subsequent resentments that moves the reader.

Welcome, Silence is an absorbing account. Since schizophrenia is a disorder that typically appears in late adolescence and early adulthood, this book might have particular appeal to high school students as well as to parents and teachers who have a personal and professional interest in an often disabling and tragic disease.

■ O'Neill, Cherry Boone. *Dear Cherry: Questions and Answers on Eating Disorders.* Continuum, 1985. 138pp. (0-8264-0357-3) Reading Level: Grades 7–12. (BL 15 My85; KR 1 Je85; LJ 1 S85)
Disability: Emotional disturbance; Eating disorders

Dear Cherry is a follow-up to Cherry Boone O'Neill's 1982 best-seller, *Starving for Attention.* After the publication of that book, in which O'Neill recounts her struggle with bulimia and anorexia, she received thousands of letters, all of which she answered personally in her own handwriting. *Dear Cherry* is a compilation of some of these letters and her responses to them. Introductory chapters summarize O'Neill's experiences with eating disorders and give a helpful, accurate summary of their underlying causes as well as an explanation of appropriate therapies. A seven-page bibliography of articles, largely medical and scholarly in nature, concludes the book.

Analysis: The letters themselves and the responses are reproduced verbatim. They make for fast-paced, sometimes gripping reading. Factual and obviously real, they often deal with matters of life and death. The copy of the book used to write this review was borrowed from a large university library collection. It had circulated heavily and was liberally penciled, testifying to its importance to the young, college-aged population that forms the clientele of the library. It is quite readable and could easily be handled by readers as young as those in fifth grade and as old as those in high school and beyond.

■ Packard, Russell. *The Psych Wards: From Behind a Psychiatrist's Door.* Paul S. Eriksson, 1984. 236pp. (0-8397-6904-0) Reading Level: Grades 10–12. (BL 1 F85; PW 9 N84)
Disability: Emotional disturbance

The author kept a diary of his first 18 months of training in psychiatry at a military hospital. His book is in the form of diary entries.

The first half of the book refers to the young doctor's experiences first on a locked, then on an open ward of the hospital, where most of the patients are very young men from the various armed services. Packard is at the same time trying to learn psychiatry in the medical bureaucracy of a military system and to actualize himself as a young husband and father.

The second half of the book opens with the arrival of newly released POWs from Vietnam. Packard's struggles intensify in both his work and his marriage. He eventually decides to "come back to medicine" by changing his focus to neurology, although he views his year of psychiatry as personally and professional enriching.

In a single-page addendum, "seven years later," the subsequent careers of Packard and his close staff associates are listed. Readers learn that the author divorced, remarried, and went into private practice as director of a neurology and headache management clinic.

Analysis: The diary entries are spontaneous, off the top of the head, often humorous musings of a very young person enduring the physically and intellectually intense and trying regimen of the first year of medical internship. These make fast and interesting reading. By the end of the adventure, Packard has realized his manhood and is ready to embark enthusiastically on his professional career. The book can be viewed as a vivid day-by-day struggle of a young person's making the transition from adolescence to adulthood in the special environment of a mental hospital. That environment gives a unique view into the problems of the young patients (and their dependents) who cannot adjust to military life.

■ Piersall, Jim, and Al Hirshberg. *Fear Strikes Out: The Jim Piersall Story.* Little, Brown, 1955. 217pp. Reading Level: Grades 7–12. (BL 1 Je55; HB D55; KR 15 Ap55; LJ 15 Ap55)
Disability: Emotional disturbance

Jim Piersall, who was born in 1929, grew up in Waterbury, Connecticut, in the difficult depression years. His mother, a gentle woman, had a number of breakdowns during his childhood and often had to spend months in a state institution. Piersall's father was a house painter, who had large ambitions for his son and groomed him to be a major-league ball player from the time he was a little boy. Piersall loved sports and especially baseball; by the time he was 17, he was a rookie with the Boston Red Sox as a center fielder. During the off season, he got jobs to support himself and soon, his parents and a wife.

Piersall had always been tense, prone to worries and headaches. Despite marriage to a young woman whom he loved, the birth of a daughter, and success as a ball player, his tensions and anxieties increased. He often slept badly and was short tempered and argumentative with his colleagues. Finally, in 1952, he ended up in the Westborough State Hospital in Massachusetts, after seven months of crazy antics on the field, fist fights, and other aberrant behavior. Shock treatment erased most of his memories of this period; when he came to himself in the hospital it was August, but the last event he remembered at first had been walking into a hotel lobby in Florida the previous January. His doctor and family had to tell him what had happened, for he could hardly even recall the birth of his second daughter that spring. As he recovered, he read the newspaper clippings his wife had saved for him, with sports articles that described his increasingly erratic behavior. Helped by a wise psychiatrist and a loving, supportive wife, Piersall recovered. In the final pages of the book, he describes his association with a support group called Fight Against Fears, his satisfying off-season job as goodwill ambassador for a company, and his baseball comeback.

Analysis: With the wisdom of hindsight, Piersall can look back at his life and see the early indications of the illness that was eventually to bring him to a halt. He has come to the point where he can recognize and talk frankly about his symptoms and breakdown, and he and his coauthor have written a convincing account of his thoughts and experiences. Though of course Piersall has not been a familiar name in the sports world for many years, young readers with an interest in baseball might be particularly attracted to this book.

■ Pike, Bonnie. ***Three Brass Monkeys.*** Susan Hunter, 1988. 81pp. (0-932419-11-0) Reading Level: Grades 10–12.
Disability: Psychosis

This play was a semifinalist in the National Play Awards of 1984 and has been sponsored by organizations involved in mental health and prevention of child abuse and family violence. It is based on therapy sessions conducted by James F. Smith with a troubled woman who gained insight into the various parts of her psyche and her past, thereby achieving her regeneration.

In a foreword, the therapist gives some facts about his patient. When she was 4 years old, in 1939, she was brutally raped. She then watched while her father beat the rapist to death. "A conspiracy of silence and deception by her Southern aristocratic mother and Irish immigrant father strengthened the girl's repression of the experience, and she retreated into psychosis." For 40 years, she had various hospitalizations and shock treatments to no avail. Finally, she went through seven years of cathartic psychotherapy, which the play encapsulates.

The two acts are projections of the mind of Kathleen Kelly (50/Katy), who is 50 years old and returning to her apartment in Atlanta after burying her mother. She is bent on suicide until the climax of the play, when she is able to acknowledge her repressed selves and repressed memories. 13/Katy is the young girl who was orphaned when her beloved father went to jail for his crime and whose mother became incompetent to care for her. 30/Katy, a no-nonsense nursing supervisor, rejected all advances of love, so as not to admit to the early physical brutalization that led to her fear of closeness. Other people also intrude on her memory, including her father, mother, and uncle.

Part of the property list for the play is the statuette of the three brass monkeys who hear no evil, see no evil, speak no evil. At the end of the play, the three monkeys "finally at peace among themselves, form a portrait of unity and integration" (p. 79).

Analysis: Whereas a play is best seen rather than read, this "read" is powerful and disturbing. The crushing consequences of sexual abuse, violence, abandonment, dehumanization, deceit, and prejudice are examined in a compelling, sometimes humorous manner. Fortunately, the play offers catharsis, as well as the underlying message that truth can heal.

■ Purl, Sandy, and Gregg Lewis. *Am I Alive?: A Surviving Flight Attendant's Struggle and Inspiring Triumph over Tragedy.* Illus. Harper & Row, 1986. 185pp. (0-06-250691-9) Reading Level: Grades 10–12. (LJ 1 Ap86; PW 21 F86; SLJ S86)
Disability: Posttraumatic stress syndrome

Sandy Purl, a flight attendant, survived a plane crash in New Hope, Georgia, that killed many passengers and crew members. After she had recovered physically, she spent four years trying to recover emotionally. Plagued by posttraumatic stress syndrome, she had reactions very similar to those suffered by Vietnam veterans. The nightmares and hallucinations that she experienced, together with her inability to function in everyday life, broke up her marriage and threatened not only her career but also her very ability to survive.

After a disastrous but brief relationship with another man, who made no effort to empathize with her or even attempt to understand what she was experiencing, and an equally disastrous professional relationship with a therapist who terminated her therapy because he had fallen in love with her and ultimately had a breakdown himself, she found a number of people who were helpful to her, including an excellent therapist. She eventually recovered enough to return to work.

Sandy now views life differently from before her experience, when she would have described herself as a self-centered, relatively superficial person. Nowadays she gives time and effort to helping flight attendants who have undergone experiences similar to hers. She works with various groups such as the flight attendant unions to improve the treatment of individuals like herself who have survived plane crashes, and she makes personal contact with survivors. She also volunteers her off-duty time and her free flight privileges to help organizations that work with children in Latin America. She provided services such as delivering items to their orphanages as well as transporting some of their adoptees to new homes in the United States. She has also remarried.

Sandy gives much credit for her recovery to various people whom she met along the way and to a newfound religious belief. She has managed to forgive the airline for which she worked at the time (now a part of Republic Airlines) and the various individuals therein who treated her very callously. In addition, she has forgiven various others, who either abandoned her or were indifferent to her during the course of her emotional problems.

Analysis: As a good story about the true experiences of a young woman, this book should provide high-interest reading for high school students and possibly for more mature junior high school students who are avid readers.

■ Rapoport, Judith L. *The Boy Who Couldn't Stop Washing: The Experience and Treatment of Obsessive-Compulsive Disorder.* Dutton, 1989. 260pp. (0-525-24708-4) Reading Level: Grades 9–12. (NYTBR 26 F89; PsyT D88; PW 18 N88)
Disability: Obsessive-compulsive disorder (OCD)

In the introduction, the author, a psychiatrist, describes her intention to research what she initially assumed to be rare mental disorders, namely obsessions and compulsions; the latter refer to ritualistic and excessive repetition of behaviors by otherwise reasonable children and adults; the former refer to intrusive, "crazy" thoughts that interfere with the well-being of otherwise normal people. She discovered that the number of sufferers from these problems is indeed high. Inasmuch as pharmacological and behavioral therapies have benefited many of them, Rapoport has been motivated to reach with a readable, nontechnical book the millions estimated to have obsessive-compulsive disorder.

Early on, Rapoport's research was given publicity on several television shows. Many people called in to say they had similar problems that seemed so shameful, they were apt to hide their awful secret from their relatives, spouses, and closest friends. Much of the book comprises the stories of over 20 children and adults who came for therapy with the author, and in one case with a colleague. The most common problem was that of ritual washing—a process that could take hours and cause pain.

One woman had literally pulled out all of her hair since the time she was a teenager. Some people were plagued with unaccounted-for guilt, or doubts, or recurrent tunes in the head. Against all reason, these patients felt they simply had to think or do certain things, and they were most relieved when they could be helped to be rid of these obsessions and compulsions.

Rapoport ends her book with some speculations and philosophizing. She postulates a neurological defect in the brain that releases an atavistic pattern of stored knowledge similar to the instinctive survival mechanisms of animals. These include cleansing, grooming, nesting, and ritual display. She ponders the problem of the meaning of free will and of knowing; these seem to be awry in her subjects.

An Obsessions and Compulsions Checklist and other helpful information follow.

Analysis: Rapoport has undoubtedly accomplished her purpose of bringing obsessive-compulsive disorders "out of the closet" with this national best-seller. It may become the "fashionable" disorder of the 1990s, although this was obviously not her intent. Any reader will probably look at his or her own idiosyncratic quirks and rituals with new thoughtfulness, and some may find real help and understanding for a serious problem.

The book makes interesting reading. The bizarre case studies are fascinating in the same way that psychological thrillers and "freak shows" tend to be.

■ Schiff, Jacqui Lee. *All My Children.* Pyramid, 1972. 240pp. (o.p.) Reading Level: Grades 10–12. (BL 1 Je71; KR 1 N70; LJ 1 Ja71; PW 2 N70)
Disability: Emotional disturbance

Jacqui and Moe Schiff were mental health workers—she a social worker, he a counselor. They were raising Jacqui's three children from her first marriage. The pair had met in the San Francisco area at a graduate seminar on transactional analysis, a therapy to which Jacqui was dedicated and which Moe incorporated into his practice as well. When they finished their education, the couple and the children moved to the Charlottesville, Virginia, area.

One day Jacqui agreed to see Dennis, a violent, nineteen-year-old who was a well-known fringe character on the campus of the University of Virginia. He had been mentally ill for some time, and his friend, who was acquainted with Jacqui, felt that at this point, Dennis was an emergency case. He arrived, "his long thin face . . . twisted into hard angry lines. His mouth hung loose and dripped saliva. His long, matted dirty hair and beard were caked with dandruff." Jacqui soon concluded that he was "paranoid, delusional, homicidal—and dangerous" (pp. 29–30).

Even through his ramblings, his frustration at not being able to find help was clear, and Jacqui agreed to place him in a therapy group that she was conducting. At one session, his reactions to the recollection of a beating by his father were so strong that she set up a private session for him later that week to pursue the situation further. During this session, Dennis went into a violent psychotic episode, which Jacqui, with Moe's help, allowed, even encouraged, to continue, not the usual path of treatment. It culminated with Dennis's curling up in a fetal position, crawling onto her lap, trying to nurse, and falling peacefully asleep.

Dennis, later renamed Aaron, became Jacqui's and Moe's "son," and, following the tenets of transactional analysis, they began a reparenting program with him, a technique that Jacqui had seriously considered for many years but had never attempted before. The two, aided by their three sons, who apparently adapted well in this unusual environment, proceeded to take in other seriously ill youngsters and attempted to reparent them. Eventually, this sideline evolved into a full-time residential treatment center. They have had outstanding to moderate to poor results, depending upon the child with whom they worked. Nearly all of these children, however, had been considered untreatable by usual methods.

Analysis: Schiff, aided by writer Beth Day, tells a good story. It is exciting and dramatic and often reads more like good fiction than nonfiction. Teenagers will find it interesting reading, even though the story is set in the early 1970s.

Another aspect that lends interest to this book is that transactional analysis and the reparenting technique are alive and well today, although they have never come into mainstream use by most "establishment" psychotherapists.

■ Spungen, Deborah. *And I Don't Want to Live This Life.* Illus. Villard, 1983. 404pp. (0-449-20543-6) Reading Level: Grades 10–12. (BL 15 S80; LJ 15 S83; PW 29 J183)
Disability: Drug addiction

The author wrote this book sometime after her elder daughter, Nancy, was stabbed to death by her lover—punk rock star Sid Vicious. She dedicates the book to her husband, two surviving children, and Nancy. The focus of the book is on the 20 years of Nancy's life.

Nancy was an unexpected first baby, who ended her young mother's plans for higher education and a career. She arrived early, with a prolapsed umbilical cord. She suffered from AB incompatibility and severe bilirubin instability, both of which necessitated painful medical procedures. Upon getting home from the hospital, she was healthy but evinced a pattern of extreme physical activity. She was unable to stay sleeping, even for a few hours, without medication. She was an early talker who was inclined to tantrum if she did not get her own way. Very early, her parents decided she was uncontrollable, and they gave up setting any limits on her behavior. When she was almost 4, her distraught parents had her first evaluation done at a child guidance clinic. She was diagnosed as very bright and essentially normal, apart from a slight visual-motor delay.

In school, Nancy was a superb student, but she showed signs of what would become a lifelong problem in making friends. As if in recompense, she often cruelly manipulated her younger sister and brother. By the time she was 7, she always won power struggles with her parents, who were convinced that something was physically wrong with her. Meanwhile, her mother felt trapped in her domestic life, and her father spent more and more time away from home. In retrospect, Spungen attributed much of the family's unhappiness to Nancy. She blamed her daughter for a yearlong affair she had when she was 27, although she rationalized at the time that she was retaliating for her husband's presumed infidelity.

Nancy became enthralled with rock music at the age of 9, and she soon became an underage "hippie" and political activist, protesting the Vietnam war. When her behavior became more erratic and asocial, she was again evaluated by a psychiatric clinic that advised therapy for her and her parents. Despite the therapy, Nancy's acting-out behavior worsened and became violent. After Nancy's death, Spungen learned that the new evaluation included "almost adult-like paranoid schizophrenic ideation" (p. 102), validating her mother's opinion that she was not a normal child. She left school and displayed an increasing amount of violent, hallucinatory, and even suicidal behavior. She was committed to several institutions and even did well in one of them until the directors were transferred. She always returned home, now on drugs. She had a pattern of losing jobs, playing rock music, and disrupting her family's equilibrium. Spungen felt that Nancy had too much influence on her siblings. They, too, took drugs, began to party, and at one point wrecked the family car.

When she was seventeen, Nancy's parents financed an apartment for her in New York in order to get rid of her. There she became a go-go dancer in Times Square and became addicted to heroin. She went on to London, where she linked up with a punk rock group and began her ill-starred relationship with Sid Vicious. The couple came back to the states for some performances and were somewhat reluctantly allowed in the Spungen home. Shortly thereafter, at age 20, Nancy was stabbed to death. Spungen later received a letter from Sid Vicious that proclaimed his complete devotion to Nancy. She wondered if her daughter had put him up to the crime, since she had long ago decided to die young. Sid Vicious died of an overdose while out on parole.

For a long while, the Spungen family was devastated by these events. Deborah made her peace in part by organizing a group for parents of murdered children, thus turning her sorrow and her love for her daughter into a constructive force. Even in death, Nancy's personality seemed to dominate the family.

Analysis: This is a sad but compelling story of a mismatch between parents and child. Difficult and impetuous Nancy apparently needed firm limits and unconditional love. Her well-meaning parents alternated between overindulgence and extreme anger and blame. The professionals involved seemed to have confounded the escalating problems.

The writing is quick paced and vivid. Black-and-white photographs enhance the descriptions of this fascinating but tragic girl and her family. It is a tribute to Spungen's honesty that she includes details that do not always support her conclusions about her daughter's motivations. A rebellious youngster might well identify with Nancy's plight and also achieve some understanding of the pain of her parents, who tried so hard but failed.

■ Stein, Patricia M., and Barbara C. Unell. *Anorexia Nervosa: Finding the Life Line.* CompCare, 1986. 95pp. (0-89638-084-X) Reading Level: Grades 7–12. (CH N87; RSR Su87)
Disability: Anorexia

The authors of this brief but excellent book about anorexia nervosa begin by interviewing seven persons—six women and one man—who are recovering from anorexia nervosa. The accounts of their lives and illnesses vary. Always, in their childhood, either they or a family member had undue concern about eating or about weight and appearance, and always, low self-esteem enters their description of themselves. Beside these similarities, their accounts are varied.

The biographical section covers 42 pages; then the rest of the book discusses what anorexia is and what can be done about it. A list of organizations, a bibliography, and suggestions for additional reading are included at the end of the narrative. Two of the chapters are written by physicians. One of the authors, Stein, is a dietician/counselor who works with patients who have eating disorders.

Analysis: This is an excellent book for teens who are interested in eating disorders or who have eating disorders. Authoritative and straightforward, it is also understandable, brief enough to capture the attention of most readers, and helpful even if only portions are read. Highly recommended.

■ Wallace, Marjorie. *The Silent Twins.* Illus. Ballantine, 1987. 320pp. (paper 0-345-34802-8) Reading Level: Grades 10–12. (KR 1 S86; LRB 8 My86; TLS 28 S86)
Disability: Elective mutism

Haverfordwest is a remote town in West Wales, where the Royal Air Force had a base. Here, Aubrey Gibbons and his wife had come from Barbados, in the West Indies. Gibbons, a controller, supported five children, including identical twin daughters, June and Jennifer. The book traces the unusual development of these girls up to their early 20s, when they became known to the author, who relies on interviews with the parents and with professionals and on extensive writing by the twins to construct the story of their life. Numerous black-and-white photographs appear throughout.

The twins had had an uneventful early life, except that, at 3 years old, they only spoke in two- or three-word sentences. They went to school at the usual time but were moved from base to base, where they were virtually the only black children, and very reclusive. In some schools they were shunned for their race and their behavior. They read fluently by the age of 8, but they still did not speak at home or at school, except to their younger sister.

When they were 11, some educational experts in Wales began to concern themselves about these strange girls who spoke a high-speed "patois" with each other, and played endless, elaborate fantasy games with their dolls, hibernating in their upstairs room. Various attempts to help them with speech therapy, special education, and physical separation were all for naught. When they became school leavers, they were put on the dole, which they left their room to collect once a week. They communicated their wants to the family through scrawled notes.

In their private world, the twins' doll play turned to story writing; they wrote adventures in an imagined American setting, replete with violence and intrigue and in stark contrast to the drab and lonely surroundings of their actual existence. They spent their welfare money on writing courses and classic books. Some of their works were eventually accepted for publication, and they are quoted in the book, along with many sections of their detailed, personal diaries.

For a while, the twins bound their developing breasts in an effort not to grow up. Finally their strong sexuality demanded expression, and they began to make rather inappropriate overtures to various boys in the community. At the same time they began some minor shoplifting.

Finally, the twins turned to a five-week orgy of vandalism and arson. They seemed to court their eventual detection and remand to prison. After lengthy delays, they were tried and committed indefinitely to Broadmoor Hospital, labeled as dangerous psychopaths. In the hospital, the staff tried and gave up on most therapy. By the end of the book, the twins were separated for the most part and sedated as well. They had given up drawing, creative writing, and serious reading. They continued to express their hopelessness in their diaries. The girls had only each other, and they lived in a bind of love and hate, envy and jealousy. "Like twin stars, they are caught in the gravitational field between them, doomed to spin round each other for ever. If they come too close, or drift apart, both are destroyed" (p. 7).

The author likens the twins to the Brontë sisters, who also created a literary world so different from their cold and isolated home life. Unfortunately for the Gibbons, at every step, events seem to have conspired to make a waste of the lives of these brilliant, passionate girls.

Analysis: This is a compelling, yet depressing book. It thoroughly explores the strange characteristics of the silent, identical twins, who almost seemed to act as one troubled person. However, little explanation other than metaphorical description is offered for the depth of their mutual pathology. This book has probably gratified the twins' fervent wish to be outstanding; Their strange story will surely become a classic in the annals of twin study.

■ Wigoder, David. *Images of Destruction.* Routledge and Kegan Paul, 1987. 272pp. (0-7102-1085-X) Reading Level: Grades 10–12. (BL 15 S87; NYTBR 1 IN87; PW 28 Ag87.)
Disability: Manic-depression

David Wigoder, a successful, highly intelligent British accountant and computer consultant, has written an autobiographical account of his years of struggle with a disorder that, after many years, was diagnosed as manic-depression. His youth was spent largely with a mother who also had this disorder, although for years he never made the connection between his mother's problems and his own.

Analysis: Wigoder relates his various breakdowns and treatments in realistic and sometimes harrowing detail. Even the summary of his life is traumatic: "By the time I was forty I had destroyed two successful careers, served a prison sentence [for the attempted murder of his wife], been made legally bankrupt, lost a treasured professional qualification, attempted to kill two people, and isolated myself from most of my family and friends" (p. 12). By the end of the book, having finally been properly diagnosed and treated, Wigoder is in a recovering state and well able to write this perceptive, high-interest volume, which is highly recommended for mature teen-aged readers.

LEARNING DISABILITIES

■ Coman, Carolyn. *Body and Soul: Ten American Women.* Illus. Hill, 1988. 134pp. (Paper 0-940595-16-8) Reading Level: Grades 10–12. (BL 1 Ap88; PW 11 Mr88; SLJ S88)
Disability: Dyslexia

Author Carolyn Coman set out to write a book about ten women in nontraditional jobs but ended up, instead, writing about ten women, each one unique in her own right, whose lives make strong statements of individuality, purpose, freedom, and creativity. One of these ten women is Doreen Lopes, a neglected child raped twice before the age of 14, the single mother of three children, who defines her greatest problem in life as her inability to read.

When Doreen's daughter showed signs of reading problems, she and a friend mustered the courage to confront the school's principal and ask that the child be tested for dyslexia. Eventually Doreen herself was diagnosed as dyslexic, and she began the long road to overcoming this problem, which ultimately led her not only to learn to read but also to enroll in college.

Analysis: Like the women in the other chapters, Doreen tells her story in her own words, accompanied by vibrant, vivid photographs taken by noted photographer Judy Dater. Doreen is an excellent role model for young women of all socioeconomic classes, whether or nor they are physically, mentally, or emotionally challenged. Highly recommended for teenage readers.

■ Dwyer, Kathleen M. *What Do You Mean I Have a Learning Disability?* Illus. by Barbara Beirne. Walker, 1991. 38pp. (0-8027-8102-0) Reading Level: Grades K–3.
Disability: Learning disabilities

This is a photographic essay told by 10-year-old Jimmy, who thinks he is stupid. He is forgetful and awkward, and worst of all, he has such problems with reading, writing, math, and even speaking, that everyone, including Jimmy, assumes that he is not very bright. Jimmy eventually is tested, found to have learning disabilities, and given special training that ultimately results in great improvement in his schoolwork and his self-esteem.

Jimmy's story is a true one, told in a child's words and heavily illustrated with photographs of Jimmy at key stages and with examples of his written work. The author operates a private clinic for children and adults with learning disabilities.

Analysis: Highly recommended for children in the middle elementary grades for its straightforward explanation of what learning disabilities are and what can be done about them.

The author indicates a readership range of grades K to 4; however, the title is classified above as suitable for grades K–3 in order to fit into the grade ranges established for this bibliography.

■ Fleming, Elizabeth. *Believe the Heart.* Strawberry Hill, 1984. 180pp. (0-89407-061-4) Reading Level: Grades 6–12. (LJ 1 My84)
Disability: Dyslexia

This story is written by a mother about her own life and that of her five children, now young adults, all of whom have been diagnosed as having hereditary dyslexia.

Fleming discusses her own undiagnosed problems in school, where she was usually considered a dummy because she had so much difficulty learning to read and spell. At the end of World War II, she had graduated from high school but felt she had few prospects for her future. She married a young man who had been in the Navy, and together they struggled to establish themselves and the babies that began to arrive.

Fleming's most difficult challenge came after the family of six had lived happily in a Pennsylvania community for some time. At the time of her fifth pregnancy, her husband left her, and she became determined to assume the responsibility for her children. Still struggling with her dyslexia, she took college courses, received counseling, and achieved self-understanding, which helped her to guide and encourage her children as well.

In the second half of the book, each offspring tells his or her own story, with particular reference to learning problems in school. At the book's end, a daughter is a speech pathologist, a son is director of the Law Library of the U.S. Department of Commerce, another daughter is a graduate in architectural drafting, and two sons are still in college.

In the final chapter, "Positive Advice," Fleming philosophizes on the difficulties and solutions of the problems of dyslexia. An appendix lists 21 pages of resources reprinted from an Academic Therapy publication. A general bibliography follows.

Analysis: The book is to be recommended because it is an engaging, although very subjective account by people who have been diagnosed as dyslexic. The basic intelligence and enthusiasm of each person is evident, and it might be hard for a reader who is not learning disabled to believe that such tasks like spelling, so automatic to most, can be so onerous to persons who eventually achieved a measure of academic sucess. The feeling of being misunderstood, of being different from the "average" person, is clearly expressed.

The author states that the book is written to "keep the simple sentence structure of the dyslexic to help the reader enter into the world of dyslexia" (Introduction). The sentence structure does not seem remarkable. However, there are a number of spelling errors, and one son repeatedly misspells the name of the college which he attends. This is never commented on or explained.

Author Fleming has resolved her problems with her own learning difficulties by formulating certain concepts, which, again, are acutely subjective. She refers to the "dyslexic . . . as a new breed." She also draws scientific conclusions from newspaper journalism to back some of her concepts. However, while some of her ideas must be taken with a grain of salt, her perceptions and struggles are well described and instructive.

■ Hampshire, Susan. *Every Letter Counts.* Illus. Bantam, 1990. 388pp. (0-593-01886-9) Reading Level: Grades 7–12. (Books F90)
Disability: Dyslexia

Susan Hampshire is a well-known British actress, whose book *Susan's Story: An Autobiographical Account of My Struggle with Dyslexia* (see *Accept Me as I Am,* 1985) chronicled her life as a learning-disabled person. The new book was written to show the positive side of being dyslexic and to give to those who are not dyslexic a clear understanding of what the disability entails. Eighty percent of the royalties from sales are earmarked for two charities concerned with the problem in England.

The main body of the book consists of taped interviews conducted by the author. While some were conducted at the Dyslexic Institute for adults, Hampshire has literally gone around the world for others. Some names have been changed to protect anonymity. However, a number of "celebrity" dyslexics have allowed their name to be used in order to inspire fellow sufferers. An introductory paragraph before each testimonial explains what the subject has done in life and how Hampshire came to meet the person. The book print is deliberately large and well spaced, with numerous block headings for reading ease. Jokes, cartoons, and quotations are interspersed in the text.

In the first part, Hampshire reviews her own childhood. Sandwiched in birth order between two bright sisters, she knew she was different by age 3. Because of her obvious problems with reading and writing, her parents took her to many specialists, but she was not diagnosed as dyslexic until she was 16. At that time, she suffered a nervous breakdown and tried to commit suicide. After leaving school and spending five months in a mental institution, she decided to take her life into her own hands. She entered the beauty world and became manager of a shop at 19. She went on into acting on the stage, in motion pictures, and in television.

The subjects for the 60 or so interviews came from many walks of life: from taxi driver, soldier, and electrician to researcher, dentist, and member of Parliament. Common themes are repeated over and over: Respondents as children believed themselves stupid, and they experienced humiliation in school, frequently abetted by ignorant or cruel teachers. Most felt relief when they were finally diagnosed as having a specific learning problem that others shared as well. All found joy in discovering something they could do well to earn themselves a livelihood. Many attested that their problems had made them fighters and survivors, thereby contributing to their considerable success in life.

At the end of the book, there are three appendixes: one is addressed to parents, another illustrates dyslexic spelling, and a third lists various references.

Analysis: The number and variety of people located by Hampshire with the common denominator of dyslexia is surprising. These range from children of kings and presidents to a few blue-collar workers. Most of the interviewees went through the English educational systems, whose intricacies may be lost on the American reader. The warm and upbeat feeling to the book comes in part from the fact that most of the accounts are transcripts of personal interviews that the author conducted with many interesting people. The essays do begin to have a certain sameness about them—a strength, in that the important points become very clear, but somewhat at the expense of freshness.

These stories should, as Hampshire hopes, inspire and teach others with similar difficulties, fears, and potentials. The oft repeated accounts concerning teachers' use of humiliating and cruel methods with atypical students might provide a lesson for educators. There are some testimonies as well about understanding teachers who contributed greatly to the happiness and eventual success of their struggling pupils.

This book continues a practice also prevalent in the United States, which takes great pains to distinguish learning-disabled people from "stupid and thick" people. That kind of elitist putdown of those who are not so "bright and intelligent" is unfortunate and really unnecessary. In this book, the subjects' high intelligence is stressed over and over; indeed, some are eminent in science, mathematics, the arts, and so on. This is a very select subgroup who are not necessarily representative of the larger group of more ordinary people with learning problems.

■ Levinson, Harold N. *Smart But Feeling Dumb.* Warner, 1984. 236pp. (0-446-51307-5) Reading Level: Grades 10–12. (BL 1 D84)
Disability: Dyslexia

Dr. Levinson is clinical associate professor of psychiatry at New York University Medical Center. Through his experience with his patients, with research, and with his own daughters, he has come to believe that dyslexia is caused by inner-ear dysfunction and that the dysfunction itself may be the result of a variety of causes, including genetic inheritance and disease. An earlier book, *A Solution to the Riddle Dyslexia,* was a scientific text; *Smart But Feeling Dumb* is written for the general reader. Drawing on many case studies and on written material from his patients and from parents, Levinson lays out and supports his thesis. In 14 chapters, he discusses such topics as treatment of the disorder by medication, education, and psychotherapy, the relationship between phobias and dyslexia, and variations of dyslexia. The book concludes with several appendixes, a bibliography, and an index.

Analysis: Levinson's argument is persuasive. He is absolutely certain that he has found both the cause and the successful treatment of dyslexia, and the testimony of his patients supports his claim. Some patients who sought his advice had previously been misdiagnosed by eminent physicians, and, while he does not name names, he does not hesitate to point out their errors. He cautions readers repeatedly against self-medication, emphasizing the importance of carefully monitored treatment. The case studies he presents demonstrate remarkable improvement in skills and self-image; as his title makes clear, dyslexic people must fight not only against their disability with its resultant frustrations and the feeling of living in a world askew but must deal also with those who see them as lazy and dumb.

While not everyone may agree with Dr. Levinson's thesis, it bears careful consideration. His book can be recommended to young adults with learning disabilities as well as to their parents and teachers; in addition, young people who contemplate a career in education would find it valuable.

■ MacCracken, Mary. *Turnabout Children: Overcoming Dyslexia and Other Learning Disabilities.* Little, Brown, 1986. 258pp. (0-316-55540-1) Reading Level: Grades 7–12. (BL 1 D86; Inst Ag88; RT N87)
Disability: Dyslexia

Since writing her last three books (see *Accept Me as I Am,* 1985), the author returned to college to become certified as a teacher of learning-disabled children. After that accomplishment, she decided to set up a private practice, first in an office complex, to see children for individual tutoring. Later she moved the practice to an addition to her home.

Most of the chapters of the book are written about four boys and one girl who have come to her for help. Each has unique and formidable learning problems that have prevented progress at school and have disrupted their family life. Their frustrations and bad feelings about themselves, as well as their specific learning inadequacies, are detailed, yet these children are revealed to be basically intelligent, charming, and courageous.

MacCracken's philosophy includes strong parental involvement. Some of the parents have suffered their own inner turmoil, including in one case a secret and severe dyslexia. Such parents had been rejected themselves as children. MacCracken also likes to work closely with her pupils' classroom teachers, and she describes team efforts with regular and special education teachers who are her allies in "turning about" her young students.

A brief appendix lists and annotates a series of tests the author uses for evaluation of learning disabilities.

Analysis: MacCracken uses liberally the professional terminology current in the field of learning disabilities, but she is sparing of technical details that might bore the general reader. She describes her teaching strategies simply and fully enough to bring a tutoring session alive. She is always aware of the whole child, and, as described in her previous books, she attends masterfully to the often overwhelming emotional needs of her young charges. The vignettes are presented in a straightforward but compelling style that has the reader pulling with the author for the children's hard-won but impressive successes.

A common theme in the book is the newly achieved insight on the part of teachers, parents, and the children themselves with regard to learning needs and difficulties. It should be noted that all but one of the "turn-about" children were affluent and from intact families. They had considerable intellectual potential, and theirs were success stories. The one poor child was spirited out of town early in the tutoring process, because his mother was escaping a highly abusive husband. Some readers might find some of these cases overoptimistic. However, MacCracken's acceptance of differences and her appreciation of each child's unique gifts are compelling and inspiring.

■ Smith, Bert Kruger. *Dilemma of a Dyslexic Man.* Hogg Foundation for Mental Health, 1973; 1968. 23pp. Reading Level: Grades 9–12. (PGJ N69)
Disability: Dyslexia

This short pamphlet was originally printed for the Twentieth Annual Conference of the Southwest Foundation. It briefly summarizes the life of an extraordinary 30-year-old man, Dwayne, who is a painter, a song lyricist, a guitar player, and a good conversationalist on learned subjects. He can neither read nor write because he has dyslexia. For most of his life he was branded as either stupid or lazy, and he himself thought that he was either damaged or stupid. He has absorbed the large amounts of knowledge that he possesses by listening to educational television, to tapes, and to individuals. The last four pages consist of a most literate response that Dwayne dictated for the pamphlet as he worked on a piece of clay sculpture. At that point he had taken some community college courses as a noncredit student and was about to enroll formally in a full-time college program.

Analysis: This brief, poignant tale would be especially helpful and inspirational to teenagers with similar language disabilities. Dwayne has an extreme form of dyslexia that had not responded to the treatments available at the time the book was written and later reprinted. A weakness, however, is that the information is rather old at this point, having been written in 1968 and revised in 1973, but the fundamental message of struggle with disability at least remains the same.

■ Smith, J. David. *Minds Made Feeble: The Myth and Legacy of the Kallikaks.* Illus. Aspen Systems Corp., 1985. 205pp. (0-87189-093-3) Reading Level: Grades 10–12. (CH 23 N85; KR 1 Mr85; LJ 15 My85)
Disability: Learning disabilities

In 1912, a respected psychologist and proponent of social Darwinism, Henry Goddard, published a book, *The Kallikak Family: A Study in the Heredity of Feeble-Mindedness.* Goddard had met Deborah Kallikak (last name fictitious) in the Training School for Feeble-Minded Girls and Boys in Vineland, New Jersey. He hired a young woman, Elizabeth Kite, to investigate Deborah's genealogy back to the American Revolution. The original Kallikak presumably started two lines of descendants: one out of wedlock with a feeble-minded woman, and the other with his lawful wife. Kite and Goddard adjudged the majority of progeny from the illegitimate line to be "morons" (a term Goddard invented), and degenerates. The progeny from the legitimate line were found to be prominent and respectable persons up to the present day.

During Goddard's lifetime, new discoveries in genetics, coupled with a closer examination of his flawed experimental methodology, brought his study into disregard. However, until the present book, the real Kallikak story had been uninvestigated and untold. The author has turned to historical records, including photographs, and to a reexamination of the original study, to "reveal for some, and to remind others of, the tragedy of Deborah Kallikak's life of needless confinement, and of the thousands of other lives that have been similarly wasted." (p. 9)

Chapter Three chronicles Deborah's life from her illegitimate birth at a "poor farm," or alms house, through her abandonment and consequent institutionalization from age 8 to her death in 1978 at 89. Pictures and text reveal a winsome, talented, and productive person whose diagnosis as feeble-minded was based solely on academic test performance. In her daily life, she demonstrated woodworking and musical abilities, and skill in caring for children and nursing the sick. She had many friends with whom she maintained an active correspondence. Smith surmises that Deborah would be classified today as a normal person with a specific academic learning disability that should not have led to her confinement and segregation for 81 years.

Many of Goddard's and Kite's findings are reinterpreted to reach conclusions exactly opposite to those originally proposed. Smith, in reviewing records of the "bad" Kallikak family, discovered that the descendants were, in the main, farmers and blue-collar workers who raised children and contributed to community life. Many were among the working poor, who did not have the advantages that accrued to the "good" Kallikak family down through the generations.

Smith traces the eugenics movement to its later terrible consequences. A model sterilization law was declared constitutional by the United States Supreme Court in 1927. It was adopted in Hitler's Germany in 1933. The eugenics philosophy led to laws banning interracial marriage in the United States and in Germany. Under the Nazis, an estimated 1 million people deemed defective were eliminated in a euthanasia campaign. This thinking was ultimately extended to justify the genocide of the Holocaust.

Even after World War II, the myth of the Kallikaks was perpetuated, in part to prevent racial integration. Smith discusses some of the better known advocates of this point of view. He ends with a short epilogue and an index.

Analysis: Although this book is a well-referenced scholarly work, it reads like a piece of investigative journalism. The author is to be commended for tracing the influence of an early, flawed work through subsequent history to its vestiges in the modern day. Rather than preach or extol, Smith is inclined to quote the eugenic proponents themselves to illustrate the virulence of their positions.

■ Ungerleider, Dorothy. **Reading, Writing, and Rage: The Terrible Price Paid by Victims of School Failure.** Foreword by Bruce Jenner. Jalmar, 1985. 221pp. (0-91-5190-42-7) Reading Level: Grades 10–12. (BL 15 Ja85; LJ 15 Mr85; PDK O85)
Disability: Learning disabilities

The author, an educational therapist, has created the fictionalized educator Diana to make a coherent story of her actual own work and research into the life of the boy she calls Toni Petri. The book is based on hours of interviews with significant persons in the story, as well as much written documentation.

. Toni was the only son of an older couple that seemed to have more than their share of emotional miseries and financial insecurities. They were well meaning with each other and their son, but they made a discordant and eccentric family. Toni was an unusually large and clumsy boy with developmental lags, asthma, and allergies. He was finally diagnosed as having phoria, a condition resulting in intermittent double vision. He was obviously intelligent and thoughtful and a mastermind with mechanical things. His school life had been plagued by an unfortunate mismatch of teachers and other academic specialists; he developed severe reading problems and suffered a poor self-image. His parents felt defeated in their efforts to find help for him.

At the time "Diana" began working with him, he was a lethargic, cynical 15-year-old at school but an enthusiastic auto mechanic and motorcycle rider in his neighborhood. She first enticed him to learn to read by using the driver's manual, and she won his trust by her empathy and honesty.

Misunderstandings and mishaps continued at school. Eventually, Toni quit to marry his already pregnant young girlfriend. He later hurt his back while eking out a living with a trucking firm and felt that he was unjustly treated by the insurance company. He had always been prone to contain his anger until it erupted in a violent outburst. He awoke one morning with a plan to shoot his employers, but on his long drive to the plant, gun ready, he managed to total his truck.

The story ends with the young couple's life fairly well stabilized. However, their eldest daughter had just been identified by the school authorities as having "something wrong" with her, so history was repeating itself. Diana felt that her efforts on Toni's behalf were worth it when he reflected, "Mrs. Cotter, you didn't completely teach me to read, but you taught me something I never knew before. You taught me that I *could* read. I guess the rest is up to me, isn't it?" (p. 203).

Analysis: This fast-paced, emotion-laden narrative realistically portrays the interconnections between the physical, psychological, sociological, and chance happenings that can tip the balance of a child's life toward school failure, unstable personality, and delinquency. As an educator, Ungerleider focuses on the shortcomings of the school system and of educational remediation. She is remarkably tolerant of her student's anger and inappropriate responses, as well as of his sad, ineffective parents. Her ability to see the world from their perspective was probably crucial to her relatively successful intervention with the troubled teenager, and it is certainly instructive to readers who have grappled with their own learning disabilities.

MENTAL RETARDATION

■ Bakely, Donald C. *Bethy and the Mouse.* Faith & Life, 1985. 164pp. (0-87303-111-3) Reading Level: Grades 7–12.
Disability: Mental retardation; Microcephaly; Down's syndrome

Donald Bakely is a minister who at the time he wrote this book was executive director of Cross-Lines Cooperative Council in Kansas City. His fifth child, Matthew, was born with part of his brain either missing or underdeveloped, a condition that might have been caused by the severe food poisoning his mother had had when she was two months pregnant; Matthew, whom the family nicknamed The Mouse, died at age 5. He was never able to speak or stand or, indeed, to function independently, although he did seem to understand and respond to his family. Bethany, the seventh child in the family, was born 16 years after Matthew, when her parents were in their late 40s, and it was immediately obvious that she had Down's syndrome, but her condition was much less acute than Matthew's. Her parents took her as a 1-month-old to the Infant Development Center of the Shawnee Mission Medical Center, and the staff there guided her early years. Bethy's portion of the book ends with her entrance into regular kindergarten, probably the first Down's syndrome child ever to do this in Kansas.

Bakely has written most of his text in free verse form, punctuated with reports on Bethy's progress from the Infant Development Center. Black-and-white photographs of both children illustrate the book.

Analysis: Although he acknowledges pain and dismay, Bakely believes that children like Matthew and Bethy are "God's gifts in special packages." He feels that the whole family was positively affected by them and that such children are sent "to be the example of the best God has to offer—love." The section on Bethy is much longer than that on the Mouse, and she emerges from her father's description as an engaging little girl who delights her parents and siblings. While she is clearly different from so-called normal children in appearance and slower in her development, she shares many characteristics with other youngsters.

To some readers Bakely's choice of the free verse form may seem strange and perhaps a barrier. Much of the text is devoted to the author's thoughts and to vignettes, while the most specific details of Bethany's development come in the brief progress reports. Young people who are interested in mental retardation might want to read this book in conjunction with others on the same subject written by both parents and professionals.

■ Becker, Ruth M. *Jon: Lessons in Love.* Illus. Northwestern, 1984. 88pp. (0-8100-0196-9) Reading Level: Grades 10–12.
Disability: Mental retardation; Apraxia

The author is an instructor in nursing at the University of Arizona. She writes, "I would like to share with you how my husband and I came to accept the retardation of our son Jon in the framework of Christ's love." The royalties from the book are to go to the Care for the Mentally Retarded Fund of the Special Ministries Board, Wisconsin Evangelical Lutheran Synod. An admiring foreword was written by the family's pastor in Tucson, and by Jon's grandmother. The various chapters each end with some half dozen bible verses for reflection.

The story begins with Jon's birth as the fourth child of a high school math teacher and his wife, who was about to reenter nurses' training. By the time the little curly-headed baby was 5 weeks old, his parents became aware of a lethargy and unresponsiveness that signaled what would turn out to be mental retardation and autistic behavior. The grieving mother tried to reconcile the love of God with this burden that she felt unable to bear. After a clinical evaluation and definitive diagnosis when he was 1, his parents instituted a home program to teach Jon to eat with a spoon, pull up, and respond to cues. He had occasional seizures and many debilitating infections.

Jon entered a preschool for retarded children when he was 2. He was taken regularly to church and took part in Christian ritual at home. He slowly learned to identify prayers and hymn and to recognize pictures of Jesus. In a speech clinic, he was diagnosed as apraxic, that is, he could hear and comprehend to some extent, but he could never acquire much speech. At 6 he went to a special school, where he began to learn simple counting, colors, and manual signs. He learned to swim and dive.

Ruth Becker maintained a constant dialogue with God in order to increase her understanding of the blessings He bestowed in the form of Jon's progress, in the many caring people they met because of Jon, and in the compassion of their other children. She wrestled with unworthy thoughts, such as "Why me?" She became active in the Association for Retarded Citizens. She spoke as an antiabortion advocate in a special education class, stressing that in her family, at least, the retarded child was a blessing. Eventually several foster children joined the family as well.

Becker chronicles many experiences with Jon, one of the most harrowing being an incident of physical abuse inflicted on 8-year-old Jon by a new, inexperienced teacher in his school. Progress for Jon was slow but sure, and he became a person in his own right in his mother's eyes.

When Jon was 11, the family reluctantly placed him in a group home, because his father had become ill, so it was too difficult to have him at home. The book ends with Jon 12, happy in his new situation and still a delight to his family.

Analysis: Becker has faith in a personal, Christian God who plans all things in her life according to His purposes, and she views herself as an instrument of this purpose. While she believed her retarded son to be a special gift and message from God, she and her family worked long and diligently to help Jon become all he could. She is honest enough to acknowledge her negative feelings, although she is apt to see them as a fault on her part. Jon comes across as a winsome personality, still lacking some self-control but progressing nicely in a supportive environment. The few black-and-white photographs show an alert, happy boy.

■ Bergman, Thomas. *We Laugh, We Love, We Cry: Children Living with Mental Retardation.* Photographs by Thomas Bergman. Gareth Stevens, 1989. 48pp. (1-55532-914-4) Reading Level: Grades 2–6. (BCCB F90; BL 15 Ja90; KR 1 N89)
Disability: Mental retardation

In this book, originally published in Sweden in 1977, Bergman focuses on two sisters, aged 5 and 6, both of whom are developmentally delayed. In addition to their mental retardation, they do not speak, and they have serious physical disabilities requiring therapy. Both are learning sign language. Anna Karin, the older, has been evaluated to see if there is any structural reason for her inability to speak; none has been found, and she is going to be taught to make speech sounds. Both children are mainstreamed. Anna Karin used to go to a special school but is now in regular kindergarten; Asa is in a day care center with normally functioning children. The girls are shown in many activities with their parents, at therapy sessions, and in their classrooms. The last pages of the book are devoted to informational material.

Analysis: Despite their different physical appearance, their difficulty in walking and balance, and their developmental delays, these little girls appear responsive, outgoing, alert to their world, and happy. Both text and photographs make clear their joy in interacting with other children and their hurt when they are left out. The author stresses the hard work required by their therapies and says, "Sometimes they don't seem to be going very fast, but they are going steadily." As in the other books in this series, the pages at the end provide valuable information, answers to questions, and suggestions. One question that readers might well ask, however, is not addressed: how did it happen that two such children were born to normal parents? Even if the answer is unknown, it would have been well to raise the issue. However, this is a minor omission in an otherwise fine book.

■ Canning, Claire E. *The Gift of Martha.* Illus. Children's Hosp. Medical Center of Boston, 1975. 30pp. Reading Level: Grades 7–12.
Disability: Mental retardation; Down's syndrome

"Forget her, mother. She will never know the difference, and it will be the best thing by far for all the family" (p. 12). A well-meaning pediatrician spoke these words to Claire Canning in December 1971 shortly after she had given birth to her fifth child, Martha, who has Down's syndrome. Despite this dire warning, echoed four more times by other equally sincere physicians whom Canning describes as middle-aged family men so bound up in success that they could not accept anything less than a perfect human being, she and her family, after looking at institutions for Martha, decided to keep her at home.

Martha spent part of her time at Crystal Springs Nursery and part at home. Claire's greatest surprise when caring for Martha was the discovery that she was really like her other four infants except for limp muscular response. When a pediatrician at Boston Children's Hospital received a grant to study children with Down's syndrome, Crystal Springs referred the Cannings to him, and Martha and her parents, respectively, began various forms of physical therapy and counseling, which ultimately resulted in better development for Martha and the facilitation of a really positive attitude on the part of all the family members, including the four teenage children, who were very accepting of their new sister. The book ends with Martha at 4, deeply loved by her family and accepted by neighbors and family friends.

Analysis: Claire Canning presents a realistic picture of both the joys and the difficulties of working with a developmentally delayed infant and toddler within her home setting. She is gently but firmly critical of the early information and advice that she received after her daughter was born and very complimentary and supportive of the attitude of those involved in the research program at Boston Children's Medical Center and at the Crystal Springs Nursery. Beautiful black-and-white photographs taken by Martha's father, Joseph, illustrate the text. Highly recommended.

■ Craig, Mary. *Blessings: An Autobiographical Fragment.* Morrow, 1979. 128pp. (0-688-03456-X) Reading Level: Grades 10–12. (KR 1 My79; LJ 1 S79; PW 30 Ap79)
Disability: Hurler's syndrome (gargoylism); Down's syndrome

Craig's story begins in 1956 near the town of Derby in the Midlands of England. There she gave birth to her second son, who was diagnosed several years later as having the rare disorder called Hurler's syndrome, or gargoylism. Little Paul was severely retarded and he was difficult to manage. The Craigs were nominal Catholics, and they took the boy in his wheelchair to Lourdes. Other attempts at cure included a hospital stay when Paul was left in Poland, but all were to no avail. In 1965, Mary Craig delivered another boy, this one with Down's syndrome. In all she would have two normal and two handicapped youngsters to care for.

She was exhausted and in abject despair during the course of these events, and she mournfully appealed to God to help her find some meaning to her hard life. Shortly thereafter, she read about the Home for Concentration Camp Survivors, operated by Sue Ryder, an Englishwoman, with whom she began a long association. This remarkable member of the resistance movement went to Poland after World War II to help clear up the devastation. Ever since, she had dedicated her life to caring for those who survived the Holocaust, as well as the sick and disabled in all age groups wherever the need was the greatest. Craig rode in Ryder's truck on one mercy mission all over Poland and Czechoslovakia. The trip was fraught with hardship but also with wonderful adventures. They visited Auschwitz, the extermination camp in which many of those they met had been interned. The courage and compassion of those who had suffered the worst of life's horrors helped Craig to achieve the sense of perspective and acceptance that she had been seeking.

When Paul was 10, Craig was summoned to Poland to get him. Weak and sick, he fell out of bed and died of a heart attack shortly after returning to the family home. Craig meditates on the value of Paul's life in opening her eyes to the redemptive power of suffering: "If Paul had helped me towards even a little understanding, how could I agree that he had lived to no purpose? He had taught me a lesson, quite unwittingly, and now that he was no longer there, I owed it to him not to forget" (p. 104).

In the last section of the book, Craig reviews the successful development of her two nondisabled boys. She also describes the happy life of the brother who has Down's syndrome. Nicky learned to walk and talk by the time he was 4, although he has remained incontinent. At age 13, he has an exuberant and friendly personality, with a strong sense of fun. He attends a special school and perhaps will have the prospect of community living as an adult. Between caring for him, his mother has carved out a career in journalism, writing, and broadcasting, often drawing on the experiences of her life. The present book is intended as the final word on the subjects included. Craig ends with an essay on the meaning and justification of human suffering.

Analysis: As the author says of herself, she has wanted to avoid all hint of romanticism or self-pity in telling her story. She writes hoping to give comfort by sharing her experiences, just as others have given to her in her need. The tone of her writing is often spiritual but not overly religious. Her narration is vivid and often humorous, despite some agonizing descriptions of victims of suffering. The text is easier reading than that of many British books. It reads almost as if it had been spoken, perhaps because much has been culled from talks and broadcasts that Mary Craig has given.

■ Dorris, Michael. **The Broken Cord.** Harper & Row, 1989. 300pp. Reading Level: Grades 10–12. (LJ Jl89; NYTBR 30 Jl89)
Disability: Fetal alcohol syndrome (FAS); Learning disabilities

Dorris, an anthropologist and novelist, has written his memoirs that commence when, at age 26, he became a single, adoptive parent. He was given Adam, a 3-year-old Native American boy who had been removed from the care of an abusive, alcoholic mother. His initial conviction was that his love and solicitude could reverse the child's already arrested physical and mental development. Meanwhile, he, half Indian himself, joined the faculty of Dartmouth College to head a new program in Native American studies.

Adam began to experience seizures due to brain lesions. He was also inclined toward weight loss and fevers. As the father began to acknowledge the depth of Adam's problems, he determined to delve into the boy's past to understand their origin. It transpired that Adam's mother had died of alcohol poisoning at age 33. Her plight was similar to many young women on the Indian reservations.

Dorris adopted two more Indian children—a boy and a girl. Then, at a college reunion, he met a former classmate, Louise Erdrich, who would later become his wife and the mother of these and their biological children. She is also a professional writer, and she contributed the foreword to the book. Many professionals did their best to assist Adam, whose education proceeded by fits and starts. In his adolescence he was enrolled in special vocational education classes and eventually in some supportive employment. His future did not look very optimistic.

Dorris continued to study the problem of alcohol abuse among Native Americans, specifically in Adam's tribe, the Sioux. In his visits, he was astonished to find a number of teenagers who resembled and acted like his son. They had the distinctive characteristics of full-blown fetal alcohol syndrome: (1) significant growth retardation both before and after birth, (2) measurable mental defect, (3) altered facial characteristics, (4) other physical abnormalities and (5) documentation of maternal alcoholism (p. 148).

Gradually Dorris began to apprehend the terrible and permanent damage a drinking mother could inflict on her unborn child. He cites evidence that even small amounts of alcohol can contribute to fetal alcohol effect (FAE). Moreover, an impaired generation of children who reach childbearing age tend to perpetuate the irresponsible behavior of their parents, hence producing new victims. This seems, indeed, to be the case on many Indian reservations and increasingly so in American society at large and in other parts of the world. The narrative ends with a verbatim account that Adam Dorris wrote about his life. Some of his entries recall, from his standpoint, events in his father's story. The book closes with a lengthy bibliography of technical articles on FAS.

Analysis: This fast-moving, well-written, and very personal account has many strengths: The portrayal of Adam gives FAS a human face. A simple but accurate explanation of this phenomenon, whose incidence is 7,500 American babies each year, is helpful. This, coupled with opinions quoted from a number of experts, reinforces the exhortation that pregnant woman should abstain from drinking alcoholic beverages. Dorris acquaints the reader with aspects of Native American culture that make FAS a particularly serious problem on Indian reservations. In addition, completely apart from consideration of disability, he adroitly describes and contrasts his dominant and his minority culture as he cycles between them. He reveals the beauty and the tragedy that are still the legacy of the nation's management and mismanagement of its original inhabitants. Lastly, Dorris raises ethical questions with regard to the rights of women and of their unborn. These issues are timely and of critical import.

The contribution of Adam's story illustrates the honesty, but sparsity, of his intellect.

■ Edwards, Jean, and David Dawson. *My Friend David: A Source Book about Down's Syndrome and a Personal Story about Friendship.* Illus. Ednick Communications, 1983. 125pp. Reading Level: Grades 10–12.
Disability: Mental retardation; Down's syndrome

The first 39 pages of this remarkable little book consist of a handwritten autobiography, written by David Dawson, a man who was then 46 years old, born with Down's syndrome. Clearly, simply, and with very few errors, David tells the story of his life, beginning with his birth as the twin brother of Douglas, who does not have Down's, and his mother's subsequent refusal to institutionalize him.

Jean Edwards, a university professor and director of a center for people with Down's, then tells what David's friendship has meant to her. David is one of her clients, and the two have become good friends. The third part of the book explains what Down's is and step-by-step, what one should do as the parent of a Down's child. This resource section, complete with addresses of organizations, lists of books, and practical suggestions on how to cope, as well as how to help, can be extremely valuable to parents, teachers, and anyone who deals with children in any way. It gives excellent information on training, education, employment, adult day care, and all aspects of living with Down's.

Analysis: The ultimate value of this book is its presentation of David as a very real and very normal human being—someone almost anyone would like to claim as a friend. Highly recommended.

■ Jansen, Larry. *My Sister Is Special.* Illus. by Nan Pollard. Standard, 1984. Unp. Reading Level: Grades PS–1.
Disability: Down's syndrome

Larry Jansen has written this short book in the voice of his son, Matthew, who is talking about his younger sister, Rachel. Matthew begins by telling the reader what he and then Rachel like and don't like. After a page on the differences in the preferences and appearances of all people, he says, "Everyone is special, because God made us." Then he introduces the different ways in which Rachel is special because she has Down's syndrome. She is slow to learn some things, she may always live with her parents and never be a "mommy" herself, but she too is made by God. Though she may need help in some areas, there's much that she can do; she's also loving and fun to be with. She teaches her brother that it doesn't matter what people look like or who they are—she teaches him about love: "She teaches me that God loves me, even though I may not be perfect. I love my sister, and she loves me. She is a person whom God created."

A Note to Parents and Teachers at the end talks about the author's hope that his book will help correct existing bias based on ignorance, and he suggests questions that can be discussed with children.

Full-color illustrations.

Analysis: Though written like fiction, this book is apparently fact and is dedicated "To Matthew Jansen, a very special big brother." The text is simple and easily understood by young readers. The illustrations are less successful; mediocre in quality, they do not present Rachel as a real Down's syndrome child. Nevertheless, the book could be used with pre-school and elementary school children, perhaps in conjunction with a photo-essay such as *Someone Special, Just Like You,* by Tricia Brown (Holt, 1984), *Don't Forget Tom,* by Hanne Larsen (Crowell, 1978), or *Jon O.: A Special Boy,* by Elaine Ominsky (Prentice-Hall, 1977). As indicated in the passages quoted above, the book presents a religious viewpoint.

■ Jones, Ron. *Say Ray.* Illus. Bantam, 1984. 181pp. (0-553-24330-7)
Reading Level: Grades 10–12. (LATBR 5 Ag84; PW 1 Je84; SLJ Ja85)
Disability: Mental retardation

Ray, a man in his 20s, tested in the mentally retarded range. Consonant with the deinstitutionalization policy of the state of California, he quali-fied for community placement in a seedy welfare home run by the aging, slovenly Mrs. Burr. His case was being managed by a dedicated but overworked social worker, Miss Croce. When the story begins, he has been spending his days in a repetitive routine on the street and in the public playground, where he is tolerated by adults and liked by children. Once, in his desire to please, Ray agrees to dress as Rudolph the Red-Nosed Reindeer in the local merchants' Christmas parade. He did not understand the logistics of his task, and eventually he was beaten up by fraternity boys on a romp in the middle of the cold night.

Also in his boarding house was an elderly "couple," the Rogers, who had been removed from years in a state institution. It transpired that Ray had inherited quite a bit of money from his father's estate. Mrs. Burr's shady nephew, John Butler, getting wind of this, managed to get himself declared Ray's legal guardian. One step ahead of social service and Mrs. Burr, who also smelled money, Butler took Ray and his friends the Rogers in a trailer to Mexico, where they joined a hippie commune. After the Rogers hitchhiked home, their strange account led Miss Croce to investi-gate Ray's abduction.

Meanwhile, Butler and Ray, experiencing a precarious friendship, con-tinued their adventures in Mexico, including an abortive bank heist and starting a taxi business. Then the maladroit and venial Butler abandoned Ray and in the end disposed of most of his inheritance. However, Ray got himself back to San Francisco. With the help of the social workers and the court, he got out from the clutches of Mrs. Burr, and his finances were placed under the supervision of the public guardian's office. His experi-ences had matured him. He got a job with McDonald's. He married and had a child, and the family lived with his wife's mother. He is still entwined in the thicket of welfare bureaucracy, but he is a happy, fulfilled man.

Analysis: This well-crafted story was written by the author of *The Acorn People* (see *Accept Me as I Am,* 1985) and, again, describes with empathy and humor the lives of society's most vulnerable members. Since 1978, Jones has been physical education director for the Recreation Center for the Handicapped in San Francisco. He had access to people and documents in the States and in Mexico to help him research and re-create Ray's story. There is a surreal aspect to this voyage of an innocent "simpleton" who brings love and magic into a world whose complexities and evil he cannot fully understand. Jones' social message is clear: When marginal people are given a chance, they can become productive members of society.

■ Mulkern, Micki. *Erin: Mourning Journey to Joy.* Illus. Pine Hill, 1976. 77pp. (Paper) Reading Level: Grades 10–12.
Disability: Mental retardation

Elisabeth Kubler-Ross has written this book's introduction, in which she expresses the belief that the work can help others who are confronted with severely retarded children to understand their emotions and to find purpose and meaning in their situation. The author has divided her book into the four stages of mourning that Kubler-Ross has conceptualized.

Mulkern begins with the uneventful birth of her second daughter, Erin. During the baby's first year, she was slow to develop. The pediatrician suggested retardation, but her mother denied the possibility. She was always a happy, loving child. At 2, the diagnosis was confirmed. She attended a preschool class for retarded children when she was 3. Her mother became very angry at God and considered drowning Erin.

At this point, Mulkern began Gestalt therapy sessions, and information from tapes relevant to that experience are included. Despite the help, her marriage ended, and she temporarily lost her nursing job. Quotes from her journal reflect on this difficult time in her life. She said of Erin, "She's such a love, but such a heart ache" (p. 16). Her thoughts were recorded on a videotape, "A Different Kind of Loving," for medical students.

With bleak prospects for Erin's development, Mulkern began guiltily to consider institutionalization for her daughter. These deliberations appear in journal form. Finally, she placed her in Hacienda de Los Angeles, in Phoenix, Arizona (to which organization the proceeds of this book will be donated). She enticed artist Ted DeGrazia to do a print for a fund-raising project that garnered $30,000 for a new Hacienda school.

She entered a nurse practitioner's course at the university, which led to a new job and new career. Later, Mulkern went to an invited workshop with Elisabeth Kubler-Ross. During its course, she visited Erin, who now spoke in simple sentences but did not seem to recognize her particularly. She suddenly experienced the unconditional love that flowed between her and her daughter. Finally, she had gone from mourning to joy.

Black-and-white photographs show the author and her girls at various stages in their lives. A bibliography of self-help books follows.

Analysis: Mulkern's journals record the stream of consciousness of a conflicted mother. Her free-verse poems, written to her daughters, usually express some resolution of her feelings. Her story seems heartfelt, and the reader can rejoice with her in her final, loving triumph. She generously acknowledges the help she has received from Hacienda de Los Angeles, professionals, and a host of good friends. In the photographs, Erin appears as a winsome child.

■ Pastor-Bolnick, Jamie. **Winnie, "My Life in the Institution": A Memoir of a Special Woman.** Martins/Marek, 1985. 248 pp. (0-312-88230-0) Reading Level: Grades 7–12. (LJ 1 N85; NYTBR 1 D85)
Disability: Mental retardation

As a child, the author lived near the large state school-hospital for 1,700 mentally retarded women and briefly encountered a resident, Winnie, who was in her early 20s. Fifteen years later, Bolnick returned to the institution as a summer worker. Winnie had achieved a reputation with the professionals because she had written a "book," in longhand and in pencil, titled "My Life in the Institution," to prove that she was not mentally retarded. The "book" forms the core of Winnie's story, but the author elicited most of the account from taped interviews that she edited, so it is presented in Winnie's voice. Winnie had total recall of many events and even seemed to relive them as she spoke.

Winnie's story begins in 1938 when she was 6, with her car ride to the institution with her uncaring foster mother. With no explanation, she was taken for various exams, sedated, placed in different groups, and always told that her mother would be back for her.

She was initially frightened by the shouts and screams coming from the building with incorrigibles and "low grades," by a woman in a wheelchair menstruating through diapers, and by the night seizures of her cottage companions. She waited in vain for her parents to come for her or even to see her on visiting days. In her sadness and with her many frustrations, she was frequently "in troubles."

The chapters are titled chronologically up to Winter–Spring 1964. Winnie had many adventures ranging from being almost strangled by a sadistic nurse to actually learning to read. She made a first trip ever to a restaurant with her sister, and eventually she attempted a life outside the institution in a nursing home. The last chapter found her back in the institution, writing her book, in the realization that "It's [the institution] only better for us 'cause we're used to it here" (p. 246).

An epilogue explains that Winnie was unsuccessfully placed in another nursing home and finally died at age 44 of cancer in an institution near her sister's home.

Analysis: This book affords a rare glimpse of a perspective and a world that most of us can know only from the outside. Many of Winnie's problems were common to all children: she had to live in a world she did not make or understand, and she had to struggle for the self-control, skills, and autonomy that would make her acceptable. Her tragedy was that she had been orphaned at 2 and placed with foster parents who could not cope with her differences, so wrote her out of their lives.

Her story is very easy reading, and her adventures are absorbing in their own way. Older readers will catch the heart-rending comments she makes about being different, hoping for a better life, wanting human closeness. Young adults may question, as the author does in the epilogue, a system that squandered so much of her potential.

The book certainly, by negative example, supports the trend toward deinstitutionalization and normalization that has humanized life for many people.

And the author helped Winnie find dignity and self-respect in her life by facilitating the publication of her story.

■ Philips, Caroline. *Elizabeth Joy.* Lion, 1984. 144pp. (o.p.) Reading Level: Grades 7–12. (BL 15 Ja86)
Disability: Down's syndrome

Caroline Philips's first child, Elizabeth Joy, is a Down's syndrome child born when Philips was in her late 20s. This is the story of Elizabeth's first two years and of her mother's struggle to come to terms with her baby's disability. Early in the book, the author describes how she had become a believing Christian as a teenager; her husband Mark is a minister, and, during the period she writes about here, they live in an unnamed English town. The young parents are supported by the love and interest of their families and friends, their church community, a mother's group, and some—but not all—professionals.

Elizabeth's condition was diagnosed at birth. Caroline Philips recognized it when she first held her daughter in her arms, even before word came from the doctors: "I looked down at the tiny person in my arms: an expression, or was it the shape of her face, reminded me of something. And then I knew. 'She's a mongol isn't she?' I said to the nurse. 'They don't know yet,' she replied. But I knew. I bravely said that I was a Christian and God must have a good purpose in giving her to us. The nurse praised my attitude, but I said to my daughter, 'You'll be the brainiest mongol out,' and I tried hard not to cry." Philips struggles with the ideas suggested in this passage: the belief that Elizabeth's condition is part of God's plan and the determination that the parents will do everything possible to nurture her abilities. Sometimes this leads Philips to a competitive race, hoping that her work with Elizabeth will keep the baby from falling too far behind the norm for her age and certainly not behind the levels attained by other Down's syndrome children. In her introduction she recognizes this; she refers to the range of potential found in Down's children, hopes that readers will not focus on comparing their children to Elizabeth, and writes: "The stress on her progress in the account of the first year of her life reflects my difficulty in coming to terms with her limitations rather than any intrinsic value we would place on her ability to achieve."

Philips made use of many resources as she learned to care for Elizabeth. She joined a Down's group, she had friends with normally endowed children, and she got ideas for stimulating activities from her reading; eventually, Elizabeth went to a small playgroup for normal children. The Portage program, developed in Portage, Wisconsin, for educationally delayed children, was particularly helpful in their home activities. This teaching method "is based on behavior modification. Praise is the major reward and demonstration and prompting are the ways to teach the skills. Another essential process is the breaking down of the skills into tiny parts which a child can learn slowly." Elizabeth's progress was sometimes discouraging, but at other times she made clearly observable gains. At 23 months, as the book ends, she is walking and is beginning to talk; she has started to enjoy hearing stories rather than just looking at the pictures as previously, engages in imaginative play with make-believe, and can manage such activities as puzzles and painting. She has always been a sweet-natured child. As she grows, her sense of humor develops and so does her sense of independence. The evaluation done by an educational psychologist indicates that she is not far behind the average for her age, though her speech is clearly delayed; he finds that "her level of play was good, particularly her imaginative play, and also that she was a good learner." Looking to the future, her parents and the psychologist agree "that Elizabeth would continue to learn most through normal playgroups and nursery school"; special education might be needed later on.

Throughout these first two years, her parents, for all the ups and downs, remain firm in their Christian faith and their belief that God directs their life. The book ends with a postscript describing the birth of the Philips's second child, a healthy, normal baby boy. Philips includes a bibliography of books both by professional and by the parents of Down's syndrome children and the addresses of associations in Chicago and in Hamilton, Ontario.

Analysis: This is a very appealing book, as well as an informative one. Philips's honesty and intelligence make her an astute observer both of Elizabeth's development and of her own struggles to accept completely this child and the reality of her limitations. Elizabeth clearly has more abilities and more potential than many Down's syndrome children, yet sometimes the struggle to help her to master what normal babies pick up with much less conscious and intensive guidance can be frustrating, repetitive, and boring. For all their faith, her parents are saddened by Elizabeth's difference. They struggle to "learn acceptance, and to relax with who Elizabeth is, not always striving to move her on for our sake, but to help her be as complete a person as she can be, for her own sake." In doing so, they feel they will begin to understand God's intention as an indication of God's love. Actually, of course, all parents must strive to accept and love their children for themselves and not for their achievements.

The theme of Christian faith underlies this book as it does Philips's life, yet it is not intrusive. Readers who do not share her beliefs can nevertheless enjoy the book and learn from it. Philips writes clearly and fluently. The book could certainly be read by youngsters from the age of 11 or 12 years who have an interest in the subject.

■ Rimland, Ingrid. *The Furies and the Flame.* Arena, 1984. 281pp. (0-87879-418-2) Reading Level: Grades 10–12. (LATBR 8 J184) *Disability:* Mental retardation

Ingrid Rimland is a novelist, a child therapist in private practice, and an activist interested in the education of children with disabilities. Now a Californian, she was born in a Mennonite community in the Soviet Union and immigrated with her Mennonite parents and other community members to a settlement in the Paraguayan jungles after World War II. She grew up there, married as a teenager, and gave birth to her first child, Erwin, who as an infant was overdosed with anesthesia by the village doctor and badly brain damaged. Later, she and her husband moved to Canada, where she bore another child.

Rimland's years of trying to help Erwin led her to a university education and personal and professional growth. She obtained degrees in special education and has written a novel about Mennonite life—*The Wanderers*—and two other books, including this autobiography. She has a deep and abiding love and respect for Mennonite life and culture, about which she writes dramatically, intertwined in the story of her life and Erwin's.

Her formative experience with him, however, has caused her personally to reject many of its traditional beliefs and customs. In the introductory chapter, she says, "Let this be known: it was a ghoulish thing to happen to a baby. Don't cheapen grief by telling me it was God's will—how could that be? Don't say it was my cross to bear—I did not choose it. Don't tell me in smug ignorance that in the end his tragedy was meant to strengthen me—life's balances can't be that simple" (p. 3). She goes on to say, "Like Abraham, I wrestled with God for my son" (p. 4).

Rimland's tireless efforts to help Erwin led her to a new life, and both factors ultimately played into her separation and divorce from her husband. Ultimately, concerned both that Erwin needed more than she could give him at home as he matured and that her younger son, Rudy, needed more than she could give him with Erwin to care for, she found a group living facility for Erwin, who since has attended a public high school and graduated from it. She reprints some of his letters to her; they are remarkable in both content and feeling.

Analysis: Rimland is a gifted writer. Mature teens should enjoy the description and the drama as her narrative unfolds. Highly recommended.

8

BOOKS DEALING WITH
MULTIPLE/SEVERE AND VARIOUS
DISABILITIES

*It is not the perfect, but the imperfect who have need
of love.*

—Oscar Wilde

The first section of this chapter, Multiple/Severe Disabilities, covers individuals, each of whom has several significant disabilities. The second section, Various Disabilities, consists of stories of people who have different disabilities, such as those in a hospital, for example, or of several different people in a collective biography.

Annotations are alphabetical by author in each section.

MULTIPLE/SEVERE DISABILITIES

■ Busselle, Rebecca. *An Exposure of the Heart.* Norton, 1989. 288pp. (0-393-02547-0) Reading Level: Grades 10–12. (LJ 1 Ap89; NYTBR 12 Mr89)
Disability: Multiple/severe disabilities

Rebecca Busselle is a photographer who spent a year in 1983 taking pictures at Wassaic Developmental Center, a big institution for those now termed "developmentally disabled," located in Upstate New York. Busselle lives a short distance from the facility in a small town whose residents have had, in her words, "an intimate, uneasy relationship with Wassaic," which, next to IBM, employs the second-largest number of people in Dutchess County. Busselle and her family moved there because her husband found a position at Wassaic as an architectural planner. Like other similar institutions, Wassaic has undergone many changes in the last 20 years, following revelations of the inhumane conditions at Willowbrook, another New York State facility; most changes have brought improvement.

There are no pictures in this book. Instead, Busselle uses words to describe her experience, from her first encounter with a resident with a head hideously deformed by hydrocephaly. The others she met on that day were variously deformed and disabled, and she left without taking a picture, so horrified and repelled that she thought she would have to give up the project and return her grant. However, she forced herself to go back.

Arranged by the seasons, the book describes the people she came to know at Wassaic, both residents and staff, and the scenes and lives she observed. She formed relationships, the central one with a profoundly retarded child named Emily, who was the same age as her 12-year-old son, Max. Busselle interweaves the story of her Wassaic experience with her own life, memories, reactions, and with its effect on her own family, particularly on Max and on her daughter Katrina, who was 13 when the year at Wassaic began.

The book concludes with a bibliography of books that Busselle found helpful. "Some have given me visual information, some have given historical context, others have broadened my perspective on different disabling conditions."

Analysis: Busselle has written a moving, compelling book, as absorbing as a novel. A vivid writer, she describes both what she sees and what she feels with graphic detail and sometimes painful honesty. Some of the residents at Wassaic are remote and inaccessible, unable to communicate except with rage or silence. Emily, developmentally a toddler, cannot speak but has developed a body language that Busselle gradually learns. Their relationship is central to the book. Others, like the four elderly women whom Busselle takes home for Christmas Eve supper, are painfully articulate; fully aware of their situation, describing themselves as having been "put away," they long for another life. Busselle's family reacts in different ways to her work and to her efforts to include Emily and the elderly quartet in their home life. The account starts in winter and ends at Christmastime, when Emily at last leaves Wassaic to move to a residential facility near her grandmother. An afterword brings the story and the central figures to 1987.

Busselle's work is informed throughout by her respect and her humanity. She is sensitive not only to the lives of Wassaic's residents but also to the staff members who care for them—sometimes with harshness and even brutality, but more often with realistic compassion laced with black humor. She is aware too of her own ambivalences and frailties, which she sometimes sees reflected in the responses of her children, particularly Max. An unusual and outstanding book, *An Exposure of the Heart* could be recommended to high school readers, both to those with a particular interest in disabling conditions and to a wider group who are attracted to accounts of human experience in whatever form it takes.

■ de Vinck, Christopher. *The Power of the Powerless: A Brother's Lesson.* Doubleday, 1988. 153pp. (0-385-24138-0) Reading Level: Grades 7–12. (BL 15 Mr88; PW 15 Ja88; WSJ 2 Je88)
Disability: Multiple/severe disabilities

Christopher de Vinck is a high school teacher and a poet. His older brother Oliver was born with multiple impairments, probably due to an incident during their mother's pregnancy (she was made unconscious by fumes from a coal stove). Oliver could not see or hear or walk; he lived for 32 years, lying on the same bed in the same room, fed and bathed and nurtured by his parents and his five brothers and sisters. De Vinck's essay about Oliver was printed first in the *Wall Street Journal* and later re-printed in the *Reader's Digest.* He had many letters from readers with similar stories to tell, and he visited the families of several severely disabled children. His book includes some of the letters and describes the visits. De Vinck and his family were profoundly affected by Oliver, who, inert and unknowing, exerted an influence on all their lives; other families attest to similar experiences. The book has an introduction by Father Henri J. M. Nouwen and an afterword by Fred Rogers.

Analysis: De Vinck's narrative begins with Oliver's death and the publication of his essay and then weaves back and forth between present and past, between his life with his wife and three children and his childhood in the "house of Oliver." Though at times repetitive and perhaps excessively artless, the book is a moving account of love and acceptance, of a joyous reaching out and affirmation. Each of the disabled persons described here has become an intrinsic part of her or his family, each has exerted unexpected power. Even Lauren, who died after a day of life, altered her parents forever.

Though de Vinck sometimes acknowledges the difficulty and pain of caring for severely disabled children, his recurrent note is one of affirmation. "Because of Oliver," he writes frequently—because of Oliver, he grew up to be a particular kind of person, a particular kind of son, brother, teacher, husband, father, and writer.

Young adult readers who can respond to a quiet book, without plot or suspense, may find here a resonance for their own lives; certainly they will have a greater appreciation of what it means to grow up with a sibling who, while utterly helpless, becomes a dominant member of the family.

■ Rosenberg, Maxine B. *Finding a Way: Living with Exceptional Brothers and Sisters.* Illus. by George Ancona. Lothrop, Lee & Shephard, 1988. 48pp. (LB 0-688-06873-1) Reading Level: Grades 2–6. (BL 1 D88; KR 1 N88; SLJ F89)
Disability: Asthma; Diabetes; Spina bifida

Rosenberg and Ancona have collaborated on several fine books for young readers, including *My Friend Leslie,* about a friendship between an able-bodied child and one with multiple impairments (see *Accept Me as I Am,* 1985). Here, they focus on three youngsters who have siblings with disabilities: Danielle's older brother has diabetes, Danny's younger brother and sister have asthma, and Rachel's older brother was born with spina bifida. Text and pictures show both the ways in which these disabilities make family life exceptional and the activities and relationships that can be found in many ordinary households. Each healthy sibling expresses both positive and negative feelings, with emphasis on the former. Two pages of general comments introduce the text. The book concludes with an essay addressed to parents, written by Stephen Greenspan, Ph.D., a professor of educational psychology and acting director of Connecticut's University Affiliated Program on Developmental Disabilities.

Analysis: Both writer and photographer display great sensitivity to family dynamics and to the complex relationships between siblings when they are complicated by health problems. Using direct quotes and narration, Rosenberg lets youngsters give voice to their feelings of jealousy and resentment at the special attention required by their brothers and sisters. Whereas most of the fine black-and-white photographs show smiling faces and happy activity, others catch children and parents in pensive moods. As Greenspan points out in the afterword, this is a book to stimulate discussion and encourage understanding.

The large print, generous margins, and many pictures make this a book to share with children as young as 7 or 8. Since the oldest siblings are 11 and 13, it can also appeal to readers in this higher age group. While the book is generally well designed, the three segments flow into each other without a break, which can be confusing. The range of the book is necessarily limited by the decision to focus on three disabilities, all physical; in addition, all the families are white and appear to be middle-class and suburban. The book could have been given wider appeal had author and illustrator chosen at least one urban and/or nonwhite family. Nevertheless, these criticisms do not negate the importance of the book's contribution to the understanding of disabilities and their effect on both healthy and impaired family members.

VARIOUS DISABILITIES

■ Aaseng, Nathan. *Winners Never Quit: Athletes Who Beat the Odds.* Illus. Lerner, 1980 (LB 0-8225-1060-X) Reading Level: Grades 4–9. (BL 1 O80; SLJ D80)
Disability: Various disabilities

A collection of ten brief biographies of athletes who overcame various disabilities to achieve outstanding success in their field, this work teeters on the brink of the stereotype of people with disabilities as somehow set apart and on a higher plane than others. However, it avoids falling into the abyss because of the introductory chapter, in which the author identifies these athletes as "extra effort" heroes who compensated for their disability by trying so hard that they became stars. He states: "But when the extra effort heroes battle to the top, players and fans may still marvel at their performance, but they no longer envy these stars," because they realize their achievement was the result of hard work rather than talent and luck.

Eight of the ten athletes have physical disabilities or health problems: Rocky Bleier (football), Wes Unseld (basketball), Larry Brown (football), Kitty O'Neill (Olympic diver and later Hollywood stuntperson), John Hiller (baseball), Tommy John (baseball), Bobby Clarke (baseball), and Tom Dempsey (football). Of the remaining two, Lee Trevino (golf) overcame poverty that made it difficult for him to get started as a golfer, and Ron LeFlor (baseball) overcame behavioral problems that landed him in prison, where he started his baseball career.

Analysis: Recommended for upper elementary and junior high school students as a provider of some inspiration on the profitability of effort and hard work and on the possibility of competing despite disabilities and differences.

■ Anderson, Peggy. *Children's Hospital.* Harper & Row, 1985. 532pp. (0-06-015089-0) Reading Level: Grades 10–12. (BL Je85; KR 1 Ap85; NYTBR 23 Je85)
Disability: Various disabilities

Exploring in minute detail the lives of six very sick children, Peggy Anderson spent five years researching, organizing, and writing this book. It is more than the story of these children. Anderson's intent, from the very beginning, she says, was "to explore the responses of those involved when a child is struck down by serious illness or injury: to discover how—or whether—the child, the family, and the hospital staff members attempting to save or cure the child are able to tolerate the intolerable."

The answer to this question, in brief, was "yes," and the staff at Children's Hospital of Philadelphia, where Anderson did her research, comes out looking far better than most of the health care professionals who are described in the other books reviewed in this volume and in its predecessor, *Accept Me as I Am.*

The six children are Mark, age 15, who has cystic fibrosis; Candy, a 6-year-old, born with a badly malformed face; Jody, 18 months old, who has already had 12 operations in attempts to correct multiple birth defects; Gina, an 8-year-old, who has leukemia; Brandon, a placenta previa baby, born very prematurely with an extremely low birth weight; and Freddy, age 9, who sustained massive injuries when thrown through the air by a car as he was crossing a street.

Anderson follows the lives of these children, their families (or, in Jody's case, his guardian, the state welfare department), and their caregivers over a period of five months from December to May. She spent a great deal of time interviewing all those involved, especially the parents and the hospital staff, and also researching the children's illnesses. She did follow-up work with the families for up to two years after the actual time period that she chronicled in detail.

Analysis: The results of the meticulous, in-depth work are related in vivid, colorful, specific prose. Anderson is a sensitive and caring person who is able to observe and analyze the complex effects that these traumatic childhood illnesses and injuries have upon everyone whose life is affected by them. Although this is a lengthy book, it reads like a good story, and many teens will enjoy it. It is, as well, highly instructive and informational, and it seems to present the essence of a good hospital.

The book concludes with an excellent bibliography on pediatric hospitals and illnesses.

■ Astor, Gerald. *The Disease Detectives: Deadly Medical Mysteries and the People Who Solve Them.* New American Library, 1983. 217pp. Reading Level: Grades 10–12. (KR 15 Ap83; KR My83; LJ 15 Je90) *Disability:* AIDS; Hepatitis; Toxic shock syndrome

The chapters of this book are devoted to the work of various epidemiologists who study the outbreak and transmission of maladies such as Legionnaire's disease, ebola, and cholera. Vignettes about the patients, in all walks of life and circumstances, and the public health workers who attempt to unravel the mysteries of their symptoms, highlight the fragile balance between the immune system and disease organisms that constitute a healthy body.

Specific environmental and social situations that influence the state of public health are described. Physicians, as well as agencies such as the Centers for Disease Control, and patients, themselves, often become embroiled in political and economic hassles; examples include the potential liability of the military for radiation-related cancers in soldiers who witnessed nuclear explosions or that of the company that produced the tampon associated with toxic shock syndrome. Criminal investigators have contributed when, for instance, illegal drugs have become contaminated with hepatitis or salmonella.

The last chapter in the book suggests future trends in public health and possible directions for further investigations. A short bibliography and an index follow.

Analysis: Astor has been a professional writer and editor for over 25 years. His prose is lively, suspenseful, and easy to read. He puts many modern deadly diseases, including AIDS, into a broad medical and social perspective. (It should be remembered that AIDS research, in particular, has progressed considerably since the book's publication.) The opportunities for young people who might choose the field of epidemiology as a career are well detailed through many of the vignettes. The discussions of health practices are practical and pertinent.

■ Bach, Julie, ed. *Biomedical Ethics: Opposing Viewpoints.* Illus. Greenhaven, 1987. 216pp. (0-89908-396-X) Reading Level: Grades 9–12. (BL 15 S87; PW 10 J187; SLJ Je87)
Disability: AIDS; Renal disease; Heart disease; Kidney failure

This is one of more than 20 books in the Opposing Viewpoints series. This particular title covers issues important to those in the health care professions and to sick or disabled people. The five chapters contain essays with differing viewpoints purposely placed back-to-back to create a running debate. At the front of each essay, a few questions are posed to assist the reader to think critically about the facts and ideas that follow. Activities are suggested that may also facilitate critical thinking. The chapters ends with periodical bibliographies. The book concludes with a glossary of terms, a descriptive list of pertinent organizations, and a bibliography of books.

The essayists come from many fields: science, ethics, religion, and journalism. Pieces have been chosen from a variety of sources, including newspapers, popular periodicals, and professional journals. A few articles were specifically directed to high school students. Humorous black-and-white cartoons are interspersed in the text.

Chapter one raises issues around the dangers and benefits of genetic engineering in animals and people. For example, the alteration of "defective" genetic makeup is discussed. Chapter two covers progress and problems with tissue and organ transplants. The recipient of the first artificial heart, Barney Clark, had been mentioned in the introduction to the book. Now the toll of human suffering he endured and the tremendous financial investment involved are weighed against future possibilities for the procedure.

Chapter three is entitled "Should Limits Be Placed on Reproductive Technology?" An essay on artificial insemination considers the possibility of inadvertent transmission of genetic disorders and mutagenic alteration of donor sperm. The risks of acquiring infections, such as AIDS, from donor semen are posed. The merits of surrogate motherhood for disabled or ill women are balanced against those for women who elect not to bear their genetic offspring for aesthetic or career reasons. The fourth chapter discusses the pros and cons of animal experimentation for the benefit of humans. The last chapter asks, "What Ethical Standard Should Guide the Health Care System?" Here, the rights of the poor and disabled to equal treatment and health care access are covered.

Analysis: A book of this sort cannot help but be uneven in quality. The target audiences of the essays, for example, range from youth to professionals. Furthermore, some authors are undoubtedly influenced by factors, such as religious conviction, that are not mentioned in their articles. The issues are so timely that recent developments have made some information inaccurate. Nevertheless, the selections tend to be thoughtful and interesting contributions from competent people in many walks of life. No essays are contentious or irresponsible. Examples taken from real life keep the tone of the book from being overly abstract for young people. The cartoons add a welcome levity to the seriousness of the heavy issues. The questions and activities should be helpful to the individual reader and useful for sparking group discussion as well.

■ Baird, Joseph L., and Deborah S. Workman, eds. *Toward Solomon's Mountain: The Experience of Disability in Poetry.* Temple Univ. Pr., 1986. 151pp. (0-87722-416-1) Reading Level: Grades 10–12.
Disability: Various disabilities

This is an anthology of poetry about disability. It contains several of the works written by each of 35 poets, who describe in a multitude of ways their experiences as disabled persons. As the editors say in the preface, "a decade ago this anthology would have been impossible; two decades ago inconceivable . . . only at this point in history could there have been produced a volume of serious, tough-minded poetry wholly concentrated upon the experience of disability" (p. 3). Unlike the stereotyped, sentimental poetry of the past, these works, which have grown out of the disability rights movement and the new attitudes that it has fostered, are forceful, truthful, and reality oriented. "The poetry gathered here fully authenticates that new spirit abroad in the land" (p. 3).

Following the main body of poetry are several useful appendixes, including biographical sketches of contributors, a selected bibliography, and three indexes (author-title, first line, and theme).

Analysis: Mature teenagers should appreciate the honesty, emotion, and thoughtfulness of these straightforward works, all of which are eminently readable, clear, and easy to understand.

■ Bergman, Thomas. *On Our Own Terms: Children Living with Physical Disabilities.* Photographs by Thomas Bergman. Gareth Stevens, 1989 (1-55532-942-X) Reading Level: Grades 2–6. (BCCB F90; BL 15 Ja90; KR 1 N89)
Disability: Various disabilities

Like Bergman's *Finding a Common Language,* this title is in the Don't Turn Away series. Bergman has photographed and here describes children who are being treated in a clinic at the Karolinska Hospital in Stockholm, Sweden. All of them have physical disabilities due to a variety of causes, for example, spina bifida, cerebral palsy, spinal injury, and brain damage. One child was born with shortened arms and one finger on each hand; another, the most difficult to look at, lacked both arms and legs (he died of an infection after the pictures were made).

Bergman focuses on the therapy devised for each child to help her or him do as much as possible and on the close relationship between the therapists and the children. The Question and Answer section at the back includes a discussion of language: Bergman defines "spastic," "cripple," "handicap," and "disability," pointing out that "words derived from 'cripple' and 'spastic' like 'crip' and 'spaz' have no place in the vocabularies of sensitive and loving people." There is a list of "Things to Do and Think About" to help able-bodied readers become more aware of what it means to have a disability, followed by a list of sources of information, titles of children's books about people with disabilities, a glossary, and an index.

Analysis: This is an exceptionally fine book. The large black-and-white photographs have been taken by someone who sees with a sensitive and compassionate eye, yet they never sentimentalize their subjects. The clear, honest text shares these qualities. The discussion of terminology mentioned above is particularly noteworthy and could be used to spark thoughtful discussion with young readers. One possible criticism could be made of the description of spina bifida as "an inherited condition" when "a condition with a genetic component" or "congenital" would seem more appropriate; this perhaps is a result of the text having been translated from the original Swedish. This aside, the book is as good as *Anna's Silent World* and *Don't Feel Sorry for Paul*, Maxine Rosenberg's *My Friend Leslie*, and Lou Ann Walker's *Amy: The Story of a Deaf Child.*

■ Bogdan, Robert. **Freak Show.** Illus. Univ. of Chicago Pr., 1988. 322pp. (0-226-06311-9) Reading Level: Grades 10–12. (Atlan N89; TLS 17 F89) *Disability:* Physical disabilities

The author is an academic who has set out to do a professional study of the evolution and demise of the American freak show, with particular emphasis on its exploitation of "exhibits" who had physical or mental abnormalities. He contrasts his own work with that of Drimmer and Fiedler (both reviewed in *Accept Me as I Am,* 1985), saying that unlike them, he has been careful to separate the role of "freak" from the actual identity of the various individuals who assumed such a role.

A number of well-known show people are described, many of whom were notable only because of their innate significant differences. These include dwarfs, Siamese twins, microcephalic persons (pinheads), thin or fat people, and giants. Some performers were self-made freaks, such as tattooed men and women and sword swallowers. Others were simply hoaxes: those with two heads or false hair, for example. Many black-and-white photographs, often originally used by the subjects for their own promotion, illustrate the stories of these extraordinary people.

In the final chapter, the author discusses how changing societal attitudes have contributed to the virtual end of the freak show as an institution. These days, portrayal of extreme human variation is apt to be confined to medical journals, although an exception would be the graphic exhibition of disabled people to raise funds for charitable organizations. Bogdan opposes all exploitation of exceptional persons, either for the enjoyment of spectators or for the purpose of provoking fear or pity. "The job of those who want to serve people known as disabled should be to get behind the scenes, to know them as they are, not as they are presented" (p. 279).

An extensive appendix of notes and references follows the text.

Analysis: Notwithstanding Bogdan's scholarly purpose and his sincere goal of humane treatment of people with significant abnormalities, the book fascinates readers as the freak show fascinated its attendees. Bogdan himself seems aware of this when he writes, early in the book, "There will be exhibits (and it will be okay to look!)" (p. 3). The book presents a wonderful history of the carnival and circus world with the freak show as the focus. The prose and pictures memorialize the curious human beings who accepted the role of freak, and yet, in most instances, loved, had children, and lived exemplary private lives.

Bogdan ponders the ambiguous social attitudes toward people who are deviant. He invites the reader to share his fascination, admiration, and dismay over the lives of the stars of the freak show.

■ Bowe, Frank. *Personal Computers and Special Needs.* Illus. by L. D. Kerr and Lisa D. Williams. Sybex, 1984. 171pp. (0-89588-193-4) Reading Level: Grades 10–12. (Byte J185; CBR Mr85; Inst F85; LHTN O84) *Disability:* Physical problems; Sensory problems; Cognitive problems

Frank Bowe is a nationally recognized authority on the use of microcomputers by people with disabilities. He himself is hearing impaired. His book is an outgrowth of the White House Conference on Computers and Disabled Persons.

In Part One, Bowe says that this book was written for those with special needs, their families, friends, and others. It is also addressed to anybody who knows little or nothing about computers. He believes that computers are the most remarkable "reasonable accommodation" devices for disabled people ever invented. In the chapter entitled "About Special Needs," Bowe reminds readers that there are 4 million disabled people under age 16, 13 million between 16 and 65, and 8 million over 65. He gives many examples of people using computers: a blind professor of literature who has a speech synthesizer, the author of *Black and Deaf in America* pictured with his device, a deaf college student using a spell-checker program, adaptations for a wheelchair user, and so forth.

In Part Two, employment of disabled people is discussed. Bowe introduces a systems analysis specialist, totally paralyzed, who works on his back in bed. Another quadriplegic man uses a "puff-and-sip" mouthpiece in the office. A blind programmer is pictured operating the Versabraille machine. Subsequent chapters cover computer technology in the classroom and in independent living situations.

Part Three's chapters discuss software and machines adapted for people with vision impairment, hearing loss, mobility limitations, and learning disabilities. Part Four lists resources, a buyer's guide, and additional citations. An index is included.

Analysis: Some of the specific information, as opposed to general prin-

ciples, is no doubt already outdated in a field that produces new generations of computers and new software constantly. It may also be that the
European and other countries have narrowed the gap with respect to the
United States in the field that Bowe mentions. Still, his discourse rings true
because it always involves actual children and adults whose lives have been
transformed by the machines and adaptations featured in the book. He
admittedly does not explain how things work, but ample references give
the reader an opportunity to learn more. The book is discursive, interesting, and very upbeat.

■ Browne, Susan E., Debra Connors, and Nancy Stern. *With the Power
of Each Breath: A Disabled Woman's Anthology.* Cleis, 1985. 354pp.
(0-939416-09-3) Reading Level: Grades 10–12. (BL J185; LJ Ag85; PW 12
J185)
Disability: Various disabilities

Fifty-four women wrote contributions for the eight chapters that compose
this book. The chapters deal with surviving the social welfare system for
disabled persons, growing up as the disabled child in a family, rearing
children, making friends, relating to differently abled persons, developing
a positive body image, forming self-identity, and using anger construc-
tively. The contributions pertain to every topic imaginable: childbirth,
education, sexism, sexuality, employment, pain, and death, to name only
a few.
    Analysis: This is a strong, powerful, sometimes overwhelming book.
The women who wrote it are direct and frank and will no doubt anger
some readers with the bluntness of their criticisms of the way society treats
women who are disabled. They are particularly critical of those in the
medical profession, educators, and other professionals who work with
disabled women. Chapter 2, entitled "Shout Out—Using Our Anger,"
reflects much of the tone of the book, very angry and very sad. At the same
time, each chapter is also full of life, energy, and creativity.
    The editors have wisely changed very little of what the women wrote;
thus each chapter varies widely. There is no consistent writing style, level
of sophistication, or even approach. This is one of the major strengths of
the book, because it results in an intensity and a reality not found in a
literary creation. Recommended highly for high-school-level readers.

■ Cattoche, Robert J. *Computers for the Disabled.* Illus. Franklin Watts,
1986. 96pp. (0-531-10212-2) Reading Level: Grades 7–12.
Disability: Cerebral palsy; Brain damage; Visual impairment

As the title indicates, the author of what the publisher terms "A Com-
puter-Awareness First Book" has focused on computers that make it

possible for people with disabilities to communicate in new ways and to acquire skills that bring a richer and more independent life within reach. After explaining how computers work, in the following chapters, Cattoche discusses computers for physically disabled people, for children with learning disabilities, and for those with hearing and visual deficits.

Vignettes describing young people who use computers to compensate for disabilities such as cerebral palsy, brain damage, and visual impairment appear throughout. The book is illustrated with black-and-white photographs. In the last chapter, Cattoche writes about employment opportunities and independent living. A bibliography is next, followed by sections on how to buy equipment and lists of organizations, resources, manufacturers, and products; a glossary and an index complete the book.

Analysis: Though he writes in a rather dry and colorless style, Cattoche still makes it poignantly clear that computers can revolutionize the lives of disabled people. His explanations of technology are straightforward and accessible, and the book is informative for able-bodied and disabled readers alike. Of course computer programs and possibilities are always changing, so some of the information may be out-of-date. Nevertheless, the book can be a valuable source of background material as well as of encouragement.

■ Colen, B. D. *Hard Choices: Mixed Blessings of Modern Medical Technology.* Putnam, 1986. 272pp. (0-399-13139-6) Reading Level: Grades 10–12. (BL 1 Je86; NYTBR 7 S86)
Disability: Various disabilities

The author, who is the science editor of *Newsday,* discusses the ethical issues surrounding the uses of modern medical technology to begin, extend, or save human life. As such, this is an excellent introduction to the complex field of bioethics. Colen, who already has extensive bioethical writing to his credit, interviewed large numbers of medical and legal professionals in the course of writing this book. He also interviewed persons involved as patients or as the family of patients. These interviews are the meat of the book. Many are reported in great depth and illustrate vividly the myriad of complex issues that surround decisions such as whether to save the life of a profoundly retarded and physically disabled infant during a medical emergency or whether to withdraw an irrevocably brain-damaged patient from the respirator that is keeping her or him alive.

Seven sections deal with various medical situations in which bioethics plays a major role. The first one discusses genetic disorders and the dilemmas surrounding them, as illustrated by the story of a baby born with Tay-Sachs disease, his subsequent death, and his parents' continued efforts to have other children. The second section, also illustrated by a detailed case history, deals with attempts to become pregnant, while the third tells the story of fetal surgeries performed on two babies, Michael and Nicholas, and discusses the pros and cons of such treatment.

The subsequent two sections describe the birth and treatment of high-risk infants and the dilemmas surrounding medical care and treatment of multiply disabled infants who have no chance of ever becoming even minimally functional. The final two sections are about organ transplants and "the end of life" in situations in which patients are kept alive, often for years, on a respirator without any hope of ever regaining consciousness. Each section has at least one detailed case history; often there are several.

Analysis: In the foreword, Dr. John W. Scanlon of Georgetown University School of Medicine states that modern medical technology is the "social equivalent of a perfect weapon"; it maims rather than kills, "requires more personnel, more services and more resources than a merely lethal one," and demoralizes others and robs them of their will to fight (p. 9).

The book presents as many questions as it does answers. It is a sharp, to-the-point, realistic treatment of bioethical issues and an excellent introduction to them for mature teenage readers. Highly recommended for its readability, clarity, and the author's sense of humanity.

■ Coulehan, Jack. *The Knitted Glove.* Nightshade, 1991. 36pp. (1-879205-07-6) Reading Level: Grades 10–12.
Disability: Various disabilities

Jack Coulehan, a poet-physician, is also an epidemiologist and medical ethicist, who after many years of teaching at the University of Pittsburgh School of Medicine, recently joined the faculty of the State University of New York at Stony Brook.

Coulehan has published extensively in the medical field, and about five years ago, with the encouragement of a patient who is a poet, he began to write poetry. Since then his poetry has been published in magazines such as the *Kansas Quarterly, Prairie Schooner, Negative Capability, South Coast Poetry Journal,* and *Journal of the American Medical Association.* One of the poems in *The Knitted Glove,* "Anniversary," was nominated for a Pushcart Prize.

Analysis: This is a chapbook, published by a small press and containing poems by a sensitive, caring poet-physician. The content of the poems deals with the things of a physician's life—patients, pain, illness, and hospitals—but the poet describes these with beautiful, well-chosen, vivid words that are crafted into precise, often profound thoughts.

■ Drimmer, Frederick. *Born Different: The Amazing Stories of Some Very Special People.* Illus. Atheneum, 1988. 182pp. (0-689-31360-8) Reading Level: Grades 7–12. (BL 15 S88; KR 1 J188; WLB Je89) *Disability:* Various disabilities

Frederick Drimmer is the author of *Very Special People: The Struggles, Loves, and Triumphs of Human Oddities* (see *Accept Me as I Am,* 1985) and *The Elephant Man.* Here, for a younger audience, he writes short biographies of the dwarf Tom Thumb, Robert Wadlow (called the tallest man in the world), Julia Pastrana (billed as the Apewoman because of an appearance caused by deformities), the so-called Siamese twins Eng and Chang, the "elephant man" (Joseph Merrick), and Hermann Unthan, born without arms. In each case, the person being described rose above birth defects, and most were able to support themselves by using their exceptional conditions. The book is illustrated with black-and-white photographs and drawings and concludes with a selected bibliography and an index.

Analysis: Drimmer's descriptions of the deformities of his subjects are explicit and detailed, his approach compassionate without being sentimental or pitying (although the reader might wonder why he refers to Tom Thumb so repeatedly as "the little man"). In addition to recounting the events of these lives, Drimmer gives information on the nature and possible causes of the physiological abnormalities. With Robert Wadlow, for example, born in Alton, Illinois, in 1918, there is no mystery about the reason for his condition; he had overactive pituitary glands, probably caused by a tumor and not treatable by surgery at the time when he was growing up. On the other hand, the writer can only speculate about the possible causes of Julia Pastrana's multiple abnormalities.

Very Special People is not for the squeamish, because some of the conditions described might be repellent to readers, at least initially. But Drimmer's emphasis on the integrity and worth of the person living inside a strikingly different, even grotesque, body carries an important message. Adolescence is often a time of self-absorption, of concentration on appearance, and of fear of being different; to read about these special people might provide a salutary change of viewpoint for youngsters at this time.

■ Forbes, Malcolm, and Jeff Block. *Women Who Made a Difference.* Simon & Schuster, 1990. 320pp. (0-671-69552-5) Reading Level: Grades 7–12. (LJ 15 O90) *Disability:* Blindness; Birth defects; Deaf-blind; Infectious disease

Forbes, editor in chief of *Forbes* magazine, was working on this, his ninth book, at the time of his death. It consists of 100 vignettes of approximately three pages each about somewhat forgotten women who have made significant contributions in the areas of politics, science, public policy, the arts, and so on. Among these women were a few who were impaired, disabled, or worked in areas impinging on health and rehabilitation.

In the chapter about Laura Bridgeman, the legacy of this girl to deaf-blind Helen Keller, who lived 50 years later, is underscored. Bridgeman lost her senses of hearing, vision, and smell at the age of 2 as a result of scarlet fever. When she was 7, Samuel Gridley Howe accepted her into the Perkins Institute, a Boston school for the blind. There she learned reading, writing, and needlework, and she became an international phenomenon. Another chapter cites Dorothy Eustis as the woman who fought the rehabilitation establishment in order to bring guide dogs for use by blind people in the United States. Eustis eventually established the Seeing Eye School that still trains dogs today in Morristown, New Jersey.

Author Lady Mary Wortley Montagu is described as a survivor of smallpox, which left her face scarred and "deprived of her very fine eyelashes." (p. 313). When her husband was appointed ambassador to Turkey, she saw there the inoculation procedure that gave a patient a mild case of the disease and immunity from it thereafter. She had her two children inoculated. Some others in England followed suit, thereby surviving the smallpox epidemic of 1721. Despite some strong opposition, the inoculation gained general acceptance in England until Jenner developed the safer vaccine in 1796.

In 1952, Dr. Virginia Apgar developed the Apgar scale that has been used to evaluate tens of thousands of newborn babies. Later, Apgar became director of birth defects research for the March of Dimes. Dr. Frances Kelsey is noted as the Food and Drug Administration official who blocked the introduction of the tranquilizer thalidomide into the United States. Worldwide, an estimated 10,000 babies suffered birth defects related to this drug, but only nine such cases were reported here.

Clara Maas was an army nurse who died at age 25, in 1901, after volunteering to undergo immunity experiments in which she was infected with yellow fever. A commemorative stamp was issued for her in 1976. Mary Mallon, known as Typhoid Mary but immune herself, was instrumental in spreading the dread disease to many families for whom she cooked. She was found to be a "human culture tube" (p. 186).

Analysis: It is gratifying to see the inclusion of women with disabilities and contributors to related fields among the notables in the book. The accounts are sometimes a little glib and are not always strictly accurate. A case in point is Laura Bridgeman, who was not the first deaf-blind person ever to be brought out of a "dark, silent shell" (p. 46), although she may indeed have been the first one in the United States. There are some annoying errors. For example, while the table of contents is arranged alphabetically by last name, Lady Mary Wortley Montagu is listed under "W" rather than "M."

Nonetheless, the book gives a quick reference to some very interesting women who might have been better known except for their gender. At least some of the brief tales should whet readers' appetite for further reading.

■ Fradin, Dennis Brindell. *Remarkable Children: Twenty Who Made History.* Little, Brown, 1987. 207pp. (0-316-29126-9) Reading Level: Grades 4–9. (BL D87; SLJ D87)
Disability: Various disabilities

Among the 20 remarkable children of whom Fradin writes short biographies are two world-famous people whose natural gifts worked with their disabilities to make outstanding achievements possible. Louis Braille lost his sight through an accident with his father's awl when he was 3 years old and invented the Braille system of reading with raised dots when he was 15. Although those in positions of authority and power remained resistant to the system during Braille's lifetime, it has since become widely accepted. An illness at 19 months left Helen Keller deaf and blind; the story of her education, her teacher Anne Sullivan Macy, and the many contributions of her long life has been told repeatedly, but it retains its fascination.

Analysis: Fradin concentrates on the childhood of his 20 remarkable subjects, writing with clarity and economy, so that he is able to present much information in relatively little space. Readers who want more detail might be referred to longer biographies. See, for example, the annotations on books on both disabilities to be found in *Accept Me as I Am* (1985).

■ Hellerstein, David. *Battles of Life and Death: The Discoveries of a Young Doctor During His Medical Education.* Houghton, 1986. 264pp. (0-395-40459-2) Reading Level: Grades 10–12. (BL 15 Mr86; KR 1 Mr86; NYTBR 23 Mr86)
Disability: Emotional disturbance; Health problems

The author is a psychiatrist and a writer whose work has been published in many national magazines. He opens his book with a description of the oncology unit, the "Glitter Palace," of a California hospital, where he was assigned as a fourth-year medical student. He came to realize that much of the illness he was seeing was a trade-off for other diseases that doctors had treated. For instance, a young Vietnamese mother died from leukemia brought on by the cure for her Hodgkin's disease. In turn, Hellerstein rotates through pediatrics, a charity hospital, and gynecology.

On a transplant and renal unit, Hellerstein encountered children that he termed the "gray ones." The struggle to convince a family to approve a postmortem on a loved one reminded him of tales of the efforts to recover the corpses of young warriors in the Trojan Wars.

After graduation from Stanford Medical School, Hellerstein elected psychiatry for his residency. At one point he served on a burn unit, where every patient suffered excruciating physical and psychological pain, and each had a compulsive need to discuss the horrible experience. Later, in New York, he does a stint at "an inpatient unit at the best mad house in the city" (p. 232).

Hellerstein relates many childhood memories to the events of the present day. He is a fourth-generation physician in his family. By the end of the book, he has reached a bemused but mature perspective on his father, a researcher in cardiology, who had been so influential in his life and in his choice of career.

Analysis: The reader is enticed into a medical world that is at the same time fascinating, horrifying, and madcap. All of the patients described, even the dirty, homeless, or drug dazed, come across as people worthy of the interest and compassion that their modest young doctor bestows on each of them. Many of their stories lack resolution. This is appropriate, since those who survive are in an ambiguous state—helped but not necessarily cured in the hospitals that held them awhile.

The prose is incisive and fast moving. The book is one of the best of its kind.

■ Klass, Perri. *A Not Entirely Benign Procedure: Four Years as a Medical Student.* Putnam, 1987. 256pp. (0-399-13223-6) Reading Level: Grades 7–12. (LJ 1 My87; NYTBR 10 My87)
Disability: AIDS; Hemophilia; Muscular dystrophy

Klass, in her 20s, was already a published writer when she was accepted into Harvard Medical School. During the following four years, she wrote a column for the *New York Times* and also had pieces in other magazines concerning her experiences. These were collected to compose her book.

Nearly halfway through her medical training, Klass decided her school years were the best time to have a baby. While she has stuck with that opinion, she writes of her pregnancy, "as I moved around the medical school I was beginning to feel like a lone hippopotamus in a gaggle of geese" (p. 47). At times, Klass's perceptions and needs were apt to be at odds with standard medical wisdom, but she felt enriched and enlightened in her dual role as professional and patient.

She details many of the hassles and personal fears that she encounters in her preclinical and clinical years. "For the medical student, life is full of opportunities to show your ignorance," she expostulates. One entire section is devoted to the thorny medical issues every doctor must confront.

Klass does a clinical stint in India, where parents' realistic expectations about the survival and health of their sick children were so different from those at home. There, she was accompanied by her husband and little child. Later she encounters an adult patient with AIDS, followed by a hemophiliac boy at high risk for the disease. She describes a boy dying of muscular dystrophy, who is nonetheless full of smart-alecky, sick jokes.

The book ends at the end of medical school, when Klass is "almost but not quite a doctor." The book flap informs us that she is currently an intern in pediatrics.

Analysis: As Klass announces in the acknowledgments, she has a "warped sense of humor," which is delightful, but that in no way overshadows the basic sensitivity and honesty that pervade the essays. While she writes very consciously from the perspective of a woman medical student, her well-stated hopes and fears about preparation for and transition to the adult working world have a universal ring and should appeal to many young people. She illuminates the difficult issues and the sometimes unpleasant realities that the maturing person encounters. She is witty rather than pedantic and writes in a direct, interesting style.

■ Kosof, Anna. *Why Me? Coping with Family Illness.* Franklin Watts, 1986. 95pp. (0-531-10254-8) Reading Level: Grades 7–12. (BR Ja87; CBRS Ja87; SLJ D86)
Disability: Cancer; Spina bifida; Heart disease

Psychiatrist H. Paul Gabriel explains in the book's foreword that he has been practicing medicine 30 years, during which time the rate of survival of children with serious illness has continued to climb. As a consequence, the quality of their lives has become increasingly the concern of health care professionals.

The author focuses on families confronted with chronic, serious diseases, stressing how they cope with the symptoms, treatment, and convalescence. A number of survivors are introduced and discussed in the course of the eight chapters. There is a young woman severely disabled by spina bifida, who has undergone scores of operations, who is yet very happy to be alive. From the viewpoint of a teenage daughter, a mother's bout with breast cancer and chemotherapy is described. Next is the account of an 8-year-old boy who was paralyzed in a freak auto accident. In this case, family life was so disrupted that the boy's parents eventually separated. Another boy has leukemia. A father battles heart disease.

Kosof, who spent many days in a children's cancer unit to prepare for this book, reiterates that cancer is the second leading cause of death among children under 16 (accidents are first). She discusses the close relationship of medical people and the patients' families. She ends with some advice on how to approach sufferers, in view of their feelings and their problems.

Analysis: This book strives to emphasize the positive, but it frequently focuses on the dark side of chronic illness: the realities of suffering, shame, loss, and tremendous cost in terms of money and energy. Kosof's pessimism shows in her choice as a subject a plucky but atypically impaired girl with spina bifida. Terms such as "victim," "devastating," "shunned," and "terrible experience" abound. The writing is straightforward and unsentimental. The author confronts the worst with some hope and a deep respect for the survivors in her story.

■ Krementz, Jill. *How It Feels to Fight for Your Life.* Illus. by Jill Krementz. Little, Brown, 1989. 132pp. (0-316-50364-9) Reading Level: Grades 4–9. (KR 15 O89; NYTBR 12 N89; PW Z5 Ag89; SLJ O89)
Disability: Various disabilities

Jill Krementz is a well-known writer of more than 20 books, nearly all written for children, including three others in the How It Feels series. Here, she presents 14 youngsters, ages 7 to 16, who are battling a range of serious and often life-threatening conditions. The children tell their stories in their own voices, describing their disease or injuries and the treatments they receive. They discuss their feelings about illness and health, future plans, friendships, family, sports, hospitals, and medical personnel. Some mention the comfort they derive from their belief in God. Their conditions include spina bifida, leukemia, osteogenic sarcoma, asthma, epilepsy, kidney disease, and cystic fibrosis. One boy was severely burned in a laboratory accident; another was shot in the spine. Some of the families are working class, others middle class. The children are pictured in black-and-white photographs taken by Krementz.

In the final section, the acknowledgments, the author thanks the many people who helped her with this book, including medical personnel at hospitals in New York, Washington, Philadelphia, St. Paul, and Boston. She also describes sources of help for sick children and their families that she discovered in the course of writing the book—for example, the outstanding library at the Children's Hospital National Medical Center in Washington, the Medical Illness Counseling Center and the Association for the Care of Children's Health, also in Washington, and the Federation for Children with Special Needs in Boston.

Analysis: How It Feels to Fight for Your Life received an eloquent and positive review in the Sunday *New York Times* of November 12, 1989. The reviewer, Edwin J. Kenney, Jr., praised Krementz, among other things, for offering a healthy corrective to some current popular writing that says that one can cure oneself of serious illness or injury by fostering a strong, positive attitude, thus implying (or stating) that failure to recover is somehow the fault of the individual. Kenney calls this "reductive and moralistic thinking [that] reveals itself as what it truly is—miserably inappropriate and cruel—when one considers children with spina bifida, defective hearts," and the other disabilities presented in this book. He goes on to discuss the children's realistic courage and hope and the absence of "denial or magical thinking." Some weeks later, a letter to the same paper takes issue with Kenney and with Krementz, saying that the book "is part of a trend that is itself inappropriate and cruel—the trend of using selected sick people as models to 'inspire and instruct' other sick people to follow the straight and narrow path of adjustment, acceptance and insistence that illness affords opportunities for personal growth and a deeper appreciation of life."

These *are* special children; Krementz describes them in this way in her introduction, and both here and in her acknowledgments she pays tribute to the grace and courage of the youngsters and their families, and she hopes that their stories will encourage others. Nevertheless, it must be true that articulate, thoughtful, active children like these will grow and change through their life-altering experiences, which do not "afford opportunities" like a mind-broadening tour but which certainly shape development. Neither these children nor their situations are ordinary. The voices speaking here do not deny fear, anger, and intense pain; they admit envy of healthy people; they wish that their situations were different. The teenagers recognize in themselves the drive to become more independent, warring against the often unavoidable dependence caused by their conditions. But the children seem to have moved beyond self-pity and wishful thinking; if they once asked, "Why me?" they seem no longer to do so. They concentrate their energies on the struggle to deal with treatment, to improve, and, sometimes, to face inevitable decline. Some describe the differences that their conditions have caused in their friendships, and they emphasize that they are the same people they were before illness or accident struck. Although some say that they wish one parent (usually the father) were more involved in the illness, all express appreciation for the support given them by the love of their family and sometimes indicate that they could not have made it without such devotion. They know, too, that their conditions cause their family great pain as well.

The audience for Krementz's book is certainly not limited to ill or injured young people and their families, although such readers would find both the personal accounts and the mention of specific medical facilities, personnel, and agencies helpful. Classroom teachers and librarians might use it in a variety of ways, not only as a resource to explain certain disabilities but also possibly as the starting point for the issues raised by the review and letter quoted above as well as a discussion about attitudes toward illness at the present time and in past eras. The book is physically attractive, with clear type and large photographs.

■ Krementz, Jill. *How It Feels When a Parent Dies.* Knopf, 1988. 128pp. (paper 0-394-75854-4) Reading Level: Grades 4–9. (BR N88; PW 18 Mr88)
Disability: Physical disabilities; Neurological problems

Taped monologues of 18 children compose the chapters of the book. In addition, full-page black-and-white photographs display the subjects individually and in family scenes. Each child reminisces about the circumstances of his or her parent's death, which range from accidents and illnesses to suicide. Various religious rites and customs associated with burial are mentioned by some of the narrators. They describe their family's life after the death. Some report the remarriage of the surviving spouse and how they have learned to cope with the new family constellation.

The children speak introspectively on their feelings of sadness, anger, and guilt. They have all come to terms with their loss and seem to have achieved wise acceptance of their present situation. One 13-year-old girl philosophized, "You know, if I were dead and watching people, I'd much rather know that the people who loved me were happy with their memories of me than that they were moping around and always asking why I wasn't back on earth" (p. 21).

Analysis: These young people of various ages and races and different walks of life touch in wistful contemplation the deep emotions, thoughts, and conflicts that beset children who lose a parent. As the author stated in her foreword, these boys and girls have, indeed, shared bravely and generously their most private selves. Warm and expressive photographs beautifully enhance the essays.

■ Lee, Sally. *Donor Banks: Saving Lives with Organ and Tissue Transplants.* Illus. Franklin Watts, 1988. 95pp. (0-531-10475-3) Reading Level: Grades 5–9. (BCCB M88; BL 15 My88; BR S88; KR 15 Mr88; SLJ AP88)
Disability: Various disabilities

Lee opens her book with a vignette about a hospital where a number of patients are being treated. A young lawyer is receiving a cornea transplant to give her normal sight in one eye; a teenage boy will have cancerous bone in his arm replaced with transplanted bone; a little girl's severe burns are being covered with donated skin; a middle-aged man is having a heart transplant; and a teenager injured in an automobile accident is getting a blood transfusion. In the subsequent pages, the author presents information about how transplants work; chapters on banks for blood, eyes, organs, bone, and skin follow. Brief profiles of patients illustrate her points. The book concludes with a list of addresses and a glossary. There are black-and-white photographs.

Analysis: Transplant surgery has radically altered the prospects of many seriously ill and injured people, and the techniques, problems, and individual cases have received much media attention. Sally Lee deals with her complex subject in clear prose made more personal and immediate by the short case studies she includes. Although probably directed to middle school readers, the book would also be a good source for high school students.

■ Lesy, Michael. *Rescues: The Lives of Heroes.* Farrar, 1991. 213pp. (0-374-24947-4) Reading Level: Grades 10–12. (BL 15 N90; NYTBR 12 J91; PW 91 N90.)
Disability: Various disabilities

Lesy, author of seven other books and professor of literary journalism at Hampshire College, has written an anthology about heroism, in which he explores the reason that people risk their life for another. He examines the lives of nine ordinary people who have performed extraordinary deeds.

Two of the nine subjects have disabilities. In the first case, he interviews and describes Ed Roberts, who was left with quadriplegia after a case of polio that nearly killed him. Unable to breathe on his own ever since and unable to use either his arms or legs, he nevertheless went on to become independent. Furthermore, he became a leader in the disability rights movement at Berkeley, where he was a student in the late 60s and early 70s. Even before that, he and his parents had a major struggle to convince his town's high school to permit him to graduate in spite of the fact that he could not fulfill two of the requirements—physical education and driver's education. He also had to struggle to persuade the California State Department of Rehabilitation (of which he later became head) to send him to Berkeley once he finished junior college. Lesy interviewed Roberts extensively and describes him very realistically, not as a saint but as a stubborn, determined, rather egotistical man bent on a mission and able to beat any bureaucracy that exists.

The second case involving disabilities is called "A Mother and a Father." It is about Jane and Carl Smith, a fast-food counter worker and an auto factory worker, whose son, Keith, born in 1969, was autistic. Years of no diagnosis and misdiagnosis followed, and ultimately came the oft-repeated message, "Hopeless. Put him in an institution." The Smiths briefly tried this but soon decided they could do better. With no special training or education, and little money, Jane and Carl endured a myriad of problems but ultimately have succeeded in rearing Keith at home, aided by various people along the way, especially Deanna. They had worked their way through various schools and mental health facilities when a "psycho-ed. center" was opened in their area. Deanna, a special education teacher, gave the Smiths and Keith their six best years, until Keith developed bone cancer, which posed a temporary setback in his behavior as well as a threat to his life. At the time of the writing of the book, Keith's health had been stabilized.

Analysis: Lesy is an excellent writer, and his treatment of the Smiths' story is sensitive and caring. He is nearly overwhelmed by what these parents have done for their son. The other seven cases, while not about persons with disabilities, are equally engrossing. Lesy identifies with his subjects, all of whom he interviewed extensively. He is both empathic and sympathetic. He genuinely cares about and admires the various persons who are the subjects of these nine cases. Highly recommended.

■ Marion, Robert, M.D. *The Boy Who Felt No Pain.* Addison Wesley, 1990. 203pp. (0-201-55049-0) Reading Level: Grades 7–12. (BL 1 S90; KR 1 Ag90; LJ Ag90; PW 20 J190)
Disability: Various disabilities

Robert Marion is a pediatric geneticist. In this collection of essays, he writes about patients and their families whom he has known and treated over the years from the time he was a medical student. Jimmy, the child in the title piece, was brought into the hospital after he had had a convulsion. It turned out that this episode was caused by high fever and was not significant, but in the course of the examination, the doctors discovered that he had hereditary sensory neuropathy, inherited from his father, who had a much milder case. Jimmy felt absolutely no pain, no matter what was done to him, a condition that put him at serious risk since he could neither learn caution as the normal toddler does nor ever be alert to the warning signs of danger and illness.

Other illnesses and impairments Marion describes include a rare defect called incontinentia pigmenti, kidney transplant, Down's syndrome, pediatric AIDS, and spina bifida caused by fetal alcohol syndrome. In some cases, the parents were able to recover from their initial shock and sorrow and undertake loving care of their child; in others, as with Peter, a Down's syndrome baby, and Emilio, born to a mother with AIDS, the children were abandoned. Some stories have happy, even surprising, conclusions; others end with the death of the child patient.

Analysis: Marion writes with skill, a keen eye for detail, and compassion. He observes himself as well as his patients and is honest about his own reactions as doctor, friend, and parent. In one case, described in the chapter called "Galactosemia," he was cowed by his superiors into giving up his own diagnosis; he was still only a third-year medical student. It turned out that he had been right, but the knowledge came too late, and he ends the chapter: "It was from that moment of realization that I learned to trust my own instincts, and to not be intimidated by what others who are older and possibly wiser than me might believe. And whenever I'm attending on one of the pediatric wards, I make sure to tell the interns, residents, and medical students about Cassandra, and to teach them the lesson I learned from her. By telling and retelling her story, I like to think I'm helping to ensure that what happened to Cassandra never happens to another child."

This book might be of particular interest to middle and high school readers who are thinking of a career in medicine.

■ Martin, Russell. *Matters Gray and White: A Neurologist, His Patients, and the Mysteries of the Brain.* Henry Holt, 1986. 305pp. (0-8050-0087-9) Reading Level: Grades 10–12. (BL 15 O86; NYTBR 26 Ap87; PW 21 N86)
Disability: Neurological problems

Martin, a journalist, and Ferrier (a pseudonym), a clinical neurologist, had been teenage camp counselors the year of the moon walk. Ferrier, now in medical practice for ten years, agreed to permit his old friend literally to follow him around, during the course of a year, in order to observe his work with patients who are treated on the frontier of brain science. Descriptions of the various cases are woven in and out throughout the story as they come to Ferrier's office or to the hospital in the Rocky Mountain college town that is the setting of his practice. In addition, information is interspersed about neurological dysfunction and its treatment.

The first disease discussed, "An Agent from Cold Climates (Ch. 1)," is multiple sclerosis, the most common neurological problem to strike people between ages 20 and 30. Chapter 2, "Fire at Brief Moments," deals with epilepsies of children and adults. The treatments of a 4-year-old, a college coed, and a pregnant woman are described. Subsequent chapters detail the doctor's interactions with people suffering from various movement and communication disorders, pain problems, amyotrophic lateral sclerosis, and diseases of old age. Ferrier becomes a consultant when cancer or AIDS involves the brain.

An epilogue updates the progress of Ferrier's patients at the close of the year of observations. Martin philosophizes about his wholly likable friend and the art of medicine that is his passion. An index closes the book.

Analysis: Martin brings to life each of the many case histories in his story. He captures on paper the frenetic pace of a busy medical practice. His descriptions of the weather and the land are graphic. The information about brain science is presented clearly and unobtrusively. Throughout, he includes his own sensitive thoughts and reactions as an objective observer of the life and death dramas he is privileged to witness.

■ Matthews, Gwyneth Ferguson. *Voices from the Shadows: Women with Disabilities Speak Out.* Women's Pr., 1983. 192pp. (Paper 0-88961 080-0) Reading Level: Grades 8–12. (IBCB V 16 85) *Disability:* Paraplegia; Encephalitis

In 1964, the author was 16 and enrolled in a convent school in the province of Nova Scotia in Canada. During exams before the Christmas holiday, she became deathly sick from encephalitis. The disease finally subsided, but she learned that she must live the rest of her life in a wheelchair. The setbacks and challenges she has met in subsequent years motivated her to write this book, which combines autobiographical material as well as contributions from 45 disabled women whom she interviewed.

After her hospitalization, Matthews was sent to a rehabilitation center, where she began to experience the stages of shock, denial, anger, and acceptance that are typical reactions to catastrophic loss. Although it was foremost in her mind, the subject of sexuality was taboo among the rehabilitation personnel. At that time, even the professional literature concerning sex and disability focused almost exclusively on males. She was driven to sneaking around in a "rehab romance" in order to clumsily experiment with a partner to discover what options were still open to her. Although many sexual hurdles faced her, she and a college classmate married when she was 20.

Some of the women and girls who were interviewed had been disabled since birth; others became impaired by disease or accident. In all, they had 18 different crippling conditions. The author found some of her subjects living in nursing homes (these ranged from the hideous to the acceptable). Half of the interviewees had never experienced a sexual relationship. Only five had a husband, and some who had been married had been deserted by spouses after they became ill. Some of the women were single parents who were beset with crushing financial problems. Matthews points out that for many of the women, warmth and understanding were more important goals than physical relationships. However, all intimate relationships seem to be more elusive for disabled females than for their male counterparts.

The author describes her own three unsuccessful pregnancies and discusses the other women's views about opting for children and about the issue of aborting an imperfect fetus. Opinions ranged from positive to negative on these issues.

Hence, disabled women are represented as doubly handicapped: both by their disability and by their sex. In the preface, it is observed that nondisabled lesbian feminists have been known to be more sensitive than heterosexual feminists in responding to the needs of disabled women. Among the women interviewed, the overriding problem was loneliness.

A chapter is devoted both to the language that is commonly used to describe disabled people and to preferences in usage, of which everyone should become aware. Problems of accessibility, employability, and government red tape are elaborated. An extensive bibliography closes the book.

Analysis: Matthews accomplishes her goal of advocacy for disabled women and does so with humor and zest as well as seriousness. Some particulars are unique for Canadian citizens, but the shortcomings of social systems and the insensitivities of able-bodied people, even in the helping professions, appear all too similar to those in the United States. The feminist perspective and honest talk about sexuality are refreshing.

■ Meyer, Donald J., Patricia F. Vadsay, and Rebecca R. Fewell. *Living with a Brother or Sister with Special Needs: A Book for Sibs.* Univ. of Washington Pr., 1985. 110pp. (0-295-96287-9) Reading Level: Grades 4–9. (ASBYP N87; CP O86)
Disability: Various disabilities

In an introduction to the book, the authors pinpoint the main areas of need, gleaned from workshops with siblings of disabled children: the need for simple, clear explanations about the causes and the nature of handicaps (since information was frequently fragmentary or wrong) and the need for reassurance and support for their feelings about their sibling with special needs. Further, these brothers and sisters profited from sharing insights on how to solve the common problems they faced with their handicapped sibling, their parents, and their friends.

Chapter 1 explores different feelings that sibs might have toward their exceptional brother or sister, and each is illustrated by one or several small vignettes. Feelings range from anger and guilt to tolerance and special pride. Suggestions are offered on how to resolve problems that come up. For example, readers are advised to express negative feelings with "I" statements such as "I am very angry that you scribbled on my report," rather than commands or judgments such as "Don't you ever touch my homework again, pea brain."

The subsequent five chapters give simple explanations about various kinds of handicapping conditions, including mental retardation, sensory and behavior problems, and congenital problems. Causes of defects are given. Amniocentesis is explained briefly. More than one page is given to the relationship of child abuse to handicapping conditions.

Chapter 7 is entitled "Education and Services for Children with Handicaps and Their Families." Public Law 94-142 is explained. Physical and occupational therapy, infant intervention, and respite care are discussed. Chapter 8 deals with possible living arrangements and job possibilities for disabled people. References are given to help locate a genetic clinic, should the sib be worried about transmitting a defect.

An appendix lists for young readers a few books about handicaps, and there is a list of resources.

Analysis: A book on the elementary reading level that emphasizes problems of normal siblings of handicapped children is a welcome addition to the literature. The authors, who have run numerous sibling groups, write in an informal direct manner to get to the heart of the many conflicting feelings that arise among those who live with disability. They should be commended for tackling several important issues that are often overlooked even in professional literature. One is the subject of child abuse and neglect as causes of disability; a second is amniocentesis and its ramifications, about which the authors remain morally neutral.

In several respects, the book is not as inclusive or direct, and therefore not as responsive, about some children's situations. There seems to be a tacit assumption that the sibling reader has an intact family. Such an assumption should not be made about able-bodied children in American society, and even less so when there is a handicapped child involved. (Indeed, the stress of having a handicapped child may push a couple over the edge to marital breakup, engendering agonizing feelings for all family members.) The second topic, somewhat superficially discussed, is the probable death or shortened life span of some handicapped brothers or sisters, with which siblings must come to terms. However, the authors frequently suggest that siblings go for help to persons and organizations that might help them with both of these difficult situations.

■ Park, Leslie D. *How to Be a Friend to the Handicapped: A Handbook and Guide.* Vantage, 1986. 147pp. (0-317-44671-1) Reading Level: Grades 10–12.
Disability: Cerebral palsy; Paraplegia; Severe disabilities

This book provides concrete information and ideas to facilitate the quality of interaction between handicapped and nonhandicapped people. Some of the advice is directed toward the latter group, as the title suggests, but some is most appropriate for those who are disabled as well, such as the section on personal hygiene and grooming. Some suggestions are particularly relevant for caretakers. Park is a rehabilitation professional with more than 30 years of work with disabled people. He draws numerous illustrative examples from his experiences. He speaks of children, adults, and the elderly who have severe or mild physical or mental disabilities and discusses their role in the workplace, the home, and the community.

Among the tips and ideas about improving social relationships is a section dealing with the kinds of gifts that might be most appreciated by a handicapped friend. Park gives his own solution to the problem of handicapped beggars. He gives. And he offers guidelines for buying products from companies serving the disabled. Serious safety concerns are addressed throughout the book. Specific rules are suggested for special situations; for example, what provisions should be made if a disabled person is a smoker. Helpful technical aids and devices, from a hot water regulator on a spigot to a mouth-switch-operated word processor, are covered.

Analysis: This lively book reflects a spirit of caring and generosity. Park refers to his work as a reference book that one would turn to if needing specific advice, for example, about how to push a person in a wheelchair. However, it reads quickly and is interesting overall for its enthusiastic approach and a number of fresh ideas. The advice offered is not in the least patronizing or moralistic.

The illustrative examples serve to remind readers that it is people, first of all, who should be kept in mind, not a generic, "the handicapped," as the titled unfortunately suggests. There is a gentle use of humor in the instruction on proper and improper conduct in relationships.

In an uncharacteristic lapse, Park advocates a tickling spree with young cerebral palsied children, to the point where they laugh hysterically. However, this is not good advice.

In sum, this is a most imaginative, yet practical guide for people confronted with disability.

■ Pekkanen, John. *Donor: How One Girl's Death Gave Life to Others.* Little, Brown, 1984. 214pp. (0-316-69792-3) Reading Level: Grades 7–12. (SLJ S86)
Disability: Organ transplants; Kidney failure; Visual impairment

The story commences with the evening on which 17-year-old Lisa Kelly was run over as she crossed the highway on her way to the shopping mall.

The circumstances of her happy life form a prelude to the hospital scene where she is declared brain dead and where her loving family are helped to decide to donate her still healthy organs for transplant.

Subsequent chapters describe the disparate histories and lives of the recipients of the deceased girl's organs. The youngest was 3 years old when he was given a lifesaving kidney only 48 hectic hours after Lisa's death. Little Matthew had already endured seven major operations in his short life. The eldest patient, who was 68, regained partial sight as a result of receiving one of Lisa's corneas.

The fates of the recipients are all the more favorable because of these medical procedures, although they had to struggle with organ rejection and other difficult problems. Lisa's family eventually met with the flourishing young Matthew and his ever grateful parents to see what their gift of life had meant for others.

One of the medical heroes of the book is Jo, the nurse who first approached the grieving family about the possibility of organ donation. Time is always of the essence; live organs have a short life and must often be transported long distances to compatible donors; the would-be recipients are deteriorating physically, yet must often wait months or years for the parts they need. Jo interpreted organ donation as a healing process whereby relatives can be reconciled to the otherwise senseless death of a loved one. Jo has advocated far and wide in speeches to lay and medical groups.

Analysis: The author has humanized the emerging field of organ harvest and transplant by including in each instance the case histories, thoughts, and feelings of all the players in the medical drama. Whereas the subtitle of the book might suggest simplistic success, the vignettes within illustrate the countless vicissitudes encountered by transplant patients. Along the way the reader acquires much pertinent information.

■ Perske, Robert. *Circles of Friends: People with Disabilities and Their Friends Enrich the Lives of One Another.* Illus. by Martha Perske. Abingdon, 1988. 94pp. (0-687-08390-7) Reading Level: Grades 4–12. *Disability:* Various disabilities

Judith Snow, one of the persons whose story is told in this book, is a university-educated Canadian woman born with muscular dystrophy, which caused her to have quadriplegia. She suddenly found herself ineligible for the personal care assistance that she needed to survive outside an institution. Just before she was to lead a workshop on understanding people with disabilities, she collapsed, exhausted by her efforts to cope with everyday life alone. Five friends "circled around" and gave her both personal assistance and assistance with moving the bureaucracy to help her. The group became known as the Joshua Committee, because the members made walls tumble down. Again, this theme is a common thread through so many books about people with disabilities—the rigidity, coldness, and even cruelty that the medical and human services establishments exhibit toward people who are seriously ill or disabled.

Analysis: Consisting of true stories about people with disabilities and about nondisabled persons who have become their friends, this collection is highly recommended for a wide variety of readers all the way from fourth grade through high school. The stories are chatty and highly personalized. Excellent black-and-white illustrations and an attractive page format make the book appealing. Some of the stories are about children; others, about adults. All are readable, and all emphasize the integration of persons with disabilities into everyday social, educational, and working life through close personal relationships with nondisabled persons or, as the title states, circles of friends such as those described in the story from which the title is taken, "Friends Circle to Save a Life."

■ Richter, Elizabeth. *Losing Someone You Love: When a Brother or Sister Dies.* Illus. by Elizabeth Richter. Putnam, 1986. 80pp. (0-399-21243-4) Reading Level: Grades 4–12. (BL 15 Ap86; KR 1 Mr86; SLJ Ag86) *Disability:* Emotional disturbance

In a brief foreword, Richter affirms the need for boys and girls to work through their feelings when their sibling dies. She expresses the hope that the results of her interviews that compose the book will be of help to those children and their parents who must go through "this lonely crisis" (p. 11).

There are 15 chapters, each a first-person account by a sibling who has lost a brother or sister. The narrators range in age from 10 to 24 and represent a number of religions and races. The youngest sibling to die had sudden infant death syndrome; the two eldest were 19 and died from Cooley's anemia and a car crash, respectively.

Each respondent discusses the circumstances surrounding the death and his or her feelings about the tragedy, such as sadness, fear, or anger. Some felt guilt about being the survivor. They reminisce about happy times with their absent sibling and about occasional regrets. Each ends with reflections on how they have been able to resolve their grief and to get on with their life. Some of them talk of individuals and circumstances that were particularly helpful to them in the crisis.

Full-page black-and-white photographs, either portraits or family shots, portray all but one of the participants in the project. The acknowledgments mention Compassionate Friends, a national organization of bereaved parents.

Analysis: The language in this book sounds like a transcription of kids'

speech rather than like a prepared text. The stories are told simply and in a low-key manner, but the facts are wrenching. The young people express profound insights and wisdom, naturally and with candor. Adults, as well as children, might learn from this book. The author's illustrations capture the warmth and sensitivity of her informants and their families.

■ Sacks, Oliver. *The Man Who Mistook His Wife for a Hat and Other Clinical Tales.* Summit, 1985. 223pp. (0-671-55471-9) Reading Level: Grades 10–12. (EJ S87; NYTBR 1 Ap90; YR W88)
Disability: Brain tumors; Mental retardation; Tourette's syndrome

Sacks is a neurologist, who had published 8 of the 24 chapters in this book in various popular or professional sources, beginning in 1970. In these, he has revived the nineteenth-century tradition of clinical tales in order to describe lives that have been cut across and transformed by neurological disorder. Rather than espouse the present trend of impersonal neurological science, he emphasizes the relationship of pathological processes to the unique biographies of his various patients.

Part 1, "Losses," begins with the story of an elderly musician, which gives the book its title. Dr. P., who had a growing brain tumor that would eventually take his life, had lost the ability to recognize faces and people. Furthermore, he did not "know" that he had lost this ability. He not only tried to put on his wife's head, but he patted parking meters, evidently taking them for children. His considerable gifts as a musician, teacher, and scholar remained intact, so he was able to live to the end as an eccentric tragicomic character.

Part 2, "Excesses," begins with the story of Witty Ticcy Ray, a young man who had had Tourette's syndrome of violent, multiple tics since he was 4. The reactions of intelligent and desperate Ray to his infirmity had shaped his life through school, college, and marriage. His self-diagnosis led to a referral to Sacks, who promised possible control of his symptoms, but by a treatment that would also subdue the inspired energy and frivolity associated with "Touretters." Ray's struggle for a good life and an ultimate resolution of his dilemma transcended his sickness and liberated his spirit. In Part 3, "Transports," unusual subjective experiences of the reminiscence, memory, and sensual impressions of young and old people are described. These are related to, but not completely determined by, various epilepsies or mind-altering drugs.

The Part 4 title of the book, "The World of the Simple," refers to the world of the retarded, which the author typifies by the word "concreteness"—"neither complicated, diluted, or unified by abstraction" (p. 164). Sacks recounts tales about retarded people who nevertheless have some amazing capabilities in areas such as memory, computation, and drawing.

The author had discussed earlier the normal five senses that constitute the sensate world for most of us. "But there are other senses—secret senses, sixth senses, if you will—equally vital, but unrecognized and unlauded" (p. 68). The "simple" people in the tales have learning abilities and problems in still scientifically mysterious areas.

Sacks concludes his book with the words of a Japanese teacher known for remarkable success in helping autistic children become professionally accomplished artists: "The secret in developing Yanamura's talent was to share his spirit. The teacher should love the beautiful, honest retarded person, and live with a purified, retarded world" (p. 223).

Analysis: The fact that the author is a neurologist lends credence to his descriptions of the strange and amazing predicaments of the heroes and heroines of his tales. He is also a practiced writer, although his charming style might seem a bit old-fashioned. A young reader might grow impatient with the extensive footnotes and bibliographic notes (like those used by Freud and other analysts whose clinical tales the author admires).

What makes this book outstanding is its humanistic and artful approach to the human beings who have both helped Sacks achieve new insights into the working of the human psyche and mystified and delighted him. He is reverent in his faith in the potential of every human being and adamant that people must be allowed to use their abilities in order to develop or even maintain them. His point of view is beautifully summarized in a discussion of the struggle of one young man with Tourette's syndrome to overcome the extraordinary barriers to individualization and actualization. He writes, "For the powers of survival, of the will to survive, and to survive as a unique inalienable individual are, absolutely, the strongest in our being: stronger than any impulses, stronger than disease. Health, health militant, is usually the victor" (pp. 119–20).

■ Saxton, Marsha, and Florence Howe, eds. *With Wings: An Anthology of Literature By and About Women with Disabilities.* Feminist Pr., 1987. 167pp. (0-935312-61-7) Reading Level: Grades 10–12. (BL 15 Je87; WRB J187)
Disability: Various disabilities

With Wings is one of several anthologies dealing with the experience of being both disabled and a woman. It includes essays by several prominent authors, such as Alice Walker, who confront disabilities, and by other disabled women. Marsha Saxton, a consultant, trainer, and organizer of peer counseling for persons with disabilities and one of the coeditors of this volume, has contributed a short essay about her own several experiences as a young child waiting for surgery in the ward of a Shriners hospital for "crippled" children. Nancy Mairs, the writer, who has multiple sclerosis, writes an essay on being a cripple, a word that she prefers in referring to herself because it is more honest. These women, and the others whose contributions appear, represent varied ages, races, and socioeconomic levels. Their commonality is disability.

Analysis: These selections display consistently high quality. Rage, hostility, humor, warmth, and, above all, strength characterize the works and the lives of these women. It is a dense book and not easy to read cover to cover. Rather, it is excellent for dipping, for picking and choosing according to the reader's interests and/or needs of the moment.

High school students, particularly young women, would find all these works accessible, appealing, and informative.

■ Siegel, Mary-Ellen, and Hermine M. Koplin. *More Than a Friend: Dogs with a Purpose.* Illus. by Stephanie Bee Koplin. Walker, 1984. 133pp. (0-8027-6558-0) Reading Level: Grades 4–9. (BL 1 My85)
Disability: Various disabilities

The authors describe dogs that have been trained to help people in a variety of ways: as companions, guards, assistants in daily life, search dogs, and guides. The focus is not only on disabilities, but those presented include blindness, deafness, and both temporary and permanent loss of mobility. Siegel and Koplin write about the training required, the types of dogs used, and their characteristics; give historical information; and focus on individual dogs and people who are also pictured in the black-and-white photographs. A glossary, a list of sources for information, a bibliography, and an index complete the book.

Analysis: Informative and clear, this book is a useful addition to the literature about dogs as helpers for people with disabilities. There is a certain sameness to the remarks ascribed to individuals, in a way that each one's personal voice seems to some extent to have been edited out, but the illustrations are livelier. (To add to the homogeneous quality, there is no ethnic variation; everyone shown is white.) Despite this cavil, the book is well worth recommending to young readers, who would respond both to the information presented and to the fluent expository style.

■ Simmons, Richard. *Reach for Fitness: A Special Book of Exercises for the Physically Challenged.* Illus. Warner, 1986. 316pp. (0-446-51302-4) Reading Level: Grades 10–12. (BL 1 Je86; LJ 15 My86; PW 14 Mr86)
Disability: Various disabilities

Richard Simmons, exercise and diet guru of television, has written a book on good nutrition and proper exercise especially geared for the use of physically challenged persons of all ages. He has also established the

Reach Foundation to carry on the work that he has begun in teaching physically challenged persons practical ways of exercising regularly and eating properly. A long appendix (pp. 217–315) presents medical information on various disabilities, particularly any factors that might conflict with a general exercise program, and also presents any exercise or nutrition tips that specialists in those particular disabilities might want to pass on.

Analysis: This is an upbeat, inspirational approach both to physical fitness and to disabilities, in keeping with Richard Simmons' whole approach. On the surface, it may appear that it is not a book about people with disabilities but rather a book for them. Actually, it is both, because Simmons narrates the stories of many disabled children and adults with whom he has worked. In addition, the book is full of wonderful pictures, very graphic and realistic, of persons with disabilities in the process of learning or carrying out their exercise program. Highly recommended for a wide variety of audiences.

■ Skurzynski, Gloria. *Bionic Parts for People: The Real Story of Artificial Organs and Replacement Parts.* Illus. by Frank Schwartz. Four Winds, 1978. 147pp. (0-590-07490-3) Reading Level: Grades 7–12. (BL 1 F79; KR 15 S78; SLJ S79)
Disability: Amputations; Blindness; Deafness; Kidney failure

This work was a Junior Literary Guild selection, chosen as an outstanding title for older readers. The author has also published five picture books for children.

Five chapters of the book each concentrate on a specific part of the body and the possible replacements, both artificial and transplanted. In each chapter, an explanation of the organ function is given. Black-and-white photographs and drawings illustrate the text.

The book opens with a description of a doctor watching helplessly as a 22-year-old man died of kidney failure in Holland. Dr. William Kolff began secret research during the Nazi occupation that led to his development of the dialysis machine. His continuing research at the University of Utah has led to an experimental portable and wearable artificial kidney.

Chapter two covers mobility aids for blind people, from guide dogs to the implantation of electrodes into the visual cortex. Chapter three discusses aids for deaf people, including experimental cochlear implants. In chapter four, the still problematic procedures involving the artificial heart and heart transplants are covered. Chapter five begins with a picture of Teddy Kennedy, Jr., son of the senator from Massachusetts, who lost his leg to cancer when he was 12 years old. The construction of prostheses is described, including the new Utah Arm, operated by electromyographic signals from the amputee's stump, back, and shoulder. Special prostheses designed for thalidomide children are mentioned as well.

Chapter six concentrates on the types of biomedical material that have been used in various artificial body parts, from metals to polymers, stressing the limitations each imposes. Chapter seven lists other artificial parts with which researchers are experimenting, in animals and in people. The last chapter offers vitae of nine men who have contributed to the research and development discussed in the book. An index is included.

Analysis: This book is clearly written, and the illustrations enhance the text. Much attention is paid to developments on the forefront of bionic research. Therefore, the content seems less dated than that of other, similar works from the 1970s. The author rightly emphasizes that some of the bionic parts are not very helpful to people now but may be in the future.

■ Stearner, S. Phyllis. *Able Scientists—Disabled Persons: Biographical Sketches Illustrating Careers in the Sciences for Able Disabled Students.* Illus. John Facila, 1984. 65pp. (0-916655-00-8) Reading Level: Grades 10–12.
Disability: Various disabilities

Dr. S. Phyllis Stearner is herself an able disabled scientist, for she has cerebral palsy. Educated first in special schools, she eventually earned a Ph.D. at the University of Chicago and went on to a 35-year career as a radiobiologist in the Division of Biological and Medical Research at Argonne National Laboratory.

In this book, she presents brief biographical sketches of 27 men and women with a variety of disabilities such as blindness, deafness, postpolio condition, osteogenesis imperfecta, cerebral palsy, and rheumatoid arthritis. Each sketch is illustrated with a black-and-white photograph of the subject. All 27 have achieved success as scientists; for example, they work as physicists, biologists, computer programmers, chemists, engineers, meteorologists, and mathematicians. Although they encountered difficulties in achieving their educational and professional goals, most of these obstacles were presented by the prejudices of others, for example, university administrators. Their families and sometimes their teachers and other scientists provided support and role models.

A postscript about the author, written by Marcia W. Rosenthal, describes some of the work Stearner has done both at Argonne and elsewhere at the national level to achieve equal physical, educational, and occupational access for those with disabilities.

The text includes a list of selected resources.

Analysis: Written with clear focus, Stearner's book gives the reader a convincing and inspiring picture of what bright, able, motivated people can achieve in the field of science. As the author points out in her introduction, two Nobel Prize winners have had significant disabilities (Sir John W. Cornforth, deafness, Chemistry, 1975, and James B. Sumner, accidental amputation, Chemistry, 1946). While not omitting harsh facts about the difficulties overcome by her subjects, Stearner recognizes that some barriers have been reduced or eliminated, and she writes with optimism.

The text has been printed in two columns and in small print, the lines closely set together. Therefore it may at first present a visually uninviting aspect. However, good senior high school readers should be able to overlook this, and the stories of the individuals presented should attract both able-bodied and disabled readers alike.

■ Stilma, Lize. *Portraits.* Trans. by Lous Heshusius and Adrian Peetoom. Mosaic, 1986. 94pp. (0-88962-337-6) Reading Level: Grades 7–12. (Queens Q Su88; Stand Sp88)
Disability: Mental retardation; Down's syndrome; Autism

Stilma is from northern Holland, of Frisian origin. She began her writing career in her 50s. This is her first book to be translated into English. One of the translators, Heshusius, also a native of the Netherlands, has taught special and regular education there and in North America. Currently, he is associated with York University in Toronto. Peetoom left the Netherlands for Canada in 1954 to work in educational publishing. Each translator supplies a short introduction.

The book has three sections dividing the 55 verbal portraits, each a page or two in length. The prose is simple and sparse and arranged in free-verse style. Each vignette consists of an encounter or a conversation or a story about a child or adult, who is usually disabled and often stigmatized. "I can take your hand and introduce you to each of them," said the author.

Most of the pieces are about institutionalized people, ranging from severely disabled infants in a baby ward to adults who may be elderly but are childlike. Some are residents of towns, perhaps "crazies," who are tolerated but not integrated into society. One portrait is in the voice of a man who has isolated himself after running down a 5-year-old boy years ago. The themes of social rejection and loneliness recur, balanced by descriptions of the wisdom and honesty that exceptional persons, even children, so often possess. In the portrait "In Times Gone By," the narrator describes a walk taken with a retarded man with a memory for details such as license plate numbers. As the encounter ends, the man says, "You remember what you have to remember. That's why you live in a normal home. And I live here." The narrator concludes, "Fate has been discussed and nothing can change it" (p. 61).

Analysis: This book is original and direct in its presentation. The portraits are brief but poignant, and the humanity of all the protagonists shines through. Some offerings express a religious faith; all are spiritual in focus. The disabled people tend to be characterized as virtuous and long suffering, while many "normals" are shown as somewhat heartless. The institutions are portrayed as physically adequate (which they may indeed be in Holland).

■ Ward, Brian R. *Overcoming Disability.* Illus. Franklin Watts, 1988. 48pp. (0-531-10645-4) Reading Level: Grades 4–6. (SL Ag89; SLJ Jl89; TES 24 F89)
Disability: Various disabilities

Part of a series called Life Guides, *Overcoming Disability* discusses 17 disorders, including asthma, diabetes, sensory impairments, cancer, and cystic fibrosis. A brief introduction defines the term "disability," and the next section helps readers imagine what it might be like to experience a condition such as muscular dystrophy or cerebral palsy. Each condition is presented in text and color photographs and sometimes in drawings and diagrams as well. Key words appear in boldface. Nearly all the people pictured are children or young people. A typical entry might describe the condition and its causes, its effects, and its treatment. The book concludes with a section called "Positive approaches to handicap and disability," emphasizing the desire of children with impairments to be accepted as people and treated like others and to live as fully as possible. Readers are urged to offer friendship and encouragement to those with disabilities, rather than show fear and pity. One of the illustrations in this section shows a woman who was a thalidomide baby and has no arms or legs but is pictured feeding her own infant by holding the spoon in her mouth.

The book concludes with a list of organizations devoted to particular disabilities, a glossary, and an index.

Analysis: This is a visually attractive book, with well-chosen illustrations, large type, and wide margins. Much concentrated information is presented, but the clearly written text keeps the material readable and accessible. Like many authors currently writing about these subjects for children, Ward's approach combines understanding and empathy but eschews sentimentality. He emphasizes the many ways in which youngsters with disabilities can cope with their situation, and he points out that the children he describes want to be accepted as themselves—seen as people, rather than as disabling conditions.

This could be a valuable short reference book for school libraries and classroom collections, particularly where children with disabilities are mainstreamed.

■ Weiner, Florence. *No Apologies: A Survival Guide and Handbook for the Disabled, Written by the Real Authorities—People with Disabilities and Their Families.* Illus. St. Martin's, 1986. 188pp. (0-312-57523-8) Reading Level: Grades 10–12. (BL 1 J186; LATBR 17 Ag86; PW 30 My86) *Disability:* Various disabilities

No Apologies is a guide for living with a disability, written, as the preface states, "by the *real* authorities—people with disabilities and their close family members" (p. xii). The author/editor, Florence Weiner, is a disability rights activist whose 24-year-old sister received a spinal cord injury in an automobile accident.

Weiner spent four years conducting interviews and researching this book in the United States, England, France, and Germany. The result is a lively, well-illustrated collection of articles about every facet of living with a disability. The articles are grouped under seven main headings: (1) Who we are, (2) Living/making it with a disability, (3) Who wouldn't want me (sexuality), (4) Doctors, hospitals, helping professions, (5) Education is a right, (6) Work and money, and (7) Organizing. Some of the chapters are written by people with disabilities, others by Weiner herself.

Analysis: This attractive quarto-sized, paperback volume features large type, many photographs of people who are disabled as they go about their daily lives, checklists and quotes inset into the main text, a chapter listing voluntary organizations, an index, and a bibliography. It is upbeat but realistic, often using wry humor to convey its point. Its primary use is as a handbook for persons with disabilities. It would also, however, be a good teaching tool to illustrate the practical problems that differently abled persons face and how they deal with them. Recommended for the high school years.

■ Weiss, Ann E. *Bioethics: Dilemmas in Modern Medicine.* Enslow, 1985. 122pp. (0-89490-113-3) Reading Level: Grades 7–12. (BCCB Ja86; BL 1 N85; SLJ D85) *Disability:* Genetic abnormalities; Kidney failure; Down's syndrome; Sickle cell disease; Heart disease

The author's recent title, *God and Government: The Separation of Church and State,* was chosen as a notable children's trade book of the year by the National Council for the Social Studies. In the present work, her aim is to survey the many complex issues in the new field of bioethics. The book was reviewed by the director of the Institute of Society, Ethics and Life Sciences, the Hastings Center, prior to publication.

Eleven chapters cover a wide range of subjects, such as the sale of organs for transplant, human experimentation, reproductive choice, the right to die, and the cost factor in medical decision making. Thought-provoking actual cases are often presented. For example, the case of the infant Baby Doe is reviewed. He was born with Down's syndrome and was allowed to die rather than be allowed to have a simple operation that could have saved his life.

A number of individuals are quoted directly, and many differing opinions are presented. Weiss stresses the urgent need for people to address the issues she raises. She very frequently asks questions that stimulate readers to resolve these issues in their own mind.

Analysis: This commendable book covers a vast amount of material in lively, readable prose. However, the presentation of so many points of view could conceivably confuse the young, or not even so young, reader. The book might be used most effectively in conjunction with group discussion or as an introduction to further study of bioethics.

Weiss takes pains to explore many sides of an issue, sometimes including extremist positions. Such evenhandedness is admirable to some extent, but it might imply that all arguments are equally valid. For example, she writes, "A few unscrupulous white doctors might go so far as to tell blacks who are not sickle-cell carriers that they *do* have the gene for the disease, these people fear" (for the purpose of curtailing black population growth, p. 66). Such a surmise does not seem helpful in illuminating the other serious issues regarding genetic counseling. In the same section, she errs in her statement that sickle-cell anemia is a disease that strikes *only* black people. The qualifying word should have been "predominantly."

■ White, Peter. *Disabled People.* Illus. Watts, 1990. 64pp. (0-531-17146-9) Reading Level: Grades 4–9. (SL Ag89)
Disability: Various disabilities

White has divided his book into six chapters whose titles (e.g., "All the Things We're Not," "One of the Crowd," and "Fit for Work") indicate his theme. In his one-page introduction, he writes, "In this book we'll be suggesting that having a body which doesn't conform to some imaginary 'normal' standard may well create inconveniences, but it doesn't make you 'weird.' " He discusses such subjects as choosing between special schools and mainstreaming, difficulties faced by disabled people in finding jobs, dating and marriage, and treatment of people with mental handicaps and mental illnesses. A final chapter suggests ways in which one can best offer help to people with disabilities. The text is broken up by quotations

printed against a colored background and by case studies also set off by background and is illustrated with color photographs. At the end are a short list of sources of help, a brief glossary, and an index.

Analysis: White, who is himself blind (a fact that is introduced casually), writes with clarity and force. His descriptions are realistic and informative and are set against his recurring emphasis on the importance of recognizing that people are not disabilities.

In addition to presentation of a variety of impairments, the author includes information on laws regarding employment of disabled people. The color photographs are both appealing and instructive, and the quotations and case studies bring a personal note to the text. In format, the book is uneven: there is no table of contents, top and bottom margins are skimpy, and the red band that runs across the tops of the pages might be distracting to some readers. Nevertheless, this is a book well worth sharing with youngsters, either in a classroom setting or at home.

■ Zola, Irving Kenneth. *Missing Pieces: A Chronicle of Living with Disability.* Temple Univ. Pr., 1982. 246pp. (0-87722-232-1) Reading Level: Grades 9–12. (KR 1 D81; LJ 1 Mr82)
Disability: Orthopedic disabilities; Chronic illness

This book grew out of the author's writings about his experiences in a special village, Het Dorp, in Holland, that was designed and built in the 1960s for severely disabled and chronically health impaired adults. Zola was a sociology professor in his 30s, whose bout with polio at age 16 and subsequent automobile accident required him to wear a back and leg brace and to use a cane. Thus, the project he undertook on his sabbatical leave from Brandeis University was of personal as well as professional interest to him.

Zola made a preliminary trip to the village to establish professional contacts. Het Dorp had 400 disabled residents living in various configurations of private living quarters. An equal number of staff members served the community. About half of the residents engaged in some kind of work opportunities, paid or unpaid. Recreational and community activities were encouraged. Adaptive equipment was individually designed to facilitate independence in the activities of daily living and in the workplace.

On his weeklong return visit, Zola was determined to live as much as possible like a fellow resident. He shed his braces for a wheelchair, the conveyance used by 80 percent of the village members. As he shared the daily routine and the role of a handicapped person, he began to realize his own ambivalence toward the "normal" and "invalid" groups, and the subtle putdowns and prejudices he could discern in each.

Much of the book is written as an hour-by-hour journal, as Zola

learned to master the routine and the environment as a wheelchair user, and as he made friends with his neighbors and with a few staff members. By the end of his stay, he had uncovered old memories and old hurts pertaining to his earlier experience with disease and hospitalization. He became aware that he straddled two worlds, the normal and the invalid—pronunciation of the latter, in Dutch, significantly accenting the second syllable.

In conclusion, Zola waxes philosophical about the patronizing and dehumanizing aspects of any institutions into which disabled people are forced. He discusses the ways even well-meaning people tend to subjugate people who cannot be, or are not allowed to be, in the mainstream of society. He describes short but often poignant exchanges with the residents of Het Dorp. He ends with affection and nostalgia for his friends there and with a renewed respect for people like them, who choose to struggle and carry on their life as best they can.

Analysis: Zola gives the rare residents'-eye view (wheelchair-high) of a setting generally regarded as a utopia for disabled and chronically ill adults. The reasons for his ambivalence toward this place are well illustrated and seem amply justified. His writing becomes more abstract at the end of the book, belying his professional identification as a sociologist. For those interested in the issues of alienation and stigma, it is well worth bearing with his musings.

The author does a service by being open about "unmentionables," such as how he managed toileting when unable to stand, and problems of sex and sexuality. In contrast, he only tantalizes by his mention of his failed marriage and his apparently strained relationship with his daughter. He does reveal himself to be a self-searching, witty, and warm personality in this interesting book.

AUTHOR INDEX

The Author Index covers all entries in this volume and annotated entries from *Accept Me as I Am* (R. R. Bowker, 1985). All numbers refer to page numbers. Page numbers preceded by an A indicate a page number in *Accept Me as I Am*.

TITLE INDEX

The Title Index covers all entries in this volume and annotated entries from *Accept Me as I Am* (R. R. Bowker, 1985). All numbers refer to page numbers. Page numbers preceded by an A indicate a page number in *Accept Me as I Am*.

SUBJECT INDEX

The Subject Index covers the annotated entries that appear in this volume and annotated entries from *Accept Me as I Am* (R. R. Bowker, 1985). All numbers refer to page numbers. Page numbers preceded by an A indicate a page number in *Accept Me as I Am.*